Lecture Notes in Computer Science   14724

Founding Editors

Gerhard Goos
Juris Hartmanis

The series Lecture Notes in Computer Science (LNCS), including its subseries Lecture Notes in Artificial Intelligence (LNAI) and Lecture Notes in Bioinformatics (LNBI), has established itself as a medium for the publication of new developments in computer science and information technology research, teaching, and education.

LNCS enjoys close cooperation with the computer science R & D community, the series counts many renowned academics among its volume editors and paper authors, and collaborates with prestigious societies. Its mission is to serve this international community by providing an invaluable service, mainly focused on the publication of conference and workshop proceedings and postproceedings. LNCS commenced publication in 1973.

Panayiotis Zaphiris · Andri Ioannou
Editors

Learning and Collaboration Technologies

11th International Conference, LCT 2024
Held as Part of the 26th HCI International Conference, HCII 2024
Washington, DC, USA, June 29 – July 4, 2024
Proceedings, Part III

 Springer

Editors
Panayiotis Zaphiris 🆔
Department of Multimedia and Graphic Arts
Cyprus University of Technology
Limassol, Cyprus

Andri Ioannou 🆔
Department of Multimedia and Graphic Arts
Cyprus University of Technology
Limassol, Cyprus

Research Center on Interactive Media, Smart
Systems and Emerging Technologies
(CYENS)
Nicosia, Cyprus

ISSN 0302-9743   ISSN 1611-3349 (electronic)
Lecture Notes in Computer Science
ISBN 978-3-031-61690-7   ISBN 978-3-031-61691-4 (eBook)
https://doi.org/10.1007/978-3-031-61691-4

Foreword

This year we celebrate 40 years since the establishment of the HCI International (HCII) Conference, which has been a hub for presenting groundbreaking research and novel ideas and collaboration for people from all over the world.

The HCII conference was founded in 1984 by Prof. Gavriel Salvendy (Purdue University, USA, Tsinghua University, P.R. China, and University of Central Florida, USA) and the first event of the series, "1st USA-Japan Conference on Human-Computer Interaction", was held in Honolulu, Hawaii, USA, 18–20 August. Since then, HCI International is held jointly with several Thematic Areas and Affiliated Conferences, with each one under the auspices of a distinguished international Program Board and under one management and one registration. Twenty-six HCI International Conferences have been organized so far (every two years until 2013, and annually thereafter).

Over the years, this conference has served as a platform for scholars, researchers, industry experts and students to exchange ideas, connect, and address challenges in the ever-evolving HCI field. Throughout these 40 years, the conference has evolved itself, adapting to new technologies and emerging trends, while staying committed to its core mission of advancing knowledge and driving change.

As we celebrate this milestone anniversary, we reflect on the contributions of its founding members and appreciate the commitment of its current and past Affiliated Conference Program Board Chairs and members. We are also thankful to all past conference attendees who have shaped this community into what it is today.

The 26th International Conference on Human-Computer Interaction, HCI International 2024 (HCII 2024), was held as a 'hybrid' event at the Washington Hilton Hotel, Washington, DC, USA, during 29 June – 4 July 2024. It incorporated the 21 thematic areas and affiliated conferences listed below.

A total of 5108 individuals from academia, research institutes, industry, and government agencies from 85 countries submitted contributions, and 1271 papers and 309 posters were included in the volumes of the proceedings that were published just before the start of the conference, these are listed below. The contributions thoroughly cover the entire field of human-computer interaction, addressing major advances in knowledge and effective use of computers in a variety of application areas. These papers provide academics, researchers, engineers, scientists, practitioners and students with state-of-the-art information on the most recent advances in HCI.

The HCI International (HCII) conference also offers the option of presenting 'Late Breaking Work', and this applies both for papers and posters, with corresponding volumes of proceedings that will be published after the conference. Full papers will be included in the 'HCII 2024 - Late Breaking Papers' volumes of the proceedings to be published in the Springer LNCS series, while 'Poster Extended Abstracts' will be included as short research papers in the 'HCII 2024 - Late Breaking Posters' volumes to be published in the Springer CCIS series.

I would like to thank the Program Board Chairs and the members of the Program Boards of all thematic areas and affiliated conferences for their contribution towards the high scientific quality and overall success of the HCI International 2024 conference. Their manifold support in terms of paper reviewing (single-blind review process, with a minimum of two reviews per submission), session organization and their willingness to act as goodwill ambassadors for the conference is most highly appreciated.

This conference would not have been possible without the continuous and unwavering support and advice of Gavriel Salvendy, founder, General Chair Emeritus, and Scientific Advisor. For his outstanding efforts, I would like to express my sincere appreciation to Abbas Moallem, Communications Chair and Editor of HCI International News.

July 2024   Constantine Stephanidis

HCI International 2024 Thematic Areas
and Affiliated Conferences

- HCI: Human-Computer Interaction Thematic Area
- HIMI: Human Interface and the Management of Information Thematic Area
- EPCE: 21st International Conference on Engineering Psychology and Cognitive Ergonomics
- AC: 18th International Conference on Augmented Cognition
- UAHCI: 18th International Conference on Universal Access in Human-Computer Interaction
- CCD: 16th International Conference on Cross-Cultural Design
- SCSM: 16th International Conference on Social Computing and Social Media
- VAMR: 16th International Conference on Virtual, Augmented and Mixed Reality
- DHM: 15th International Conference on Digital Human Modeling & Applications in Health, Safety, Ergonomics & Risk Management
- DUXU: 13th International Conference on Design, User Experience and Usability
- C&C: 12th International Conference on Culture and Computing
- DAPI: 12th International Conference on Distributed, Ambient and Pervasive Interactions
- HCIBGO: 11th International Conference on HCI in Business, Government and Organizations
- LCT: 11th International Conference on Learning and Collaboration Technologies
- ITAP: 10th International Conference on Human Aspects of IT for the Aged Population
- AIS: 6th International Conference on Adaptive Instructional Systems
- HCI-CPT: 6th International Conference on HCI for Cybersecurity, Privacy and Trust
- HCI-Games: 6th International Conference on HCI in Games
- MobiTAS: 6th International Conference on HCI in Mobility, Transport and Automotive Systems
- AI-HCI: 5th International Conference on Artificial Intelligence in HCI
- MOBILE: 5th International Conference on Human-Centered Design, Operation and Evaluation of Mobile Communications

List of Conference Proceedings Volumes Appearing Before the Conference

1. LNCS 14684, Human-Computer Interaction: Part I, edited by Masaaki Kurosu and Ayako Hashizume
2. LNCS 14685, Human-Computer Interaction: Part II, edited by Masaaki Kurosu and Ayako Hashizume
3. LNCS 14686, Human-Computer Interaction: Part III, edited by Masaaki Kurosu and Ayako Hashizume
4. LNCS 14687, Human-Computer Interaction: Part IV, edited by Masaaki Kurosu and Ayako Hashizume
5. LNCS 14688, Human-Computer Interaction: Part V, edited by Masaaki Kurosu and Ayako Hashizume
6. LNCS 14689, Human Interface and the Management of Information: Part I, edited by Hirohiko Mori and Yumi Asahi
7. LNCS 14690, Human Interface and the Management of Information: Part II, edited by Hirohiko Mori and Yumi Asahi
8. LNCS 14691, Human Interface and the Management of Information: Part III, edited by Hirohiko Mori and Yumi Asahi
9. LNAI 14692, Engineering Psychology and Cognitive Ergonomics: Part I, edited by Don Harris and Wen-Chin Li
10. LNAI 14693, Engineering Psychology and Cognitive Ergonomics: Part II, edited by Don Harris and Wen-Chin Li
11. LNAI 14694, Augmented Cognition, Part I, edited by Dylan D. Schmorrow and Cali M. Fidopiastis
12. LNAI 14695, Augmented Cognition, Part II, edited by Dylan D. Schmorrow and Cali M. Fidopiastis
13. LNCS 14696, Universal Access in Human-Computer Interaction: Part I, edited by Margherita Antona and Constantine Stephanidis
14. LNCS 14697, Universal Access in Human-Computer Interaction: Part II, edited by Margherita Antona and Constantine Stephanidis
15. LNCS 14698, Universal Access in Human-Computer Interaction: Part III, edited by Margherita Antona and Constantine Stephanidis
16. LNCS 14699, Cross-Cultural Design: Part I, edited by Pei-Luen Patrick Rau
17. LNCS 14700, Cross-Cultural Design: Part II, edited by Pei-Luen Patrick Rau
18. LNCS 14701, Cross-Cultural Design: Part III, edited by Pei-Luen Patrick Rau
19. LNCS 14702, Cross-Cultural Design: Part IV, edited by Pei-Luen Patrick Rau
20. LNCS 14703, Social Computing and Social Media: Part I, edited by Adela Coman and Simona Vasilache
21. LNCS 14704, Social Computing and Social Media: Part II, edited by Adela Coman and Simona Vasilache
22. LNCS 14705, Social Computing and Social Media: Part III, edited by Adela Coman and Simona Vasilache

47. LNCS 14730, HCI in Games: Part I, edited by Xiaowen Fang
48. LNCS 14731, HCI in Games: Part II, edited by Xiaowen Fang
49. LNCS 14732, HCI in Mobility, Transport and Automotive Systems: Part I, edited by Heidi Krömker
50. LNCS 14733, HCI in Mobility, Transport and Automotive Systems: Part II, edited by Heidi Krömker
51. LNAI 14734, Artificial Intelligence in HCI: Part I, edited by Helmut Degen and Stavroula Ntoa
52. LNAI 14735, Artificial Intelligence in HCI: Part II, edited by Helmut Degen and Stavroula Ntoa
53. LNAI 14736, Artificial Intelligence in HCI: Part III, edited by Helmut Degen and Stavroula Ntoa
54. LNCS 14737, Design, Operation and Evaluation of Mobile Communications: Part I, edited by June Wei and George Margetis
55. LNCS 14738, Design, Operation and Evaluation of Mobile Communications: Part II, edited by June Wei and George Margetis
56. CCIS 2114, HCI International 2024 Posters - Part I, edited by Constantine Stephanidis, Margherita Antona, Stavroula Ntoa and Gavriel Salvendy
57. CCIS 2115, HCI International 2024 Posters - Part II, edited by Constantine Stephanidis, Margherita Antona, Stavroula Ntoa and Gavriel Salvendy
58. CCIS 2116, HCI International 2024 Posters - Part III, edited by Constantine Stephanidis, Margherita Antona, Stavroula Ntoa and Gavriel Salvendy
59. CCIS 2117, HCI International 2024 Posters - Part IV, edited by Constantine Stephanidis, Margherita Antona, Stavroula Ntoa and Gavriel Salvendy
60. CCIS 2118, HCI International 2024 Posters - Part V, edited by Constantine Stephanidis, Margherita Antona, Stavroula Ntoa and Gavriel Salvendy
61. CCIS 2119, HCI International 2024 Posters - Part VI, edited by Constantine Stephanidis, Margherita Antona, Stavroula Ntoa and Gavriel Salvendy
62. CCIS 2120, HCI International 2024 Posters - Part VII, edited by Constantine Stephanidis, Margherita Antona, Stavroula Ntoa and Gavriel Salvendy

https://2024.hci.international/proceedings

Preface

In today's knowledge society, learning and collaboration are two fundamental and strictly interrelated aspects of knowledge acquisition and creation. Learning technology is the broad range of communication, information, and related technologies that can be used to support learning, teaching, and assessment, often in a collaborative way. Collaboration technology, on the other hand, is targeted to support individuals working in teams towards a common goal, which may be an educational one, by providing tools that aid communication and the management of activities as well as the process of problem solving. In this context, interactive technologies not only affect and improve the existing educational system but become a transformative force that can generate radically new ways of knowing, learning, and collaborating.

The 11th International Conference on Learning and Collaboration Technologies (LCT 2024), affiliated with HCI International 2024, addressed the theoretical foundations, design and implementation, and effectiveness and impact issues related to interactive technologies for learning and collaboration, including design methodologies, developments and tools, theoretical models, and learning design or learning experience (LX) design, as well as technology adoption and use in formal, non-formal, and informal educational contexts.

Learning and collaboration technologies are increasingly adopted in K-20 (kindergarten to higher education) classrooms and lifelong learning. Technology can support expansive forms of collaboration; deepened empathy; complex coordination of people, materials, and purposes; and development of skill sets that are increasingly important across workspaces in the 21st century. The general themes of the LCT conference aim to address challenges related to understanding how to design for better learning and collaboration with technology, support learners to develop relevant approaches and skills, and assess or evaluate gains and outcomes. To this end, topics such as extended reality (XR) learning, embodied and immersive learning, mobile learning and ubiquitous technologies, serious games and gamification, learning through design and making, educational robotics, educational chatbots, human-computer interfaces, and computer-supported collaborative learning, among others, are elaborated in the LCT conference proceedings. Learning (experience) design and user experience design remain a challenge in the arena of learning environments and collaboration technology. LCT aims to serve a continuous dialog while synthesizing current knowledge.

Three volumes of the HCII 2024 proceedings are dedicated to this year's edition of the LCT 2024 conference. The first focuses on topics related to Designing Learning and Teaching Experiences, and Investigating Learning Experiences. The second focuses on topics related to Serious Games and Gamification, and Novel Learning Ecosystems, while the third focuses on topics related to VR and AR in Learning and Education, and AI in Learning and Education.

The papers of these volumes were accepted for publication after a minimum of two single-blind reviews from the members of the LCT Program Board or, in some cases, from members of the Program Boards of other affiliated conferences. We would like to thank all of them for their invaluable contribution, support, and efforts.

July 2024   Panayiotis Zaphiris
                                                                Andri Ioannou

11th International Conference on Learning and Collaboration Technologies (LCT 2024)

Program Board Chairs: **Panayiotis Zaphiris**, *Cyprus University of Technology, Cyprus*, and **Andri Ioannou**, *Cyprus University of Technology, Cyprus* and *Research Center on Interactive Media, Smart Systems and Emerging Technologies (CYENS), Cyprus*

- Miguel Angel Conde Gonzalez, *University of Leon, Spain*
- Fisnik Dalipi, *Linnaeus University, Sweden*
- Camille Dickson-Deane, *University of Technology Sydney, Australia*
- David Fonseca, *La Salle, Ramon Llull University, Spain*
- Alicia Garcia-Holgado, *Universidad de Salamanca, Spain*
- Francisco Garcia-Penalvo, *University of Salamanca, Spain*
- Aleksandar Jevremovic, *Singidunum University, Serbia*
- Elis Kakoulli Constantinou, *Cyprus University of Technology, Cyprus*
- Tomaz Klobucar, *Jozef Stefan Institute, Slovenia*
- Birgy Lorenz, *Tallinn University of Technology, Estonia*
- Nicholas H. Müller, *Technical University of Applied Sciences Würzburg-Schweinfurt, Germany*
- Fernando Moreira, *Universidade Portucalense, Portugal*
- Anna Nicolaou, *Cyprus University of Technology, Cyprus*
- Antigoni Parmaxi, *Cyprus University of Technology, Cyprus*
- Dijana Plantak Vukovac, *University of Zagreb, Croatia*
- Maria-Victoria Soule, *Cyprus University of Technology, Cyprus*
- Sonia Sousa, *Tallinn University, Estonia*

The full list with the Program Board Chairs and the members of the Program Boards of all thematic areas and affiliated conferences of HCII 2024 is available online at:

http://www.hci.international/board-members-2024.php

HCI International 2025 Conference

The 27th International Conference on Human-Computer Interaction, HCI International 2025, will be held jointly with the affiliated conferences at the Swedish Exhibition & Congress Centre and Gothia Towers Hotel, Gothenburg, Sweden, June 22–27, 2025. It will cover a broad spectrum of themes related to Human-Computer Interaction, including theoretical issues, methods, tools, processes, and case studies in HCI design, as well as novel interaction techniques, interfaces, and applications. The proceedings will be published by Springer. More information will become available on the conference website: https://2025.hci.international/.

General Chair
Prof. Constantine Stephanidis
University of Crete and ICS-FORTH
Heraklion, Crete, Greece
Email: general_chair@2025.hci.international

https://2025.hci.international/

Contents – Part III

AI in Learning and Education

VR and AR in Learning and Education

Learning 3D Matrix Algebra Using Virtual and Physical Manipulatives: Qualitative Analysis of the Efficacy of the AR-Classroom

Samantha D. Aguilar[1]([✉]) [iD], Heather Burte[2] [iD], James Stautler[1] [iD],
Sadrita Mondal[1] [iD], Chengyuan Qian[1] [iD], Uttamasha Monjoree[1] [iD], Philip Yasskin[1] [iD],
Jeffrey Liew[1] [iD], Dezhen Song[1,3] [iD], and Wei Yan[1] [iD]

[1] Texas A&M University, College Station, TX, USA
{samdyanne,james.stautler,sadritamondal,cyqian,uxm190002,
yasskin,jeffrey.liew,wyan}@tamu.edu
[2] Carnegie Mellon University, Pittsburg, PA, USA
hburte@andrew.cmu.edu
[3] Mohamed bin Zayed University of Artificial Intelligence, Abu Dhabi, United Arab Emirates
dzsong@mbzuai.edu

Abstract. The AR-Classroom application aims to teach three-dimensional (3D) geometric rotations and their underlying mathematics using virtual and physical manipulatives. In an efficacy experiment, undergraduates completed six 3D matrix algebra rotation questions and were assigned to interact with virtual (N = 20) or physical (N = 20) manipulatives in the AR-Classroom. While completing these rotation questions, researchers documented the participants' reported thoughts, feelings, and perceptions (i.e., qualitative data). A thematic analysis of participants' reports revealed four prevalent themes regarding participants' learning experience: (1) Difficulty using traditional methods, (2) Reliance on resources, (3) Pattern recognition, and (4) Developing an understanding of 3D matrix algebra. Participants struggled to complete rotation matrices when only using information from the question and the model; when unsure how to solve the matrix, participants utilized any available resources. Moreover, participants could identify similarities among matrices, demonstrated after using AR-Classroom repeatedly. The findings indicate that the AR-Classroom may aid students in improving their mathematical skills. Suggestions for future research on the AR-Classroom and efficacy experiments are discussed.

Keywords: User Experience (UX) · Augmented Reality (AR) · Educational Technology · Embodied Learning · Math Learning

1 Introduction

Traditional methods for teaching and learning mathematics are well-documented as complex for students and instructors. Students struggle to visualize mathematical shapes and objects, particularly in the three-dimensional space, and to grasp abstract concepts

© The Author(s), under exclusive license to Springer Nature Switzerland AG 2024
P. Zaphiris and A. Ioannou (Eds.): HCII 2024, LNCS 14724, pp. 3–16, 2024.
https://doi.org/10.1007/978-3-031-61691-4_1

related to mathematical theory [1, 2]. Moreover, students struggle to understand geometry subjects, and their educators have problems finding suitable and practical teaching aids. These difficulties appear to persist across levels of school and often continue into higher education [3–5], which can negatively impact students wanting to pursue majors within science, technology, engineering, or mathematics (STEM).

Most STEM instruction uses multiple representations to illustrate complex or abstract concepts, a practice built on evidence that multiple representations can enhance learning. While many interventions seek to integrate abstract concepts and embodied mechanisms to enhance learning [6], a recent review [7] showed that theories of conceptual learning and embodied learning often make conflicting predictions about the effectiveness of virtual and physical manipulatives alone. Thus, designing effective interventions that combine multiple forms of manipulatives and stimulation may allow for deeper learning of abstract mathematical concepts. From a pedagogical perspective, educational applications utilizing augmented reality (AR) technology can provide a situated and embodied approach to learning [8–10] as the learned knowledge occurs within a specific context and is marked by the embodiment, enhancing the learner's knowledge acquisition.

Educational applications using AR technology have the potential to provide an innovative solution to mathematical learning issues. AR allows teachers and students access to immersive and interactive learning experiences enhanced by the intentional integration of real and virtual stimuli [11–13]. A review by Ahmad and Junaini [14] found that AR usage in math teaching and learning provides students with an interactive learning process, increased understanding, and enhanced visualization. For the matrix algebra underlying geometric transformations, AR allowes learners to interact with simplified complex and abstract mathematical theory information through virtual and physical stimuli. Combining AR technology and multiple forms of physical and virtual manipulatives, the AR-Classroom educational application may provide an effective intervention for learning geometric transformations and their underlying mathematical theory.

2   AR-Classroom

AR-Classroom aims to teach two-dimensional (2D) and three-dimensional (3D) geometric rotations and their mathematics. It provides a virtual and physical interactive environment to facilitate embodied learning, making it more engaging and straightforward to learn 3D matrix algebra. The AR-Classroom app comprises a virtual and physical workshop and a model registration tutorial. Users can perform rotations by manipulating the application's X-, Y-, and Z-axes sliders to rotate a virtual model (i.e., virtual workshop, Fig. 1). Alternatively, they can rotate the physical LEGO space shuttle (i.e., physical workshop, Fig. 2). The virtual and physical workshops of the AR-Classroom share similar features, such as a green wireframe model superimposed onto the LEGO space shuttle to visualize the rotation transformations, color-coded X-, Y-, and Z-axes lines, degree or radian representations of rotation angles, Z-axis direction manipulation, multiple types of model views, and 2D or 3D matrices.

2.1 Previous Research on AR-Classroom

Previous user studies on similar educational technology applications for learning geometric transformations and their mathematics have informed the development of AR-Classroom and its research. The iPad application BRICKxAR/T, developed by Shaghaghian and colleagues [15], used AR to display the mathematical concepts behind geometric transformations by visualizing the entries within transformation matrices. Using an iterative approach, Aguilar and colleagues [16] conducted two usability tests to investigate the usability of the BRICKxAR/T app's AR and non-AR workshops, the first to evaluate usability in its starting condition and the second to investigate the impact of changes made based on the original usability study's findings. Guided by the BRICK-xAR/T development and usability studies, the AR-Classroom app was developed as further described in Yeh et al. [17].

Several usability tests on the AR-Classroom assessed user-app interactions, the functionality of app features, overall ease of use, and the effectiveness of iterative changes made to the app. First, Aguilar et al. [18] conducted usability tests of the AR-Classroom in its starting version; based on the findings from this test, recommendations were formulated to address issues and enhance users' experience. Next, a second usability test was conducted to investigate how changes made to the app based on the first usability test impacted its discoverability and usability. The changes made to the virtual and physical workshops of AR-Classroom improved usability and enhanced user-app interactions. However, based on the results of the updated usability test, there were still salient issues in user-app interactions. Finally, Aguilar et al. [19] conducted a third usability test to investigate the cumulative impact of changes made to the AR-Classroom. Through this iterative approach to usability testing, the current version of the AR-Classroom is deemed satisfactory, as it demonstrates an improved user experience, increased ease of use, and an overall increase in users' understanding of the app's functionality.

The data and procedures derived from previous studies on the BRICKxAR/T and AR-Classroom apps informed the development and execution of the present learning experiment and the importance of qualitative data for answering questions about the impact of AR educational technology on students' learning.

2.2 Phenomenological Research

Using a phenomenological approach, the current study explored participants' qualitative experience while interacting with the AR-Classroom's virtual or physical workshop to learn 3D matrix algebra. Phenomenological research is a qualitative approach that assumes understanding concepts, opinions, or experiences depends on individuals' descriptive reports of the occurrence [20, 21]. Qualitative research guided by phenomenology investigates the profound knowledge and experience of the participants through their description of how the experience made them think, feel, and act during specific situations rather than using the exploration of numeric patterns that traditionally provide a broad overview of findings. Phenomenological research design is beneficial for topics in which the researcher needs to go deep into the audience's thoughts, feelings, and experiences, such as Human-Computer Interactions [22], and can broaden our understanding of the complex phenomena involved in learning, behavior, and communication prevalent within the STEM disciplines [23–25].

2.3 Learning Experiment Using AR-Classroom

The present study investigated users' experiences learning 3D matrix algebra using AR-Classroom (i.e., the phenomenon) via two experimental groups (virtual or physical). The study focused on the qualitative data (i.e., user-reported experience and observations) collected from the experiment. In contrast, another paper will focus on quantitative differences between the experimental and active control groups [26]. Using the qualitative data, the paper answers two research questions on the AR-Classroom's efficacy: 1) How effective is the AR-Classroom in teaching introductory 3D matrix algebra? 2) What mathematical concepts related to matrix algebra do students learn from using the AR-Classroom application?

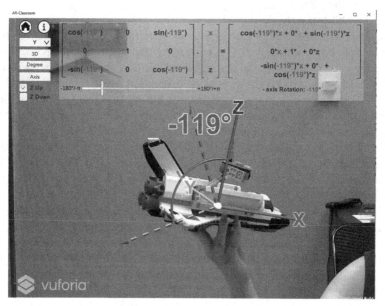

Fig. 1. AR-Classroom: Virtual workshop Y-axis rotation with degrees, and axis visualization (i.e., dotted axes for the LEGO space shuttle's body frame).

3 Methods

Participants were recruited via a research sign-up system in the Department of Psychological and Brain Sciences at Texas A&M University. The experiment took 2 h, and participants received research credit for participation. A total of 60 participants were included in the experiment, with each participant being randomly assigned to the virtual condition (N = 20), the physical condition (N = 20), or the control condition (N = 20). For this study, this paper focuses on the forty participants in the two experimental groups to investigate the qualitative findings of learning using the AR-Classroom app. Participants in the virtual condition (N = 20) were mostly in their freshmen year, with the mean

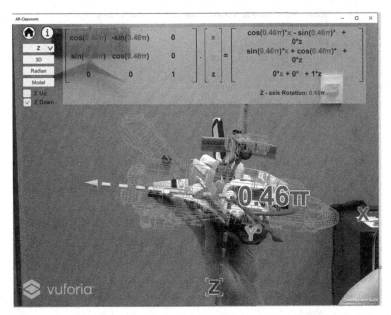

Fig. 2. AR-Classroom: Physical workshop Z-axis rotation with radians, and model visualization (i.e., green wireframe). (Color figure online)

age being approximately 19 years old, and with twelve identifying as male and eight as female. The majority of the virtual condition participants reported experience with 2D matrices, and an even split of participants with and without 3D matrices experience. The physical condition participants shared similar characteristics as the majority were in their freshmen year, with the mean age being approximately 19 years old; however, eight identified as male and twelve as female, and all had experience with both 2D and 3D matrices.

3.1 Procedures

The two experiment conditions followed similar procedures, except for completing different workshops. Participants completed a pre-test with questions regarding demographic information, previous experience with matrix algebra, measures of spatial visualization abilities, and math abilities and confidence. After completing the pre-test, participants watched an introductory video on matrix algebra that provided a brief overview of key concepts and terminology as a primer for students and a second video on setting up the LEGO space shuttle while interacting with the AR-Classroom. After watching the videos, the AR-Classroom application was run on the desktop computer with a webcam, and participants were given the LEGO space shuttle Depending on the participant's assigned experimental condition, rotations about the X-, Y-, and Z-axes are performed either by manipulating the rotation slider for the virtual condition or by physically rotating the LEGO space shuttle for the physical condition. Interacting with one of the workshops on the AR-Classroom, participants completed six 3D matrix algebra questions in a rotation booklet while being recorded.

Rotation #2 - Rotation by 90 degrees counterclockwise about the y-axis

2. We would like to understand the matrix which describes a rotation by 90° counterclockwise about the y-axis.

Step A: Fill in the matrix in the answer booklet using the LEGO model and instructions below

Again, let this matrix be $R = \begin{pmatrix} a & b & c \\ d & e & f \\ g & h & i \end{pmatrix}$. Hold the shuttle so you are looking at the tip of its left wing (the y-axis).

(a) Notice that the z-axis (the antenna) is still up but the x-axis (the nose) is now on your left. Rotate the shuttle by 90° counterclockwise about the y-axis. The wings stay along the y-axis, i.e. $(0, W, 0)$ moves to $(0, W, 0)$.

$$\begin{pmatrix} a & b & c \\ d & e & f \\ g & h & i \end{pmatrix} \begin{pmatrix} 0 \\ W \\ 0 \end{pmatrix} = \begin{pmatrix} 0 \\ W \\ 0 \end{pmatrix}$$

(b) The antenna moves to where the nose was, i.e. $(0, 0, A)$ moves to $(A, 0, 0)$.

$$\begin{pmatrix} a & b & c \\ d & e & f \\ g & h & i \end{pmatrix} \begin{pmatrix} 0 \\ 0 \\ A \end{pmatrix} = \begin{pmatrix} A \\ 0 \\ 0 \end{pmatrix}$$

(c) The nose moves to down, opposite to where the antenna was, i.e. $(N, 0, 0)$ moves to $(0, 0, -N)$.

$$\begin{pmatrix} a & b & c \\ d & e & f \\ g & h & i \end{pmatrix} \begin{pmatrix} N \\ 0 \\ 0 \end{pmatrix} = \begin{pmatrix} 0 \\ 0 \\ -N \end{pmatrix}$$

(d) Use this information to fill in the entries in Matrix R on Answer Sheet 2.

Answer Sheet #2: Rotation by 90° counterclockwise about the y-axis.

Step A: Fill in Matrix R using the instructions in the Rotation Booklet and the Lego Shuttle:

Matrix R

Step B: Fill in Matrix R' using the AR Classroom – Workshop 1 Virtual and the Lego Shuttle:

Hold the shuttle in front of the AR Classroom App and again rotate it **90° counterclockwise about the y-axis.** Remember to set the AR Classroom: Dimension = 3D, Angle = Degrees

Matrix R'

STEP C: Does the Matrix R' displayed by the AR Classroom agree with the Matrix R? If not, ask the experimenter for help.

Fig. 3. Example of 3D Matrix Algebra Rotation Questions (90° about the y-axis; Top) and Rotation Booklet (virtual condition; Bottom).

The rotation booklet consisted of three problems on 90-degree and three problems on 30-degree rotations about the X-, Y-, and Z-axes (Fig. 3). The rotation booklet questions were guided by a scaffolding teaching approach in which learners are guided towards a greater understanding, skill acquisition, and learning independence through less direct instruction of a concept [27]. Each of the three sets progressively provided less supporting information as participants worked through the rotation booklet. The first 90-degree rotation question was thoroughly explained so the participant understood how each of the nine values in the matrix was created. The second rotation question was presented with a shortened explanation, requiring students to use what they learned from the first rotation. The third rotation question contained the most basic explanation. The 30-degree rotation questions followed this same progression. Participants were instructed to first complete Matrix R (Fig. 3, Bottom) only using the instructions in the rotation booklet and the LEGO space shuttle (Fig. 3, Top), after doing so, they were then prompted to use the AR-Classroom to check their work and complete Matrix R' (Fig. 3, Bottom) and compare their answers for both.

While working through the problems, participants were instructed to think aloud and explain what they were trying to do, if the task was easy or challenging, why they found it easy or challenging, and any general thoughts related to their experience with the app. During the experiment, a research assistant documented the participant's feedback. After interacting with the app, participants completed a post-test with the same spatial visualization abilities, math abilities, and confidence measures from the pre-test.

4 Results

Qualitative investigation provides a detailed description of participants' experiences during an experiment. Thematic analysis, a method for analyzing qualitative data, provides a systematic way for researchers to identify meaningful patterns and themes within the data collected. The analysis aims to understand the complexity of meanings in the data by searching for meanings and determining how these patterns can be organized into themes to explain experiences [28, 29]. Thematic analysis findings can uncover the deeper meanings of the experiences being studied and help identify common experiences shared by the group, which can then be used to conclude the overall phenomenon being studied.

For the present study, the thematic analysis included transcribing materials, coding data into themes, and summarizing the participants' learning experience using AR-Classroom (Table 1). Derived themes highlighted four broad findings related to matrix algebra learning:

1. Difficulty using traditional methods
2. Reliance on resources
3. Pattern recognition
4. Developing understanding of 3D matrix algebra.

4.1 Difficulty Using Traditional Methods

For participants in both the virtual and physical conditions ($N = 40$), the findings of the thematic analysis revealed that participants found it difficult to relate how matrix operations correspond to geometric transformations and they lacked an understanding of the trigonometric functions involved in spatial rotations. For rotation question 1, Matrix R, participants either failed to fill out the entire matrix or created a rotation

Table 1. Participants' matrix algebra learning experience using AR-Classroom (N = 40).

Theme	Description	Significant Example(s)
Difficulty using traditional methods	The connection between geometric transformations in a 3D coordinate space and matrix operations were difficult when solving without the AR-Classroom's aid	"I'm not sure how I was supposed to be getting the numbers…" "So, like as far as filling this in and saying x, y and y and then there's the whole matrix I guess that's where I'm confused"
Reliance on resources	Participants needed assistance completing the matrix using only the worksheet and model and relied heavily on previous notes and rotation questions to find solutions	"[I] don't really understand, just using past notes" "The instructions are telling me the same things as I have here [notes], the same formulas"
Pattern recognition	Participants demonstrated a rudimentary understanding of the correlation between rotations and changes in matrices and patterns in three-dimensional rotations after using the AR-Classroom repeatedly	"It follows the same formula. Pretty much if you can pick up the formula, you can do it even if you don't understand" "….this question had a 001 here there should be a 001 on this too"
Developing understanding of 3D matrix algebra	After repeated use of the AR-Classroom application, participants were able to provide a more detailed reasoning for how they solved the matrix and displayed a greater understanding of the rotations	"I didn't try to find [a] pattern I just kind of remembered from before"

matrix incorrectly (N = 18), often putting in numbers and letters unrelated to the 90-degree rotation counterclockwise about the X-axis. Though participants appeared to approach question 2, Matrix R, with less apprehension than the first rotation question, they were still unable to solve the transformation matrix correctly. Participants reported being confused about where the numbers go in the columns based on the rotation (N = 6); "I'm not sure how I was supposed to be getting the numbers…". The main concerns documented related to difficulty completing the transformation matrix using traditional methods, as participants expressed great difficulty understanding how the 3D coordinates of the space shuttle pre- and post-rotation are represented in a 3D matrix. One participant in the physical condition expressed their disconnected understanding between the axes and the matrix by stating, "So, like as far as filling this in and saying x, y, and y and then there's the whole matrix, I guess that's where I'm confused".

Regarding participants' understanding of the trigonometry underlying the rotations, participants needed help utilizing and relating the trigonometric functions (sine, cosine) to the matrices and their corresponding geometric transformations (N = 12). Trigonometric functions presented an additional difficulty for participants with weaker math backgrounds throughout all presented tasks; some clarification was needed with the function of sign usage ($\pm$) in the matrices. This difficulty was further exposed as participants had trouble completing a 30-degree X-axis rotation because there was confusion about whether a value was positive or negative (N = 4), often resulting in failure to have the right solution (N = 15). Participants often attempted clockwise rather than counterclockwise rotation (N = 6) and rotated on the incorrect axis (N = 11). Participants often asked the experimenter, "Do I rotate it like this or?" or "Which way do I like to rotate it? This way or the other way?" Participants in both conditions appeared to demonstrate less confidence in their approach to completing a 30-degree rotation matrix about the X-, Y-, or Z-axis. Even though they had completed three 90-degree rotations about these axes in the previous questions, when the problems shifted from 90-degree to 30-degree rotation, participants in the virtual condition struggled the most with six participants needing clarification about what numbers to use in the matrix.

4.2 Reliance on Resources

Another prevalent theme in both conditions was a reliance on previous notes taken, instructions provided, and participants' answers to earlier rotation questions. Participants needed assistance completing the matrix using only the worksheet and model and, therefore, relied heavily on previous notes and rotation questions to find solutions. This was initially observed in their understanding and ability to solve the first transformation matrix as four participants in the virtual and four in the physical condition read through the instructions and then flipped back to the front page of the rotation booklet to reread notes, unit circles, or matrix information. Moreover, participants needed help starting the rotation questions. They would prompt the experimenters to provide more detailed instructions on matrix algebra, such as which types of values should go where on the matrix and how those numbers are obtained (N = 11).

As participants progressed through each question, their utilization of the resources provided persisted and adapted as they reached the 30-degree rotation questions. Participants began to connect that the introductory video provided the answers for solving problems. If participants recognized this (and took notes), they could fill out the corresponding parts with the angles in the question. Thus, participants utilized previous notes and answers as a template for completing the problem rather than solving it for themselves (N = 15). Participants used previous information and notes; one participant even stated, "The instructions are telling me the same things as I have here [notes], the same formulas". By the last rotation question, half of the participants still utilized notes from the videos and previous matrices as a template for completing the problem rather than demonstrating an understanding of the math involved (N = 10).

4.3 Pattern Recognition

In conjunction with utilizing their notes and past problems to complete the matrix rotation, participants also began to identify patterns in the types of matrices. "It follows the same formula. Pretty much if you can pick up the formula, you can do it even if you don't understand". When solving for rotation question 3, Matrix R, participants in both conditions began to use pattern recognition to complete the matrix (N = 11). For this question, rather than solving the matrix by learning how the rotations work, participants would use earlier problems and the patterns of the numbers to guess how to complete the matrix (N = 7). However, as participants progressed to question 4, participants understood what a 30-degree rotation looked like and recognized that it was similar to the previous problems (N = 12). It was clear that participants recognized the similarities between the 90- and 30-degree sets as one noted, "It's pretty similar to the first problem except instead of 90, you're just doing 30". By the final rotation question, several participants in the virtual condition (N = 5) demonstrated a clear understanding that regardless of the degree of rotation, rotations about the same axis will have the same values in some elements in the matrix "....this question had a 0 0 1 here there should be a 0 0 1 on this too".

4.4 Developing Understanding of 3D Matrix Algebra

After interacting with the AR-Classroom to complete four of the six rotation matrix questions, participants in both conditions were able to provide more detailed reasoning for how they solved the matrix and displayed a greater understanding of the rotations. In the physical condition, participants were able to understand that rotations along one of the three principal axes could be represented as a rotation of the shuttle's cross-section on a plane formed by the other two axes (e.g., a rotation along the Z-axis could be viewed from the perspective of looking directly at the XY plane). In comparison, participants in the virtual condition demonstrated a greater understanding of counterclockwise rotation as participants seemed to be less confused than on previous questions about the direction the rotation needs to be (N = 5). Finally, rather than relying on previously identified patterns, virtual condition participants finished filling out the final Matrix R (i.e., 30-degree counterclockwise rotation about the Z-axis) very quickly, with little help from the model or previous notes (N = 12), a participant stated: "I didn't try to find [a] pattern I just kind of remembered from before".

5 Discussion

The present study investigated AR-Classroom's efficacy in teaching introductory 3D matrix algebra and what mathematical concepts related to matrix algebra students learn from using the app. Four prevalent themes emerged from a thematic analysis of the participants' learning experience: (1) Difficulty using traditional methods, (2) Reliance on resources, (3) Pattern recognition, and (4) Developing understanding of 3D matrix algebra.

Participants displayed less confidence and more apprehension when solving the matrix rotation without the aid of the AR app. They often relied on their resources, such as notes or previous problems or began searching for patterns to ease the cognitive load it may take to solve the rotation. Such findings are not surprising, as previous literature asserts that students often use memorized formulas to solve problems and have difficulty solving problems that require visualization skills [30]. However, the AR-Classroom app eliminates the need for solid spatial skills, allowing students to visualize and physically manipulate complex spatial relationships and abstract concepts. Additionally, recognizing the patterns underlying spatial rotations is a foundational component of geometry learning, as previous research demonstrates that students often struggle with connecting spatial rotations and their underlying mathematical theories [31].

Finally, the connection between geometric transformations in a 3D coordinate space and matrix operations was easier when solving the problem with the AR-Classroom's aid. After using the AR-Classroom across multiple rotation questions, participants demonstrated a rudimentary understanding of the correlation between the rotations and changes in matrices and patterns in three-dimensional rotations. Therefore, 3D matrix algebra and geometry learning using the AR-Classroom app helps with learning by helping students understand the appearance of 3D objects in different directions and involve them in the learning process through interaction with virtual and physical manipulatives within a real-world environment.

5.1 Limitations and Future Research

The study examined the qualitative data extracted from the AR-Classroom's efficacy experiment using a rigorous qualitative methodology protocol to investigate participants' learning experiences using AR-Classroom. The data was collected via two researchers' observations of the participants during the intervention with corresponding recordings and analyzed by examining the researchers' notes, transcribing video recordings, coding results to identify patterns, and generating themes to describe participants' experiences. However, additional qualitative methods such as post-intervention interviews regarding the students' acquired knowledge of 3D matrix algebra and open-ended survey questions about their strategies for learning during the intervention will strengthen the present findings and provide additional prevalent themes. Future qualitative studies on the AR-Classroom should implement additional qualitative data collection methods to provide a robust understanding of learning using the application. The AR-Classroom's efficacy in teaching 3D matrix algebra must be further studied using different methodological approaches and content-specific research questions. For example, efficacy could be gauged using a longitudinal study to examine the educational gains on targeted rotation concepts through repeated use of the AR-Classroom application, or by conducting a case study of implementing the intervention in a STEM or math-based classroom. Expanding how our research team conceptualizes and measures learning outcomes using the AR-Classroom provides further validation of the app's potential success as a learning tool.

6 Conclusion

The paper reviewed the qualitative findings of the AR-Classroom efficacy experiment and provided recommendations for future research on AR-Classroom and similar technologies. The initial findings from the present study and its quantitative counterpart (Burte et al., Submitted to HCII 2024) suggest that matrix algebra learning interventions delivered by AR-Classroom may be helpful and lead to improvements in mathematical skills. After repeatedly using the AR-Classroom, students recognized the patterns and similarities between types of spatial rotations and their representations. They demonstrated a fundamental understanding of the mathematical theory underlying 3D spatial rotations. Guided by the data-informed and iterative approach previously used to improve the educational technology AR-Classroom and its predecessor, BRICKxAR/T, our research team, and tech development team will use the present findings to develop new versions of the app targeted at the current studies identified strategies students use to learn matrix algebra and develop a new learning experiment with revised procedures, measures, and data collection approaches to validate the app's efficacy further.

Acknowledgments. This material is based upon work supported by the National Science Foundation under Grant No. 2119549. We appreciate the support from our undergraduate learning and assessment research team, Adalia Sedigh, Grace Girgenti, Hana Syed, and Megan Sculley.

Disclosure of Interests. The authors have no competing interests to declare that are relevant to the content of this article.

References

1. Cesaria, A., Herman, T.: Learning obstacles in geometry. J. Eng. Sci. Technol. **14**(3), 1271–1280 (2019)
2. Noto, M.S., Priatna, N., Dahlan, J.A.: Mathematical proof: the learning obstacles of preservice mathematics teachers on transformation geometry. J. Math. Educ. **10**(1), 117–126 (2019)
3. Jones, K., Tzekaki, M.: Research on the teaching and learning of geometry. In: The Second Handbook of Research on the Psychology of Mathematics Education, 109–149 (2016)
4. Lehrer, R., et al.: Developing understanding of geometry and space in the primary grades. In: Designing Learning Environments for Developing Understanding of Geometry and Space, pp. 169–200. Routledge (2012)
5. Mulligan, J.: Looking within and beyond the geometry curriculum: connecting spatial reasoning to mathematics learning. ZDM Math. Educ. **47**, 511–517 (2015)
6. Abrahamson, D., Lindgren, R.: Embodiment and Embodied Design (2014)
7. Rau, M.A.: Comparing multiple theories about learning with physical and virtual representations: conflicting or complementary effects? Educ. Psychol. Rev. **32**(2), 297–325 (2020)
8. Akçayır, M., Akçayır, G.: Advantages and challenges associated with augmented reality for education: a systematic review of the literature. Educ. Res. Rev. **20**, 1–11 (2017)
9. Ibáñez, M.B., Delgado-Kloos, C.: Augmented reality for STEM learning: a systematic review. Comput. Educ. **123**, 109–123 (2018)
10. Wu, H.K., Lee, S.W.Y., Chang, H.Y., Liang, J.C.: Current status, opportunities and challenges of augmented reality in education. Comput. Educ. **62**, 41–49 (2013)

11. Rohendi, D., Wihardi, Y.: Learning three-dimensional shapes in geometry using mobile-based augmented reality. Int. J. Interact. Mob. Technol. **14**(9) (2020)

12. Scavarelli, A., Arya, A., Teather, R.J.: Virtual reality and augmented reality in social learning spaces: a literature review. Virtual Reality **25**, 257–277 (2021)

13. Pellas, N., Mystakidis, S., Kazanidis, I.: Immersive virtual reality in K-12 and higher education: a systematic review of the last decade of scientific literature. Virtual Reality **25**(3), 835–861 (2021)

14. Ahmad, N., Junaini, S.: Augmented reality for learning mathematics: a systematic literature review. Int. J. Emerg. Technol. Learn. (iJET) **15**(16), 106–122 (2020)

15. Shaghaghian, Z., Burte, H., Song, D., Yan, W.: Design and evaluation of an augmented reality app for learning spatial transformations and their mathematical representations. In: 2022 IEEE Conference on Virtual Reality and 3D User Interfaces Abstracts and Workshops (VRW), pp. 608–609. IEEE (2022)

16. Aguilar, S.D., Burte, H., Shaghaghian, Z., Yasskin, P., Liew, J., Yan, W.: Enhancing usability in AR and non-AR educational technology: an embodied approach to geometric transformations. In: Zaphiris, P., Ioannou, A. (eds.) HCII 2023. LNCS, vol. 14041, pp. 3–21. Springer, Cham (2023). https://doi.org/10.1007/978-3-031-34550-0_1

17. Yeh, S.H., et al.: AR-classroom: augmented reality technology for learning 3D spatial transformations and their matrix representation. In: 2023 IEEE Frontiers in Education Conference (FIE), pp. 1–8. IEEE (2023)

18. Aguilar, S.D., et al.: AR-Classroom: investigating user-app-interactions to enhance usability of AR technology for learning two and three dimensional rotations. In: Stephanidis, C., Antona, M., Ntoa, S., Salvendy, G. (eds.) HCII 2023. CCIS, vol. 1957, pp. 249–256. Springer, Cham (2023)

19. Aguilar, S.D., et al.: AR-classroom: usability of AR educational technology for learning rotations using three-dimensional matrix algebra. In: 2023 IEEE Frontiers in Education Conference (FIE), pp. 1–8. IEEE (2023)

20. Frauenberger, C., Good, J., Keay-Bright, W.: Phenomenology, a framework for participatory design. In: Proceedings of the 11th Biennial Participatory Design Conference, pp. 187–190 (2010)

21. Neubauer, B.E., Witkop, C.T., Varpio, L.: How phenomenology can help us learn from the experiences of others. Perspect. Med. Educ. **8**, 90–97 (2019)

22. Valentine, K.D., Kopcha, T.J., Vagle, M.D.: Phenomenological methodologies in the field of educational communications and technology. TechTrends **62**, 462–472 (2018)

23. Carambas, J.R., Espique, F.P.: Lived experiences of teachers and students in distance education: shift from traditional to online learning. Educ. Technol. Q. **2023**(4), 422–435 (2023)

24. Said, G.R.E.: Metaverse-based learning opportunities and challenges: a phenomenological metaverse human-computer interaction study. Electronics **12**(6), 1379 (2023)

25. Timario, R.R., Lomibao, L.S.: Exploring the lived experiences of college students with flexible learning in mathematics: a phenomenological study. Am. J. Educ. Res. **11**(5), 297–302 (2023)

26. Burte et al.: Submitted to HCII (2024)

27. Anghileri, J.: Scaffolding practices that enhance mathematics learning. J. Math. Teach. Educ. **9**, 33–52 (2006)

28. Sundler, A.J., Lindberg, E., Nilsson, C., Palmér, L.: Qualitative thematic analysis based on descriptive phenomenology. Nurs. Open **6**(3), 733–739 (2019)

29. Braun, V., Clarke, V.: Can I use TA? Should I use TA? Should I not use TA? Comparing reflexive thematic analysis and other pattern-based qualitative analytic approaches. Counseling Psychother. Res. **21**(1), 37–47 (2021)

30. Battista, M.T.: The development of geometric and spatial thinking. Second Handb. Res. Math. Teach. Learn. **2**, 843–908 (2007)
31. Pereira, L.R., Jardim, D F., da Silva, J.M.: Modeling plane geometry: the connection between geometrical visualization and algebraic demonstration. J. Phys.: Conf. Ser. **936**(1), 012068 (2017)

Exploring the Impact of Virtual Presence in Digital Meetings: A Comparative Study

Hakan Arda[✉] [iD] and Karsten Huffstadt [iD]

Technical University Würzburg-Schweinfurt, Sanderheinrichsleitenweg 20,
97074 Würzburg, Germany
{Hakan.Arda,Karsten.Huffstadt}@thws.de

Abstract. Virtual Reality can help to solve problems. By creating a virtual space, people can discuss, work and simply be creative with each other as if they were together in a physical place. The virtual presence and therefore the appearance of the chosen avatar plays an important role. Depending on how we represent ourselves, we are perceived differently by other humans, that applies to the virtual as well as to the real reality. For this reason, this paper has taken as a goal to find out whether the virtual presence becomes more immersive and instructive through a realistic representation than with generic avatars. To achieve this goal, first a look at the past was taken. Then, based on well-founded theoretical constructs such as the Uncanny Valley Effect, the SECI model, and the Design Thinking, a methodology was developed that makes it possible to achieve this goal. This methodology was then carried out with a case study. The result of the study shows that there is a significant difference between generic and lifelike avatars and that this has an impact on vividness, credibility, and attention. This finding can now be used as a tool for different purposes and can be explored more deeply through continued research.

Keywords: Virtual Reality · SECI · Uncanny Valley

1 Introduction

There is an accelerated digitalization of the meeting modality. Formal and informal communication is increasingly taking place online. Especially the generation of knowledge in creative processes is a challenge without physical presence. Collaboration in geographically distributed teams not only leads to new flexibility, but also to challenges due to the spatial distance. Unimagined challenges await, especially in the areas of communication, the transfer of knowledge, and the development of shared knowledge spaces or networks. Virtual teams are slow and prone to errors, especially in the exchange of information [1, 2]. Several specific challenges, such as social and cultural distance, the localization of relevant knowledge sources, misunderstandings in communication, and a lack of formal rules and reflection opportunities, lead to the question of what small and medium-sized enterprises (SMEs) can improve in knowledge management about virtual collaboration. The Covid 19 pandemic has also accelerated these challenges by normalizing home offices and necessitating virtual teamwork. This was particularly problematic

P. Zaphiris and A. Ioannou (Eds.): HCII 2024, LNCS 14724, pp. 17–34, 2024.
https://doi.org/10.1007/978-3-031-61691-4_2

for SMEs because most of their work processes were not adapted to this rapid virtual shift. The pandemic shift from traditional work models to the increased use of mobile and hybrid forms of work highlighted the need for a reinvention of virtual working for both organizations and business informatics [3].

Currently, virtual meetings take place on various virtual platforms and technically suitable solutions, for example Microsoft Teams, Zoom and Cisco Webex [4]. The most important requirements for these tools are the exchange of media, such as text, sound, or images, as well as collaboration features such as screen sharing, shared lists or white-boards. These video conferencing systems and collaboration tools have found their place in the working world. They already easily cover the most important formal communi-cations by enabling digital meetings and collaboration. But what they have in formal factors, they lack in informal ones. For example, body language is usually shortchanged, or the focus of attention is not even considered. It's easy to forget that in virtual meetings, the pixels on the screens are real people [5]. Due to the lack of non-verbal communication, virtual teams in video conferences also lack cohesion and trust. The use of virtual reality (VR) for virtual meetings could be a possible solution to address these challenges and create an immersive and trustworthy environment [6]. This seems particularly promising in the areas of knowledge transfer [7] and digital communication [3]. For example, the Management of a Scientific Institute explains how the rapidly increasing use of infor-mation technologies can help companies realize efficiencies in an emerging knowledge society [8, 9]. They have developed a knowledge management framework to help SMEs prepare for future changes. In doing so, they show how urgent help is needed to keep up with technological progress. Another study by Philippe et al. [10] shows the vari-ous applications of VR with realistic examples, including behavioral therapy, machine assembly, flight simulation, physics at school, and many more.

2 Theoretical Framework

The aim of this work is to find out which type of virtual presence is best suited to increase immersivity and willingness to collaborate. Specifically, whether a realistic representation through a digital persona is better suited for dialogue between humans or problem solving than a generic avatar. Mori et al.'s [11] Uncanny Valley effect, which describes the reduction of immersivity through too "human like" appearance and behavior, plays a particularly important role here. According to Mori et al. [11], if the digital persona resembles its creator too much without being perfect, this can have serious consequences on the perception and acceptance of the people involved. To address this challenge, this work explores the use and impact of realistic personas in VR on humans and how they differ from other avatar types. By figuring out which type is best suited for this, measures can be taken to improve people's experience even before VR collaboration tools are developed.

2.1 Problem Statement

The current state of VR is one of rapid growth, innovation, and expanding applications. VR has made significant strides since its inception, with improved hardware, more accessible devices, and a growing ecosystem. Content creation and diverse applications also remain areas for growth [12]. While there is a wide range of VR content available, the ecosystem would benefit from more high-quality and compelling experiences across various domains, including gaming, education, healthcare, architecture, and more. This is proven based on an large survey of 1,784 German VR users, that showed that gaming motives, perceived content quality, content reach, system quality, and barriers to VR use significantly influence the experience of VR gaming and thus behavioral intention [12]. Encouraging developers to create innovative and engaging content and fostering collaborations between content creators and industry sectors can drive the growth and adoption of VR.

Furthermore, social interaction and collaboration in VR have immense potential but require more development. For example, traveling together in pandemic times [13] or replacing real classrooms with virtual ones [14] are only a small part of what is possible. Creating seamless and intuitive ways for users to connect, communicate, and share experiences within virtual environments can enhance the social aspect of VR and open new possibilities for virtual gatherings, events, and teamwork. In conclusion, the current state of VR is one of progress and promise, but there are still challenges to overcome. Advancements are needed in areas such as realism, comfort, interaction, affordability, content creation, and social interaction. By addressing these challenges, VR can continue to evolve and expand its impact in entertainment, education, training, design, communication, and beyond.

2.2 Related Work and Research Questions

The virtual appearance, or the visual representation of oneself and others in VR, has the potential to profoundly impact how people behave and interact within virtual environments. This behavior, in turn, can significantly influence the immersivity of the VR experience and individuals' willingness to learn. In VR, users can embody virtual avatars that represent them in the virtual space. These avatars can range from realistic representations of oneself to stylized or abstract forms. The choice of virtual appearance can have psychological and social implications on users' behavior and sense of presence [15, 16]. For example, Zebrowitz and Montepare [15] write in their paper that a person's face has an impact on behavior, empathy, and perception. The humans' perceptual systems have evolved to extract useful information from moving, talking faces that are attached to bodies, and that we are likely to learn more about how the face perception system works if we study it in more ecologically valid contexts. Another example comes from the work of Forsythe [16] about the influence of the applicant's clothing on the interviewer's hiring decision. She wrote that masculine clothing has a significant impact on perceptions of all management characteristics studied. Applicants were perceived as more energetic, aggressive, and received more favorable hiring recommendations when they wore masculine clothing. When individuals have the opportunity to customize or select their virtual appearance, it can foster a sense of ownership and identification with the avatar. This sense of ownership and agency can influence how individuals behave in the virtual environment. Research has shown that when people perceive their avatars as extensions of themselves, they are more likely to engage in prosocial behaviors, collaborate with others, and exhibit positive social interactions [17].

The willingness to learn in VR can also be influenced by the virtual appearance. Research has shown that when learners are embodied in virtual avatars that resemble experts or successful individuals, they may experience a phenomenon called "self-efficacy" [18]. This refers to the belief in one's own abilities to successfully perform a task. When learners have a high level of self-efficacy, they are more motivated and willing to engage in learning activities, leading to improved learning outcomes. However, challenges persist in achieving realistic and convincing virtual appearances. Uncanny Valley, a concept in computer graphics and robotics [11], describes the discomfort people experience when encountering human-like entities that are not quite convincingly realistic. Striking the right balance between realism and avoiding the Uncanny Valley is an ongoing challenge in VR development. The topic of Uncanny Valley will be explained further in the following chapters.

2.3   The Uncanny Valley

The Uncanny Valley effect is a psychological phenomenon that describes the unease or discomfort people experience when encountering human-like entities that are almost, but not quite, convincingly realistic. The term "Uncanny Valley" was coined by robotics professor Masahiro Mori in 1970 [11]. The concept suggests that as the appearance or behavior of humanoid entities becomes increasingly close to human-like, there is a point at which they elicit a strong negative emotional response before eventually becoming indistinguishable from real humans.

The causes of the Uncanny Valley effect can be attributed to several factors. One key factor is related to perceptual incongruity. When an entity's appearance, movements, or behavior deviate from our expectations of natural human behavior, it triggers a cognitive dissonance. The brain perceives subtle deviations as anomalies, creating a feeling of discomfort and unease. An example of the emergence of this feeling comes from the work of Ding and Moon [19], who found out that Pixar films deliberately animate people as cartoonish, because too realistic animation seems unbelievable [19]. The consequences of the Uncanny Valley effect can vary among individuals. Some common reactions include feelings of revulsion, aversion, or a sense of eeriness. The discomfort experienced can result in a diminished sense of presence and engagement, impacting the overall immersive experience. It can also affect the perception of credibility, trust, and likability of the entity, leading to negative attitudes and reduced acceptance [20]. To mitigate the Uncanny Valley effect, several countermeasures have been proposed. One approach is to carefully design and adjust the appearance and behavior of humanoid entities to minimize the deviations from human norms [21–23]. Gradual exposure to increasingly human-like features, allowing individuals to become acclimated to the appearance, can also help reduce the uncanny feeling. Improvements in animation, rendering, and motion capture technologies can contribute to more realistic and natural movements, reducing the perceptual incongruity. Incorporating subtle imperfections and individual variations can also enhance the authenticity and acceptance of humanoid entities [19]. Additionally, contextual factors can influence the perception of the Uncanny Valley effect [24, 25]. Providing appropriate context and clear explanations about the nature of the entity can help individuals understand and accept the deviations. Framing the experience as stylized or intentionally non-human can also alleviate the discomfort associated with the uncanny feeling. By carefully considering the design, behavior, and context, it is possible to mitigate the negative emotional response, improve acceptance, and create more engaging and comfortable experiences.

2.4 Knowledge Generation

To find out whether virtual presence has a significant impact on cognition and willingness to learn, this paper builds on Nonaka and Takeuchi's conceptualization of knowledge generation [8].

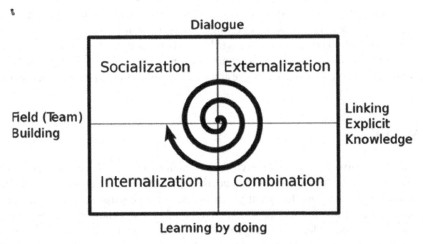

Fig. 1. SECI model according to Nonaka and Takeuchi [8].

In their model, Nonaka and Takeuchi specify four knowledge generation modes as processes of interplay between implicit and explicit knowledge that led to the creation of new knowledge (see Fig. 1). Implicit knowledge is personal, intuitive knowledge, e.g., how to ride a bicycle, which requires personal experience and learning-by-doing. Explicit knowledge, on the other hand, is formal and documentable knowledge, such as how to inflate a bicycle tire. Compared to intuitive knowledge, explicit knowledge is much easier to convey [3]. Because intuitive knowledge always requires the initiative of the person being taught. According to Nonaka and Takeuchi [8], the process of knowledge generation can be divided into the different phases of socialization, externalization, combination and internalization. This method of conceptualization is referred to by the acronym SECI. The transformation of implicit to explicit knowledge occurs in the phases of socialization and externalization, while the return of explicit to implicit knowledge occurs in the phases of combination and internalization.

Socialization is the acquisition of knowledge in operational or organizational cooperation. In the process, new implicit knowledge emerges that is built up through informal interaction. An example of this is the everyday collaboration with colleagues in the office. Externalization is the transformation of implicit knowledge into explicit knowledge through documentation and experience sharing. This also includes, for example, the expert interviews from qualitative research. Combination refers to the merging of previously unrelated knowledge domains and involves the collection, processing, and sorting of existing explicit knowledge. For example, through discussions with other interested parties. Internalization is the internalization of explicit knowledge absorbed by organizations into individually held and organizationally embedded implicit knowledge. This includes, for example, the experience gained from experiments.

Following the work of Schenk et al., Design Thinking is also chosen as a method for generating knowledge in this master thesis. Design thinking is a recognized and controlled knowledge creation process and therefore offers great potential for prototypical application research [26–28]. The goal of Design Thinking is to develop innovative and user-oriented products and services by means of creative problem solving. This work takes a similar approach here but changes the premise and focuses on the dialogue between two people. The aim is to discuss solutions that can be applied in the real world, thus closing the knowledge gaps, and refining the previous work. The Design Thinking phase, finding ideas, is also the focus here and is illustrated by the following experimental set-up.

3   Method

Looking at the current practical research environment related to VR, research is mainly conducted with the improvement of the underlying technology, which has now reached a high level of maturity and technical progress [29, 30]. In contrast, academic research is mainly concerned with social factors such as collaborative behavior and body-based communication in knowledge exchange in VR [31]. Based on the discrepancy between these two fields, a research gap emerges regarding the understanding of the potential, benefits, and added value of the technology between practical application and theoretical research [3]. To close this research gap, the goal of this work is to test the Virtual Presence with a realistic application scenario and thus bring the different perspectives closer. The basic assumption here is that the Virtual Presence is reinforced by realistic avatars, again helping to increase knowledge generation. To prove this assumption a bridge between the core properties of VR immersion, presence and interactivity [32, 33], and the knowledge generation model SECI socialization, externalization, combination, and internalization [8] is built in this thesis. A similar approach was taken by Schenk et al. [3] in their work, with the difference that in their work the focus is on VR as a collaboration tool in general. Here, the focus is specifically on avatars and their impact on the aspects of VR and SECI.

H1–H4 assume a positive influence of immersion, H5–H8 a positive influence of presence, and H9–H12 a positive influence of interactivity on the four SECI aspects socialization, externalization, combination, and internalization. A detailed overview with formulated hypotheses can be found in Table 1. This method of hypothesis generation is based on previous studies to ensure the applicability and comparability of the data [3, 6, 26, 34].

Table 1. Hypothesis Overview [3]

Hypothese	Description
H1	Experiencing and recognizing the realistic avatar (*immersion*) had a positive impact on *SECI socialization*
H2	Experiencing and recognizing the realistic avatar (*immersion*) had a positive impact on *SECI externalization*
H3	Experiencing and recognizing the realistic avatar (*immersion*) had a positive influence on the *SECI combination*
H4	Experiencing and recognizing the avatars (*immersion*) had a positive impact on *SECI internalization*
H5	The physical presence of the realistic avatar (*presence)* had a positive impact on *SECI socialization*
H6	The physical presence of the realistic avatar (*presence*) had a Positive influence on *SECI externalization*
H7	The physical presence of the realistic avatar (*presence*) had a positive influence on the *SECI combination*
H8	The physical presence of the realistic avatar (*presence*) had a positive impact on *SECI internalization*
H9	The possibility of interacting with a realistic avatar (*interactivity*) had a positive impact on *SECI socialization*
H10	The possibility of interacting with a realistic avatar (*interactivity*) had a positive impact on *SECI externalization*
H11	The possibility of interaction with a realistic avatar (*interactivity*) had a positive influence on the *SECI combination*
H12	The possibility of interaction with a realistic avatar (*interactivity*) had a positive impact on *SECI internalization*

3.1 Case Study

The Avatars. The appearance of the avatar plays the most important role in this work. There are many ways to create a lifelike or stylized digital persona. In this thesis, four of the possibilities are used for the study: One way is to scan the user completely for a lifelike avatar. Scanning people to create virtual avatars is a process that involves capturing the physical features of real individuals and translating them into digital representations. This process primarily relies on cameras and specialized software and high-definition cameras to achieve accurate and realistic virtual avatars. The Polycam application uses the cameras to generate a 3D model of the person, which is then imported into the Untiy [35] software and made VR-ready. In Unity, the avatar is then transformed into a moving VR avatar by connecting the head mounted display (HMD) with the corresponding body parts (see Fig. 2).

Another way to create a more stylized avatar is with the help of the tool Ready Player Me. Creating an avatar using the Ready Player Me is a straightforward process [36]. To

Fig. 2. From left to right; the generic, - stylized, - mixed, - and lifelike avatar.

begin, open your web browser and navigate to their website. On the website, you'll find a button or link that invites you to create your avatar. After following the individual steps described, an avatar is generated. Once the avatar (see Fig. 3) is ready, it will be available for download. Depending on your intended use, the avatar will be provided in a format that suits your purpose.

One advantage of Ready Player Me is that no other hardware is required apart from a browser capable device. The avatar has all the necessary things like mesh, textures, and skeleton right after the download and can be controlled directly with the HMD. However, because no photos are taken by cameras, the degree of realism of the avatar is significantly limited here. To compensate for this factor there is a third way to create avatars, which takes the advantages of lifelike and stylized avatars and creates a mix of both worlds. For avatars that are supposed to resemble a real person as much as possible, the face probably plays the most important role. The face reflects the behavior, empathy, and perception of the person [15, 16]. The website Avaturn makes use of this characteristic and offers avatars that are created quickly but are still very realistic [37]. To do this, the software uses the same technique as when Polycam scans people but limits it to the user's face. This requires three biometrically taken photos of the user's face. Next, the remaining body parts such as hair, torso, arms, and legs are created using the Ready Player Me-like character creator tool. The result is an avatar that at first glance looks very similar to the original (see Fig. 2), but on closer inspection shows significant differences. Which in itself is not a problem, because an avatar that is too similar to humans can be subject to the Uncanny Valley effect and thus lowers the immersion [19].

In addition to the digital persona, an avatar without any connection to the human is also included as a control group for the tests. This is the character model Space Robot Kyle (see Fig. 2). This generic looking robot provides all the necessary features to create a VR avatar, without specifying a gender or body shape. Because the robot does not try to resemble a human being, the risk for Uncanny Valley is very low [11] and thus, allow to control if there are significant differences between realistic or generic avatars. The four types of avatars: lifelike, stylized, mixed, and generic, are the basic variable for the experimental design of the paper.

Questionnaire. To analyze and evaluate the results of the case study implementation, a questionnaire was used to collect quantitative and qualitative data from the participants. The questionnaire is based on previous studies in the research field [3, 6, 26, 34, 38, 39]. This ensures applicability and comparability.

The questionnaire includes a total of 57 questions. These include 4 personal questions, 48 quantitative questions divided into 4 sections per avatar, 5 questions about the course of the conversation, and 4 additional free-text questions related to the avatars themselves and a question about which avatar they thought was the best. The control of the hypotheses will mainly take place with the quantitative questions. These questions were developed and based on the hypothesis generation method by Schenk et al. [3] Each section of the VR factors Immersion, Presence and Interactivity have one question each on the different SECI properties Socialization, Externalization, Combination, and Internalization. In this context, the immersion section particularly targets the emotional perception of the interlocutor of the subjects. Presence, on the other hand, is intended to assess the appearance of the person opposite. And finally, the interactivity describes the interaction of both parties.

3.2 Structure of the Case Study

The case study proceeds in three steps. At the beginning, the participants are informed about the upcoming events. It is explained that this is a role play, in which the respondent takes on the role of a politician and I take on the role of various journalists from various newspapers. Then both parties meet in the virtual space in VRChat. The test person has a generic avatar without any certain resemblance. His opposite is one of the four avatars lifelike, stylized, mixed or generic.

The second step is the beginning of the discussion. The journalist asks if the politician knows the last generation. Depending on the answer, either a short explanation based on an example of the last generation or directly the question about the politician's opinion on the topic follows. Based on the politician's opinion, an argument against or for the last generation now follows. The politician may respond to this argument. Afterwards, the journalist proposes a possible solution to the issue and discusses whether it is within the politician's possibilities. This discussion continues until a compromise has been reached or the attempt to find one has been declared a failure by both parties. After the discussion there is a short break in which the respondent is allowed to answer the first part of the questionnaire. The discussion will take place four times in total. Each time the appearance and the newspaper of the avatar changes. After each round, the participant has time to fill in the survey questions. After the fourth round, the discussion ends, and the final phase is initiated.

In the last phase, the respondent is informed about the topic and is asked to fill in the volunteer feedback questions about the avatars. Afterwards, there is a farewell, and the test is successfully completed. For time and organizational reasons, the individual cases take place partly in a closed laboratory at the university but also remotely on the user's own computer at home.

4 Results

4.1 Data Analysis

A total of 30 subjects participated in the study. This experimental group is divided into 29 male and one female participant. The age of the participants ranged from 16 to 50 years old, with most of the participants being between 20 and 28. Experience in VR/AR was rated by the probands themselves on a scale of 1 for no experience at all and 5 for very much experience. The average score was 2.20. The average test time was 57:10 min. This includes the interviews and the time to complete the survey.

The professional background was mainly students. There were 15 bachelor's and master's students, 4 computer scientists and 6 other non-informatics professions. As a computer scientist or prospective computer scientist in college, mild to moderate experience with VR or AR can be expected. However, actual findings cannot be deduced from this, because every course of study has a different focus, and the topic of VR and AR was not included in the subjects' basic studies. Therefore, the experience values of the probands are an approximate estimation of their own interest and experience.

Table 2. Survey results by group and question per hypothesis in mean values.

Hypotheses/Group	Lifelike	Mixed	Stylized	Generic
H1	4.83	4.50	4.37	4.23
H2	4.30	4.30	4.07	3.93
H3	4.57	4.27	4.13	4.47
H4	4.53	4.17	4.13	4.03
H5	1.57	1.93	1.60	1.97
H6	1.47	1.80	1.43	2.27
H7	1.20	1.50	1.20	1.23
H8	1.27	1.53	1.50	1.50
H9	4.37	4.03	4.07	3.30
H10	4.57	4.27	4.23	4.00
H11	4.80	4.40	4.40	4.40
H12	4.60	3.97	3.40	3.93

For the processing of the quantitative questions, the survey results were distributed to the respective avatar groups (see Table 2). Each hypothesis was treated accordingly with at least one question from the survey. These questions were asked in the survey with a five-point Likert scale, 1 meaning I do not agree at all and 5 meaning I fully agree. The results of the question items were considered individually during the evaluation and analyzed using the free program GNU PSPP version 1.6.2. Due to the sample size of $N = 30$, a test of the normal distribution of the samples can be omitted. The results were then tested in a T-test with independent samples, since the values for the individual avatars were recorded by different subjects. This T-test is used to determine whether the mean values of the corresponding samples are different and thus whether there is a statically significant difference between the sample mean values all pairs of groups. To be able to look at the T-test, the variance homogeneity or equality must still be tested. The condition of the variance homogeneity is calculated with the Levene-test [40]. Since the null hypothesis of this work states for all hypotheses that all variances are homogeneous, the significance must be higher than 0.05. If the variance is below 0.00, the null hypothesis must be rejected and statistical significance by the T-value must not be assumed. For example, the hypotheses H2, H3, H5, and H17-H10 scored above 0.05 on the Levene-test (see Table 3). That means in the next step these hypotheses can be considered on the value of the T – test. In the case of an equality of variance, 2 types of the T-test can be used. If there is no assumption that, for example, a sample has a higher or lower value, then the 2-sided T-test must be considered. On the other hand, if there is a presumption of an effect, the 1-sided T-test is used [40]. In both cases, we assume a confidence interval of 95%, which in turn means that we test the T test value at $\alpha = 0.05$.

Table 3. Results of the comparison pair lifelike and generic.

Hypothese	Levene – Test Value	T – Test Value 2 Sd.	T – Test Value 1 Sd.
H1	,000	,003	,0015
H2	**,590**	,154	,0770
H3	**,168**	,571	,2855
H4	,030	,063	,0315
H5	**,621**	,204	,1020
H6	,047	,003	,0015
H7	**,819**	,835	,4175
H8	**,169**	,300	,1500
H9	**,074**	**,000**	**,0000**
H10	**,339**	**,007**	**,0035**
H11	,001	,048	,0240
H12	,001	,012	,0060

Based on these assumptions, we find a significant difference between the lifelike and generic avatar in hypotheses H9 and H10 (see Table 3). Both hypotheses have a significant level under $\alpha = 0.05$ in the 2-sided as well as the 1-sided T-test. H9 for both tests with 0.00 and H10 for the two-sided test with 0.007 and for the one-sided test with 0.0035. Thus, we can reject the null hypotheses for H9 and H10 and accept the alternative hypotheses. Apart from this comparison pair, there was no further static significance in the other comparison groups. In the following chapters the hypotheses that have been adopted will be examined in greater depth in terms of content and impact.

4.2 Qualitative Questions

The last part of the survey dealt with the qualitative questions. These are primarily opinions on whether a lifelike avatar is more suitable than a generic avatar and why they think that is the case. These questions were not mandatory to complete the test. When asked which avatar was the best, 6 voted for the generic, 3 for stylized, 4 for mixed and the majority with 17 for the lifelike avatar. When asked if they would prefer a realistic avatar to an unrealistic avatar, the respondents answered yes 16 times and no 7 times. In addition, 6 other participants gave free-text answers, such as "It depends on the situation. In an interview yes" or "I don't care as long as the avatar comes across as likeable". When asked why they decided to use a real avatar or why they decided against it, the opinions were very detailed. When asked if they would choose a realistic avatar if everyone in the room also had a realistic avatar 21 respondents answered yes and 5 answered no.

The last question was about the suggestions of the respondents to make the avatars more realistic. The answers were mostly related to the facial expressions of the realistic avatars. Especially the eyes and the mouth were mentioned by many as needing improvement. For example, one respondent said "Integrate subtle movements, like blinking, breathing or small twitches. This gives the avatar the feeling of being alive". Another said "Insert a mouth animation. So that the mouth moves when speaking. (I don't know if this is possible without special technology, maybe just by recording the microphone)". In general, the degree of life authenticity was relatively high, as can be read in the following statements "If possible upscale the quality of the avatars, otherwise add more animations in the face, otherwise Very well done", "I think they are all very well done", and "Nothing at all".

5 Discussion

The lifelike avatar had the greatest effect on knowledge generation for all avatar types tested. In this scenario, especially on the SECI aspects socialization and externalization. These aspects were positively influenced. One reason why SECI socialization increased can be derived from the definition of the term. Socialization represents the acquisition of knowledge through collaboration. This creates new implicit knowledge that is built through informal interactions. The special thing here is that it was strongest in the VR area of interactivity. Which in turn means that through the possibility of interaction with a lifelike avatar, it was possible for the probands to generate more informal knowledge than with a generic avatar.

Another reason why socialization has increased through interactivity with a lifelike avatar can be gleaned from the statements of the probands themselves. For example, respondent 10 says that the right appearance attracts more attention to the other person. However, according to the statement, this only applies if one hits the right center point, in relation to the Uncanny Valley effect. This makes it possible to achieve the same effect as in advertising: attention through curiosity. Another statement also directly addresses the appearance of the avatar.

Respondent 29 says that the realistic look of the avatar increases the feeling of well-being. This feeling of well-being is a very important factor that only comes about when the avatar is not in the Uncanny Valley and thus not creates discomfort. Because the avatar is realistic enough to attract attention, it helps the subject to engage in the conversation. The subject also mentions that it is also situational. This is indicated by the statement that "while others prefer the freedom and creativity of an unrealistic avatar". This means that depending on the person or situation, the appearance can play a very important role on the attention and the resulting knowledge transfer through interactions. In addition to SECI socialization, an effect was also observed in externalization. This involves the transformation of implicit knowledge into explicit knowledge. This can occur, for example, through expert interviews. Experts, because of their accumulated knowledge, are consulted in different categories to ensure that the information researched or conveyed is credible. The feeling of credibility also played a major role in the interviews here. The realistic appearance of the avatar made it easier for the subjects to believe the journalist. This effect also speaks for why the factor VR interaction was positively influenced. The gained belief promoted the participation in the interview because the subjects were put in the situation of a real-looking discussion about the last generation. A similar effect can be found in other studies from other research fields, such as testing new drugs with placebos. In this study, it means that the realistic appearance of the avatar made the journalist's statements more believable, giving the discussion a degree of meaningfulness. This meaningfulness in turn made it easier for the subjects to participate in the discussion.

This effect of credibility is reflected in the statement of respondent 11. The respondent says that especially in serious or important topics, a person who can be better imagined in the role helps to attract more attention. This statement is consistent with the fact that explicit knowledge comes from proving implicit knowledge, such as when interviewing a credible expert. It is important that the expert or in this case the journalist looks appropriate to his role. Respondent 11 considers the age of the journalist, who must not look too old or young. Accordingly, it is necessary to pay attention to how the journalist is imagined and how he looks, so that it also influences the credibility.

Based on the results of the case study and the statements of the test persons, it can now be seen that a realistic appearance of an avatar has clear advantages when generating knowledge. On the one hand, the targeted use of lifelike avatars can promote attention through the importance of the situation. This in turn leads to a livelier discussion. On the other hand, it is also possible to let the avatar appear as an expert in his field by fulfilling certain specific roles. This helps to clarify the facts and thus radiates credibility. This credibility, then helps to maintain the seriousness of the situation and directs the attention entirely to the corresponding topic. Thus, the realistic appearance plays a very important role on the interaction in the virtual world and can serve as a tool for generating knowledge.

6   Scientific Placement

The findings of this thesis are part of the broad research spectrum of VR. The field of research has grown significantly in recent years, because on the one hand the hardware prices have fallen and on the other hand the quality of the experience has increased.

This created a real hype around VR and with the change into a digital meeting age the breeding ground for research was laid. A topic which influences VR very much is the Uncanny Valley effect [11]. This effect is the focus of research when it comes to representing real things in the virtual world. The concept suggests that as the appearance or behavior of humanoid entities becomes more and more human-like, there is a point at which they will evoke a strong negative emotional response, before eventually becoming indistinguishable from real human beings. This phenomenon is also reflected in the overall results of this study. These points come from the results of the survey (see Table 2) and were added up. Because questions 8–12 were asked negatively, the results have been converted to positive. To do this, the average of all the results for each question was subtracted from the possible 5 points. The difference is then the new score and is added to the remaining points. With this calculation, the generic avatar scored 45.32, the stylized avatar scored 47.15, the mixed avatar scored 47.07, and the lifelike avatar scored 51.06 points. The generic avatar achieves the lowest number of points of all avatars. If we now increase the realism level, such as the stylized avatar, then the points also increase. Until we reach a point where the points drop again, as the points of the mixed avatar show us. This means that the mixed avatar falls right into the Uncanny Valley and generates fewer points despite its greater realism. However, if you use an alternative method to create lifelike avatars, the number of points increases again, and the uncanny valley effect no longer occurs. This means that, with the help of the avatars, we were able to show that the Uncanny Valley Effect exists and how important the research by Mori et al. [11] was at the beginning of the development of VR. Because there is currently no scientifically substantiated method for ranking avatars based on Uncanny Valley, the results mentioned here are only assumptions and must be validated by further research work.

Another scientific work that influenced this paper was the findings of e.g., Schenk et al. [3] in their study. Here, a demonstrated positive effect was immersion on internalization. Internalization means that implicit knowledge is transformed into explicit knowledge through trials and thus falls into the area of "learning by doing". These attempts took place in the case study of Schenk et al. in the context of an "Escape Room". If we would now change the scenario of this work to the same way, we would probably get a similar result in the area of internalization and combination. This means that the findings in VR always depend on the scenario of the case study. Conversely, this means that methods such as Design Thinking can also be used to depict other scenarios that also occur in reality. To do this, a process must be divided into its individual steps, as in the example of this work, understanding, observing, defining point of view, and finding ideas. In this way, a scenario can be developed that can be seamlessly transferred to the virtual world.

7 Conclusion

The past has shown that with every step VR takes, the goal of being a fully functional communication platform that is in no way inferior to conventional meeting tools is getting closer and closer. This change comes on the one hand with hurdles, such as technical requirements, which must be solved little by little, but also with potential to significantly improve the typical way of working we know today. It doesn't take much more time for a product that can be fully exploited for the world of work to come onto the market. The entertainment world is already taking advantage of VR and using HMDs to create their own subworlds. This creates new ways to meet, talk, work, and live together without having to be in the same place.

The goal of this paper was to determine if the virtual presence becomes more immersive and educational through a digital persona. To do this, a research environment was built that allowed a discussion to take place in the virtual world. This included a mapping of a real space and the development of 4 individual avatars. Each of the avatars from this study represented a different level of realism. The theoretical constructs used were the Uncanny Valley effect for degree of affinity, the SECI model for knowledge generation, and Design Thinking as a process for integrating a working discussion. As an example, for a comparable study and as a basis for the theoretical construction for this thesis, the study of Schenk et al. [3] was used.

The results of this paper show that there is a significant positive difference between generic and lifelike avatars in terms of knowledge generation in the areas of socialization and externalization. This finding can be used specifically to generate more knowledge in different scenarios, such as lectures, job interviews, or doctor's consultations. A lifelike avatar helps focus attention on the important issues, reflecting the seriousness of the situation. In addition, a lifelike avatar can also represent the role of an expert and thus give more importance to the reproduced statements. To achieve these advantages, the avatar must also consider the appropriate factors, such as modeling, textures, and movements. This also includes the scenario in which the avatar is located. This is true for all examples mentioned here. If you follow these rules, you can expect a positive influence on the creation and consolidation of knowledge.

To find out if other areas of VR are influenced by the appearance of avatars, further research can be done in this area. An example of future work would be to examine what impact a lifelike avatar would have on aspects of the SECI model when the scenario takes place not only in dialogue, but in craft development in VR. For example, the premise could be the creation of a new city district where the subjects must decide together as a team where to place the different types of buildings. Through such a premise, it would be possible to start a dialogue on the one hand, promote interactivity through the tangibility of virtual objects, and most importantly address Nonaka and Takeuchi's [8] "learning by doing". This is just one examples of what is currently possible. If technology continues to evolve and people's fascination with VR continues, there will always be ways to represent reality in VR. The idea of "Virtual Reality" is finally here and we are among the first to try out what will be possible in the future.

References

1. Rosen, B., Furst, S., Blackburn, R.: Overcoming barriers to knowledge sharing in virtual teams. Organ. Dyn. **36**, 259–273 (2007). https://doi.org/10.1016/j.orgdyn.2007.04.007
2. Olson, G.M., Zimmerman, A., Bos, N.: Scientific Collaboration on the Internet. MIT Press, Cambridge (2008)
3. Schenk, J., Kurik, J., Gelberg, J., Lischka, A.: Wissensmanagement in virtuellen Welten: Wissensgenerierung in virtual reality-Umgebungen. HMD **59**, 159–176 (2022). https://doi.org/10.1365/s40702-021-00814-z

4. Woodruff, P., Wallis, C.J.D., Albers, P., Klaassen, Z.: Virtual conferences and the COVID-19 pandemic: are we missing out with an online only platform? Eur. Urol. **80**, 127–128 (2021). https://doi.org/10.1016/j.eururo.2021.03.019

5. Kessler, R.: Teamarbeit in Zeiten der Pandemie: co-creation und Entscheidungsfindung – Herausforderung im virtuellen Raum. Now. New. Next – Organisationsberatung (2020)

6. Mueller, J., Hutter, K., Fueller, J., Matzler, K.: Virtual worlds as knowledge management platform - a practice-perspective. Inf. Syst. J. **21**, 479–501 (2011). https://doi.org/10.1111/j.1365-2575.2010.00366.x

7. Wallet, G., Sauzéon, H., Rodrigues, J., N'Kaoua, B.: Use of virtual reality for spatial knowledge transfer. In: Feiner, S., Thalmann, D., Guitton, P., Fröhlich, B., Kruijff, E., Hachet, M. (eds.) VRST08: The ACM Symposium on Virtual Reality Software and Technology; 27–29 October 2008; Bordeaux France, pp. 175–178. ACM, New York (2008). https://doi.org/10.1145/1450579.1450616

8. Nonaka, I., Takeuchi, H.: The knowledge-creating company: how Japanese companies create the dynamics of innovation. Long Range Plan. **29**, 592 (1996). https://doi.org/10.1016/0024-6301(96)81509-3

9. Liao, S.: Knowledge management technologies and applications—literature review from 1995 to 2002. Expert Syst. Appl. **25**, 155–164 (2003). https://doi.org/10.1016/S0957-4174(03)00043-5

10. Philippe, S., et al.: Multimodal teaching, learning and training in virtual reality: a review and case study. Virtual Reality Intell. Hardw. **2**, 421–442 (2020). https://doi.org/10.1016/j.vrih.2020.07.008

11. Mori, M., MacDorman, K., Kageki, N.: The uncanny valley [from the field]. IEEE Robot. Automat. Mag. **19**, 98–100 (2012). https://doi.org/10.1109/MRA.2012.2192811

12. Kunz, R.E., Zabel, C., Telkmann, V.: Content-, system-, and hardware-related effects on the experience of flow in VR gaming. J. Media Econ. **34**, 213–242 (2022). https://doi.org/10.1080/08997764.2022.2149159

13. Hiramatsu, M., Asagiri, S., Amano, S.G., Takanashi, N., Kawagoe, S.K., Kamegai, K.: Virtual ALMA tour in VRChat: a whole new experience (2022). https://doi.org/10.48550/arXiv.2208.10740

14. Cahyadi, P., Wardhana, D.I.A., Ansori, W.I., Farah, R.R.: Enhancing students' english speaking ability through vrchat game as learning media. JORLE **3**, 54 (2022). https://doi.org/10.33365/jorle.v3i2.2135

15. Zebrowitz, L.A., Montepare, J.M.: Social psychological face perception: why appearance matters. Soc. Pers. Psychol. Compass **2**, 1497 (2008). https://doi.org/10.1111/j.1751-9004.2008.00109.x

16. Forsythe, S.M.: Effect of applicant's clothing on interviewer's decision to hire. J. Appl. Soc. Pyschol. **20**, 1579–1595 (1990). https://doi.org/10.1111/j.1559-1816.1990.tb01494.x

17. Yee, N., Bailenson, J.: The proteus effect: the effect of transformed self-representation on behavior. Hum. Commun. Res. **33**, 271–290 (2007). https://doi.org/10.1111/j.1468-2958.2007.00299.x

18. Nissim, Y., Weissblueth, E.: Virtual reality (VR) as a source for self-efficacy in teacher training. IES **10**, 52 (2017). https://doi.org/10.5539/ies.v10n8p52

19. Ding, L.I., Moon, H.-S.: Uncanny valley effect in the animation character design - focusing on avoiding or utilizing the uncanny valley effect. Cartoon Animat. Stud. **43**, 321–342 (2016). https://doi.org/10.7230/KOSCAS.2016.43.321

20. Kim, B., de Visser, E., Phillips, E.: Two uncanny valleys: re-evaluating the uncanny valley across the full spectrum of real-world human-like robots. Comput. Hum. Behav. **135**, 107340 (2022). https://doi.org/10.1016/j.chb.2022.107340

21. Haring, K.S., Satterfield, K.M., Tossell, C.C., de Visser, E.J., Lyons, J.R., Mancuso, V.F., et al.: Robot authority in human-robot teaming: effects of human-likeness and physical embodiment on compliance. Front. Psychol. **12**, 625713 (2021). https://doi.org/10.3389/fpsyg.2021.625713

22. DiSalvo, C.F., Gemperle, F., Forlizzi, J., Kiesler, S.: All robots are not created equal. In: Verplank, B., Sutcliffe, A., Mackay, W., Amowitz, J., Gaver, W. (eds.) DIS02: Designing Interactive Systems 2002, 25–28 June 2002, London, England, pp. 321–326. ACM, New York (2002). https://doi.org/10.1145/778712.778756

23. Ackerman, E.: Why every social robot at CES looks alike? IEEE Spectr. (2017)

24. Kätsyri, J., Förger, K., Mäkäräinen, M., Takala, T.: A review of empirical evidence on different uncanny valley hypotheses: support for perceptual mismatch as one road to the valley of eeriness. Front. Psychol. **6**, 390 (2015). https://doi.org/10.3389/fpsyg.2015.00390

25. Łupkowski, P., Rybka, M., Dziedzic, D., Włodarczyk, W.: The background context condition for the uncanny valley hypothesis. Int. J. Soc. Robot. **11**, 25–33 (2019). https://doi.org/10.1007/s12369-018-0490-7

26. Vogel, J., Schuir, J., Thomas, O., Teuteberg, F.: Gestaltung und erprobung einer virtual-reality-anwendung zur unterstützung des prototypings in design-thinking-prozessen. HMD **57**, 432–450 (2020). https://doi.org/10.1365/s40702-020-00608-9

27. Vogel, J., Schuir, J., Koßmann, C., Thomas, O., Teuteberg, F., Hamborg, K.-C.: Let's do design thinking virtually: design and evaluation of a virtual reality application for collaborative prototyping. In: ECIS 2021 Research Papers (2021)

28. Fromm, J., Radianti, J., Wehking, C., Stieglitz, S., Majchrzak, T.A., vom Brocke, J.: More than experience? - on the unique opportunities of virtual reality to afford a holistic experiential learning cycle. Internet High. Educ. **50**, 100804 (2021). https://doi.org/10.1016/j.iheduc.2021.100804

29. Biene, R., et al.: Augmented und virtual reality (2023)

30. Zobel, B., Werning, S., Metzger, D., Thomas, O.: Augmented und virtual reality: stand der technik, nutzenpotenziale und einsatzgebiete. In: de Witt, C., Gloerfeld, C. (eds.) Handbuch Mobile Learning, pp. 123–140. Springer, Wiesbaden (2018). https://doi.org/10.1007/978-3-658-19123-8_7

31. Fu, X., Zhu, Y., Xiao, Z., Xu, Y., Ma, X.: RestoreVR: generating embodied knowledge and situated experience of Dunhuang mural conservation via interactive virtual reality. In: Bernhaupt, R., et al. (eds.) CHI 2020: CHI Conference on Human Factors in Computing Systems, 25–30 April 2020, Honolulu, HI, USA, pp. 1–13. ACM, New York (2020). https://doi.org/10.1145/3313831.3376673

32. Walsh KR, Pawlowski SD. Virtual reality: a technology in need of is research. In: CAIS (2002). https://doi.org/10.17705/1CAIS.00820

33. Ryan, M.-L.: Narrative as Virtual Reality: Immersion and Interactivity in Literature and Electronic Media. The Johns Hopkins University Press, Baltimore (2015)

34. Schulze, A., Hoegl, M.: Knowledge creation in new product development projects. J. Manag. **32**, 210–236 (2006). https://doi.org/10.1177/0149206305280102

35. Unity. Echtzeit-Entwicklungsplattform von Unity | 3D, 2D, VR- und AR-Engine (2024). https://unity.com/de. Accessed 12 Jan 2024

36. ReadyPlayerMe. Integrate a character creator into your game in days - Ready Player Me (2024). https://readyplayer.me/de. Accessed 12 Jan 2024

37. Avaturn. Avaturn | Realistic 3D avatar creator (2024). https://avaturn.me/. Accessed 12 Jan 2024

38. Bandera, C., Keshtkar, F., Bartolacci, M.R., Neerudu, S., Passerini, K.: Knowledge management and the entrepreneur: insights from Ikujiro Nonaka's dynamic knowledge creation model (SECI). Int. J. Innov. Stud. **1**, 163–174 (2017). https://doi.org/10.1016/j.ijis.2017.10.005

39. Farnese, M.L., Barbieri, B., Chirumbolo, A., Patriotta, G.: Managing knowledge in organizations: a Nonaka's SECI model operationalization. Front. Psychol. **10**, 2730 (2019). https://doi.org/10.3389/fpsyg.2019.02730

40. Walther, B.: T-Test bei unabhängigen Stichproben in SPSS durchführen. Björn Walther (2022)

A Biometric-Based Adaptive Simulator for Driving Education

Paola Barra[1] , Carmen Bisogni[2](✉) , and Chiara Pero[2]

[1] Parthenope University of Naples, 80133 Naples, Italy
paola.barra@uniparthenope.it
[2] University of Salerno, 84084 Fisciano, Italy
{cbisogni,cpero}@unisa.it

Abstract. Distracted driving emerges as a global threat, significantly contributing to the alarming toll of 1.3 million annual traffic fatalities. This paper presents an innovative solution employing a Unity-based driving simulator with biometric features to tackle distracted driving across educational and technological domains. The simulator uses the popular Mediapipe Solutions library and uncomplicated camera setups to capture pivotal biometric parameters: head rotation, gaze direction, and eyelid opening. The fusion of these parameters creates an immersive user experience, enabling self-assessment of distraction levels within simulated nighttime scenarios. The simulator incorporates alerts for incorrect gaze direction or signs of drowsiness, employing an acoustic signal. Furthermore, the simulator activates car headlights upon the driver's proximity to the dashboard, indicating compromised visibility. The proposed solution's efficacy is confirmed through experiments conducted under diverse conditions, including scenarios with sunglasses, eyeglasses, and low luminosity. With minimal hardware and software requirements, the simulator emerges as a valuable educational tool for drivers, holding potential for integration into assisted driving systems. The results highlight its significant contribution to road safety, effectively addressing the pervasive issue of distracted driving through a comprehensive and accessible framework.

Keywords: driver simulator · assisted driving · biometrics · adaptive simulator

1 Introduction

Annually, road traffic accidents claim around 1.3 million lives worldwide, as reported by the World Health Organization (WHO) [25]. Recent statistical insights shed light on distracted driving as a prominent contributor to accidents. Distracted driving, encompassing visual, manual, and cognitive distractions, emerges as a significant threat to road safety. Further complicating this challenge is driver drowsiness, positioned as the second leading cause of accidents, following alcohol consumption. Symptoms such as fatigue, yawning, and attention deficits heighten the associated risks.

P. Zaphiris and A. Ioannou (Eds.): HCII 2024, LNCS 14724, pp. 35–49, 2024.
https://doi.org/10.1007/978-3-031-61691-4_3

The term "*distraction*" is described as the "diversion of the mind, attention, etc. from a particular task" [26]. In the context of distracted driving, it refers to any activity that diverts attention away from the primary task of driving. Maintaining full attention is paramount for safe driving, and engaging in non-driving activities increases the risk of accidents [17]. Distraction is classified into three types: manual, visual, and cognitive [9]. Manual distraction involves the driver participating in activities such as using a cellphone, eating, or drinking. Visual distractions shift the driver's eyes and focus away from the road, while cognitive distraction occurs when the driver's mind is not concentrated on driving, such as talking to a passenger, daydreaming, or becoming lost in thoughts. Given that driver distraction and inattention are the primary causes of vehicle crashes, it is essential to identify instances of driver distraction and implement countermeasures to ensure safe driving.

The ongoing progress in Advanced Driver Assistance Systems (ADAS) has significantly contributed to enhancing road safety by providing crucial support throughout the driving process [24]. These cutting-edge technologies rely on a multitude of sensors to actively monitor the vehicle's surroundings, issuing timely warnings or taking preventive measures to mitigate potential hazards such as obstacles, lane departures, and speed infractions. The realm of ADAS includes various systems such as automatic emergency braking, forward collision warning, blind spot warning, and lane departure warning, all of which provide transient interventions in critical situations. In the contemporary automotive landscape, the continual evolution of ADAS is directed towards ensuring a secure and stress-free driving experience. Figure 1 shows various state-of-the-art ADAS features along with the corresponding sensors employed in their implementation.

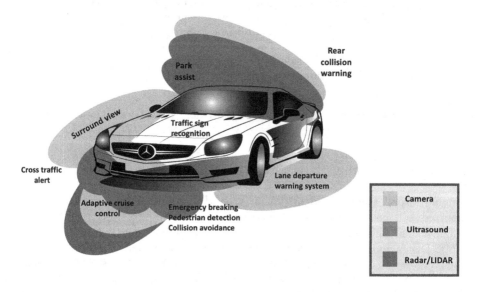

Fig. 1. State-of-the-art ADAS features and implementing sensors.

The seamless integration of multi-source data, specifically biometric information designed for driving scenarios and integrated with existing vehicle sensors, represents a significant leap forward in reinforcing ADAS security. Facial and eye movement indicators, including head rotation, eye blinks, and gaze direction, are conventionally utilized for deducing driver cognitive states [14]. Real-time head rotation recognition assumes a pivotal role in driver behavior analysis and monitoring attention levels [11,29,34]. Conversely, insights into gaze direction provide a detailed understanding of the driver's focal point, enabling precise interventions by ADAS. In controlled environments, gaze can be tracked with remarkable accuracy, particularly with the introduction of affordable devices in recent market offerings. On the other hand, eye-related metrics have demonstrated promising results in determining the driver's fatigue state [20,21,28]. Last but not least, monitoring the distance from the windscreen yields valuable data regarding driver posture and positioning, providing a complementary layer to existing sensor inputs.

Based on these premises, this study introduces an innovative driving simulator for distraction assessment and education, underscoring the practical integration of automated solutions into assisted driving scenarios. These include obstacle detection systems, assisted driving features, and drowsiness prevention mechanisms. By offering a comprehensive approach to tackling distracted driving and alleviating the risks linked to driver drowsiness, the simulator aims to reshape driving education for safer roads. The use of accessible biometric data capture techniques, especially through camera-based systems, introduces a pragmatic dimension to the proposed methodology. In essence, the main contributions can be summarized as follows:

- Development of a driving simulator for distraction assessment and education, allowing drivers to assess their distraction levels in simulated scenarios and offering a valuable tool for enhancing awareness of safe driving practices.
- Utilization of biometric features as distraction indicators, including head rotation, gaze, distance from the windscreen, and eyelid opening. These parameters serve as effective indicators of driver distraction levels during simulated driving experiences.
- Camera-based biometric data collection for practical implementation by using a simple camera for capturing biometric features. An RGB camera on a PC is employed for educational driving, while a near-infrared camera can be strategically positioned on the car dashboard for assisted driving scenarios.

The rest of this article is organized as follows: In Sect. 2, we provide an overview of recent literature, in particular on the themes of distraction detection and drowsiness detection while driving; in Sect. 3, we propose our framework with details about the biometrics techniques involved and the types of alerts; in Sect. 4, we present the framework developments and the findings of the test we conducted with such a framework, other than highlighting the open challenges and future directions; in Sect. 5, we resume our work and provide a complete but concise overview of the overall insights and future paths.

2   Literature Review

2.1   Distraction Detection

Exploring ADAS in the field of Computer Vision poses challenges given its pivotal role in enhancing automotive safety. According to [4], there are four categories deemed effective in measuring and identifying driver distraction: behavioral (such as eye and head movements), performance-based (including vehicle lateral and longitudinal control), psychological (utilizing driver electrocardiographic and electroencephalographic methods), and subjective (employing self-assessment questionnaires and expert evaluations) [8]. Among these, the first two categories, behavioral and performance-based, are the most commonly utilized for driver distraction analysis. Among these, the most frequently employed for driver distraction analysis are the first two [22].

Gaze direction and head pose estimation stand out as widely used attributes. For instance, in [5], the focus was on identifying a specific type of driver distraction–specifically, the rotation of the driver's head caused by a change in the yaw angle. The research involved training multiple classifiers on diverse video frames to evaluate and identify driver distraction. The authors demonstrated that the method utilizing motion vectors and interpolation outperformed other approaches in effectively detecting the rotation of the driver's head. Choi et al. [13] employed advanced deep learning techniques to classify a driver's gaze zones. Through the analysis of camera images, the sequential arrangement of these gaze zones offers valuable insights into the driver's behaviors, encompassing aspects like drowsiness, focus, or distraction. To achieve robust face detection, a combination of a Haar feature-based face detector and a correlation filter-based MOSS tracker is utilized. The study successfully identified nine gaze zone categories, indicating where the driver is looking while driving. Continuing in this line of investigation, Vora et al. [31] conducted a study to investigate systems capable of adapting to diverse drivers, cars, perspectives, and scales. Utilizing Convolutional Neural Networks (CNNs), they categorized a driver's gaze into seven zones, fine-tuning both AlexNet and VGG16 through three distinct input preprocessing techniques. The findings highlighted that concentrating on the upper half of the face yielded superior results compared to employing the entire face or face+context images for effective classification. A very recent study aims to identify instances of distraction by focusing on the true driver's focus of attention (TDFoA) [16]. The process involves two primary stages: predicting TDFoA and determining the Driver Distraction Degree (DDD) based on the driver's focus of attention (DFoA) and TDFoA. To accomplish this, they introduced a deep 3D residual network with an attention mechanism and encoder-decoder (D3DRN-AMED). This model is specifically designed to operate on successive frames using convolutional Long Short-Term Memory (LSTM), effectively minimizing the impact of momentary distractions by considering historical variations in driving scenarios. For an in-depth overview of driver distraction methods, a recent literature review is available in [18].

2.2 Drowsiness Detection

Artificial Intelligence-based systems designed for detecting driver drowsiness have explored various approaches by analyzing the geometric configuration of facial features [12]. Some methods focus exclusively on head pose along with the spatial relationships between specific facial elements [15]. Conversely, other approaches center on the eyes, considering factors such as eye orientation and gaze [3,20,23]. To overcome limitations associated with individual approaches, such as restricted applicability to specific scenarios or being confined to frontal-face driving scenarios, there is a need for a hybrid model that integrates both head pose and eye status [29]. In [35], a Deep Cascaded Convolutional Neural Network is utilized for face detection, followed by the application of the Dlib library to identify facial landmarks. Subsequently, the Eyes Aspect Ratio (EAR) is calculated, and a Support Vector Machine is employed to classify the drowsiness state. Another strategy, outlined in [30], integrates multimodal information, encompassing driver posture, blinks, vehicular data, and Heart Rate Variability (HRV), to discern both slight and severe drowsiness. In [33], a hierarchical temporal Deep Belief Network is deployed to detect drowsiness states in drivers, incorporating high-level facial and head features. Likewise, [36] employs a Neural Network architecture for drowsiness detection, analyzing motions through spatio-temporal representation learning. A particularity of this approach involves automatic scene understanding through an optimization algorithm, achieving a balance between drowsiness detection and scene comprehension. The analysis of multimodal data is further delved into in [6], where fusion also entails emotion detection. This approach combines information derived from yawning, eye movements, and lip gestures, contributing to a comprehensive approach for drowsiness detection. A comprehensive analysis of vehicle metrics, facial and body expressions, as well as physiological signals, aiming to enhance driving safety through adaptive interactions with the driver, is discussed in [2].

3   Proposed Framework

The proposed framework revolves around a sophisticated technology adept at discerning and mapping a driver's facial features, leveraging a strategically positioned webcam. The biometric data obtained includes:

– Facial rotation
– Gaze direction
– Distance assessment
– Eye closure

Primarily designed for integration within assisted driving frameworks, the technology vigilantly monitors the driver's attentiveness, detects signs of fatigue or drowsiness during the driving experience, and triggers high-beam illumination as the driver approaches the webcam. The workflow of the framework is depicted in Fig. 2.

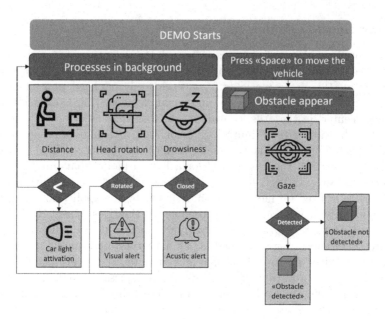

Fig. 2. Workflow of the proposed method. (Those graphs has been designed using images from Flaticon.com www.flaticon.com. Authors of the icons: Freepik, surang, mj.)

Python serves as the programming language, offering a versatile selection of modules. The acquisition of biometric data involves the utilization of the MediaPipe and OpenCV libraries, complemented by essential data manipulation tools such as NumPy, itertools, math, and socket. More details can be found in the following subsections.

Facial Rotation Estimation. Face pose detection is achieved through the MediaPipe package, which employs methodologies for facial mapping utilizing 468 specific landmarks. These landmarks are strategically positioned on the nose, ears, eyes, and mouth, enabling the estimation of facial rotation. The face mesh is obtained by a convolutional neural network like MobileNetV2-like [27] with customized blocks for real-time performance. The rotation estimation is performed by the OpenCV function named "solvePnP" (Perspective-n-Point), designed to estimate face pose based on a set of points encompassing both 2D and 3D coordinates, along with the camera matrix and distortion coefficients. The primary concept involves estimating the position by utilizing the 3D coordinates of N points and their corresponding 2D projections.

Gaze Direction. Once the face mesh is obtained by the method above mentioned, the eye coordinates are used to create a mask for cropping the eye region. Subsequently, a gaussian and median blur are applied to remove the noise from the eye image. The eye is processed in three equal parts vertically. A pixel counter function is called to count the black pixel for each part of the eyes (right, center, left). Since the pupil is known as a black (or near black) pixel in the image, we can obtain the pupil position by counting. We will then have the right, left, or center positions of the gaze. For more detail, please refer to the code available at [1].

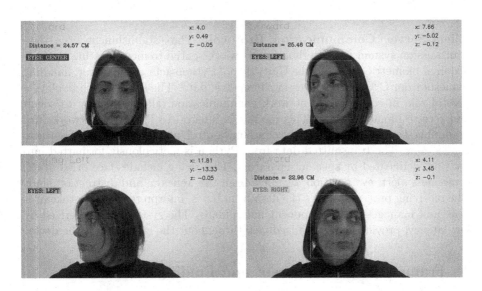

Fig. 3. Biometric-based measures to perform drowsiness detection, distance estimation, gaze position and head rotation.

Distraction and Drowsiness Detection. Distraction detection is accomplished by analyzing previously obtained information, specifically facial rotation. To determine eye closure, landmarks on the eyelids of both eyes–particularly those at the center–are utilized. The closure of an eye is identified when the distance between landmarks on the upper and lower rims is very small. Importantly, each eye is monitored independently, ensuring that the individual closure of one eye does not trigger a drowsiness alert.

Two potential warning types are implemented: distraction and drowsiness. Distraction is recognized when the driver fails to maintain a forward gaze for a specific duration. This may occur due to various reasons, such as engaging in conversation with passengers, turning attention towards them, looking at the radio or phone, or gazing out of the window. Drowsiness detection involves identifying the closure of both eyes for a specific duration. Both scenarios prompt an auditory signal, with its tempo increasing over time to alert the driver to remain attentive while driving. Time calculations for these detections are facilitated by the use of the "time" library, providing practical methods for time management.

Webcam-Based Distance Measurement. Utilizing the OpenCV library and Haar-cascade files for face detection, the system gauges the driver's distance from the webcam. Calibration involves capturing a reference image with a known distance and face width and subsequently computing the focal distance using the known parameters. The aim of this part is to automatically activate the car lights when needed. All of the above-mentioned techniques are integrated, as depicted in Fig. 3.

Client-Server Communication Protocol. The establishment of a data transmission system from Python to C# was essential to incorporating Python-acquired biometric data into the Unity demo. Python acts as the server, handling requests from C# for the necessary biometric data. The socket module plays a pivotal role in coordinating network communication, allowing Unity to solicit and receive biometric data. This module is integral to Python's Network Programming Toolkit, facilitating the creation, control, and management of network connections. The transmitted data from Python is meticulously formatted into a string, delineated by specific separators. This string includes face orientation, drowsiness alert, eye position, distance from the webcam, and distraction alert. The receiving process decodes the data from bytes, interprets them via tokenization, and manages each component individually. The system, characterized by low latency, provides real-time feedback throughout the execution of the demo.

4   Framework Development and Findings

The biometric data-driven simulator was developed within Unity, a versatile game engine created by Unity Technologies for game and interactive content development. The simulator showcases a driving scenario on a straight road at night and employs assets from the Unity Asset Store, such as the "Modular Lowpoly Streets" package for road construction and the "AllSky" package for creating the night skybox.

A car image was positioned in front of the camera, and a script was implemented to guide the camera's movement, simulating a moving vehicle. The car features a spotlight that simulates low beams, dynamically adjusting its range and intensity as the driver approaches the webcam, similar to high beams (Fig. 5). Upon starting the demo, the car begins its movement along the road, encountering strategically placed obstacles.

The simulator incorporates an obstacle detection system, where the car identifies obstacles (depicted as red cubes; see Fig. 6) along the road, triggering alerts on the screen. When the driver directs their attention towards an obstacle, it transitions to green, signifying the system's acknowledgment of the driver's attentiveness. However, if the driver becomes distracted or closes their eyes for a specific duration, an escalating and intensifying auditory warning signal is initiated by the car. This setup aims to simulate real-world driving scenarios and test the driver's responsiveness to potential hazards (Fig. 4).

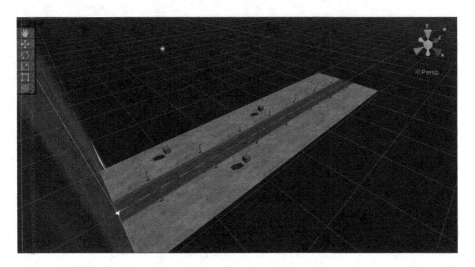

Fig. 4. Unity Simulation scene with lighting.

In order to prove the effectiveness of the method, we tested it under various scenarios:

- **Eyeglasses** The framework is robust in the case of eyeglasses. None of the involved methods presented a decrease in performance with the use of eyeglasses.
- **Sunglasses** The framework is robust in the case of sunglasses for the methods involving the pose of the user and the alert regarding distraction detection. Due to the absence of a visible pupil, the method is not able to work in this case to detect the gaze of the user and the closing eyes. For this reason, the drowsiness alert and obstacle detection will not work in this case.
- **Partially occluded face** Since the method involved uses landmark prediction, even in the case of partially occlusions, the framework is able to work without decreasing in performance. In particular, for the lower part of the face that is occluded, like the mouth, the nose, or both, the method works as usual. If the upper part is partially occluded (as an example, one eye is occluded), only the drowsiness detection will fall because it is calibrated to detect both eyes closed. However, this is a characteristic of the framework that can be easily modified as needed.
- **Low brightness** When the face is not sufficiently illuminated during the demo, both the accuracy of the gaze detection and the distance estimation decrease. This means that the obstacle detection and the car light activation functions are no longer reliable. In contrast, the landmarks are correctly detected, and the distraction and drowsiness alerts work as usual. This problem could be overcome by considering the use of a near-infrared camera. Those particular cameras are also able to capture the facial image at very low brightness, which would more realistically simulate a real car environment during night driving. In this case, the ability of Mediapipe to detect facial landmarks

Fig. 5. Unity Simulation: lighting variations (Top: Off, Bottom: On).

should be tested, since there is not, to the best of our knowledge, a literature on accuracy decreasing when using near-infrared cameras. However, other methods, like dlib [19], have been proven to be easily trainable on different input data, as in the case of the depth image of faces [10].

Based on our observations, we can define different paths for future directions of the work:

- **From 2D simulation to VR** Unity, which has been used to build the driving simulator, also provides a version, Unity3D, that allows you to create 3D environments. For this reason, a possible path would be to move the simulation from 2D to 3D in order to make the experience more immersive

Fig. 6. Unity Simulation: recognized obstacle (Top: Driver's Detection, Bottom: Driver's Perspective).

for the learner. In this case, however, the facial landmark and the eye position should be captured by different devices. The integrated gaze devices in the visors for the second case [32], and the webcam as usual in the first case, since Mediapipe is able to work also in case half the face is occluded.

- **From 2D simulation to AR** Other than VR, one possibility could be to test the demo in a context of mixed reality, where the car seat, the illumination conditions, the steering wheel, and the accelerator are real, and the moving road and the appearance of the obstacle are simulated. This would help not only in the immersive learning of the driver but also in the calibration of sensors.

- **From 2D simulation to car** One possible test to conduct would be to mount a camera on the dashboard of a real car, integrate the above-mentioned sensors, and test the alarms installed in the demo to obtain feedback from experienced drivers on possible improvements to the learning phase and calibration.

5   Conclusions

The continuous evolution of technology is making the integration of simulation techniques into user educational processes increasingly seamless. This study specifically focuses on safe driving practices, introducing a simulation framework designed to replicate a driving scenario while considering its intricate elements. These encompass critical aspects like obstacle detection, identification of drowsiness, distraction management, and addressing challenges posed by low luminosity. The techniques presented in this work, combined with an autonomous driving algorithm as [7], could prevent accidents. The proposed framework is versatile and compatible with personal computers equipped with RGB cameras, including integrated options. It capitalizes on established biometric analysis algorithms to evaluate the aforementioned driving situations. The framework not only identifies potential issues but also provides users with diverse alerts and feedback mechanisms to enhance their driving skills. Moreover, the adaptability of the framework extends to immersive experiences in virtual reality and augmented reality settings. This potential integration aims to elevate the user experience, contingent upon the availability of appropriate hardware devices. The incorporation of structured feedback, manifesting as alerts, facilitates the translation of insights gained within the simulation environment into tangible perspectives for assisted driving scenarios.

Our future endeavours involve refining biometric techniques tailored to three applications: 2D simulations, 3D simulations, and assisted driving contexts. Additionally, we plan to conduct comprehensive testing using images from various input sources under diverse and challenging conditions. This includes scenarios where visors partially or fully cover the driver's face, using near-infrared images, and experimenting with different camera positions, such as mounting the camera on the dashboard. In summary, the proposed simulation framework addresses immediate concerns related to driving distractions and demonstrates adaptability for emerging technologies like virtual reality and augmented reality. The structured feedback mechanism ensures that the insights gained from the simulation environment contribute meaningfully to assisted driving, promising a safer and more informed driving experience for users in diverse conditions.

Acknowledgment. We would like to thank Marco Pastore, a 'Graphics and Interaction' student, for his assistance with the game graphics as part of his internship and bachelor thesis.

References

1. Gaze detector using mediapipe. https://github.com/Asadullah-Dal17/Eyes-Position-Estimator-Mediapipe. Accessed 25 Jan 2024
2. Aghaei, A.S., et al.: Smart driver monitoring: when signal processing meets human factors: in the driver's seat. IEEE Signal Process. Mag. **33**(6), 35–48 (2016)
3. Akshay, S., Abhishek, M., Sudhanshu, D., Anuvaishnav, C.: Drowsy driver detection using eye-tracking through machine learning. In: 2021 Second International Conference on Electronics and Sustainable Communication Systems (ICESC), pp. 1916–1923. IEEE (2021)
4. Aksjonov, A., Nedoma, P., Vodovozov, V., Petlenkov, E., Herrmann, M.: Detection and evaluation of driver distraction using machine learning and fuzzy logic. IEEE Trans. Intell. Transp. Syst. **20**(6), 2048–2059 (2018)
5. Ali, S.F., Hassan, M.T.: Feature based techniques for a driver's distraction detection using supervised learning algorithms based on fixed monocular video camera. KSII Trans. Internet Inf. Syst. (TIIS) **12**(8), 3820–3841 (2018)
6. Altameem, A., Kumar, A., Poonia, R.C., Kumar, S., Saudagar, A.K.J.: Early identification and detection of driver drowsiness by hybrid machine learning. IEEE Access **9**, 162805–162819 (2021)
7. Anzalone, L., Barra, P., Barra, S., Castiglione, A., Nappi, M.: An end-to-end curriculum learning approach for autonomous driving scenarios. IEEE Trans. Intell. Transp. Syst. **23**(10), 19817–19826 (2022). https://doi.org/10.1109/TITS.2022.3160673
8. Arun, S., Sundaraj, K., Murugappan, M.: Driver inattention detection methods: a review. In: 2012 IEEE Conference on Sustainable Utilization and Development in Engineering and Technology (STUDENT), pp. 1–6. IEEE (2012)
9. Baheti, B., Talbar, S., Gajre, S.: Towards computationally efficient and realtime distracted driver detection with mobileVGG network. IEEE Trans. Intell. Veh. **5**(4), 565–574 (2020)
10. Bilotti, U., Bisogni, C., Nappi, M., Pero, C.: Depth camera face recognition by normalized fractal encodings. In: Foresti, G.L., Fusiello, A., Hancock, E. (eds.) Image Analysis and Processing - ICIAP 2023. LNCS, vol. 14233, pp. 196–208. Springer, Cham (2023). https://doi.org/10.1007/978-3-031-43148-7_17
11. Bisogni, C., Cascone, L., Nappi, M., Pero, C.: IoT-enabled biometric security: enhancing smart car safety with depth-based head pose estimation. ACM Trans. Multimedia Comput. Commun. Appl. **2**, 1–24 (2024)
12. Bisogni, C., Hao, F., Loia, V., Narducci, F.: Drowsiness detection in the era of industry 4.0: are we ready? IEEE Trans. Ind. Inform. **18**(12), 9083–9091 (2022). https://doi.org/10.1109/TII.2022.3173004
13. Choi, I.H., Hong, S.K., Kim, Y.G.: Real-time categorization of driver's gaze zone using the deep learning techniques. In: 2016 International Conference on Big Data and Smart Computing (BigComp), pp. 143–148. IEEE (2016)
14. Dubs, A., et al.: Drive a vehicle by head movements: an advanced driver assistance system using facial landmarks and pose. In: Stephanidis, C., Antona, M., Ntoa, S. (eds.) HCII 2022. CCIS, vol. 1580, pp. 502–505. Springer, Cham (2022). https://doi.org/10.1007/978-3-031-06417-3_67
15. Friedrichs, F., Yang, B.: Camera-based drowsiness reference for driver state classification under real driving conditions. In: 2010 IEEE Intelligent Vehicles Symposium, pp. 101–106. IEEE (2010)

16. Huang, T., Fu, R.: Driver distraction detection based on the true driver's focus of attention. IEEE Trans. Intell. Transp. Syst. **23**(10), 19374–19386 (2022)
17. Kaplan, S., Guvensan, M.A., Yavuz, A.G., Karalurt, Y.: Driver behavior analysis for safe driving: a survey. IEEE Trans. Intell. Transp. Syst. **16**(6), 3017–3032 (2015)
18. Kashevnik, A., Shchedrin, R., Kaiser, C., Stocker, A.: Driver distraction detection methods: a literature review and framework. IEEE Access **9**, 60063–60076 (2021)
19. Kazemi, V., Sullivan, J.: One millisecond face alignment with an ensemble of regression trees. In: 2014 IEEE Conference on Computer Vision and Pattern Recognition, pp. 1867–1874 (2014). https://api.semanticscholar.org/CorpusID:2031947
20. Khan, M.Q., Lee, S.: Gaze and eye tracking: techniques and applications in ADAS. Sensors **19**(24), 5540 (2019)
21. Ledezma, A., Zamora, V., Sipele, Ó., Sesmero, M.P., Sanchis, A.: Implementing a gaze tracking algorithm for improving advanced driver assistance systems. Electronics **10**(12), 1480 (2021)
22. Li, W., Huang, J., Xie, G., Karray, F., Li, R.: A survey on vision-based driver distraction analysis. J. Syst. Architect. **121**, 102319 (2021)
23. Maior, C.B.S., das Chagas Moura, M.J., Santana, J.M.M., Lins, I.D.: Real-time classification for autonomous drowsiness detection using eye aspect ratio. Expert Syst. Appl. **158**, 113505 (2020)
24. Nidamanuri, J., Nibhanupudi, C., Assfalg, R., Venkataraman, H.: A progressive review: emerging technologies for ADAS driven solutions. IEEE Trans. Intell. Veh. **7**(2), 326–341 (2021)
25. World Health Organization, et al.: Global status report on road safety 2023: summary. In: Global Status Report on Road Safety 2023: Summary (2023)
26. Regan, M.A., Hallett, C., Gordon, C.P.: Driver distraction and driver inattention: definition, relationship and taxonomy. Accid. Anal. Prev. **43**(5), 1771–1781 (2011)
27. Sandler, M., Howard, A.G., Zhu, M., Zhmoginov, A., Chen, L.C.: MobileNetV2: inverted residuals and linear bottlenecks. In: 2018 IEEE/CVF Conference on Computer Vision and Pattern Recognition, pp. 4510–4520 (2018). https://api.semanticscholar.org/CorpusID:4555207
28. Schwehr, J., Willert, V.: Driver's gaze prediction in dynamic automotive scenes. In: 2017 IEEE 20th International Conference on Intelligent Transportation Systems (ITSC), pp. 1–8. IEEE (2017)
29. Sharara, L., et al.: A real-time automotive safety system based on advanced AI facial detection algorithms. IEEE Trans. Intell. Veh., 1–12 (2023)
30. Sunagawa, M., Shikii, S.i., Nakai, W., Mochizuki, M., Kusukame, K., Kitajima, H.: Comprehensive drowsiness level detection model combining multimodal information. IEEE Sens. J. **20**(7), 3709–3717 (2019)
31. Vora, S., Rangesh, A., Trivedi, M.M.: On generalizing driver gaze zone estimation using convolutional neural networks. In: 2017 IEEE Intelligent Vehicles Symposium (IV), pp. 849–854. IEEE (2017)
32. Wei, S., Bloemers, D., Rovira, A.: A preliminary study of the eye tracker in the meta quest pro. In: Proceedings of the 2023 ACM International Conference on Interactive Media Experiences, IMX 2023, pp. 216–221. Association for Computing Machinery, New York (2023). https://doi.org/10.1145/3573381.3596467
33. Weng, C.H., Lai, Y.H., Lai, S.H.: Driver drowsiness detection via a hierarchical temporal deep belief network. In: ACCV Workshops (2016)
34. Yang, Y., Liu, C., Chang, F., Lu, Y., Liu, H.: Driver gaze zone estimation via head pose fusion assisted supervision and eye region weighted encoding. IEEE Trans. Consum. Electron. **67**(4), 275–284 (2021)

35. You, F., Li, X., Gong, Y., Wang, H., Li, H.: A real-time driving drowsiness detection algorithm with individual differences consideration. IEEE Access **7**, 179396–179408 (2019)
36. Yu, J., Park, S., Lee, S., Jeon, M.: Driver drowsiness detection using condition-adaptive representation learning framework. IEEE Trans. Intell. Transp. Syst. **20**(11), 4206–4218 (2018)

Learning 3D Matrix Algebra Using Virtual and Physical Manipulatives: Statistical Analysis of Quantitative Data Evaluating the Efficacy of the AR-Classroom

Heather Burte[1]($\boxtimes$) , Samantha D. Aguilar[2] , James Stautler[2] ,
Sadrita Mondal[2] , Chengyuan Qian[2] , Uttamasha Monjoree[2] , Philip Yasskin[2] ,
Jeffrey Liew[2] , Dezhen Song[2,3] , and Wei Yan[2]

[1] Carnegie Mellon University, Pittsburgh, PA 15213, USA
hburte@andrew.cmu.edu
[2] Texas A&M University, College Station, TX 77843, USA
{samdyanne,james.stautler,sadritamondal,cyqian,uxm190002,
yasskin,jeffrey.liew,wyan}@tamu.edu, dzsong@mbzuai.edu
[3] Mohamed Bin Zayed University of Artificial Intelligence (MBZUAI), Abu Dhabi, UAE

Abstract. The Augmented reality (AR) allows digital information to be overlayed onto a physical plane that users can manipulate. Using the unique capabilities of AR, the AR-Classroom learning tool aims to teach three-dimensional (3D) geometric rotations and their mathematics using virtual and physical manipulatives. In an efficacy experiment, undergraduates completed pre-test measures of matrix algebra and spatial thinking skills, were assigned to interact with virtual ($N = 20$) or physical ($N = 20$) manipulatives in the AR-Classroom, or to complete active control activities ($N = 20$), and then completed post-test measures of matrix algebra and spatial thinking skills. Using a series of ANCOVAs, pre-test accuracy on matrix algebra and spatial thinking tests significantly predicted matrix algebra post-test accuracy. There were no significant group differences indicating that all three groups showed similar improvement in matrix algebra skills. Further ANCOVAs revealed that the virtual and physical conditions showed marginally significant improvements on matrix algebra questions that were taught by the AR-Classroom, specifically rotations and rotations combined with translations. These initial findings indicate that the AR-Classroom may aid students in improving their mathematical skills. Suggestions for future improvements to the AR-Classroom and efficacy experiments on the AR-Classroom are discussed.

Keywords: User Experience (UX) · Augmented Reality (AR) · Educational Technology · Embodied Learning · Math Learning

P. Zaphiris and A. Ioannou (Eds.): HCII 2024, LNCS 14724, pp. 50–64, 2024.
https://doi.org/10.1007/978-3-031-61691-4_4

1 Introduction

1.1 Learning Using Augmented Reality

Mathematical concepts can be challenging for many students to visualize, particularly when those concepts are abstract, dynamic, and/or involve multi-dimensional spaces [1, 2]. These challenges extend to their instructors as they struggle to find teaching aids that address or alleviate these challenges. If not appropriately addressed, students who struggle with mathematical concepts in younger grades may continue to struggle well into higher education [3–5]. Difficulties in learning mathematical concepts can impede students from pursing science, technology, engineering, or mathematics (STEM) degrees and careers.

Multiple representations are frequently used to enhance conceptual learning. This is why it is common for STEM instructional material to use multiple representations to illustrate complex or abstract concepts. Another approach is to use embodied learning where students physically interact with either virtual or physical manipulatives to enhance their learning. While numerous interventions have sought to integrate embodied learning with abstract conceptual learning [6], theories on conceptual and embodied learning often conflict about the effectiveness of using virtual or physical manipulatives alone [7]. Therefore, learning interventions designed for teaching abstract mathematical concepts might be more effective when they combine multiple manipulatives and stimulation. Augmented Reality (AR) technology can do just that. AR can provide both situated and embodied approaches to learning [8–10] as students' learning is contextually situated while the student physically interacts with that specific context. Combining both approaches may enhance knowledge acquisition of challenging concepts.

AR-enabled educational technologies could be an innovative solution to the challenges instructors and students face in engaging with complex mathematical topics. AR can be used to intentionally integrate real and virtual stimuli within immersive and interactive learning experiences [11–13]. Using AR for the instruction of mathematical concepts has been found to provide an interactive learning process that enhances understanding and visualization [14]. AR also has the potential to simplify complex and abstract mathematical theory thereby allowing learners to interact with the content through virtual and physical stimuli. With this in mind, the AR-Classroom application was developed to leverage AR capabilities combined with physical and virtual manipulatives. This paper investigates the efficacy of the AR-Classroom as a learning intervention targeting geometric transformations and their underlying mathematical theory.

1.2 Foundational Research on the BRICKxAR/T

The development of and research on the AR-Classroom has been informed by usability tests and learning efficacy research conducted on the BRICKxAR/T application. BRICKxAR/T is a predecessor to the AR-Classroom. It was an educational technology application that ran on an iPad so that users could move around and interact with LEGO models [15]. This embodied approach was designed to support learning the mathematical concepts behind geometric transformations. One version of the BRICKxAR/T used AR technology to visualize axes of rotation along with the entries within transformation matrices. Another version did not use AR (non-AR) and served as a comparison for evaluative purposes.

The BRICKxAR/T's user experience was evaluated by a series of usability tests: a benchmark usability test provided initial user interactions with the BRICKxAR/T, recommendations for improvements were made based on the benchmark usability test, then some recommendations were implemented, and finally a follow-up usability test was run to identify changes in user interactions [16]. This series of tests revealed that making changes to initial instructions and a demo video resulted in users rating the app as more intuitive and easier to use, users more often sought out and effectively used in-app instructions, and better understood the relationship between the LEGO model, AR wireframe overlay on the LEGO model, and the rotation matrix. In addition, a learning efficacy experiment conducted on BRICKxAR/T found that scores on a math test significantly improved from pre-test to post-test [17]. Participants who interacted with the AR-enabled workshop tended to show greater improvements compared to the non-AR workshop. Participants reported that the BRICKxAR/T was interesting and useful, and participants engaged with the AR workshop for longer than the non-AR workshop. On the basis of these promising research findings, the AR-Classroom was developed to expand the use of AR technology and to compare the use of physical versus virtual manipulatives teach matrix algebra concepts.

1.3 AR-Classroom Capabilities

The AR-Classroom application was developed in a way that makes challenging and not (typically) visible concepts more interactive, visible, and intuitive [18]. These features are designed to engage students in embodied learning which may lessen the demand on their spatial thinking skills and support more intuitive understanding of mathematical concepts. More specifically, the AR-Classroom utilizes AR technology to teach two-dimensional (2D) and three-dimensional (3D) geometric rotations and their mathematics using virtual and physical manipulatives.

AR-Classroom consists of a model registration tutorial and two workshops: virtual and physical. In the model registration tutorial, users are introduced to registering the LEGO space shuttle with the AR-Classroom. In the workshops, users perform rotations by utilizing the application's X, Y, and Z axes sliders to rotate a virtual model (i.e., virtual workshop, Fig. 1) or by using a physical space shuttle LEGO model (i.e., physical workshop, Fig. 2). Each workshop displays a green wireframe model superimposed onto a LEGO model to represent the rotation transformations, color-coded axis lines, degree or radian representations, Z-axis direction (up versus down) manipulation, different model views, and 2D or 3D matrices.

1.4 Previous Research on the AR-Classroom

After the initial development of the AR-Classroom, several usability tests have been used to assess user-app interactions, app feature functionality, app ease of use, and the impact of iterative app improvements. First, a set of usability tests were run [19]. These tests included a benchmark usability test, recommendations for changes to the AR-Classroom based on the benchmarked usability, changes made to the AR-Classsrsoom,

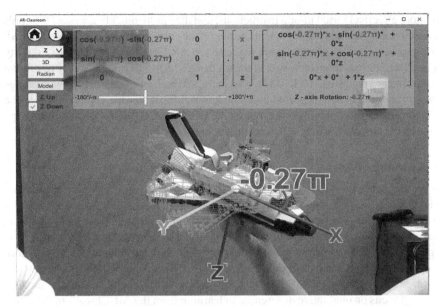

Fig. 1. The AR-Classroom's Virtual workshop with a Z-axis rotation and angle in radians.

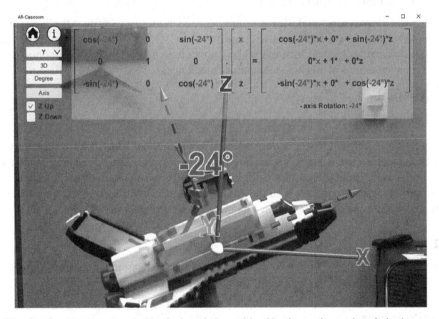

Fig. 2. The AR-Classroom's Physical workshop with a Y-axis rotation and angle in degrees.

an updated usability test, and a comparison between benchmarked usability and usability after the recommended changes were made. After changes were made, the usability of both workshops was improved as users could more easily set up the LEGO space shuttle, they more effectively used in-app instructions, and they more quickly accessed the app's features. Even with these improvements, salient issues in user-app interactions remained. Next, another round of changes were made to the AR-Classroom and a third usability test evaluated the cumulative impact of these changes [20]. The third usability test found that the changes made to the AR-Classroom increased metrics of user experience, ratings of ease of use, and better supported user's understanding of how the app functioned. The findings derived from previous research on the BRICKxAR/T and AR-Classroom apps informed the current learning efficacy experiment.

1.5   Learning Efficacy Experiment on the AR-Classroom

The present study investigated the AR-Classroom's efficacy in teaching undergraduate students the basics of matrix algebra using three learning conditions: using the AR-Classroom's virtual workshop, using the AR-Classroom's physical workshop, and completing active control activities that were designed not to train matrix algebra skills. The purpose of using two experimental conditions was to compare students' matrix algebra learning after using virtual or physical manipulatives. This paper will focus on quantitative differences between the experimental and active control groups. In contrast, another paper will focus on qualitative differences in learning from the AR-Classroom [21]. The current study asked two broad research questions about the AR-Classroom's efficacy in teaching the basics of matrix algebra:

1. How does matrix algebra skill and/or confidence change after using the AR-Classroom application, compared to an active control?
2. How does using physical versus virtual manipulatives in the AR-Classroom contribute to changes in matrix algebra skill and/or confidence?

2   Method

2.1   Participants

Sixty Texas A&M University undergraduates were recruited using the Department of Psychological & Brain Sciences' research sign-up system (Table 1). These students received research course credit for participating in the experiment. Each participant was randomly assigned to interact with the AR-Classroom's virtual workshop ($N = 20$) or physical workshop ($N = 20$), or they completed the active control activities ($N = 20$).

2.2   Design

The efficacy experiment utilized a three between-subjects learning conditions (virtual, physical, active control) by two within-subjects test (pre and post) design.

2.3   Procedures

Participants in the virtual and physical conditions completed the following in a two-hour session: a pre-test, interacted with the AR-Classroom's virtual or physical workshop (based on their assigned condition), and a post-test. Participants in the active control condition completed the following in a two-hour session: a pre-test, completed assessments and activities about spatial thinking and analogies, and a post-test.

Table 1. Demographics and Previous Experience with Matrices by Learning Condition.

Heading level	Virtual Workshop	Physical Workshop	Active Control
Year of schooling	13 freshmen 5 sophomores 1 junior	12 freshmen 5 sophomores 2 juniors 1 senior	14 freshmen 4 sophomores 2 seniors
Mean Age	19.1 years old	19.0 years old	18.6 years old
Gender	12 men 8 women	8 men 12 women	5 men 15 women
Experience with 2D Matrices	19 had experience 1 did not	19 had experience 1 did not	17 had experience 3 did not
Experience with 3D Matrices	10 had experience 10 did not	14 had experience 6 did not	5 had experience 15 did not

2.4 Pre-test Materials

All three learning conditions followed the same pre-test: demographic and experience survey, the Purdue Spatial Visualization Test-Visualization of Rotations, and a matrix algebra test with confidence ratings.

Demographics and Experience Survey. Participants answered multiple-choice questions about their year of schooling, age, gender, major, previous experience with 2D and 3D matrices, and level of experience (5-point scale from 1 = "not at all familiar" to 5 = "extremely familiar") with video games, 3D modelling, and AR.

Purdue Spatial Visualization Test-Visualization of Rotations (PSVT:R). The PSVT:R is a commonly used assessment of spatial visualization skills that is composed of 20 problems. In this assessment, participants see diagrams of 3D object in a starting orientation and a finishing orientation after an unknown rotation on one or more axes has been completed. The participant must identify a diagram of a second 3D object that has been rotated in the same manner as the first 3D object. They are presented with the second 3D object in a starting orientation and must select the correct finishing orientation from a set of five options. Performance on the PSVT:R is calculated as a percentage of correctly answered problems.

Matrix Algebra Test with Confidence Ratings. The matrix algebra test was composed of sixteen multiple-choice questions, each followed by a confidence rating. The questions were developed by a mathematics professor to cover simple to complex matrix algebra concepts. Low complexity questions required identifying transformations based on diagrams, and identifying the center, direction, vector, and/or angle of a transformation (Fig. 3). Moderate complexity questions required identifying a 3×3 rotation matrix that represents a given transformation or identifying the transformation from a given 3×3 rotation matrix (Fig. 4). High complex questions required identifying a 4×4 rotation matrix that represents a given translation and transformation, or the inverse (Fig. 5). The concepts in the matrix algebra test included rotations, which were the focus of the

AR-Classroom's current capabilities, and also translations and scaling, which were only covered in the introductory video on matrix algebra. Performance on the matrix algebra test was calculated as a percentage of correctly answered questions.

After each of the 19 matrix algebra questions, participants were asked to rate their confidence in their answer. Participants rated their confidence on a 5-point scale from 1 = "Not at all confident (I guessed)" to 5 = "Completely confident (I know I answered correctly)". Average confidence ratings were calculated.

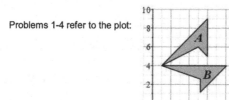

Problems 1-4 refer to the plot:

1. What transformation (motion) is applied to quadrilateral *A* to get quadrilateral *B*?
    a.   translation
    b.   rotation   Correct Answer
    c.   reflection
    d.   dilation (scale)

Fig. 3. An example of a low complexity question from the matrix algebra test that requires identifying transformations based on a diagram.

12. What type of 3D transformation is performed by the matrix
$$M = \begin{pmatrix} \cos\theta & 0 & \sin\theta \\ 0 & 1 & 0 \\ -\sin\theta & 0 & \cos\theta \end{pmatrix}?$$
    a.   Rotation about the x axis
    b.   Rotation about the y axis   Correct Answer
    c.   Reflection through the plane $x\cos\theta + z\sin\theta = 0$
    d.   Reflection through the plane $x\cos\theta - z\sin\theta = 0$

Fig. 4. An example of a moderate complexity question from the matrix algebra test that requires identifying the transformation represented by a given 3×3 rotation matrix.

2.5   AR-Classroom Interaction Materials

After completing the pre-test, participants watched introductory videos on matrix algebra and the AR-Classroom. The introductory video on matrix algebra covered key concepts and terminology to remind students of previous coursework in matrices or to provide foundational understanding if students lacked previous coursework in matrices. The introductory video on the AR-Classroom taught students how to set-up a LEGO space

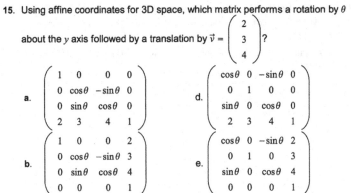

Fig. 5. An example of a high complexity question from the matrix algebra test that requires identifying the transformation represented by a given 3×3 rotation matrix.

shuttle model for use with the AR-Classroom. After watching the two videos, a desktop computer with a webcam was used to run the AR-Classroom application.

To guide participants through using the AR-Classroom, they followed a rotation booklet with three questions (one question for each of X-, Y-, and Z-axes) on 90-degree counterclockwise rotations (Fig. 6) and three questions (one question for each axis) on 30-degree counterclockwise rotations (Fig. 7). Each question included two rotation matrices that students would fill out: one was filled out using the rotation booklet and the other was filled out using the AR-Classroom (Fig. 8).

Each set of three questions followed a similar progression. The first rotation question was thoroughly explained so that the participant understood how each of the 9 values in the matrix were found. The second rotation question was presented with a shortened explanation, requiring the student to use what they learned from the first rotation. The third rotation question contained the most basic explanation. For each of the six rotation questions, participants would read the rotation booklet and use the LEGO space shuttle to fill out a rotation matrix. Then the AR-Classroom with the LEGO space shuttle were used to allow the participants to see how the rotation was performed and to check if their rotation matrix was correct or not. In this way, the learning session was self-paced and allowed students to correct their own mistakes. An experimenter was available for questions throughout the learning session but tried to direct the participant to answer their own questions using the rotation booklet and AR-Classroom.

The primary difference between the physical and virtual learning conditions is in how participants interacted with LEGO space shuttle and the AR-Classroom. For both workshops, participants hold the LEGO space shuttle in front of the webcam and the AR-Classroom presents 3D visualizations of axes and angle of rotation superimposed onto the video of the participant holding the space shuttle. In the virtual workshop (Fig. 1), participants use a dropdown box to select the axis of rotation and then move a slider to change the angle of rotation. By moving the slider, they rotate the axes superimposed onto the stationary shuttle and the rotation matrix is updated with every movement of the slider. In the physical workshop (Fig. 2), participants use a dropdown box to select

Rotation #1 - Rotation by 90 degrees counterclockwise about the x-axis

1. We would like to understand the matrix which describes a rotation by 90° counterclockwise about the x-axis.

Step A: Fill in the matrix in the answer booklet using the LEGO model and instructions below

Let this matrix be $R = \begin{pmatrix} a & b & c \\ d & e & f \\ g & h & i \end{pmatrix}$. If $X = \begin{pmatrix} x \\ y \\ z \end{pmatrix}$ is any point on the shuttle, then this rotation moves the point X to the point

$$RX = \begin{pmatrix} a & b & c \\ d & e & f \\ g & h & i \end{pmatrix} \begin{pmatrix} x \\ y \\ z \end{pmatrix} = \begin{pmatrix} ax + by + cz \\ dx + ey + fz \\ gx + hy + iz \end{pmatrix}$$

We want to determine the numbers $a, b, c, \cdots, i$. Pick up the shuttle, hold it so you are looking directly at the nose (the x-axis). Then the y-axis (the left wing) is on your right and the z-axis (the antenna) is up. Rotate it counterclockwise by 90°.

(a) Notice the nose did not move, i.e. the point $(N, 0, 0)$ moved to the point $(N, 0, 0)$, or

$$\begin{pmatrix} a & b & c \\ d & e & f \\ g & h & i \end{pmatrix} \begin{pmatrix} N \\ 0 \\ 0 \end{pmatrix} = \begin{pmatrix} N \\ 0 \\ 0 \end{pmatrix}$$

Using the rotation matrix at the top for reference, we can formulate:

$$a(N) + b(0) + c(0) = N \tag{1}$$
$$d(N) + e(0) + f(0) = 0 \tag{2}$$
$$\vdots$$

Use this to determine a, d, g.

Fig. 6. The first step of instructions for rotation #1 from the rotation booklet. These instructions guide students through using the LEGO space shuttle model to fill in an empty rotation matrix.

Rotation #6 - Rotation by 30 degrees counterclockwise about the z-axis

6. We would like to understand the matrix which describes a rotation by 30° counterclockwise about the z-axis.

Step A: Fill in the matrix in the answer booklet using the LEGO model and instructions below

Again let this matrix be $R = \begin{pmatrix} a & b & c \\ d & e & f \\ g & h & i \end{pmatrix}$. Hold the shuttle so you are looking down from above at the antenna. Hold the shuttle so the x-axis (the nose) is on your right and the y-axis (the left wing) is forward. Rotate the shuttle by 30° counterclockwise about the z-axis. The antenna does not move, i.e. $(0, 0, A)$ moves to $(0, 0, A)$.

The nose moves to 30° from the x-axis toward the y-axis but stays in the xy-plane, i.e. $(N, 0, 0)$ moves to $(N \cos 30°, N \sin 30°, 0)$. Check the sin and cos and the signs against the figure.

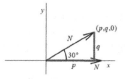

Fig. 7. The first step of instructions for rotation #6 from the rotation booklet. These instructions guide students through using the LEGO space shuttle model to fill in an empty rotation matrix.

Answer Sheet #2: Rotation by 90° counterclockwise about the y-axis.

Step A: Fill in Matrix R using the instructions in the Rotation Booklet and the Lego Shuttle:

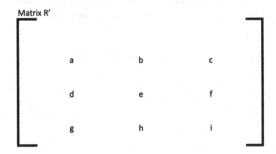

Matrix R

$$\begin{bmatrix} a & b & c \\ d & e & f \\ g & h & i \end{bmatrix}$$

Step B: Fill in Matrix R' using the AR Classroom – Workshop 1 Virtual and the Lego Shuttle:

Hold the shuttle in front of the AR Classroom App and again rotate it **90° counterclockwise about the y-axis**. Remember to set the AR Classroom: Dimension = 3D, Angle = Degrees

Matrix R'

$$\begin{bmatrix} a & b & c \\ d & e & f \\ g & h & i \end{bmatrix}$$

STEP C: Does the Matrix R' displayed by the AR Classroom agree with the Matrix R? If not, ask the experimenter for help.

Fig. 8. For each of the 6 questions, students filled out the rotation matrix on the top using the rotation booklet and filled out the rotation matrix on the bottom using the AR-Classroom.

the axis of rotation and then physically rotate the shuttle along the axis of rotation. The rotation matrix is updated with the rotation of the shuttle along the selected axis of rotation. It should be noted that the AR-Classroom will present participants with a warning message if they physically rotate the shuttle along an axis that does not match the axis they selected using the dropdown box.

2.6 Active Control Materials

The active control group did not interact with the AR-Classroom. Instead, they spent an equivalent amount of time doing the following: watching the introductory video on matrix algebra, completing two spatial thinking tests, a worksheet that used analogies to teach how spatial thinking can help solve problems, and another version of the same two spatial thinking tests. While spatial thinking is involved in matrix algebra and in understanding the visualizations used in the AR-Classroom, completing the active control activities should not train participants in the skills and concepts tested by the matrix algebra test.

2.7 Post-test Materials

All three learning conditions completed a post-test composed of the PSVT:R and matrix algebra test with confidence ratings.

3 Results

3.1 Pre-test

Between-subjects ANOVAs were run to test if there were any differences between the learning conditions (Table 2). There were no significant differences ($ps > .05$) between the learning conditions in experience with video games, 3D modelling, and AR (ratings closer to 5 represent experience), PSVT:R accuracy, matrix algebra accuracy, and matrix algebra confidence (ratings closer to 5 represent confidence). Participants across all three learning conditions were the most experienced with video games but not experienced with 3D modelling or AR. Participants struggled with the PSVT:R and the matrix algebra test, and they were not confident in their matrix algebra understanding.

Table 2. Mean Pre-Test Scores by Learning Condition.

	Virtual Workshop	Physical Workshop	Active Control
Experience with video games	3.4	3.1	2.7
Experience with 3D modelling	1.6	1.7	1.7
Experience with Augmented Reality	1.7	1.7	1.5
PSVT:R Accuracy	63%	61%	64%
Matrix Algebra Accuracy	50%	53%	52%
Matrix Algebra Confidence	2.5	2.3	2.3

3.2 Post-test

Between-subjects ANOVAs were run to test if there were any differences between the learning conditions (Table 3). There were no significant differences ($ps > .05$) between the learning conditions in PSVT:R accuracy, matrix algebra accuracy, and matrix algebra confidence. Participants across all three learning conditions improved slightly on the PSVT:R and the matrix algebra test, and their confidence improved. However, the learning conditions did not significantly differ from one another.

3.3 Changes in from Pre-test to Post-test

Using ANCOVAs, we investigated group differences in post-test PSVT:R accuracy, matrix algebra accuracy, and matrix algebra confidence after controlling for variation in their respective pre-test performance. There was a significant difference in PSVT:R

Table 3. Mean Post-Test Scores by Learning Condition.

	Virtual Workshop	Physical Workshop	Active Control
PSVT:R Accuracy	67%	71%	67%
Matrix Algebra Accuracy	61%	65%	60%
Matrix Algebra Confidence	3.4	3.5	3.2

accuracy from pre-test to post-test, $F(1, 55) = 97.17, p < .001$, meaning that participant performance on the PSVT:R improved from the beginning to the end of the experiment. However, there were no significant group differences for accuracy on the matrix algebra test, $F(2, 55) = 1.34, p = .27$. This means that all three learning conditions improved equally, so the learning experience did not impact their spatial thinking skills. This is expected as we did not hypothesize that interacting with the AR-Classroom or completing the active control activities would improve participants' spatial thinking.

For matrix algebra accuracy, there was a significant improvement from pre-test to post-test, $F(1, 55) = 35.16, p < .001$. However, there were no significant group differences for accuracy on the matrix algebra test, $F(2, 55) = 0.67, p = .51$. While participants showed improved performance on the matrix algebra test, there were no group differences in post-test accuracy (Fig. 9). A similar pattern was found for matrix algebra confidence. There was a significant improvement in matrix algebra confidence from pre-test to post-test, $F(1, 53) = 26.31, p < .001$; however, there were no significant group differences, $F(2, 53) = 0.26, p = .78$. Unfortunately, we did not find evidence that following the rotation booklet and interacting with the AR-Classroom improved matrix algebra accuracy and confidence compared to the active control. This result conflicts with our hypothesis that the two workshop groups would improve more than the active control.

It could be that individual differences, such previous experience with matrix algebra or other participant characteristics and PSVT:R accuracy, might add help explain the lack of group differences. Therefore, we ran a series of ANCOVAs that included variables collected in the pre-test. The only significant predictor of matrix algebra accuracy was PSVT:R accuracy, $F(1, 54) = 27.13, p < .001$, and the only significant predictor of matrix algebra confidence was PSVT:R accuracy, $F(1, 52) = 23.01, p < .001$. As expected because of the tightly coupled relationship between spatial thinking and mathematical reasoning, spatial thinking skills are predictive of improvements in matrix algebra accuracy and confidence, regardless of learning condition.

To further evaluate the AR-Classroom's efficacy in teaching matrix algebra, we conducted a more detailed analysis on the matrix algebra test. The matrix algebra test was composed of three problem types: translations (which were not taught by the AR-Classroom), rotations (which were taught by the AR-Classroom), and translation with rotations (more challenging problems than what was taught by the AR-Classroom). We hypothesized that there would be no group differences for translation problems because none of the groups received training in translations beyond an explanation in the introduction to matrix algebra video. We hypothesized that there would be group differences for rotation and translation with rotation problems, such that the physical and virtual groups will outperform the active control group. This is because the two workshop groups received training in these concepts through completing the rotation booklet and using the AR-Classroom.

Using ANCOVAs, we investigated group differences in post-test matrix algebra accuracy after controlling for variation in pre-test matrix algebra accuracy. As expected, there were no significant group differences for translation problems, $F(2, 56) = 1.44$, $p = .24$ (Fig. 9). The result confirms our hypothesis that participants did not improve their understanding of translation problems because they received minimal instruction about translations. There was a marginal group difference for rotation problems, $F(2, 56) = 2.52$, $p = .09$ (Fig. 9). Using adjusted means, there was a trend that physical workshop participants were the most accurate ($M = 52\%$), virtual ($M = 44\%$) were moderately accurate, and control participants were the least accurate ($M = 43\%$). There was a marginal group difference for translation with rotation problems, $F(2, 55) = 2.68$, $p = .08$ (Fig. 9). Using adjusted means, there was a trend that virtual participants were the most accurate ($M = 58\%$), physical ($M = 41\%$) were moderately accurate, and control participants were the least accurate ($M = 34\%$). While these two findings were not statistically significant, they both are in alignment with our prediction that participants

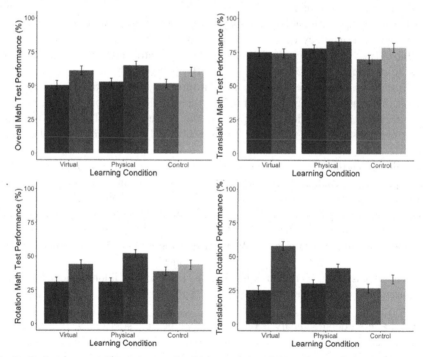

Fig. 9. Performance on the entire matrix algebra test (top left), only translation problems (top right), only rotation problems (bottom left), and translation with rotation problems (bottom right) for all three learning conditions split by pre-test (left bar; darker color) and post-test (right bar; lighter color). (Color figure online)

who completed the rotation booklet and interacted with the AR-Classroom would be more accurate on these problems compared to the active control group.

4 Discussion

The efficacy of the AR-Classroom was evaluated using a learning experiment followed by quantitative analyses presented in the current paper and qualitative analyses presented in companion paper [21]. The findings from both papers suggest that the matrix algebra learning interventions delivered by AR-Classroom may be helpful and lead to improvements in mathematical skills. While performance on the matrix algebra test improved equally for all learning groups, there was a trend that students who used the physical workshop were more accurate on rotation problems and that students who used the virtual workshop were more accurate on translation with rotation problems. This suggests that the both workshops were supporting the learning of concepts covered in the rotation booklets and AR-Classroom. Unfortunately, it remains unclear if using physical versus virtual manipulatives resulted in different learning outcomes. Future work on the AR-Classroom will include integrating the rotation booklet activities into the application itself and continuing to improve user-app interactions. Future learning efficacy research on the AR-Classroom will include larger sample sizes to increase the power to detect meaningful differences between learning groups, balancing groups by gender and spatial thinking skills to reduce the impact of individual differences within the learning groups, and a more comprehensive matrix algebra test to more clearly identify changes in conceptual knowledge. In conclusion, the development of and research on the AR-Classroom and its predecessor, BRICKxAR/T has been guided by a data-informed and iterative approach. This approach has been fundamental in understanding how students interact with educational technologies along with how students engage with complex mathematical concepts using interactive materials and AR.

Acknowledgments. This material is based upon work supported by the National Science Foundation under Grant No. 2119549. Thank you to our Research Assistants who assisted with data collection and analysis: Adalia Sedigh, Grace Girgenti, Hana Syed, and Megan Sculley.

Disclosure of Interests.   The authors have no competing interests to declare that are relevant to the content of this article.

References

1. Cesaria, A., Herman, T.: Learning obstacles in geometry. J. Eng. Sci. Technol. **14**(3), 1271–1280 (2019)
2. Noto, M.S., Priatna, N., Dahlan, J.A.: Mathematical proof: the learning obstacles of preservice mathematics teachers on transformation geometry. J. Math. Educ. **10**(1), 117–126 (2019)
3. Jones, K., Tzekaki, M.: Research on the teaching and learning of geometry. In: The Second Handbook of Research on the Psychology of Mathematics Education, pp. 109–149 (2016)
4. Lehrer, R., et al.: Developing understanding of geometry and space in the primary grades. In: Designing Learning Environments for Developing Understanding of Geometry and Space, pp. 169–200. Routledge (2012)

5. Mulligan, J.: Looking within and beyond the geometry curriculum: connecting spatial reasoning to mathematics learning. ZDM Math. Educ. **47**, 511–517 (2015)
6. Abrahamson, D., Lindgren, R.: Embodiment and embodied design (2014)
7. Rau, M.A.: Comparing multiple theories about learning with physical and virtual representations: conflicting or complementary effects? Educ. Psychol. Rev. **32**(2), 297–325 (2020)
8. Akçayır, M., Akçayır, G.: Advantages and challenges associated with augmented reality for education: a systematic review of the literature. Educ. Res. Rev. **20**, 1–11 (2017)
9. Ibáñez, M.B., Delgado-Kloos, C.: Augmented reality for STEM learning: a systematic review. Comput. Educ. **123**, 109–123 (2018)
10. Wu, H.K., Lee, S.W.Y., Chang, H.Y., Liang, J.C.: Current status, opportunities and challenges of augmented reality in education. Comput. Educ. **62**, 41–49 (2013)
11. Rohendi, D., Wihardi, Y.: Learning three-dimensional shapes in geometry using mobile-based augmented reality. Int. J. Interact. Mob. Technol. **14**(9) (2020)
12. Scavarelli, A., Arya, A., Teather, R.J.: Virtual reality and augmented reality in social learning spaces: a literature review. Virtual Reality **25**, 257–277 (2021)
13. Pellas, N., Mystakidis, S., Kazanidis, I.: Immersive virtual reality in K-12 and higher education: a systematic review of the last decade of scientific literature. Virtual Reality **25**(3), 835–861 (2021)
14. Ahmad, N., Junaini, S.: Augmented reality for learning mathematics: a systematic literature review. Int. J. Emerg. Technol. Learn. (iJET) **15**(16), 106–122 (2020)
15. Shaghaghian, Z., Burte, H., Song, D., Yan, W.: Design and evaluation of an augmented reality app for learning spatial transformations and their mathematical representations. In: 2022 IEEE Conference on Virtual Reality and 3D User Interfaces Abstracts and Workshops (VRW), pp. 608–609. IEEE (2022)
16. Aguilar, S.D., Burte, H., Shaghaghian, Z., Yasskin, P., Liew, J., Yan, W.: Enhancing usability in AR and non-AR educational technology: an embodied approach to geometric transformations. In: Zaphiris, P., Ioannou, A. (eds.) HCII 2023. LNCS, vol. 14041, pp. 3–21. Springer, Cham (2023). https://doi.org/10.1007/978-3-031-34550-0_1
17. Shaghaghian, Z., Burte, H., Song, D., Yan, W.: An augmented reality application and experiment for understanding and learning spatial transformation matrices. Virtual Reality **28**(1), 1–18 (2024)
18. Yeh, S., et al.: AR-classroom: augmented reality technology for learning 3D spatial transformations and their matrix representation. In: 2023 IEEE Frontiers in Education Conference (FIE), pp. 1–8. IEEE (2023)
19. Aguilar, S.D., et al.: AR-classroom: investigating user-app-interactions to enhance usability of AR technology for learning two and three dimensional rotations. In: Stephanidis, C., Antona, M., Ntoa, S., Salvendy, G. (eds.) HCII 2023. CCIS, vol. 1957, pp. 249–256. Springer, Cham (2023). https://doi.org/10.1007/978-3-031-49212-9_31
20. Aguilar, S.D., et al.: AR-classroom: usability of AR educational technology for learning rotations using three-dimensional matrix algebra. In: 2023 IEEE Frontiers in Education Conference (FIE), pp. 1–8. IEEE (2023)
21. Aguilar, S.D., et al.: Learning 3D matrix algebra using virtual and physical manipulatives: qualitative analysis of the efficacy of the AR-classroom. In: Zaphiris, P., Ioannou, A. (eds.) HCII 2024, LNCS, vol. 14724, pp. 3–16. Springer, Cham (2024). https://doi.org/10.1007/978-3-031-61691-4_1

An Inquiry into Virtual Reality Strategies for Improving Inclusive Urban Design Concerning People with Intellectual Disabilities

Guillermo Franganillo-Parrado[(✉)] [iD], Luis A. Hernández-Ibáñez[(✉)] [iD],
and Viviana Barneche-Naya[(✉)] [iD]

VideaLAB, Universidade da Coruña, A Coruña, Spain
{guillermo.franganillo,luis.hernandez,viviana.barneche}@udc.es

Abstract. The potential of Virtual Reality (VR) as a tool for enhancing skills and promoting community participation has gained attention. This inquiry aims to assess the current state of research on the application of VR in inclusive urban design for people with intellectual disabilities (ID). The literature was synthesized, and three primary research questions were addressed using the Preferred Reporting Items for Systematic Reviews and Meta-Analyses (PRISMA) guidelines. A total of 18 original research articles were identified from reputable sources, including *Cyberpsychology & Behavior*, *Urban Studies* and *Virtual Reality*. The inquiry found that VR interventions hold promise for promoting independent living skills, enhancing cognitive performance, and improving social skills. Additionally, it highlighted the importance of urban encounters for the well-being and autonomy of individuals with ID. However, this investigation also identified limitations, such as potentially excluding relevant studies published in non-English languages or non-peer-reviewed sources. In conclusion, this inquiry presents a comprehensive synthesis of the current literature on the use of VR in inclusive urban design for individuals with ID. The analysis presents findings that contribute to the understanding of the potential benefits and challenges associated with VR technology in this field.

Keywords: Virtual Reality · VR · Intellectual Disabilities · Learning Disabilities · Inclusive Urban Design · Urban Accessibility

1 Introduction

The use of VR in inclusive urban design for individuals with ID has gained significant attention in both research and practice. This inquiry draws on a variety of studies that have investigated the potential of VR technology to meet the needs of people with ID in urban environments. [1] highlighted the rehabilitative potential of VR for individuals with ID. They emphasized its role in skill development and cognitive enhancement. The authors' findings suggest that VR can be an effective tool for improving the lives of people with ID. [12] investigated the feasibility of using natural interfaces and virtual environments to improve pedestrian skills in adults with autism spectrum disorders. Their

P. Zaphiris and A. Ioannou (Eds.): HCII 2024, LNCS 14724, pp. 65–77, 2024.
https://doi.org/10.1007/978-3-031-61691-4_5

findings suggest that VR has the potential to address mobility challenges for individuals with cognitive impairments [12].

Research in this area explores various aspects of VR applications for individuals with ID. Studies have investigated the design of location-based learning experiences, the integration of VR content into life skills training, and the usability of VR vocational skills training systems for this population [14, 15], and [22]. [11] investigated the impact of VR on route learning, and shortcut performance in adults with ID. Their findings shed light on the potential benefits of VR interventions in enhancing functional abilities.

However, thematic gaps still require further investigation despite the growing body of research. While some studies have focused on specific skills training and cognitive rehabilitation using VR, there is a need to comprehensively assess the broader implications of VR in inclusive urban design for people with ID.

Moreover, the current literature mainly focuses on the usability and effectiveness of VR interventions, with little attention given to the influence of VR on the community participation and autonomy of individuals with ID in urban environments.

This inquiry article aims to evaluate the current research on using VR in inclusive urban design for people with ID. The investigation will assess VR intervention's effectiveness, usability, and impact, identify thematic gaps, and provide insights for future research and practice in this domain.

2 Methodology

The inquiry followed the Preferred Reporting Items for Systematic Reviews and Meta-Analyses (PRISMA) guidelines to ensure a comprehensive and transparent approach to synthesizing the literature. The investigation aimed to address three primary research questions to guide the analysis of the current state of research on the application of VR in inclusive urban design for people with ID.

2.1 Formulation of Research Questions

- Question 01: What is the trend of research on the use of VR as a support for people with ID in their relationship with the urban environment and how is its evolution?
- Question 02: What is the impact of VR on the perception and experience of people with ID in urban environments?
- Question 03: What are the current research's main thematic gaps and limitations on the application of VR in inclusive urban design for people with ID?

2.2 Data Search in Specialized Databases

To identify relevant studies, a comprehensive search strategy was developed. Peer-reviewed empirical studies published in English were systematically searched for using electronic databases, including Clarivate Web of Science© and Elsevier Scopus©. The search strategy included keywords related to 'virtual reality', 'urban design', and 'intellectual disability'. The search strategy was developed to identify studies that examine the use of VR to enhance inclusive urban design for individuals with ID. To narrow the search, we included alternative synonyms using Boolean OR (refer to Table 1).

To ensure an exhaustive study of the articles, it was necessary to consult not only the records found in Scopus and Web of Science, whose search yielded 13 results, but also other accredited databases such as PubMed, JSTOR, and Google Scholar, as well as the references cited in the articles, resulting in 29 other potentially relevant articles.

To ensure the relevance and specificity of the findings, the investigation excluded non-peer-reviewed studies, studies with unknown authors, and those with no full text available. Only high-quality peer-reviewed empirical research was included.

Very few references to ID+ Urban Design were found. It may be possible to improve the search by introducing other terms, although our tests did not yield the desired result.

Table 1. Database and search criteria. Source: Own elaboration

Database	Search terms	Initial results
Web of Science	((((((TS = ("virtual reality")) OR TS = ("Virtual Environment")) AND TS = ("intellectual disability")) OR TS = ("learning Disability")) OR TS = ("cognitive impairments")) AND TS = ("urban design")) OR TS = ("accessible city")	3
Scopus	"Virtual Reality" OR "Virtual Environment" AND "Urban Design" OR "City" AND "Intellectual Disabilities" OR "Cognitive Impairments" OR "Learning Disabilities"	10
Other databases (*PubMed, JSTOR and Google Scholar*)	"Virtual Reality" OR "Virtual Environment" AND "Urban Design" OR "City" AND "Intellectual Disabilities" OR "Cognitive Impairments" OR "Learning Disabilities"	10
References gathered from articles		19

2.3 Results

The inquiry procedure is outlined in Fig. 1. We identified a total of 42 studies, of which 24 were excluded after reviewing the title and abstract (see Fig. 1 for details). Therefore, we retrieved 18 studies for full-text assessment as they met the criteria and are included in this inquiry (Table 2).

The following section presents the analysis results, which are organized according to the three research questions and supported by both original research articles from the provided list of literature sources and references.

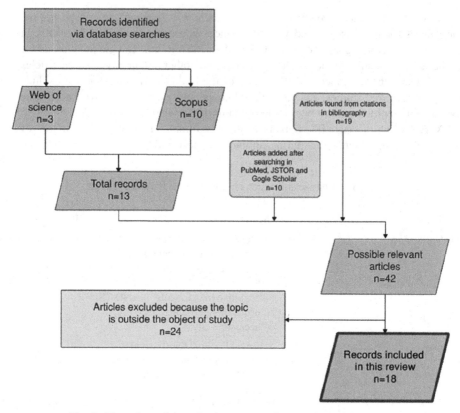

Fig. 1. Flow chart of the selection process. Source: Own elaboration.

- Question 01: What is the trend of research on the use of VR as a support for people with ID in their relationship with the urban environment and how is its evolution?

Research on using VR to support people with ID in their relationship with the urban environment has significantly evolved. Initially, the research focused on the potential of VR interventions to improve real-world skills in individuals with ID [7]. Moreover, immersive VR technology has been studied to comprehend preferences for urban squares based on living environments, indicating a wider exploration of VR in urban contexts [9].

[1] conducted a review that highlighted the rehabilitative potential of VR for individuals with ID. The authors emphasized its role in skill development and cognitive enhancement and suggested future directions for the development of more applications for independent living skills, as well as exploring interventions for promoting motor and cognitive skills. [2] explored the potential of VR in disability and rehabilitation. They focused on transferring spatial information and life skills learned in a virtual environment to the real world.

Table 2. Selected bibliography. Source: Own elaboration

Index	Paper title
1	Virtual Reality in the Rehabilitation of People with Intellectual Disabilities: Review. (Standen and Brown, 2005)
2	Virtual reality, disability and rehabilitation. (Wilson, P. et al., 1997)
3	ID Tech: A Virtual Reality Simulator Training for Teenagers with Intellectual Disabilities. (Capallera et al., 2023)
4	The effective use of virtual environments in the education and rehabilitation of students with intellectual disabilities. *(Standen, P.J. et al.,2001)*
5	Virtual reality as an assistive technology to support the cognitive development of people with intellectual and multiple disabilities. (Cunha and Silva, 2017)
6	Virtual reality and its role in removing the barriers that turn cognitive impairments into intellectual disability. (Standen and Brown, 2006)
7	Improving real-world skills in people with intellectual disabilities: an immersive virtual reality intervention. (Michalski et al., 2023)
8	Using virtual reality to provide health care information to people with intelectual disabilities: acceptability, usability, and potential utility. (Hall et al., 2011)
9	Immersive virtual reality-aided conjoint analysis of urban square preference by living environment. (Kim, S., et al., 2020)
10	From e-learning to VR-learning: An example of learning in an immersive virtual world. (Freina et al., 2016)
11	Use of a virtual-reality town for examining route-memory, and techniques for its rehabilitation in people with acquired brain injury. (Lloyd et al., 2006)
12	Virtual reality-based training for the motor development of people with intellectual and multiple disabilities. (Da Cunha et al., 2019)
13	Access to assistive technology for people with intellectual disabilities: A systematic review to identify barriers and facilitators. (Boot et al., 2018)
14	Natural interfaces and virtual environments for the acquisition of street crossing and path following skills in adults with Autism Spectrum Disorders: A feasibility study. (Saiano et al., 2015)
15	Route learning and shortcut performance in adults with intellectual disability: A study with virtual environments. (Mengue-Topio et al., 2011)
16	Universal life: the use of virtual worlds among people with disabilities (Smith, 2012)
17	Designing location-based learning experiences for people with intellectual disabilities and additional sensory impairments. (Brown et al., 2011)
18	Design insights into embedding virtual reality content into life skills training for people with intellectual disability. (Brown et al., 2016)

[3] asserts that the learning-by-doing approach shows promising results for working on learning objectives in VR and transferring them to the real world and presents stable results over time in terms of self-reported ease, satisfaction, and fatigue.

[4] investigated the use of virtual environments in educating and rehabilitating students with ID. They highlighted the potential of VR in enhancing learning experiences for this population.

[5] investigated the use of VR as an assistive technology to enhance the cognitive development of individuals with intellectual and multiple disabilities. The study demonstrated statistically significant improvements in cognitive tasks through observational analysis.

The research trend on using VR as a support for people with ID in their relationship with the urban environment has evolved from general explorations of VR benefits to more targeted investigations into specific applications. This reflects a growing understanding of the potential of VR technology in addressing the diverse needs of individuals with ID in urban contexts.

The trend towards more targeted and specialized applications of VR reflects an increasing understanding of the potential of VR technology to address specific needs and challenges faced by individuals with ID in urban settings. This suggests a maturing of research efforts, focusing on developing tailored VR interventions that cater to the unique requirements of this population in their urban experiences.

Therefore, although existing research shows a clear interest in using VR technology to enhance the urban experience for people with ID, it is important to note that the literature related specifically to urban design is limited.

- Question 02: What is the impact of VR on the perception and experience of people with ID in urban environments?

VR has been acknowledged for its potential in rehabilitating, assessing, and training skills for individuals with ID. [6] discussed the potential of VR in removing barriers that can turn cognitive impairments into ID. They emphasized the potential of VR to enhance the perception and experience of individuals with disabilities in urban environments.

It offers a safe, controlled, and repeatable training tool, providing opportunities for independent living, enhancing cognitive performance, and improving social skills [7]. Furthermore, VR has been investigated to deliver healthcare-related information to individuals with ID, demonstrating its potential usefulness in providing essential information to this population [8].

In conclusion, VR has the potential to significantly impact the perception and experience of people with ID in urban environments by providing opportunities for rehabilitation, skills training, social participation, and access to essential information. However, addressing the challenges and barriers to implementing VR effectively is crucial to ensure its inclusive and equitable utilization for individuals with ID.

- Question 03: What are the current research's main thematic gaps and limitations on the application of VR in inclusive urban design for people with ID?

The research has several thematic gaps and limitations, including a lack of inclusive research design. More studies are needed that involve individuals with ID as co-researchers, emphasizing their empowerment in the research process [18]. The lack of an inclusive research design impedes a comprehensive understanding of the needs and perspectives of people with ID in urban design initiatives.

Additionally, there is a dearth of literature exploring the experiences and perspectives of individuals with ID from low- and middle-income countries (LMICs) [16]. The lack of information results in a limited understanding of the unique challenges and opportunities related to inclusive urban design for people with ID in diverse socio-economic contexts.

Furthermore, research on VR technology for people with ID primarily focuses on the benefits of its use, with limited exploration of the current technological gaps and their impact on user experience [17]. The development of VR applications that are truly inclusive and effective for individuals with ID is hindered by this limitation.

It should be noted that the authors analyzed a sample of 16 people with ID-related problems who expressed the specific urban design problems that affect them. These problems included the following events: sidewalks occupied by fair booths, city maintenance work that requires pedestrians to change their routes, lack of street signage, and vehicle parked in a double line next to a pedestrian crossing. These events have not been found in any traceable article in scientific literature, so a research niche of high interest and social value has been located here.

In conclusion, the current research on the application of VR in inclusive urban design for people with ID has thematic gaps and limitations. These include the absence of inclusive research design, limited exploration of the experiences of individuals from LMICs, insufficient focus on technological gaps in VR applications, and the need to address a greater number of events in the urban environment, whose accessibility can be significantly improved through VR training.

2.4 Data Analysis

Through bibliometric analysis, it is possible to identify the predominant trends in the research presented in the selected articles. This analysis is based on the correlation of keywords used by the authors in their respective publications. We used VOSviewer (VOSViewer, 2023), a software specialized in constructing and visualizing bibliometric networks. The analysis uses several variables, including authors, documents, keywords, and other data.

The selection of publications was exported in plain text format. The VOSviewer analysis parameters were configured as follows:

- Type of analysis: co-occurrence
- Unit of analysis: all keywords
- Counting method: full counting
- Minimum number of occurrences of a keyword: 3
- Number of keywords to be selected: by default

After establishing the parameters, Fig. 2 illustrates the emerging trends in research based on the reviewed literature. The keywords are represented by circles that vary in size depending on the number of published papers that include them. The smaller the distance between them, the stronger the link, and the larger the distance, the weaker.

The VOSviewer analysis of the literature reveals three main interconnected research trends, represented in different colors. These trends are:

Virtual Reality. The use of VR to meet the educational needs of individuals with ID has received considerable attention in recent literature. Figure 3 presents a comprehensive

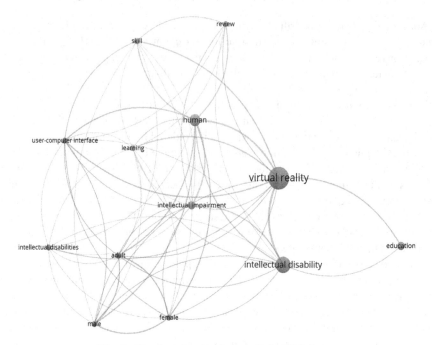

Fig. 2. Trends defined by keywords in VOSviewer

approach that highlights the potential of VR to address the specific requirements of individuals with ID, particularly in the educational domain.

The potential of VR as a tool to enhance the learning experiences of people with ID is highlighted by the connection between virtual reality, intellectual disability, and education terms.

Human. The analysis of the second trend is shown in Fig. 4. The interconnection of various concepts related to human abilities, learning, and intellectual impairment. The literature reflects an increasing focus on understanding the complex interplay between these factors and their implications for individuals with ID.

This interconnection highlights the need for a holistic approach to address the multifaceted challenges faced by individuals with ID, particularly in the context of urban design. By considering the relationships between human abilities, learning, and intellectual impairment, urban design interventions can be tailored to create environments that support the diverse needs of individuals with ID. Therefore, it is important to adopt a multidimensional approach to inclusive urban design, taking into account the complex interactions between human abilities, learning, and intellectual impairment.

User-Computer Interface. The association between the 'User-computer interface' and 'intellectual disabilities', 'adults', 'males', and 'females' suggests that it is crucial to design and implement user-computer interfaces that prioritize user-centered design approaches and cater to the diverse needs of the target user group. This contributes to developing more inclusive and effective user-computer interfaces for individuals with ID. It is important to note that the analyzed studies did not include young participants.

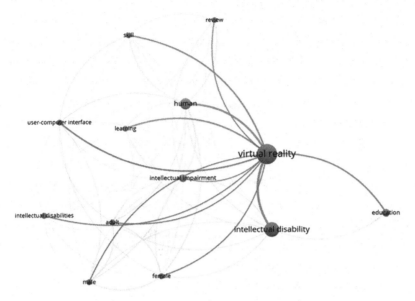

Fig. 3. *Virtual reality* connections in VOSviewer

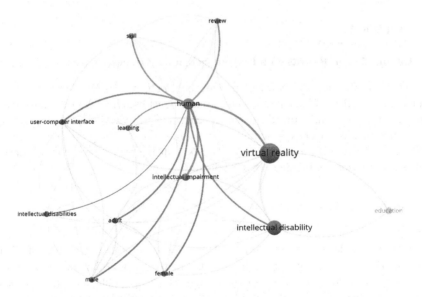

Fig. 4. Human connections in VOSviewer

In conclusion, the trend regarding 'User-computer interface' (see Fig. 5) highlights the significance of taking into account the specific requirements of adult individuals with ID.

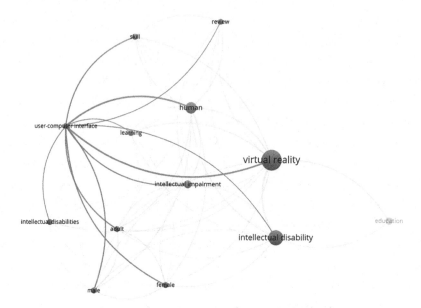

Fig. 5. User-computer interface in VOSviewer

3 Discussion

3.1 Comparison of Results with Existing Scientific Articles

The findings of this inquiry align with previous research, such as [19], which explored best practices models of VR intervention for individuals with intellectual and developmental disabilities, highlighting the potential benefits of VR interventions. However, the current investigation extends these findings by specifically focusing on the application of VR in inclusive urban design for individuals with ID, providing a comprehensive synthesis of the existing literature in this domain.

3.2 Limitations of the Study

Although the search strategy and inclusion criteria were thorough, this research may have limitations due to the lack of literature specifically addressing the application of VR in inclusive urban design for people with ID. This is particularly evident in non-scientific professional literature. The exclusion of non-English language publications and the focus on peer-reviewed articles may have resulted in the omission of relevant studies published in other languages or non-peer-reviewed sources. In addition, it is important to note that the investigation only covers existing literature and may not include emerging research in this rapidly evolving field.

It is important to consider whether additional search results could have been found in the existing literature if the search terms 'functional diversity' were used. However, this term is too broad and does not exclusively refer to intellectual disabilities.

3.3 Suggestions for Future Research

Future research should aim to address the identified gaps and limitations in the current literature. Valuable insights could be gained from studies that focus on the long-term impact of VR interventions on the community participation and autonomy of individuals with ID in urban settings. Moreover, conducting comparative studies to evaluate the effectiveness of various VR interventions and their implications for inclusive urban design could significantly contribute to evidence-based practices in this field.

It is important to note the challenges in locating scientific articles that specifically address the enhancement of the urban experience for individuals with ID using VR. This indicates that there are still areas of research that need to be explored, which we will pursue in our research as it is a topic of great interest and social significance.

A taxonomy can be proposed based on the previous evaluation, encompassing the following classifications (Table 3):

Table 3. Taxonomy of VR in Supporting People with ID in Urban Environments. Source: Own elaboration.

Types	Virtual Simulation Environments	Applications	Inclusive Urban Design
	Videogame engines		Training and Skill Development
	3D Modeling		Problem-Based Learning
Evaluation	Learning Outcomes	Challenges	Ethical Considerations
	Behavioral Analysis		Technological Constraints
	Social and Emotional Impact		Accessibility and Adaptability

This taxonomy offers a more comprehensive framework for understanding the various applications, types, evaluation methods, and challenges associated with using VR to enhance the autonomy and independence of individuals with ID in urban environments.

4 Conclusion

The inquiry has provided valuable insights into the current state of research on the application of VR in inclusive urban design for people with ID. The main results of this investigation indicate that VR interventions have shown promise in promoting skills for independent living, enhancing cognitive performance, and improving social skills [1].

The analysis emphasizes the potential impact of urban encounters on the well-being and autonomy of individuals with ID [21], highlighting the significance of even brief exchanges between strangers in shaping boundaries of social inclusion and exclusion in cities.

To investigate the application of VR in inclusive urban design for people with ID, the findings have aligned with existing literature. For example, [20] reviewed local-level inclusion-building initiatives, while [10] explored the effectiveness of the use of an IVR game by keeping high the involvement and the interest of the player and maximizing the transfer of the newly learned skills to real life. These findings contribute to understanding the potential benefits and challenges of VR technology in urban environments for individuals with ID.

All the articles highlight the importance of VR virtual reality in improving the lives of people with ID, mentioning urban design aspects such as the layout of the virtual environment as a grid of streets lined with high brick walls and buildings [13], and distractors such as cars, other people, and dogs [12], simulating a real urban environment. However, these aspects are limited, and further research is needed to uncover additional aspects.

As previously mentioned, the limitations of this study may involve the exclusion of relevant research published in languages other than English or non-peer-reviewed sources. Additionally, the focus on existing literature may not cover emerging research in this rapidly evolving field. Therefore, future research should aim to address the identified thematic gaps and limitations. This should focus on the long-term impact of VR interventions on the community participation and autonomy of individuals with ID in urban settings. Comparative studies evaluating the effectiveness of different VR interventions and their implications for inclusive urban design could contribute to evidence-based practices in this field. Research into the experiences of individuals with ID using VR applications in urban environments would enhance understanding of the benefits and challenges of VR technology in this context.

Given the scarcity of research on the topic, our research will focus on testing the potential improvements that this technology can bring to promote more inclusive urban design.

In conclusion, this inquiry has provided a comprehensive synthesis of the existing literature on the application of VR in inclusive urban design for people with ID, offering valuable insights and recommendations for future research and practice in this domain.

References

1. Standen, P.J., Brown, D.J.: Virtual reality in the rehabilitation of people with intellectual disabilities: review. Cyberpsychol. Behav.: Impact Internet Multimed. Virtual Reality Behav. Soc. **8**(3), 272–282 (2005)
2. Wilson, P.N., Foreman, N., Stanton, D.: Virtual reality, disability and rehabilitation. Disabil. Rehabil. **19**(6), 213–220 (1997)
3. Capallera, M., et al.: ID tech: a virtual reality simulator training for teenagers with intellectual disabilities. Appl. Sci. **13**, 3679 (2023)
4. Standen, P.J., Brown, D.J., Cromby, J.J.: The effective use of virtual environments in the education and rehabilitation of students with intellectual disabilities. Br. J. Edu. Technol. **32**(3), 289–299 (2001). https://doi.org/10.1111/1467-8535.00199
5. Cunha, R., Silva, R.: Virtual reality as an assistive technology to support the cognitive development of people with intellectual and multiple disabilities (2017). https://doi.org/10.5753/cbie.sbie.2017.987
6. Standen, P., Brown, D.: Virtual reality and its role in removing the barriers that turn cognitive impairments into intellectual disability. Virtual Reality **10**(3–4), 241–252 (2006). https://doi.org/10.1007/s10055-006-0042-6
7. Michalski, S.C., et al.: Improving real-world skills in people with intellectual disabilities: an immersive virtual reality intervention. Virtual Reality 1–12 (2023)

8. Hall, V., Conboy-Hill, S., Taylor, D.: Using virtual reality to provide health care information to people with intellectual disabilities: acceptability, usability, and potential utility. J. Med. Internet Res. **13**(4), e91 (2011). https://doi.org/10.2196/jmir.1917
9. Kim, S., Kim, J., Kim, B.: Immersive virtual reality-aided conjoint analysis of urban square preference by living environment. Sustainability **12**(16), 6440 (2020)
10. Lloyd, J., Powell, T.E., Smith, J., Persaud, N.V.: Use of a virtual-reality town for examining route-memory, and techniques for its rehabilitation in people with acquired brain injury. In: Proceedings of the 6th International Disability, Virtual Reality and Associated Technologies, pp. 175–182 (2006)
11. Cunha, R., Neiva, F., Silva, R.: Virtual reality-based training for the motor development of people with intellectual and multiple disabilities. Rev. Inform. Teórica Aplicada **26**(3), 40–49 (2019). https://doi.org/10.22456/2175-2745.86478
12. Saiano, M., et al.: Natural interfaces and virtual environments for the acquisition of street crossing and path following skills in adults with autism spectrum disorders: a feasibility study. J. NeuroEng. Rehabil. **12** (2015)
13. Mengue-Topio, H., Courbois, Y., Farran, E.K., Sockeel, P.: Route learning and shortcut performance in adults with intellectual disability: a study with virtual environments. Res. Dev. Disabil. **32**(1), 345–352 (2011)
14. Brown, D.J., McHugh, D., Standen, P., Evett, L., Shopland, N., Battersby, S.: Designing location-based learning experiences for people with intellectual disabilities and additional sensory impairments. Comput. Educ. **56**(1), 11–20 (2011)
15. Brown, R.A., Sitbon, L., Fell, L., Koplick, S., Beaumont, C., Brereton, M.: Design insights into embedding virtual reality content into life skills training for people with intellectual disability. In: Proceedings of the 28th Australian Conference on Computer-Human Interaction (2016)
16. Bialik, K., Mhiri, M.: Barriers to employment for people with intellectual disabilities in low-and middle-income countries: self-advocate and family perspectives. J. Int. Dev. **34**(5), 988–1001 (2022)
17. Bryant, L., Brunner, M., Hemsley, B.: A review of virtual reality technologies in the field of communication disability: implications for practice and research. Disabil. Rehabil.: Assist. Technol. (2019)
18. Johnson, K., Minogue, G., Hopklins, R.: Inclusive research: making a difference to policy and legislation. J. Appl. Res. Intellect. Disabil. **27**(1), 76–84 (2014)
19. Lotan, M., Yalon-Chamovitz, S., Weiss, P.: Lessons learned towards a best practices model of virtual reality intervention for individuals with intellectual and developmental disability. In: 2009 Virtual Rehabilitation International Conference, Haifa, Israel, pp. 70–77 (2009). https://doi.org/10.1109/ICVR.2009.5174208
20. Robinson, S., Carnemolla, P., Lay, K., Kelly, J.: Involving people with intellectual disability in setting priorities for building community inclusion at a local government level. Br. J. Learn. Disabil. **50**(3), 364–375 (2022)
21. Wiesel, I., Bigby, C., Carling-Jenkins, R.: 'do you think i'm stupid?': urban encounters between people with and without intellectual disability. Urban Stud. **50**(12), 2391–2406 (2013). https://doi.org/10.1177/0042098012474521
22. Wu, T.-F., Sher, Y., Tai, K.-H., Hong, J.-C.: Usability of virtual reality vocational skills training system for students with intellectual disabilities. In: Miesenberger, K., Manduchi, R., Covarrubias Rodriguez, M., Peňáz, P. (eds.) ICCHP 2020. LNCS, vol. 12376, pp. 123–129. Springer, Cham (2020). https://doi.org/10.1007/978-3-030-58796-3_16

English Language Learning in Primary School Children Using Immersive Virtual Reality

Alessandro Frolli[✉] , Clara Esposito , Rossana Pia Laccone ,
and Francesco Cerciello

Disability Research Centre of University of International Studies in Rome, 00147 Rome, Italy
{alessandro.frolli,clara.esposito,rossana.laccone,
francesco.cerciello}@unint.eu

Abstract. The growing prominence of Virtual Reality (VR) has captivated the attention of scholars and educators, prompting them to delve into its potential as a learning tool across diverse educational domains. Consequently, numerous literature reviews have examined and consolidated the educational applications of VR. VR refers to a type of simulated reality, constructed using computer systems and digital formats. The construction and visualization of this type of reality requires the use of hardware and software powerful enough to create a realistic and immersive experience experienced in first person. It is a perceptual enhancement, based on the generation of virtual content by a computer and their overlap with reality. VR has long been studied and described for its potential to revolutionize education as it would provide numerous benefits, including access to limited logistical experiences (such as going to the moon) or access to experiences that are physically impossible (such as being in-side a molecule). However, as Jensen & Konradsen said, it was with the release of Oculus Rift in 2013 that VR became synonymous with head-mounted display-based VR (HMD). However, there remains a dearth of recent scholarly reviews specifically focusing on the use of VR in language learning, a distinct field of interest. The aim of this paper is to investigate the relation between VR and learning a foreign language, in this case English. We compared two teaching methodologies: traditional one and VR-based in a population of 120 Italian students from the last year of primary school.

Keywords: Education · Virtual Reality · Learning · Foreign language · Language

1 Introduction

Virtual reality (VR) has rapidly gained popularity as a powerful technological tool capable of transforming the human experience in multiple domains. Its ability to create simulated environments that engage all our senses has garnered significant attention from scholars and professionals across a wide range of disciplines. VR is a promising learning tool that allows learners to immerse themselves in three-dimensional environments. It has the capability to enable interactive learning experiences since it can actively involve the learner in the learning process by re-acting dynamically to the learner's movements and behavior [1, 2]. Virtual reality is a concept that involves the creation of interactive digital environments that simulate the sensory experience of being present in a real or imagined world. This immersive engagement is made possible through the use of display devices, such as VR headsets, which transmit three-dimensional images to users, while motion tracking sensors enable interaction within the virtual environment. With this technology, learners can explore and manipulate three-dimensional (3-D) interactive environment. Pedagogical theories advocate for the utilization of virtual reality as an educational tool in school-related endeavors. Traditional pedagogical theories, such as constructivist learning, situated learning, and engagement theory, all endorse the incorporation of virtual reality into the realm of education [3–5]. Constructivist learning model has been proposed by Reigeluth [6]. Experiential learning is a concept that revolves around creating a learning environment where learners are actively encouraged to experiment. Constructivist learning is student-centric and focuses on meeting the learners' needs and helping them to construct and build on their own knowledge based on their prior experiences and knowledge [7, 8]. This process involves testing hypotheses that are based on their previous experiences and generating new knowledge and experiences to apply in new situations. This approach follows a cyclic learning process comprising four stages: concrete experience (actively experiencing and contemplating a given scenario), reflective observation (analyzing the observed outcomes), abstract conceptualization (comprehending the situation and formulating hypotheses), and active experimentation (testing hypotheses through hands-on exploration in novel scenarios) [4]. Experiential learning has gained considerable traction as a prominent pedagogical theory in the integration of virtual reality (VR) into education [9]. This is largely due to the interactive capabilities of VR technologies, especially immersive virtual environments (VEs), which empower learners to engage in active experimentation and reflective observation within a secure and authentic digital realm [5]. Learners are active, able to control their learning pace and responsible for their learning. Chen and Teh [10] have pointed out how the various technical capabilities of VR technology can support constructivist learning principles, which are congruent with the constructivist educational design principles by Dalgarno [11]. The constructivist learning principles focus on learning and learner control over content, sequence and learning strategy to construct own knowledge; authentic, contextual and discovery activity to encourage diverse ways of thinking; and interesting, appealing and engaging problem representation to provide intrinsic motivation. Though VR could support constructivist learning and research has shown a positive array of learning outcomes with desktop virtual reality, for instance, better learning in geosciences [12]; better understanding in physic concepts [7]; and positive effect on learning driving rules and regulations [13]. Numerous researches show that most students remembered what they saw in virtual reality and concluded that VR is a more significant environment than classroom [14]. The construction of learning situations enhanced by virtual reality presupposes an active teaching that leaves room for the protagonism and creativity of the students, reserving to the teacher the task of structuring the methodological-conceptual framework. VR is equipped with a myriad of capabilities that cater to the diverse needs of both the general and special population. For the neurotypicals, VR serves as a tool for professional training and school education. In training for some professions, such as pilots and doctors. VR technology in the field of education pro-vides a range of possi-bilities that enhance learning and improve educational out-comes. It enables learners to visualize complex ideas and their dynamic interconnections, while also granting access to distant or unattainable people and events due to limitations of time, distance, cost, or safety [15]. Interactive learning environments based on VR have proven to be particu-larly effective, especially in primary/elementary education [16]. For special populations, VR has the potential to serve as an ideal tool for intervention and rehabilitation, offering a realistic yet more accommodating environment. People with physical or mental condi-tions may face challenges in self-care and behavioral control, making social interactions in real-life settings uncomfortable for them. Nonetheless, many of them desire to enhance their social interaction skills for their everyday lives. This predicament can be addressed through the utilization of VR technology, which provides a secure and adjustable virtual environment (VE) where intervention can be conducted in a personalized and gradual manner, guided by therapists [17, 18]. Although immersive technologies are gaining widespread popularity and have the potential to revolutionize the field, the reduction in cost and the development of VR are relatively recent advancements. Consequently, there have been only a limited number of studies that have previously explored the benefits of VR in foreign or second language education, primarily focusing on theoretical aspects [19]. The investigation of VR technologies in foreign language teaching remains largely unexplored [20, 21]. The implementation of VR systems can prove beneficial by bring-ing language learners closer to the cultural aspects of the language and creating realistic simulations that are not even possible in the physical world. According to Lan [22] VR applications for foreign language (FL) education encompass various focuses, including visual experiences, entertainment, social networking, operation, and creation. When it comes to providing FL learners with visual experiences, VR allows them to immerse themselves in virtual worlds, providing a sense of "being there." They can witness a vol-cano, explore outer space, delve into the depths of the ocean, or wander through ancient Roman cities [23, 24]. FL learners often utilize devices such as VR goggles or Google Cardboard along with 360-degree real-world videos to enhance their visual experiences. If the goal is to incorporate entertainment into VR-based FL education, the design of VR software may focus on gamified scenarios that integrate learning materials [25]. During the gaming process, regardless of whether a headset or motion-capture technology is uti-lized, learners' motivation remains high [26]. For instance, Lan, Fang, et al. [27] created three virtual reality environments, consisting of a kitchen, a supermarket, and a zoo, to enhance the acquisition of Chinese vocabulary among college students from a university in the United States. They conducted a comparative study on the learning outcomes of 90 two-syllable Chinese words within a 15-min session, employing two different learn-ing contexts: a 2D line-drawing representation and a 3D virtual immersion setting. The study revealed that participants who experienced the 3D virtual immersion exhibited a more significant improvement in their learning trajectory compared to those in the 2D line-drawing context. Moreover, when students engage in learning while experiencing a state of flow (engagement, immersion) [28] their motivation remains high, their learning becomes autonomous, their attention is focused, and as a result, they achieve satisfac-tory learning outcomes. Csíkszentmihályi [29] defines flow as an optimal experience in which learners feel in control of their environment and are driven by specific goals [30].

On these scientific and theoretical bases, the aim of this study is to investigate if a VR teaching methods could affect in a better way learning a foreign language in students.

2 Materials and Methods

In this study, we examined 120 subjects from the fifth year of primary school and divided them into two groups of 60 subjects each. All subjects were recruited from 2 primary schools in Caserta (Italy) and were homogeneous in terms of parents' socio-cultural background; family/environmental context was not a factor influencing educational attainment in either group. Therefore, the inclusion criteria were as follows: (a) belonging to the same class level (fifth elementary grade), (b) absence of any kind of diagnosis; (c) a IQ between 95 and 105 assessed through the Raven colored Matrices [31]; (d) medium-high socio-economic class assessed through the SES scale [32].

After confirming the inclusion criteria of the sample, we divided the subjects into two randomized experimental groups consisting of 60 subjects each. The subjects of both groups had the same inclusion criteria and did not have different sociocultural factors. The language level was evaluated with MacArthur-Bates CDI [33].

In order to assess English academic skills, we assessed an English word list with 300 words. The words chosen for the questionnaire were selected from the learning units (UDA) set up for fifth graders primary school. English words target were collected in 4 macro areas regarding: house, school, nature and Free time - hobby. Every macro area had 75 words linked. They were assessed in two times: the first time (T0) was after four months since the beginning of school; the second time (T1) at the end of the school year. The two groups were provided with the two different types of interventions after the first assessment. The interventions lasted 5 months, from January to May for 2 h once a week. The data were collected and analyzed at the FINDS Neuropsychiatry Outpatient Clinic by licensed psychologists in collaboration with the University of International Studies of Rome (UNINT).

MacArthur-Bates CDI (Communicative Development Inventory): A questionnaire designed to assess the communication skills of developing children, spanning from early signs of understanding and non-verbal gestures to vocabulary expansion and the beginnings of grammar. The CDI provides standards based on a typically developing sample. It consists of two versions in checklist format: a) The Words and Gestures version, intended for children between 8 and 16 months old; b) The Words and Phrases version, intended for children between 16 and 30 months old. The Words and Gestures version includes pre-linguistic elements, assessing abilities such as name response, verbal tagging, and imitation. It presents 28 sentences, and caregivers are asked to report whether their child understands each sentence. It also lists 196 vocabulary entries, where caregivers indicate if the child "understands" or "understands and says" each item. Additionally, it includes 63 gestures categorized into five groups, including early gestures associated with social engagement and later gestures involving actions, play, and object-directed imitation. The Words and Phrases version comprises 680 vocabulary entries, and caregivers only indicate whether the child produces each item, without referencing understanding. The second part of the questionnaire covers various grammatical elements [33].

Socio-economic status questionnaire (SES): Self-administered questionnaire that allows collecting information about the level of education and professional of parents and indicates the position of the person or family within the social and economic system [32].

Raven matrices (CPM-Colored Progressive Matrices): Raven's progressive matrices measure non-verbal intelligence throughout the entire range of intellectual development, from childhood to maturity, regardless of cultural level. They are used within children between the ages of 3 and 11. Our protocol included only matrices A and B, extracted from standard test, with an additional test (AB) of 12 elements. Each sub-test required completing a series of figures with the missing one, comparing them to a model and judging their progress by an increasing degree of difficulty [31].

English word list: A list of 300 words to learn. Words were divided in 4 cluster composed of 75 each regarding 4 macro areas: Home, School, Nature, and Free time – hobby.

Every student of G1 was given HMD Oculus Meta quest 2 with the use of virtual environments on "Spatial.io". "Spatial.io" is a platform that enables collaborative experience in virtual reality. Special applications have been developed to take full advantage of the functionality offered by the platform, enabling users to interact in shared virtual environments. Moreover, it could be possible to develop English language learning apps that foster interactive and immersive experiences. Developers can create dynamic applications tailored to various learning styles and proficiency levels. These apps may incorporate virtual classrooms, interactive language exercises, role-playing scenarios, and real-time language immersion environments. Users can engage with content in a spatially-aware virtual environment, enabling seamless communication and interaction with instructors and peers. By harnessing the power of Spatial.io, English language learning apps can provide engaging, effective, and personalized learning experiences that enhance language acquisition and fluency. In this way, we use some apps in this sense to create virtual immersive environments [34].

After doubting all the inclusion criteria, we structured the intervention as follows: we divided the sample into 2 groups randomly. Both groups were given the questionnaire before the intervention at T0. In details, subjects belonging to the control group (GR1) have been subjected to the traditional type of teaching. The strategies used are those commonly used. This is characterized by frontal lessons with speaking teacher and listening children. Classes lasted 2 h, once a week for 5 months. The lessons were based on the adoption of a textbook (Happy days by Philip Curtis, Donatella Santandrea). The focus was on the repetition of the words. The topic of the day consisted in addressing general grammar and vocabulary topics specific to 5 topics: Home, School, Nature, Free time and hobby. Subjects belonging to the experimental group (GR2) have been subjected to the innovative teaching program, using Virtual Reality.

This educational approach consisted of an immersive session that enabled learning in general. The intervention takes 5 months, 2 h once a week. Subjects were equipped with an Oculus head mounted display. During the learning sessions, students were screened in a virtual classroom where specific grammar and vocabulary topics were addressed in 5 topics: Home, School, Nature, Free time and hobby. At the didactic level, in this study, two Learning Unit were created containing as teaching objectives the terminology that students should have acquired. In particular, the first Learning Unit provided the vocabulary inherent in the field of home and leisure and hobbies, while the second learning unit had as its ultimate objectives the learning of the lexicon of the sphere of school and nature. In this regard, it was decided to use Spatial.io in order to make sensory learning and contribute to the internalization of the new vocabulary to be learned. In detail, the various apps that this platform is able to offer have been taken into consideration; in doing so the students had the opportunity to manipulate and have, therefore, direct experience with the word in question because this immersive mode allowed students to contextualize that particular word. In addition, in the virtual classroom the individual terms to be learned were shown in image 3D form. Subjects had the opportunity to interact with the term in the form of a 3D image and manipulate it knowing all its characteristics. For example, at the presentation of the term "flower" in the form of a 3D object, subjects could observe it from multiple points of view, rotate it and "touch" the petals and the stem. At the end of the session, we gave each groups the same questionnaire we had given ad T0, to be refilled now at T1. Our intervention was initially thought as directed exclusively to children without any diagnosis but could be thought of as a general intervention in ordinary and special teaching. The Italian school system does not include this type of intervention as ordinary tools that underestimate its power to improve and improve soft skills and metacognitive skills.

3   Results

Data analysis was conducted using SPSS 26.0 statistical data collection software. Significance at the 1% level ($\alpha < 0.01$) was accepted. We compared the two groups (variable between - group) with T0 and T1 (variable within - time) to see if there was any improvement in the number of words in English language learning (ENGL) after instructional training. We want to check if there is an improvement between T0 and T1, but also between the two groups because they had different apprenticeships. Therefore, we performed ANOVA 2x2 mixed with repeated measurements: within (time) and between (group) factor.

1. Change Over Time (Within-Subject Factor):

   - Group 1: An increase from 156.15 words at T0 to 174.17 words at T1.
   - Group 2: A substantial increase from 157.45 words at T0 to 220.13 words at T1.

2. Between-Group Differences:

   - At T0, Group 1 had a mean of 156.15 words, while Group 2 had a mean of 157.45 words.
   - At T1, Group 1 had a mean of 174.17 words, whereas Group 2 had a higher mean of 220.13 words.

3. Interaction (Time * Group) [$F(1,118) = 75.658$, $p < 0.001$] (Table 1):

   - The change in the number of words over time is not consistent between the two groups. This is supported by the significant interaction term in the 2x2 mixed-design ANOVA.

   In summary, Group 2 not only started with a higher mean at T0 but also showed a more substantial increase in the number of words from T0 to T1 compared to Group

1. The significant interaction suggests that the effect of time on the number of words learned differs between the two groups.

Table 1. Interaction time*Group

Time	Group	Means	SD	F	P
0	1	156.15	24.74		
	2	174.17	21.78		
1	1	157.45	6.95		
	2	220.13	4.30	75.658	<0.001

4 Discussion

The results of this investigation showcase the pragmatic utilization of augmented reality in the acquisition of languages, effectively capitalizing on the distinct features of AR throughout diverse educational endeavors. This research contends that AR stands as an invaluable resource within language learning settings, albeit presenting challenges related to its technical setup and educational framework. The primary objective was to scrutinize the correlation between the incorporation of AR in acquiring a foreign language. The study aims to assess the influence of augmented reality on the learning of foreign languages. The participant pool consisted of native Italian speakers, focusing on English as the target foreign language. We juxtaposed two distinct instructional approaches: a conventional method and an approach that constructed virtual settings employing AR and HMD (head-mounted display) technology. The findings underscore the significance of both instructional methods, demonstrating successful language mastery in the target language. It is noteworthy that, in terms of statistical significance, the group utilizing augmented reality achieved even more favorable outcomes compared to the alternative group. A salient aspect noted in the examined literature was the deployment of immersive Augmented Environments (AEs). This can be attributed to the myriad advantages that AEs offer in the realm of language acquisition [35]. Aspects such as active engagement, heightened interactivity, and personalized experiences play a pivotal role in achieving positive educational outcomes [36, 37]. These augmented environments present a unique avenue to replicate real-world scenarios and culturally significant locales, enabling users to immerse themselves without the associated expenses of educational excursions [38]. Unlike other commonplace multimedia tools in language classrooms, this methodology empowers students to physically experience the culture by encountering authentic sounds, engaging with the language contextually, exploring the surroundings, and interacting with cultural elements [21]. Furthermore, this technology affords a considerable degree of flexibility in experimental design and execution. Our research reveals some notable enhancements. A conspicuous outcome is that students exhibit enthusiasm for the technology and eagerly anticipate its utilization. Despite computers becoming commonplace in educational settings, head-mounted displays remain novel, prompting students to find reasons to engage with them. This enthusiasm also serves to keep students motivated, a sentiment echoed by teachers who have observed our interventions. This showcases the efficacy of using AR as an educational tool, requiring the capture of students' attention and enthusiasm before substantive teaching can occur. However, a comprehensive overhaul of the system is necessary before widespread implementation. In our study, we observe improvements in both groups regarding the acquisition of English words. Furthermore, the group that underwent training with AR demonstrated a more pronounced enhancement. Additionally, we posit that the applied AR techniques facilitated children in learning new English words and utilizing them in conversations accurately and fluently. We expound on our findings in terms of the number of words acquired. In conclusion, disparities in motivation between groups are evident. The group exposed to AR training did not miss a lesson, with participants expressing the belief that incorporating computers, tablets, and smartphones could enhance their learning journey and heighten their enthusiasm for language acquisition. As digital natives, their familiarity with tablets and smartphones suggests that resistance to their adoption will not impede their full integration into future educational systems [39]. This study has demonstrated that integrating AR-supported methods and applications can elevate the efficacy of vocabulary instruction in primary foreign language education. It allows students to interact with virtual objects and simulations within real-world environments, creating a more captivating and immersive learning experience. Moreover, AR holds the potential to enhance students' motivation, attention, and retention of newly acquired vocabulary. Given the potential improvement in learning using AR, it is evident why researchers, organizations, and educators are exploring this technology, endeavoring to add an additional dimension to both teaching and learning in recent times.

5 Conclusion

In summary, the primary objective of this study was to compare two educational interventions. Traditional teaching methods undeniably have a positive impact on children's foundational learning skills. However, in the context of foreign language acquisition, training with virtual reality (VR) proves to be more effective. This particularly benefits metacognitive instructional interventions that consider individual differences. The results underscore that integrating VR into foreign language education is a highly effective strategy, showcasing positive impacts and significant improvements in students' learning outcomes, especially when juxtaposed with traditional teaching methods. Furthermore, participants expressed that the use of VR provides a more enjoyable and engaging learning experience. These findings underscore the immense potential of VR as a potent educational tool for foreign language learning and teaching, surpassing the efficacy of conventional and traditional methodologies. The heightened levels of motivation and satisfaction observed when using VR undoubtedly contribute to a substantial increase in the effectiveness and success of the learning process, as measured by the number of words acquired. Students' increased commitment to suggested activities and exercises further augments their learning outcomes. However, despite the encouraging evidence supporting the use of VR setups, there are noteworthy aspects that demand attention. In terms of the study sample, future research should delve deeper into the realm of virtual reality and foreign language education. To address gaps in the existing literature, subsequent investigations should include more comprehensive comparisons between VR and alternative instructional approaches. This should encompass various conventional teaching techniques, as well as the integration of different media such as videos, photos, and diverse setup configurations. Moreover, a critical aspect overlooked in all the analyzed studies was the consideration of additional elements of multisensory immersion. Conducting studies that encompass these features will provide a better understanding of potential outcomes, as the incorporation of multisensory stimuli enhances user engagement and fosters greater attention to the VR environment [40–43]. Finally, as a weakness of this study, we underscore the importance of follow-up research to verify stability over time.

Disclosure of Interests. The authors have no competing interests to declare that are relevant to the content of this article.

References

1. Chen, Y.L.: The effects of virtual reality learning environment on student cognitive and linguistic development. Asia Pac. Educ. Res. **25**(4), 637–646 (2016)
2. Christou, C.: Virtual reality in education. In: Affective, Interactive and Cognitive Methods for e-Learning Design: Creating an Optimal Education Experience, pp. 228–243. IGI Global (2010)
3. Chen, C.J.: Theoretical bases for using virtual reality in education. Themes Sci. Technol. Educ. **2**, 71–90 (2010)
4. Hedberg, J., Alexander, S.: Virtual reality in education: defining researchable issues. Educ. Media Int. **31**, 214–220 (1994)
5. Kearsley, G., Shneiderman, B.: Engagement theory: a framework for technology-based teaching and learning. Educ. Technol. **38**, 20–23 (1998)
6. Reigeluth, C.M.: What is instructional-design theory and how is it changing? In: Reigeluth, C.M. (ed.) Instructional-Design Theories and Models – A New Paradigm of Instructional Theory, pp. 5–29. Lawrence Erlbaum, Mahwah (1999)
7. Lee, E.A.L., Wong, K.W., Fung, C.C.: How does desktop virtual reality enhance learning outcomes? A structural equation modeling approach. Comput. Educ. **55**(4), 1424–1442 (2010)
8. Roblyer, M.D.: Integrating Educational Technology into Teaching, 3rd edn. Pearson Education, London (2003)
9. Zhang, M., Ding, H., Naumceska, M., Zhang, Y.: Virtual reality technology as an educational and intervention tool for children with autism spectrum disorder: current perspectives and future directions. Behav. Sci. **12**(5), 138 (2022)
10. Chen, C.J., Teh, C.S.: An affordable virtual reality technology for constructivist learning environments. In: The 4th Global Chinese Conference on Computers in Education, Singapore (2000)
11. Dalgarno, B.: Choosing learner activities for specific learning outcomes: a tool for constructivist computer assisted learning design. In: Planning for Progress, Partnership and Profit. Proceedings EdTech 1998 (1998)
12. Fung-Chun, L.I., et al.: A virtual reality application for distance learning of Taiwan stream erosion in Geosciences. In: Proceedings of the International Conference on Computers in Education, pp. 1156–1160. IEEE (2002)

13. Chen, C.J.: Are spatial visualization abilities relevant to virtual reality? e-J. Instr. Sci. Technol. **9**(2), 1–16 (2006)
14. FitzGerald, E., et al.: Dimensions of personalisation in technology-enhanced learning: a framework and implications for design. Br. J. Edu. Technol. **49**(1), 165–181 (2018)
15. Kolb, D.A.: Experiential Learning: Experience as the Source of Learning and Development. FT Press, Upper Saddle River (2014)
16. Kalyuga, S.: Enhancing instructional efficiency of interactive E-learning environments: a cognitive load perspective. Educ. Psychol. Rev. **19**, 387–399 (2007)
17. McCleery, J.P., et al.: Safety and feasibility of an immersive virtual reality intervention program for teaching police interaction skills to adolescents and adults with autism. Autism Res. **13**, 1418–1424 (2020)
18. Stewart Rosenfield, N., Lamkin, K., Re, J., Day, K., Boyd, L., Linstead, E.: A virtual reality system for practicing conversation skills for children with autism. Multimodal Technol. Interact. **3**, 28 (2019)
19. Peixoto, B., Pinto, D., Krassmann, A., Melo, M., Cabral, L., Bessa, M.: Using virtual reality tools for teaching foreign languages. In: Rocha, Á., Adeli, H., Reis, L.P., Costanzo, S. (eds.) New Knowledge in Information Systems and Technologies: Volume 3, pp. 581–588. Springer, Cham (2019). https://doi.org/10.1007/978-3-030-16187-3_56
20. Schwienhorst, K.: The state of VR: a meta-analysis of virtual reality tools in second language acquisition. Comput. Assist. Lang. Learn. **15**(3), 221–239 (2002)
21. O'Brien, M.G., Levy, R.M.: Exploration through virtual reality: encounters with the target culture. Can. Modern Lang. Rev. **64**(4), 663–691 (2008)
22. Lan, Y.J.: Immersion into virtual reality for language learning. In: Psychology of Learning and Motivation, vol. 72, pp. 1–26. Academic Press (2020)
23. Heathman, A.: Google is bringing VR to one million UK school children (2016). https://www.wired.co.uk/article/google-digital-skills-vr-pledge
24. Meyer, L.: Students explore the earth and beyond with virtual field trips. Journal **43**(3), 22–25 (2016)
25. Lan, Y.J.: The essential components of game design in 3d virtual worlds: from a language learning perspective. In: Spector, M., Lockee, B., Childress, M. (eds.) Learning, Design, and Technology, pp. 1–18. Springer, Cham (2016). https://doi.org/10.1007/978-3-319-17727-4_24-1
26. Lan, Y.J., Hsiao, I.Y.T., Shih, M.F.: Effective learning design of game-based 3D virtual language learning environments for special education students. Educ. Technol. Soc. **21**(3), 213–227 (2018)
27. Lan, Y.J., Fang, S.Y., Legault, J., et al.: Second language acquisition of Mandarin Chinese vocabulary: context of learning effects. Educ. Tech. Res. Dev. **63**, 671–690 (2015)
28. Liu, H., Song, X.: Exploring "Flow" in young Chinese EFL learners' online English learning activities. System **96**, 102425 (2021). https://doi.org/10.1016/j.system.2020.102425
29. Csikszentmihalyi, M.: Beyond Boredom and Anxiety. Jossey-Bass (2000)
30. Sun, J.C.Y., Kuo, C.Y., Hou, H.T., Lin, Y.Y.: Exploring learners' sequential behavioral patterns, flow experience, and learning performance in an anti-phishing educational game. Educ. Technol. Soc. **20**(1), 45–60 (2017)
31. Raven, J.C.: Coloured Progressive Matrices Sets A, Ab, B. Manual Sections 1 & 2. Oxford Psychologists Press, Oxford (1995)
32. Venuti, P., Senese, V.P.: A self-assessment questionnaire of parental styles: a study on an Italian sample. Ital. J. Psychol. **34**(3), 677–698 (2007)
33. Fenson, L., Bates, E., Dale, P.S., et al.: MacArthur–Bates Communicative Development Inventories, 2nd edn. Baltimore (2006)
34. www.spatial.io.com

35. Schwienhorst, K.: Why virtual, why environments? Implementing virtual reality concepts in computer-assisted language learning. Simul. Gaming **33**(2), 196–209 (2002)

36. Legault, J., Zhao, J., Chi, Y.-A., Chen, W., Klippel, A., Li, P.: Immersive virtual reality as an effective tool for second language vocabulary learning. Languages **4**(1), 13 (2019)

37. Pantelidis, V.S.: Virtual reality in the classroom. Educ. Technol. **33**(4), 23–27 (1993)

38. Alfadil, M.: Effectiveness of virtual reality game in foreign language vocabulary acquisition. Comput. Educ. **153**, 103893 (2020)

39. Belda-Medina, J., Marrahi-Gomez, V.: The impact of Augmented Reality (AR) on vocabulary acquisition and student motivation. Electronics **12**(3), 749 (2023)

40. Goncalves, G., Melo, M., Vasconcelos-Raposo, J., Bessa, M.: Impact of different sensory stimuli on presence in credible virtual environments. IEEE Trans. Vis. Comput. Graph. **26**(11), 3231–3240 (2020)

41. Romano, M., et al.: Exploring the potential of immersive virtual reality in Italian schools: a practical workshop with high school teachers. Multimodal Technol. Interact. **7**(12), 111 (2023)

42. Bisogni, F., Laccone, R.P., Esposito, C., Frolli, A., Romano, M.: Virtual reality and foreign language learning. In: ICERI 2023 Proceedings, pp. 9201–9207. IATED (2023)

43. Romano, M., Laccone, R.P., Frolli, A.: Designing a VR educational application to enhance resilience and community awareness through cultural exploration. In: ICERI 2023 Proceedings, pp. 9258–9267. IATED (2023)

Bridging Disciplinary Boundaries: Integrating XR in Communication Sciences Master's Programs

Suzanne Kieffer[1]([✉]) [iD], Sébastien Nahon[1] [iD], Damien Renard[1] [iD], and Axel Legay[2] [iD]

[1] Université catholique de Louvain, Institute for Language and Communication, Louvain-la-Neuve, Belgium
{suzanne.kieffer,sebastien.nahon,damien.renard}@uclouvain.be
[2] Université catholique de Louvain, Institute of Information and Communication Technologies, Electronics and Applied Mathematics, Louvain-la-Neuve, Belgium
axel.legay@uclouvain.be

Abstract. Extended Reality (XR) is transforming sectors like education, healthcare, and construction. With its potential for simulating real-world scenarios, XR's role in digital transformation is increasingly recognized. This shift necessitates XR education expansion beyond STEM, addressing the needs of humanities and social sciences students to understand these technologies' applications, ethics, and societal implications. This paper investigates the integration of XR into three Master's courses in communication sciences. It emphasizes the importance of practical engagement with XR through user testing, hands-on projects, and developing a critical stance towards UX and related issues. The study utilizes an exploratory case study approach, leveraging participant observation, assignments analysis, and student feedback. Findings highlight the value of XR in enhancing student engagement, understanding, and the ability to propose inclusive design solutions. Despite challenges linked to large-scale implementation and the absence of advanced programming courses in social sciences and humanities programs, XR integration serves as a powerful tool in raising awareness about designing user-friendly, secure, and inclusive immersive systems.

Keywords: XR education · Augmented reality · Virtual reality · Storyboard · User experience · Case study

1 Introduction

Extended reality (XR), an umbrella term for technologies like augmented reality (AR), virtual reality (VR), and mixed reality (MR), has emerged as a transformative force, merging the digital and physical realms [15]. The immersive nature of XR technologies, exemplified by AR and VR, has already penetrated sectors such as education, healthcare, and construction. Notably, VR has made significant inroads in healthcare, particularly in surgical simulations, owing to its capacity to simulate real-world scenarios [9]. Immersive experiences simulation,

© The Author(s), under exclusive license to Springer Nature Switzerland AG 2024
P. Zaphiris and A. Ioannou (Eds.): HCII 2024, LNCS 14724, pp. 89–105, 2024.
https://doi.org/10.1007/978-3-031-61691-4_7

and digital twins are recognized as pivotal drivers of digital transformation, with Gartner [8] asserting their more substantial role compared to other technologies. Meanwhile, challenges in XR span user experience (UX), ethical considerations, inclusion, and cybersecurity, posing multifaceted issues in the scientific domain.

In this context, the imperative arises to extend XR education beyond traditional health sciences or STEM disciplines. Humanities and social sciences students, whose professions (e.g. anthropologist, economist, lawyer) are or will be affected by digital transformation, need to comprehend and study these technologies [6]. This involves identifying current and potential applications, analyzing user attitudes, formulating recommendations for improvement, and understanding associated issues such as data protection, ethics, and inclusion. Students in communication sciences are no exception to this imperative. Broadening educational scopes ensures a comprehensive understanding of XR technologies and their societal implications [6]. This raises the following research question: *How to seamlessly and efficiently integrate XR into humanities and social sciences educational programs while preparing students for challenges associated with XR?*

Using a multiple exploratory case study design, this paper delineates the integration of immersive technologies into three courses within the Master's programs in communication sciences at Université catholique de Louvain (UCLouvain): design and evaluation of prototypes, user experience, and project management. Across these three courses, the pedagogical objectives aimed to provide students with a theoretical and practical foundation for appropriating XR technologies, identifying their key features, and fostering a critical stance toward them. The critical stance particularly concerned UX, user engagement, acceptance, or data protection. The common threads among the courses are:

1. Conducting user tests following an experimental protocol collaboratively defined by students during classes,
2. Using UX as cornerstone while defining the experimental protocol.

Additionally, students were tasked with hands-on projects, such as creating multimedia content for an AR prototype (case 1), describing interaction modalities and affordances of an existing VR prototype (case 2), and storyboarding optimistic and pessimistic VR experiences related to cybersecurity and data protection (case 3).

The paper explores the intricate ramifications of digital transformation, showcasing the viability and significance of equipping students in humanities and social sciences for the multifaceted challenges and opportunities presented by immersive technologies. Specifically, the paper delineates the instructional designs of the three courses, outlining requirements for technical and logistical support, and offering insights derived from the practical implementation of immersive technologies in these educational contexts. Subsequently, the paper examines student performance metrics, including attendance, participation, production quality, and grades, alongside solicited feedback pertaining to the instructional design of the courses. Finally, the discussion extends to the scalability of the course instructional designs, considering their applicability to larger student cohorts or undergraduate programs.

2   Background

Extended reality (XR) encompasses a broad spectrum of experiences that merge the virtual and real worlds, achieved through the integration of various immersive technologies (Fig. 1). According to [19], VR is defined as a computer-generated simulation that transports the user to a different, computer-generated environment; AR uses digital devices to overlay additional sensory information (sounds, objects, avatars, graphics, labels, etc.) on the real world, which provides contextual information that enhances appearance, delivering an enriched interactive experience; MR combines elements of AR and VR, which allows for the interactive and real-time overlay of virtual elements within the real world, providing an environment in which virtual and physical objects coexist and interact.

Fig. 1. Examples of VR (left), MR (center), and AR (right) systems. Photos by Unknown Authors licensed under CC BY (left and center), CC BY-NC (right).

2.1   Challenges Associated with XR

XR has integrated into various sectors, such as education, healthcare, marketing, pharmaceutical production, and construction, demonstrating their versatility and comprehensive applicability. Despite the transformative potential of XR, its widespread acceptance and seamless integration are challenged by a spectrum of issues spanning technical, societal, and ethical dimensions.

Technical Challenges. Advancements in XR technology have been propelled by significant strides in object detection, motion tracking, gesture recognition, and the substantial growth of artificial intelligence. These advancements have profoundly enriched the understanding of human-machine interactions. Further technological progress in 3D rendering, such as hologram projection, has enabled more realistic and immersive virtual experiences [2]. However, the high cost of XR hardware, like VR headsets, constitutes a barrier to mass adoption. Moreover, the accessibility of these technologies is restricted, especially in settings with limited resources. Lastly, the management of sensitive biometric data and the risks of cyberattacks demand robust security protocols and stringent privacy safeguards to protect user data and foster trust in these technologies [22].

UX Challenges. User experience (UX) goes beyond usability [14] and is defined as *user's perceptions and responses that result from the use or anticipated use of a system, product or service* [26]. UX is pivotal in shaping the success of XR technologies, as a well-designed UX not only ensures usability but also enriches user engagement, fostering a deep and intuitive connection with the technology. In the context of XR, UX challenges are multifaceted [12], including the creation of immersive content that is both compelling and contextually relevant, designing interactions that feel natural and intuitive, and ensuring the system's performance is seamlessly synchronized with user actions. The evolution of UX into a driver of innovation highlights its role in the deployment of XR technologies, where real-time responsiveness and adaptive interfaces are crucial for meeting user expectations and enhancing their immersive experience [17].

Societal and Ethical Challenges. While XR technologies offer immersive experiences, they bring significant societal and ethical challenges. Issues related to the collection and potential misuse of biometric data pose serious privacy risks [2]. Moreover, the immersive nature of XR technologies raises ethical considerations, particularly concerning vulnerable groups like children or individuals with mental disorders, who may be more susceptible to the psychological impacts of these technologies [25]. Furthermore, prolonged exposure to XR environments presents health concerns, while accessibility and inclusion remain pressing challenges, emphasizing the need for XR environments and interfaces that are universally accessible and non-discriminatory [3]. Addressing these societal and ethical challenges is crucial for fostering a responsible and inclusive evolution of XR technologies.

2.2   XR for Education

XR technologies facilitate the creation of immersive educational experiences that substantially enhance academic performance [7], stimulate active participation, and ultimately cultivate a learning environment that is both enriched and engaging. By replicating real-world scenarios, XR provides learners with practical exposure within a secure and controlled setting. Moreover, such simulations bridge the gap between theoretical knowledge and its practical application, an integration that proves especially pivotal in fields such as architecture, engineering, and healthcare, where grasping the practical ramifications of theoretical knowledge is paramount. At this stage, proficiency in XR technologies is crucial, proving vital for industry professionals and for those orchestrating the deployment of these technological infrastructures. For these individuals, learning XR technologies involves not only mastering the tools but also gaining a deep understanding of technological, economic, and ethical issues. In this context, the ability to identify and skillfully address technical, ethical, or user experience (UX) challenges is crucial for these future professionals.

3   Methodology

3.1   Objective and Related Approach

The paper explores strategies for seamlessly and efficiently integrating XR into educational programs, ensuring the preparation of students in humanities and social sciences for challenges associated with XR. Specifically, the paper aims to provide insights into the how-tos of XR integration:

- How to align with course learning objectives;
- How to adapt to students' profile;
- How to maintain academic performance and student engagement, particularly when students may be unfamiliar with the technology;
- How to prompt students to critically reflect on XR, encouraging a forward-looking perspective on the evolving technological landscape.

To pursue this objective, we opted for a multiple exploratory case study design. First, case study designs are suitable to address how and why questions [1], or to explore situations involving multiple variables (i.e., students' engagement or familiarity with XR) that cannot be controlled [23]. Second, we chose an exploratory approach, as XR integration in humanities and social sciences programs has no clear, single set of outcomes [1,23]. Finally, multiple cases allowed us to explore differences between cases [1].

3.2   Description of the Three Cases

We selected three case studies, each corresponding to a specific course taught in the communication sciences master's programs at UCLouvain (Table 1), based on both the relevance of XR integration in students' curriculum and the consistency of XR integration against each course' learning outcomes.

The selected cases focus on prototyping (case 1), user experience (case 2), and project management (case 3). Distinguishing features emerge in the specifics of each case. Notably, the type of prototype utilized diverges across the cases, ranging from AR in case 1 to VR in case 2 and storyboard in case 3. Additionally, students carried out user tests individually in cases 1 and 3, and in group in case 2. Although evaluation methods exhibit slight diversity, all cases place a high emphasis on group assignment, reaching 60% in case 3. Finally, the hours allocated to each course vary significantly, with cases 2 and 3 requiring twice the time compared to case 1, demanding substantially fewer hours.

All three cases share common elements: each course carries a weight of 5 European Credit Transfer and Accumulation System (ECTS), suggesting a similar level of academic commitment; the class sizes are notably consistent across different cases; and the students exhibit homogeneity in terms of socio-demographic attributes. More importantly, all three cases rely on user experience as a cornerstone, and as such, they all involve user testing.

Figure 2 depicts the instructional design in cases. All three cases involved an acclimatization phase, user testing phase, and jury. The acclimatization phase

Table 1. Description of the three cases. ECTS stands for European Credit Transfer and Accumulation System.

	Case 1	Case 2	Case 3
Course	prototyping	user experience	project management
ECTS	5	5	5
Hours	15	30	30
Semester	Spring 2023	Spring 2023	Fall 2023
Students	27	30	33
Type of prototype	AR	VR	Storyboard
Experimental protocol	collaborative	collaborative	collaborative
User test	individual	in group (13 teams)	individual
Data analysis	collaborative	collaborative	collaborative
Students' evaluation modes			
Knowledge test	-	25%	40%
Individual assignment	50%	25%	–
Group assignment	50%	50%	60%

aimed to ensure that students acquire the fundamentals in each course. For example, it included an overview of prototyping techniques in case 1, exploration of methods, practices, and UX artifacts in case 2, and a combination of agile-UX methods and techniques for project management in case 3. Additionally, case 3 introduced role-play to put into practice the theory seen during the acclimatization and enhance social interactions during class. In cases 2 and 3, a demonstration session was incorporated to familiarize students with XR technology. The user testing phase presented students with a hands-on opportunity to directly engage with XR technologies, bridging the gap between theory and practice. This phase is dynamic and integral to the curriculum. User testing involved creating the experimental protocol, carrying out the user test, and analyzing collected data. In all three cases, both the creation of the experimental protocol and data analysis took place collaboratively during classes. Students performed user test data collection individually in both cases 1 and 3, and in groups in case 2. The jury evaluation served as a significant assessment of students' comprehension and practical application of XR principles. In all three cases, we tasked students with the consolidation of results and findings in one single presentation, so as to present an integrated perspective of the phenomenon investigated.

3.3   Methods for Data Collection

We used participant observation during face-to-face classes and screened the publications on the courses' MS Teams to collect data about attendance, participation, and engagement. We analyzed group and individual assignments to

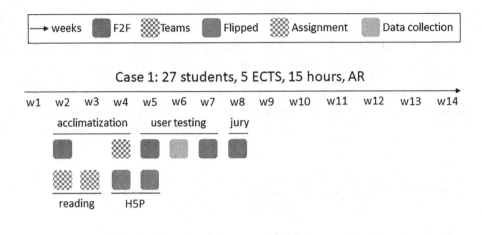

Case 1: 27 students, 5 ECTS, 15 hours, AR

Case 2: 30 students, 5 ECTS, 30 hours, VR

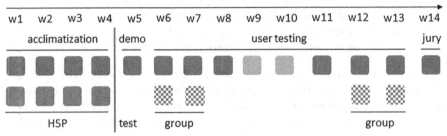

Case 3: 33 students, 5 ECTS, 30 hours, storyboard

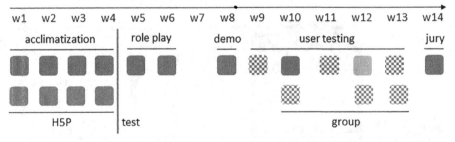

Fig. 2. Instructional design of each case. F2F stands for Face-to-Face, ECTS for European Credit Transfer and Accumulation System.

assess academic performance (quality of students production and grades). We tasked students with documenting their feedback about the system under investigation and their experience with the instructional design in a single document per working group.

3.4   Case 1

We tasked students with generating content to be incorporated into a rapid prototyping tool for AR systems. Specifically, students created in groups (5 groups) a scannable poster that would redirect to a multimedia content such as a video, image, audio (Fig. 3), therefore producing five prototypes in total, one per group. Then, students carried out user tests individually, which required them to recruit one participant who tested the five AR prototypes. Subsequently, students administered the recruited participant a questionnaire regarding user experience and engagement. At the end, the raw data was shared among all the groups, allowing them to conduct analyses based on the raw data. Students prepared the user test material in-class during week 5 and analyzed the data in-class during week 7 (Fig. 2). The material included:

- An online consent form allowing us to use data for research purposes;
- A checklist for assessing participants' performance (errors and hesitations);
- Six scales of the UX questionnaire (UEQ+) [24], namely attractiveness, efficiency, intuitive use, aesthetics, quality of content, and trust;
- The user engagement scale (UES) short form [21];
- A form allowing students to collect participant feedback.

Students presented collaboratively the results during week 8 (Fig. 2), discussing each component of the experimental design separately. For example, students emphasized the relatively mitigated results regarding both user experience and user engagement. They argued that these outcomes were "predictable" since the look and feel of the tested AR prototypes were perceived as low-fidelity by the participants. Furthermore, students highlighted the limitations of the content they created, which was evaluated as having limited engagement.

Fig. 3. AR prototypes. Example 1: users scan the poster (a), then information about next student parties appears (b). Example 2: users scan the poster (c), then a joke about the lack of electrical outlets appears (d).

3.5   Case 2

We tasked students with evaluating and formulating redesign proposals for an existing VR prototype. The VR prototype supports the arrangement of living spaces in a virtual world, including the selection of furniture and wall colors from a catalog. The immersive experience takes place under a VR headset with controllers that enable movement and interaction (Fig. 4).

Similar to case 1, case 2 also included tasks such as developing the experimental protocol, conducting user tests, and sharing and analyzing data. However, students worked in groups throughout the process, and there were slight changes in the timeline, with the preparation of experimental material spanning weeks 6–8 and analysis occurring during weeks 11–13 (Fig. 2). Like in case 1, the resulting material included a checklist for assessing participants' performance, eight scales of the UEQ+ (efficiency, dependability, intuitive use, haptics, stimulation, visual aesthetics, quality of content, acoustics), the UES short form, and a form allowing students to collect participant feedback. However, the material also included an onboarding kit for participants, and we added impression testing [12] to gather participants' initial impressions about the virtual world.

Students presented collaboratively the results during week 14 (Fig. 2), discussing each component of the experimental design separately, as well as limitations in the VR prototype. For example, students identified several inclusion-related concerns (e.g. white male hands of the avatar), and also proposed a set of recommendations for improvement (e.g. integration of auditory elements to deepen participant immersion).

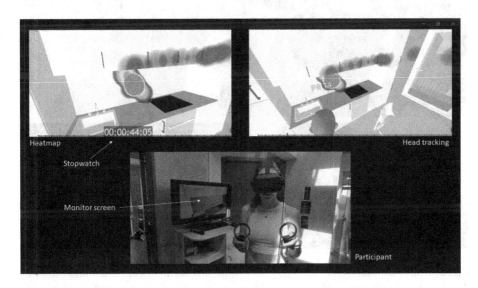

Fig. 4. VR prototype. Top: heatmap (left) and head tracking (right). Bottom: experimental setting.

3.6   Case 3

We tasked students with designing and evaluating VR scenarios through a story-board representation system. They crafted four scenarios, categorized along two dimensions: utopian versus dystopian scenarios, and the inclusion or exclusion of details about cybersecurity risks in the consent form.

Similar to cases 1 and 2, case 3 also included tasks such as developing the experimental protocol, conducting user tests, and analyzing data. In addition to the consent form, the material included scales of the technology acceptance model (TAM) questionnaire (usefulness, perceived ease of use, attitude, behavioral intention, enjoyment) adapted to VR technology [16], scales for assessing perceived cybersecurity risks [10], and a form allowing students to collect participant feedback. The students collaborated in groups, with each group producing storyboards and consent forms. Following a peer review of these works, the instructor selected one group's output (Fig. 5). Subsequently, this chosen material was utilized uniformly by all students for user testing.

During week 14, students collaboratively presented the results (Fig. 2), delving into each aspect of the experimental design. They discussed both the advantages, such as resource efficiency, and the limitations, such as low-fidelity, associated with using storyboards for user testing. Additionally, they emphasized the significance of designing experimental materials that closely match the situations one intends to generalize the results to.

Fig. 5. Top - Utopian scenario (left: introducing VR technology; right: illustrating a positive user experience). Bottom - Dystopian scenario (left: introducing a security breach; right: suggesting user's death after the headset exploded).

4   Findings

The pedagogical approach involving user testing and (re)design activities contributed to a comprehensive understanding of XR technologies and their applications. For example, students were able to grasp the advantages (e.g. capacity of simulation) and limitations (i.e. lack of inclusion) of XR technologies.

The collaborative nature of the learning experience implemented in these cases yielded positive outcomes. Table 2 presents for each case the number of students, dropouts, and mean grades. The number of students is similar among each case, with no dropouts in case 1, but a slight increase in dropout rates in cases 2 and 3 (7% and 9%, respectively). Despite broad ranges of grades, academic performance was above average, with high attendance to courses and implication in F2F and distant activities. For example, all students conducted user tests and delivered complete user data collection.

Table 2. Students' academic performances per case.

	Case 1	Case 2	Case 3
Course	prototyping	user experience	project management
Type of prototype	AR	VR	Storyboard
Experimental protocol	collaborative	collaborative	collaborative
User test	individual	collaborative	individual
Data analysis	collaborative	collaborative	collaborative
Students	27	30	33
Dropouts	0	2 (7%)	3 (9%)
Mean grades (%)	77	73	70
Range grades (%)	60–82	55–87	64–85
Course attendance	high	high	high
Students' implication	high	high	high
Critical thinking	medium	high	high

4.1   Case 1

Students identified several issues with the fast prototyping tool for AR. Key problems included the application's incompatibility with various operating systems, including some Android smartphones, and malfunctioning when attempting to scan a poster more than once or different posters in succession, necessitating an application restart. Additionally, the placement of posters in high-traffic areas posed challenges. Students' notable errors involved administrative oversights, such as two students failing to have the consent form signed.

The course was perceived as innovative, offering students a unique opportunity to explore AR within their curriculum. Highlights include the practical, hands-on experience that allowed for real-world application of classroom knowledge, conducting user tests outside the course, and learning about tools (observation grid, UEQ+, UES) beneficial for future careers in communication. The approach facilitated team-building skills, adherence to deadlines, and an ethical understanding of data collection, including the development of a confidentiality charter. Additionally, students appreciated the creative freedom to design visuals and select poster themes, enhancing their learning experience and engagement with the course material.

Within this innovative setting, the fast prototyping tool for AR has the potential to support larger student groups effectively, offering expansive educational benefits when aforementioned issues are systematically addressed.

4.2   Case 2

During user tests, students encountered several technical difficulties that impacted data collection. These challenges included poor Wi-Fi connectivity that significantly degraded image quality and caused latency in immersive sessions, as well as frequent or prolonged system crashes. The premature activation of the sleep mode on the VR headset before the commencement of user tests also contributed to stress among participants.

Errors committed by students involved deviations from the experimental protocol, such as unnecessarily prolonging the duration of impression tests beyond the specified time, a failure to accurately log encountered errors, and an omission in the collection of vital data segments. Furthermore, survey administration was compromised by translation inaccuracies and imprecise instructions, undermining the reliability of the collected data.

The course was perceived as innovative, offering students an opportunity to explore VR within their curriculum. Students proposed redesign solutions toward more equality and inclusion in the VR prototype, which is in line with the major challenges associated with immersive technologies [4,5]. From the jury's perspective, the instructional initiative provided a detailed exploration of the advantages and current challenges in incorporating immersive technologies into educational settings. Emphasis was placed on the need to develop a UX maturity model tailored to the specific demands and challenges faced by immersive technologies and their development teams. The analysis pointed out that while certain immersive experiences offer significant benefits, the complexity of human-machine interactions, especially those involving gestures and movements, requires in-depth study, modeling, and improvement.

The feasibility of conducting user tests of the VR prototype in synchronous mode was supported by the availability of four VR headsets operating simultaneously. However, accommodating a larger cohort would necessitate asynchronous testing, introducing more complex logistical considerations.

4.3 Case 3

The analysis of data collected during user tests indicated that the scenarios depicted in the storyboards did not adequately reflect the intended themes, particularly with the "utopian" scenario's inappropriate solicitation of personal information, which diverged from the project's thematic objectives. However, insights from cases 1 and 2 led to an improvement in the data collection process, specifically through the encoding of consent form and questionnaire via Moodle's feedback activity, which significantly reduced student error.

Students praised the course for its innovative approach, in particular the possibility to engage with both VR technology and related cybersecrity risks. Their feedback focused on refining the experimental protocol, notably to enhance administration of questionnaire and ensuring consistent data collection. For example, their collective input advocated for a meticulous enhancement of testing protocols, emphasizing preparatory work was deemed essential for effectively addressing participant queries, allowing participants to elaborate on their answers was suggested to deepen insights into user experiences, and streamlining questionnaires and expanding the participant pool beyond familiar circles were advised to improve data diversity and authenticity.

Storyboards emerge as a critical tool in this context, serving not just to visualize and communicate user experiences and foster creativity, but also to anchor a user-centered design approach. Importantly, they provide a pragmatic solution to the logistical challenge of equipment limitations, exemplified by the impracticality of supplying 30 headsets for 30 students. This innovative use of storyboards underscores the course's commitment to overcoming practical constraints while maintaining high educational standards and meeting learning objectives in the realm of immersive technologies.

5 Discussion

5.1 Analyzing Challenges in XR Education

Cases 1 and 2 encountered technical issues, such as operating system incompatibility (case 1 with AR) and system crashes affecting the user experience and data collection process (case 2 with VR). To facilitate effective large-scale implementation, these technical hurdles must be systematically addressed. This entails acquiring a sufficient number of smartphones or developing a system compatible with iOS for AR applications. For VR applications, it necessitates purchasing a substantial quantity of headsets and providing suitable spaces for conducting tests. By contrast, students encountered no such technical hurdles in case 3 with storyboards, demonstrating that storyboard prototypes effectively mitigate scalability challenges and technological problems and limitations associated with XR. However, storyboarding introduces considerations regarding the construction of scenarios, which must be perceived as credible by testing participants. This necessitates a careful and deliberate design process to ensure the authenticity of the content and user engagement [13].

Students consistently acknowledged the courses for their innovation, valuing the opportunity to explore XR technologies within their academic programs. This sentiment highlights the educational value seen in integrating cutting-edge technologies into the curriculum. Furthermore, the projects facilitated not only technical skills development but also soft skills, such as team building, adherence to deadlines, and an ethical understanding of data collection.

5.2   How-Tos of XR Integration

Aligning XR introduction with course learning objectives necessitates a strategic approach where XR technologies are integrated into courses that naturally support their application. This alignment implies selecting courses with learning objectives that are seamlessly complemented by XR's capabilities, such as design-oriented activities including immersive scenario prototyping or empirical data collection and analysis through XR system testing. The integration of XR should enhance the pedagogical framework, enabling students to directly apply XR technologies to solve real-world problems, thereby fostering a deeper understanding of the subject matter.

Adapting to students' profiles is crucial for the effective delivery of XR-based education. Providing students with a uniform baseline of knowledge and practical experience with XR technologies is essential. This can be achieved through targeted demonstrations and immersive experiences, considering that a significant portion of students may not have prior experience with VR technologies (30% in cases 1 and 3, 50% in case 2). Incorporating guest lectures from XR experts can demystify the technology and provide students with accessible, expert insights into XR applications, enhancing their learning experience. Moreover, master programs in social sciences and humanities do not include advanced programming courses that would allow students to develop high-fidelity prototypes. This once again positions the storyboard as a prototype facilitating the integration of XR in humanities and social sciences.

Maintaining academic performance and engagement with XR involves integrating hands-on activities like user testing and prototyping. Collaborative exercises not only solidify theoretical knowledge but also cultivate teamwork and creativity, essential in XR's dynamic field. Direct application of XR keeps students motivated and academically focused, despite new tech introductions.

Encouraging critical reflection on XR requires involving students in material creation for testing and initiating discussions on design and protocol improvements. This active involvement deepens their understanding of XR's challenges and opportunities, pushing them to think ahead about technological progress and their role in shaping future innovations.

5.3   Future Work

We delved into the variances among cases, bearing in mind the hurdles linked to large-scale implementation and the absence of advanced programming courses in social sciences and humanities programs. This enabled us to pinpoint storyboard prototypes as a solution that tackles both of these challenges simultaneously, as they simplify the introduction of XR concepts, bypassing the need for extensive programming skills and reducing reliance on expensive equipment.

Therefore, our future work will delve deeper into leveraging storyboard prototypes for XR education, with the aim of showcasing their efficacy in crafting scalable XR learning experiences accessible to students in social sciences and humanities. To enrich our understanding and validate the effectiveness of this approach, we plan to replicate case 3, aiming to produce cumulative findings and facilitate comparative analyses [1]. This endeavor will not only strengthen the evidence base but also allow for nuanced insights into the pedagogical value of storyboarding in XR education. Furthermore, we intend to broaden our research scope to include other low-fidelity prototyping methods, such as video or paper mockups, as suggested by [18]. By exploring these varied prototyping techniques, we aspire to develop a comprehensive, integrative model that enhances the adaptability and robustness of XR educational frameworksy [27]. This model will ideally support educators in effectively incorporating XR technologies into their curricula, thereby democratizing access to immersive learning experiences across diverse academic discipline.

6 Conclusion

In conclusion, the successful integration of XR technologies into educational settings requires careful consideration of course alignment, student adaptation, engagement maintenance, and the cultivation of critical thinking. By addressing these aspects, educators can not only enhance the learning experience but also prepare students to contribute meaningfully to the future of XR technology. A significant revelation of our work is the efficacy of storyboarding as an innovative approach to circumvent the dual hurdles of scalability and technical expertise in XR education. This method not only facilitates broader student involvement in XR development projects, sidestepping the necessity for advanced programming skills, but also significantly enhances collaborative processes. Finally, the integration of these technologies as learning tools enabled us to raise students' awareness of the need to design immersive systems offering a good UX [17], to integrate cybersecurity and data protection [11] and inclusion [20] into the development of these technologies.

Acknowledgement. The authors acknowledge the support provided by the Institute for Language and Communication, UCLouvain, Belgium. Appreciation is also extended to the anonymous reviewers for their insightful feedback on an earlier iteration of this work.

Disclosure of Interests. The authors have no competing interests to declare that are relevant to the content of this article.

References

1. Baxter, P., Jack, S.: Qualitative case study methodology: study design and implementation for novice researchers. Qual. Rep. **13**(4), 544–559 (2008). https://doi.org/10.46743/2160-3715/2008.1573
2. Bye, K., Hosfelt, D., Chase, S., Miesnieks, M., Beck, T.: The ethical and privacy implications of mixed reality. In: ACM SIGGRAPH 2019 Panels. SIGGRAPH 2019, Association for Computing Machinery, New York, NY, USA (2019). https://doi.org/10.1145/3306212.3328138
3. Carter, M., Egliston, B.: What are the risks of virtual reality data? Learning analytics, algorithmic bias and a fantasy of perfect data. New Media Soc. **25**, 485–504 (2021). https://doi.org/10.1177/14614448211012794
4. Dick, E.: Current and potential uses of AR/VR for equity and inclusion. Technical report, Information Technology and Innovation Foundation (2021)
5. Djamasbi, S., Strong, D.: User experience-driven innovation in smart and connected worlds. AIS Trans. Human Comput. Interact. **11**(4), 215–231 (2019). https://doi.org/10.17705/1thci.00121
6. Dong, W., Zhou, M., Zhou, M., Jiang, B., Lu, J.: An overview of applications and trends in the use of extended reality for teaching effectiveness: an umbrella review based on 20 meta-analysis studies. The Electronic Library (2023)
7. Fonseca, D., Martí, N., Redondo, E., Navarro, I., Sánchez, A.: Relationship between student profile, tool use, participation, and academic performance with the use of augmented reality technology for visualized architecture models. Comput. Hum. Behav. **31**, 434–445 (2014)
8. Gartner: What's new in the 2022 Gartner hype cycle for emerging technologies (2022). https://www.gartner.com/en/articles/what-s-new-in-the-2022-gartner-hype-cycle-for-emerging-technologies
9. Guo, X., Guo, Y., Liu, Y.: The development of extended reality in education: inspiration from the research literature. Sustainability **13**(24), 1–20 (2021). https://ideas.repec.org/a/gam/jsusta/v13y2021i24p13776-d701728.html
10. Heierhoff, S., Choun, I.H.: The impact of cybersecurity and innovation on mobility technology acceptance. In: PACIS 2023 Proceedings. No. 53 (2023). https://aisel.aisnet.org/pacis2023/53
11. Hernández-Ramos, J.L., Geneiatakis, D., Kounelis, I., Steri, G., Fovino, I.N.: Toward a data-driven society: a technological perspective on the development of cybersecurity and data-protection policies. IEEE Secur. Priv. **18**(1), 28–38 (2019)
12. Hillmann, C.: UX for XR: User Experience Design and Strategies for Immersive Technologies. DT, Apress, Berkeley, CA (2021). https://doi.org/10.1007/978-1-4842-7020-2
13. Hoffart, N., Doumit, R., Nasser, S.C.: Use of storyboards as an active learning strategy in pharmacy and nursing education. Curr. Pharm. Teach. Learn. **8**(6), 876–884 (2016)
14. Kieffer, S., Rukonić, L., Kervyn de Meerendré, V., Vanderdonckt, J.: A process reference model for UX. In: Cláudio, A.P., et al. (eds.) VISIGRAPP 2019. CCIS, vol. 1182, pp. 128–152. Springer, Cham (2020). https://doi.org/10.1007/978-3-030-41590-7_6
15. Kosko, K.W., Ferdig, R.E.: Conceptualizing a shared definition and future directions for extended reality (XR) in teacher education. J. Technol. Teach. Educ. **29**(3), 257–277 (2021). https://par.nsf.gov/biblio/10340467

16. Lee, J., Kim, J., Choi, J.Y.: The adoption of virtual reality devices: the technology acceptance model integrating enjoyment, social interaction, and strength of the social ties. Telemat. Inform. **39**, 37–48 (2019)

17. MacDonald, C.M., Sosebee, J., Srp, A.: A framework for assessing organizational user experience (UX) capacity. Int. J. Human Comput. Interact. **38**(11), 1064–1080 (2022)

18. Maguire, M.: An exploration of low-fidelity prototyping methods for augmented and virtual reality. In: Marcus, A., Rosenzweig, E. (eds.) HCII 2020. LNCS, vol. 12201, pp. 470–481. Springer, Cham (2020). https://doi.org/10.1007/978-3-030-49760-6_33

19. Milgram, P., Kishino, F.: A taxonomy of mixed reality visual displays. IEICE Trans. Inf. Syst. **77**(12), 1321–1329 (1994)

20. Naudé, W., Nagler, P.: Industrialisation, Innovation, Inclusion, vol. 43. UNU-MERIT (2015)

21. O'Brien, H.L., Cairns, P., Hall, M.: A practical approach to measuring user engagement with the refined user engagement scale (UES) and new UES short form. Int. J. Hum Comput Stud. **112**, 28–39 (2018)

22. Odeleye, B., Loukas, G., Heartfield, R., Sakellari, G., Panaousis, E., Spyridonis, F.: Virtually secure: a taxonomic assessment of cybersecurity challenges in virtual reality environments. Comput. Secur. **124**, 102951 (2023). https://doi.org/10.1016/j.cose.2022.102951, https://www.sciencedirect.com/science/article/pii/S0167404822003431

23. Quintão, C., Andrade, P., Almeida, F.: How to improve the validity and reliability of a case study approach? J. Interdiscipl. Stud. Educ. **9**(2), 264–275 (2021). https://doi.org/10.32674/jise.v9i2.2026, https://www.ojed.org/index.php/jise/article/view/2026

24. Schrepp, M., Thomaschewski, J.: Design and validation of a framework for the creation of user experience questionnaires. Int. J. Interact. Multimed. Artif. Intell. **5**, 88–95 (2019)

25. Slater, M., Gonzalez-Liencres, C., Haggard, P., Vinkers, C., Gregory-Clarke, R., Jelley, S., et al.: The ethics of realism in virtual and augmented reality. Front. Virtual Real. **1**, 1 (2020). https://doi.org/10.3389/frvir.2020.00001

26. for Standardization (ISO), I.O.: Ergonomics of human-system interaction - part 210: Human-centred design for interactive systems. Technical report ISO 9241-210:2019, ISO, Geneva, Switzerland (2019). https://www.iso.org/standard/77520.html. Accessed 30 Jan 2024

27. Yin, R.K.: Case Study Research: Design and Methods. Sage, Thousand Oaks, CA (2003)

Exploring UX: Instructional Designs for Groups in Mozilla Hubs

Kathrin Knutzen[✉] [ID], Gunther Kreuzberger[ID], and Wolfgang Broll[ID]

Virtual Worlds and Digital Games Group, Ilmenau University of Technology,
Ehrenbergstraße 29, 98693 Ilmenau, Germany
{kathrin.knutzen,gunther.kreuzberger,wolfgang.broll}@tu-ilmenau.de

Abstract. To evaluate the user experience and acceptance of Mozilla Hubs as an opportunity for educational classroom activities, we conducted user surveys involving $N = 33$ students of 5 different classes. By applying the User Experience Questionnaire (UEQ), this paper aims to gather exploratory insights into the usability, user satisfaction, learning affordances, and practicability of the platform in various instructional designs. Although there were no significant differences between groups, we see trends for differences between instructional designs. We conclude with exploratory design and practical recommendations for educators and future work.

Keywords: Mozilla Hubs · social virtual reality · user experience · education

1 Introduction

Immersive learning environments (ILEs) have experienced a surge in popularity in recent times due to their innovative nature in the field of education. This includes the utilization of social virtual reality applications like Mozilla Hubs. Research has demonstrated the efficacy of ILEs in terms of improving students' motivation, skill acquisition, and knowledge [18]. However, from a human-computer interaction-oriented perspective as with any learning tool, it is essential to also assess the usability and effectiveness of ILEs.

Usability evaluations of immersive (learning) environments focus on various metrics such as ease of use, satisfaction, immersion, motivation, and performance [8,20,23]. These metrics help gauge the efficacy of ILEs in achieving educational objectives.

Specifically, ILEs are prone to high cognitive and mental load because of the high level of interactivity and multi-sensory engagement required by (Social) VR technology [4]. Therefore, it seems fruitful to reduce the cognitive load spent on the user interface and navigation of the ILE, allowing learners to focus their attention on the educational content presented rather than spending cognitive resources on the user interface. One potential method for accomplishing this objective was examined by Petersen et al. [22]. Their study demonstrates that

P. Zaphiris and A. Ioannou (Eds.): HCII 2024, LNCS 14724, pp. 106–124, 2024.
https://doi.org/10.1007/978-3-031-61691-4_8

the instructional design and the tasks assigned to students in an ILE may impact the learning experience and outcomes. Consequently, this finding could provide a stronger rationale for employing more advanced high-immersion technologies in light of the cognitive load when the instructional design supports their implementation.

While ILEs are employed primarily in STEM- or military-related fields [7,25], they often focus on specific 3D assets or environments. However, other instructional tasks that do not prioritize the interaction with high-resolution 3D assets may also derive benefits from ILEs, provided that there exists a discernible learning advantage for the particular platform. This advantage can manifest in the form of, for instance, enhanced non-verbal communication cues, surpassing those offered by video conferencing in remote or hybrid scenarios. This enhancement facilitates engagement and promotes remote collaboration in interactive social settings for scenarios involving group work [21]. Alternatively, it can be realized through a heightened "sense of community" [12].

For a wider adoption of ILEs, it is essential to introduce more diverse and various use cases to a broader audience whose user acceptance and adoption concerning the learning affordances are yet to be explored.

To meet the growing demands for flexible study conditions and inclusive class participation, we took the opportunity to explore the features of Mozilla Hubs and implemented the platform in several classes of different courses of study with different instructional designs. The goal was to enable an online presence that promotes active class participation, increases student motivation, and reduces the risk of "Zoom fatigue" [1], and to evaluate the implementation with special regard to the user experience of students. We theorized that different instructional designs can either enhance or limit the learning potential of ILEs. This is based on how simple and useful these designs are perceived to be. The ease of use and perceived usefulness can influence how readily technology is accepted in online learning [17]. Therefore, such variations might lead to differing views on the effectiveness of platforms like Mozilla Hubs.

Based on these considerations, we proposed the following research question:

RQ: In what way do different instructional designs for larger groups on Mozilla Hubs influence the user experience?

To answer this question and to extend the use cases of social virtual reality applications, and explore the learning affordance of social virtual reality technology in higher education, we report on a series of seminars in which we implemented different classroom activities that incorporated primarily interactivity and collaboration on Mozilla Hubs. In this paper, we provide instructional designers and teachers with recommendations for classroom activities on social virtual reality platforms. Therefore, the main contributions of this paper are:

- inspiration for different instructional designs in Mozilla Hubs,
- evaluation of the Mozilla Hubs system by several diverse student groups,
- further empirical data to the nascent field of ILEs and teaching in one of the most popular social virtual reality platforms.

The remainder of this paper is structured as follows: In Sect. 2, we provide an overview of the relevance and factors in user experience and usability for educational platforms, particularly for ILEs, and review recent activities and instructional designs implemented in Mozilla Hubs settings. In Sect. 3.3, we introduce our courses, and instructional designs that were implemented in Mozilla Hubs. In Sect. 4 we describe our methodology for our user surveys in detail. In Sects. 5 to 7, we present the results and contextualize our findings, discuss our limitations, and conclude our work.

2   Related Work

2.1   Relevance of User Experience in Educational Platforms

The significance of experiences and the function that contexts play in education is of utmost importance. Dewey's [5] experiential learning theory, which applies to ILEs due to immersion and interaction features [9], posits that all occurrences are fundamentally social. Knowledge is constructed socially, procured, and exhibited based on experiences. This knowledge must be structured in real-life episodes that provide a framework for information to be learned.

In experiential learning, hence, the teacher's responsibility becomes that of a coordinator of learning materials and a catalyst for students' experiences. The educator must ensure that the setting and circumstances students are exposed to are appropriate for the knowledge being imparted. The organization of learning materials should be such that students are motivated to think intuitively and impulsively.

Consequently, the usability of educational platforms plays a vital role in learning outcomes such as in ILEs. It influences learning outcomes, learner motivation, and engagement. When a learning software is designed with a focus on usability, it becomes easier for learners to navigate, access content, and interact with the system, enhancing the overall learning experience and yielding positive outcomes [19].

Positive user experiences, facilitated by usability, contribute to learner engagement and motivation: Software that offers smooth navigation, clear instructions, and interactive features creates a sense of enjoyment and accomplishment, fostering intrinsic motivation and a desire to continue learning. Conversely, poor usability can lead to frustration, confusion, and disengagement among learners, hindering the learning process and negatively impacting motivation [24].

A well-designed and user-friendly learning software allows learners to easily access relevant materials, navigate through modules or lessons, and complete tasks efficiently [19]. This streamlined experience optimizes the use of learners' time and cognitive resources, resulting in better learning outcomes.

However, usability is only one of several factors describing the holistic user experience. Moreover, based on a former framework by Hassenzahl et al. [11] that emphasizes "the subjective nature of appealingness" and its influence on the user experience, Laugwitz et al. [15] identified six factors in user experience for software products that were eventually grouped into two categories for their development of the User Experience Questionnaire[1] that is frequently used in the human-machine-interaction field to assess user experience. On the one hand, perspicuity, efficiency, and dependability describe "ergonomic" or "pragmatic" quality aspects. On the other hand, stimulation and novelty describe hedonic quality aspects which describe "the originality of the design or the beauty of the user interface" [15]. Both categories are influenced by the overall attractiveness of a software application.

2.2 Previous Interactive Instructional Designs in Mozilla Hubs

Social VR applications such as Mozilla Hubs are used in classes among educators because of their adaptability and accessibility [3]. They enable more interaction types in a shared space as compared to traditional 2D collaboration tools, giving instructors and students the impression that they are interactive 3D avatars with more agency [21].

However, previous work has identified several usability and user experience issues that are frequently encountered when using Mozilla Hubs for larger groups of users such as in classes which is obstructive for instructional designs that rely particularly on interactivity and collaboration.

Several studies have explored the use of Mozilla Hubs in educational settings and report on benefits and fallbacks:

Peng et al. [21], Burnett et al. [3] and Brown et al. [2] implemented design tasks that were instructed to be performed collaboratively in groups. They showed enhanced student engagement and motivation. They emphasized the importance of promoting successful social interactions on the platform and creating immersive environments that increased student motivation.

Le et al. [16] report on the efficiency of virtual conferences in Mozilla Hubs and emphasize exploiting the platform's and device's functions to justify the interactivity that is expected compared to 2D streams.

Eriksson [6] shared his experience teaching a movie creation course in Mozilla Hubs, highlighting the benefits of small-group interactions for supervision meetings and stressing the Mozilla Hubs' inappropriateness for lectures due to technical issues. He also raised concerns about audio quality, user controls, and low-resolution models. Based on his experience, he suggested that the platform is best suited for meetings with fewer than 25 participants.

Hagler et al. [10] compared social presence in virtual theater tours using Mozilla Hubs and videoconferencing tools. They found only slight differences in social presence, which could be attributed to challenges with navigation controls and onboarding features.

Exams, written reports, and oral presentations are frequently used as evaluation tools in many ecological schools. Holt et al. [12] identified the sense of community created by a virtual poster session in Mozilla Hubs as one of the main advantages for non-STEM courses of study. One of the main advantages

---

[1] https://www.ueq-online.org/ [Accessed: 2024-02-01] .

of a poster session, according to the students, was engaging with classmates. Concerning the virtual environment, they valued its adaptability, novelty, and capacity for interaction. Technical issues could be resolved by repeated practice.

Hence, we summarize the following issues from previous work that need to be considered in instructional designs to not impede the user experience in Mozilla Hubs:

- audio issues with increasing number of attendants,
- issues with internet stability concerning joining or staying in rooms,
- problematic navigation controls due to poor onboarding and lack of practice,
- issues with internet stability concerning high-resolution 3D models.

3   Implementation

3.1   Platform

Leveraging the open-source capabilities of Mozilla Hubs, which offers adaptable collaborative virtual settings, avatars, and a web-based interface ensuring cross-device operability and extensive device and system compatibility, our initial approach utilized their proprietary servers. However, in consideration of our institute's imperatives regarding enhanced data autonomy for student records and an amplified degree of software client adaptability, we transitioned to an institutionally-managed instance of Mozilla Hubs Cloud[2]. This bespoke instance is hosted on servers within the European Union, providing us with decisive authority on software updates and potential server outages.

3.2   General Preparation of Classes

Several steps were taken to prepare the overall Mozilla Hubs platform that applied to all courses: We prepared an interactive asynchronous walk-through tutorial for Mozilla Hubs' navigation, interaction techniques, and functions that all students completed before the joint seminars. We have made significant improvements to the overall performance of Mozilla Hubs by utilizing the 3D modeling software Blender[3] to design our rooms such as a virtual auditorium (see Fig. 2) and models, and to optimize the polygon count, file size, and textures for a seamless experience. Based on the problems described in previous work (see Subsect. 2.2), we developed workarounds (e.g. duplicated synchronous rooms to increase participant capacity and connected them via live streams) so that we could largely avoid these problems and still be able to implement the lesson design for larger groups. Moreover, we gave our virtual rooms a campus-like appearance and feel so that our remote students may feel like they are a part of the actual on-site campus community. This was intended to foster a sense of connection and familiarity. Additionally, while working with teachers to create lessons, we have encouraged them to include movement and spatial components in their activities, leveraging proximity as a non-verbal cue in their interactive assignments and increasing active participation by students.

---

[2] Mozilla Hubs Cloud [Accessed: 2024-02-01].
[3] https://www.blender.com/ [Accessed: 2024-02-01].

3.3 Instructional Designs

We applied five instructional designs in Mozilla Hubs in four classes of three different courses of study.

Based on similar characteristics and affordances of the instructional designs, we grouped them into three overarching categories which we refer to as instructional design types, namely into Roleplay, Presentations and Lectures, and Free Exploration. In this section, we describe them briefly. In Table 1 we summarize in which class we implemented what instructional design.

Table 1. Instructional Design per Class and Course of Study

Instructional Design	Class	Course of Study
Avatar-focused Roleplay	Intercultural Communication	Communication Sciences
Environment-focused Roleplay	Media Politics	Communication Sciences
Final Presentations	Communication Systems	Engineering Sciences
Lectures	Intercultural Communication	Communication Sciences
Free Exploration	Technology-Enhanced Didactics	Teacher Education

Roleplay. During seminars with roleplays as an instructional design exercise, we emphasized the spatial movement of users to encourage active participation, while, at the same time, using proximity as a non-verbal communication cue. Moreover, since the overall user experience in social virtual reality comprises self-representation, the virtual environment, and interaction with others [14], we decided to focus on different features of the experience to be roleplayed depending on the learning affordance and intended experienced social setting.

Roleplay with Focus on Avatar Design. For more interactivity, lecturers and students were supposed to create avatars for a class about intercultural communication representing their culture in a Social VR dressing room to address their culture in their self-representation in a roleplay. Cultural rooms were made based on the Inglehart-Welzel [13] map. Four rooms were created according to students' origins. Pictures were put on walls to represent different sociocultural encounters. We decided to use pictures instead of 3D models to mind the performance of students with low internet bandwidth or insufficient hardware. In that way, students could also send pictures from their home cultures. Students could walk around between rooms and discuss cultural differences or similarities, customize their avatars using culturally-themed 3D clothes, and reflect on each other's avatar customization choices.

Users were required to move around in the scene to accommodate the distance between them and use spatial audio in smaller group discussions. A storyboard of the scene setup is provided in Fig. 1.

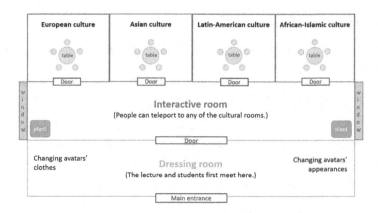

Fig. 1. Storyboard of the Roleplay and Spatial Exploration task avatar roleplay design.

Fig. 2. Parliament roleplay in the redecorated auditorium. Logos attached to the seating indicate membership to a political party.

For this activity, we divided the students into several groups and prepared several scenes with the same room contents to avoid internet issues due to too many participants in one virtual scene.

Roleplay with Focus on Environment. In the political system of Germany, public discussions in the parliament by the members of several political parties are essential for the political culture. They take place in an auditorium in which the members are seated according to their party membership. Therefore, the position of the seats has a significant meaning. For their speeches, parliament members go to the front on stage.

For a roleplay activity, students were assigned to groups that represented a political party in the parliament and were supposed to write and hold speeches. To conduct this roleplay, we repurposed our virtual auditorium into a virtual replica of the German parliament, the decoration of the virtual auditorium is illustrated in Fig. 2 and seated students according to their assigned political party. For their speeches, students were required to move to the stage. The focus of this roleplay was the room's structure instead of the avatar design.

Presentations and Lectures. Since examination regulations usually dictate the formats for educational materials, students had to prepare 2D materials but present them in three-dimensional spaces with assumingly more social presence.

Guest Lectures. In addition to the interactive seminars in the Intercultural Communication and the Media and Political Culture course, we held virtual guest lectures in the virtual auditorium replica for which the lecturers were equipped with head-mounted displays to convey more expressiveness during their lecture using gestures.

Final Presentations. To offer the remote students a common platform with more non-verbal communication cues and expressive behavior than videoconferencing tools, we held their final presentations in our virtual auditorium for which students were encouraged to use the whole stage and held subsequent small-group discussions in virtual breakout rooms.

Free Exploration. To introduce first-semester undergraduate students of teacher education to innovative educational platforms and show them the technological possibilities they can incorporate later in their classes, we held a synchronous unguided seminar session in Mozilla Hubs for which the students were equipped with Meta Quest 2 head-mounted displays. Students were free to explore the virtual campus in multiple Mozilla Hubs scenes. Students moved around freely and tried out the interactive functions of the software and discussed application scenarios for social virtual reality in teaching.

4   Survey

In this section, we describe the methodology of our surveys across all classes and instructional designs (types). Across all of our four classes in three different courses of study, we distributed online surveys to collect data for a cross-sectional between-subject research design. The structure of our instructional designs per class and per course of study is shown in Table 1.

4.1   Measurements

For the user evaluation, as our sample groups attended classes primarily remotely and sometimes even from all over the world, we relied on subjective evaluation via online surveys. In our surveys, we included questions for a thorough sample description, including their general experience with social virtual reality platforms and their demographics. Moreover, we implemented the extended version of the User Experience Questionnaire by Laugwitz et al. [15] including all 26 item pairs. The UEQ measures three subdimensions: the pragmatic qualities with scales for dependability, perspicuity, and efficiency, and the hedonic qualities with scales for novelty and stimulation that are both related to the valence dimension attractiveness. Furthermore, we included questions by Burnett et al.

Table 2. Sample description per Instructional Design type Group, * for better readability, only the first three most frequent answers are provided.

Instructional Design	n	Access Device	Nationality*	Social VR Experience	Age	Gender	Course of Study
Roleplay	10	Laptop (70%), Tablet (10%), Smartphone (20%)	Nigeria (20%), Pakistan (20%), Ghana (20%)	Never (80%), Rarely (10%), Sometimes (10%)	28.22 ± 2.39	female (90%), male (10%), other (0%)	Communication Sciences, M. A. (100%)
Presentations and Lectures	18	Laptop (61%), Tablet (16.7%), Smartphone (16.7%), Desktop-PC (5.6%)	Brazil (11%),, Germany (22.2%), India (16.7%)	Never (83%), Rarely (11%), Sometimes (5.6%)	27.39 ± 4.09	female (62%), male (38%), other (0%)	Communication Sciences, M. A. (61%), Engineering Sciences, M. Sc. (39%)
Exploration	5	VR-HMD (100%)	Germany (100%)	Never (80%), Rarely (20%)	28.6 ± 6.99	female (60%), male (40%), other (0%)	Teacher Education, B. Ed. (100%)

[3] to investigate an increase/decrease in motivation to participate in on-site classes and collaborations with fellows but changed the original scale from 1 to 7 to –3 to 3.

4.2   Sample Description

In total, $N = 37$ students of all courses filled out our survey. According to the recommendations by Laugwitz et al., [15] for the scoring of the UEQ, we excluded $n = 4$ due to inconsistent answers to our questionnaire that impacted the reliability of our questionnaire data. The overall sample is comprised of students partaking in online remote classes from 4 courses of which 3 are offered to primarily international Master's students from our university (see Table 2). The last course is for undergraduate students at a partner university who cooperated with us for a few sessions using their virtual reality head-mounted displays. Their classes' primary language is German. A thorough sample description according to the different instructional designs is given in Table 1 and Table 2.

4.3   Research Ethics

Participation in any survey was voluntary and anonymous and did not affect the students' course grades. We ensured that all class contents were imparted parallelly on alternative channels such as live streams on Webex for students who could not participate in the Mozilla Hubs activities due to, for instance, severe technical issues. All activities were discussed and reflected on in subsequent classes to ensure that the classes' contents were conveyed also outside of Mozilla Hubs in case of technical issues. Except for the final presentations, the participation in Mozilla Hubs activities did not affect the course's grades. For the final presentations, we offered the option to present on conventional video conferencing software when students faced severe technical issues with the platform or did not feel sufficiently confident in using the platform in our onboarding and test sessions.

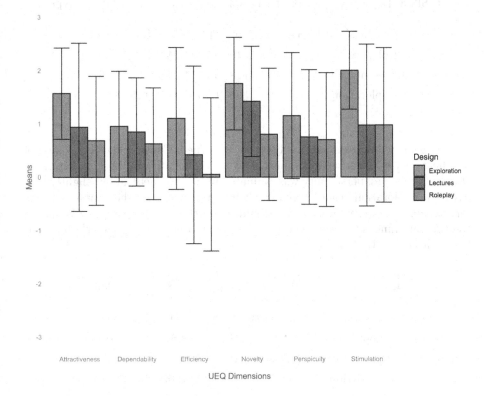

Fig. 3. Mean values and standard deviation in error bars for UEQ Subdimensions per instructional design type

5 Results

As participation in the survey was not mandatory and anonymous, our response rate in comparison to the student enrollments in all classes was fairly low, resulting in a total sample of N = 33 of all four courses. To increase the reliability of our tests, we decided to group our instructional designs based on the similarities and affordances of the designs into three instructional design types: roleplays, presentations & lectures, and exploration.

5.1 UEQ

As a first step of our analysis, we imported the responses to the UEQ analysis tool that is provided by the authors of the questionnaire[4]. Using this tool, we calculated the outcomes for all subdimensions of the UEQ and used these subsequently for further statistical analysis and group-wise comparisons (Fig. 3 and Table 3).

---

[4] UEQ Analysis Sheet [Accessed:2024-02-01].

Table 3. Descriptive statistics for Perspicuity per instructional design type

Instructional Design Type	n	M	SD	Min	Max
Roleplay	10	0.7	1.26	-1	2.5
Presentations & Lectures	18	0.75	1.25	-1.25	2.75
Exploration	5	1.15	1.18	-0.25	3

Perspicuity describes how easily a tool is learned. Considering, that values of 3 indicate a very positive and values of –3 a very negative evaluation, across all three design types, perspicuity was evaluated to be more neutral but slightly positive. the exploration group evaluated their experience to be the easiest to learn, followed by the presentation groups, and lastly the roleplay classes. Compared to other subdimensions, perspicuity was evaluated neither particularly high nor low on average (Table 4).

Table 4. Descriptive statistics for Efficiency per instructional design type

Instructional Design Type	n	M	SD	Min	Max
Roleplay	10	0.05	1.67	-2.5	2.75
Presentations & Lectures	18	0.42	1.43	-2	3
Exploration	5	1.1	1.33	-0.5	3

Efficiency measures how much effort the users perceive to spend to achieve their goals. Overall, similar to perspicuity, efficiency was evaluated to be rather neutral on average with values of around 1 and below on average. Similarly to perspicuity, the exploration design was evaluated to be most efficient, followed by presentations and lectures, and lastly by the roleplay designs. However, all three design types showed high ranges according to very high maximum evaluations of around 3 and very low minimum negative evaluations. Compared to the other subdimensions, efficiency was measured to be one of the lowest across all subdimensions (Table 5).

Table 5. Descriptive statistics for Novelty per instructional design type

Instructional Design Type	n	M	SD	Min	Max
Roleplay	10	0.8	1.03	-0.75	2
Presentations & Lectures	18	1.42	1.24	-1.75	3
Exploration	5	1.75	0.87	0.5	2.5

Novelty describes how innovative and creative the system was perceived to be. With mean evaluations of around 1 and maximum values between 2 to 3, we can describe novelty as one of the better-evaluated subdimensions. This applies also to the comparisons between subdimensions. Again, the exploration design was assessed highest, followed by presentations and lectures and, lastly the roleplay designs (Table 6).

Table 6. Descriptive statistics for Stimulation per instructional design type

Instructional Design Type	n	M	SD	Min	Max
Roleplay	10	0.98	1.38	−1.75	2.75
Presentations & Lectures	18	0.97	1.45	−2	3
Exploration	5	2	0.73	1	3

Stimulation describes how exciting and motivating the system was perceived to be. Stimulation was assessed highest for the exploration design across all subdimensions and all designs with a mean of 2 and a maximum of 3. Compared to this exceptionally high evaluation, the mean values for the other two designs differ by around 1 but also show maximum values of around 3. The minimum values are exceptionally low for roleplay, presentations, and lecture designs with negative values of around −2 (Table 7).

Table 7. Descriptive statistics for Dependability per instructional design type

Instructional Design Type	n	M	SD	Min	Max
Roleplay	10	0.62	1.02	−0.75	2.5
Presentations & Lectures	18	0.85	1.05	−0.75	2.5
Exploration	5	0.95	1.04	−0.75	2

Dependability measures how much the user felt in control using the system. Overall, we observe neutral evaluation with mean values ranging between 0 and 1 for all designs. Interestingly, for all designs, there is a high range with negative minimum values that even indicate a negative evaluation up to a highly positive evaluation for maximum values. As for all other subdimensions, exploration assessed dependability to be highest compared to presentations and lectures, and roleplay designs. Next to efficiency, dependability is one of the most negatively assessed subdimensions across all three design types (Table 8).

Attractiveness measures how the user likes or dislikes a system in general. The mean values of attractiveness show similar results to the other subdimensions as all evaluations from all 3 design types are slightly positive, but overall rather

Table 8. Descriptive statistics for Attractiveness per instructional design type

Instructional Design Type	n	M	SD	Min	Max
Roleplay	10	0.68	1.58	−1.67	2.67
Presentations & Lectures	18	0.94	1.21	−1.5	2.67
Exploration	5	1.57	0.85	0.83	3

neutral. However, the minimum and maximum values show a rather wide range of answers. Similar to the other subdimensions, the exploration design group assessed their experience as the most attractive, followed by presentations and lectures, and lastly the roleplay designs. Compared to the other subdimensions, attractiveness reached across all three design types one of the more positive evaluations.

Conclusively, comparing the three designs, the exploration design group stands out because they assessed their experience as the best in all subdimensions, followed by the presentations and lectures group. The roleplay designs were assessed as the worst for almost all subdimensions across all three design types. Considering the definition of subdimensions of the UEQ, we can summarize that all subdimensions related to the pragmatic quality of the system (dependability, perspicuity, and efficiency) are worse assessed than the hedonic qualities (Novelty and Stimulation) and the overall Attractiveness evaluation.

In the next step, we performed inferential statistic tests to see if the few differences between the evaluations could be generalized. Because the data of all 6 subdimensions were not normally distributed (as per Shapiro-Wilk tests at $p > .05$) and because of the unequal sample sizes between designs, we performed non-parametric Kruskal-Wallis tests. All results are summarized in Table 9. None of the tests were statistically significant, thus we reject the null hypothesis that there are significant differences between the groups in our sample.

Table 9. Results for non-parametric Kruskal-Wallis tests for all subdimensions of the UEQ across the three instructional design types

UEQ Subdimension	χ^2	df	p
Perspicuity	0.503	2	0.78
Dependability	0.638	2	0.72
Efficiency	1.679	2	0.43
Novelty	3.61	2	0.16
Stimulation	2.29	2	0.32
Attractiveness	0.989	2	0.61

5.2   Motivation

To evaluate in what way the implementation of Mozilla Hubs contributes to a change in motivation to participate in on-site class attendance and joint activities for more group interaction, we employed questions by Burnett et al. [3] to ask for motivation change in attending on-site classes and to interact with other student fellows from the class. Results are shown in Fig. 4 and Table 10.

The mean values of the different design types demonstrate different central tendencies among the responses. The exploration group yields the highest mean and only increase in motivation across all designs in participating in on-site classes, while the lowest mean is observed in the roleplay designs for their motivational change in engaging with on-site classes. Interestingly, the roleplay groups were the only design type that showed a stronger decrease in motivation to engage with on-site classes compared to their motivation to engage with other student peers. This indicates that participant responses vary across different instructional design types.

Analyzing the standard deviations reveals significant differences in response dispersion. Notably, the roleplay designs consistently display higher standard

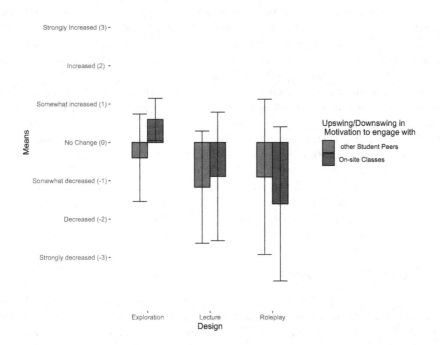

Fig. 4. Motivation upswing/downswing in engaging with on-site classes and with interacting with other student fellows per instructional design type

Table 10. Descriptive statistics of motivational changes to engage in on-site classes and with other student peers per instructional design

Question regarding motivation change	Instructional Design	n	M	SD	Min	Max
Engaging with other student peers	Roleplay	10	-0.9	2.025	-3	3
	Lectures	18	-1.167	1.47	-2	3
	Exploration	5	-0.4	1.14	-1	2
Engaging with on-site classes	Roleplay	10	-1.6	2.01	-3	2
	Lectures	18	-0.89	1.67	-3	3
	Exploration	5	0.6	0.54	1	2

deviations, indicating more diverse participant responses compared to the exploration and lecture designs. The maximum standard deviation is observed in the roleplay design for motivation to engage with other student peers, underscoring the substantial spread in participant responses for this specific group.

Concerning instructional design types, on the one hand, motivational responses towards participation in on-site classes generally exhibit a broader spectrum, ranging from a minimum mean of -1.6 for roleplays to a maximum mean of 0.6 for exploration. On the flip side, questions related to a shift in motivation regarding engagement with other student peers elicit responses within a more limited mean range, spanning from -1.167 for lectures to -0.4 for exploration. The standard deviation ranges underscore the increased variability in responses to questions addressing motivational changes concerning engagement with other student peers, extending from 1.14 to 2.02. Non-parametric Kruskal-Wallis tests show no significant differences between instructional design types, neither for motivation to engage with on-site classes ($\chi^2 = 5.35$, df $=2$, $p = .06$), nor to engage with other student peers ($\chi^2 = 1.145$, df $=2$, $p = .56$).

In conclusion, the findings underscore disparities in participant responses across instructional design types and questions. The roleplay designs, especially when involving interactions with other students, yield more diverse and variable responses.

5.3   Qualitative Feedback

Many users commented positively on their experience with the Mozilla Hubs platform. They particularly appreciated the ability to walk through and explore virtual spaces and were impressed by the precise movements of the avatars - such as raising their heads when looking up at the ceiling. The experience was a refreshing way to learn online for some. They especially praised the idea because it allowed students to feel closer to their classmates while remaining in their own space. Despite the initial uncertainty of some users who feared feeling "lost", many of them enjoyed the Social VR class after a period of adjustment.

However, there were also some criticisms and suggestions for improvement. When they experienced their classes using a VR-head-mounted display, the weight of the headset was found to be annoying by some, and a more detailed introduction to the platform was requested, as not all functions were self-explanatory for all users. Concerns regarding user interactions were also expressed, as it was difficult to view presentations when not standing directly in front of them. Some technical hurdles, such as the need to reload the page due to sound issues, and the requirements for a good internet connection as well as high-quality hardware were also raised. In addition, the lack of facial expressions in the avatars was noted, and there were suggestions to improve this with movements such as opening the mouth when speaking. Furthermore, some wished for a more immersive visual experience, more in line with the quality of video games.

Overall, the feedback was mostly positive, though it was clear that there is room for technical and design improvements to further optimize the user experience.

6   Discussion

The surge in new educational technologies has opened unprecedented avenues for learning and interaction. Our study aimed to contribute to this emerging field by focusing on Mozilla Hubs, a platform gaining popularity. However, our findings reveal that roleplay techniques face challenges due to the platform's insufficiently intuitive user interface (UI) and unstable infrastructure. Pragmatic qualities, notably for roleplays, need improvement, underscored by, for instance, low efficiency scores across all design types.

Despite suboptimal pragmatic qualities and efficiency scores, the hedonic qualities and attractiveness scores are not overtly negative. This suggests potential viability for roleplays with further enhancements on possibly other platforms. Thus, at this point, despite our efforts we see similar outcomes to, for instance, Holt et al. [12]. However, caution is advised, pending further developments in Mozilla Hubs' UI and infrastructure. Ongoing assessment is crucial, and reevaluation of roleplays' feasibility is recommended once these issues are addressed.

Surprisingly, lectures on the platform received positive feedback, indicating a potential exploration avenue. The expectation that roleplay would outperform lectures was not entirely realized, possibly due to technical issues, workload, or participants' study courses. Our study highlights high variability in outcomes, suggesting the multifaceted nature of Mozilla Hubs' UX in educational settings, influenced by, for instance, socio-cultural factors. Technical issues and intersubject differences might also contribute to this variability, impacting user experiences.

Our findings are subject to limitations, including an underpowered study with stability issues and also challenges in isolating instructional design effects in the teacher education group using VR headsets. The latter might also be a factor in the overall positive assessments by teacher education students since they were rather inexperienced with VR headsets and might have experienced a stronger initial sense of awe because of their more immersive access hardware.

Future studies should therefore ensure consistency in content, hardware, and class while varying instructional designs. Emphasizing the need for effective instructional designs, future research should assess learning success in addition to motivation and UX. In conclusion, while educational technologies like Mozilla Hubs hold immense potential, addressing UX, infrastructure, and instructional design challenges is imperative for their successful integration into virtual learning environments.

7 Conclusion

The ascent of educational technologies marks a transformative period in contemporary learning, with platforms like Mozilla Hubs steering this evolution. Our research underscores the potential of these platforms in fostering rich social interactions. Notwithstanding its potential, user feedback identified areas of improvement in Mozilla Hubs, notably the user interface and infrastructure stability. The platform's adaptability for diverse devices, including smartphones, is commendable; however, questions remain on the optimal device-interface combination.

Our observations reveal that the platform's user experience is variegated, and shaped by technical, socio-cultural, and individual user factors. This underscores the complexity of tailoring universally acceptable virtual educational platforms, considering the myriad of influencing variables. While technical issues are equally prominent in determining the platform's utility, the role of socio-cultural backgrounds that need to be considered to reach user acceptance of a broader audience and individual learning preferences cannot be understated.

However, our research is not without limitations. The underpowered nature of our study, influenced by the sample size and technical difficulties, does pose constraints on the breadth of our findings. Nonetheless, these initial insights pave the way for more rigorous, extensive, and diverse future studies. Future research endeavors should delve into refining instructional design, expanding the audience reach, and measuring not only motivation and user experience but also tangible learning outcomes.

In sum, as the educational landscape witnesses a paradigm shift with the advent of platforms like Mozilla Hubs, it is imperative to acknowledge both its promises and pitfalls. Addressing the identified challenges is not just beneficial, but necessary, to realize the full potential of such platforms. As virtual learning environments continue to burgeon in prominence, targeted research will be instrumental in optimizing their efficacy and acceptance in the global educational arena. Considering the breadth of responses, we assert that our findings underscore the critical importance of incorporating diverse samples and diverse content in the evaluation of the user experience on an educational platform, and that instructional designs in ILEs require further in-depth analyses as they did not mirror our initially assumed expectations.

Acknowledgements. This work was partially funded by the VEDIAS project at TU Ilmenau (57573356). The VEDIAS project was funded by the German Federal Ministry of Education and Research as part of the DAAD's "International Programmes Digital" call. The authors would like to thank Prof. Dr. Liane Rothenberger from the Catholic University Eichstätt-Ingolstadt, our institutional colleagues Irina Tribusean, Dr. Yi Xu, and Mira Rochyadi-Reetz, as well as Tuo Liu from the Goethe University Frankfurt, and lastly Dr. Bilal Zafar and Mendrit Shala from the Communications Research Laboratory at TU Ilmenau for their cooperation and support in their classes.

References

1. Bailenson, J.N.: Nonverbal overload: a theoretical argument for the causes of zoom fatigue. Technol. Mind Behav. **2**(1) (2021). https://doi.org/10.1037/tmb0000030
2. Brown, R., et al.: Employing mozilla hubs as an alternative tool for student outreach: a design challenge use case. In: 14th International Conference on Interactive Mobile Communication, Technologies and Learning, IMCL 2021, pp. 213–222 (2022). https://doi.org/10.1007/978-3-030-96296-8_20
3. Burnett, G., Kay, R.P., Harvey, C.: Future visions for higher education: an investigation of the benefits of virtual reality for teaching university students. In: 2021 IEEE International Symposium on Mixed and Augmented Reality Adjunct (ISMAR-Adjunct), pp. 292–297. IEEE, Bari (2021). https://doi.org/10.1109/ISMAR-Adjunct54149.2021.00066
4. Dengel, A.: What is immersive learning? In: 2022 8th International Conference of the Immersive Learning Research Network (iLRN), pp. 1–5 (2022). https://doi.org/10.23919/iLRN55037.2022.9815941
5. Dewey, J.: Experience and education: The 60th anniversary edition. The Kappa Delta Pi Lectures Series, Touchstone, New York (1997)
6. Eriksson, T.: Failure and success in using mozilla hubs for online teaching in a movie production course. In: 2021 7th International Conference of the Immersive Learning Research Network (iLRN), pp. 1–8. IEEE, Eureka (2021). https://doi.org/10.23919/iLRN52045.2021.9459321
7. Fernandes, F., Castro, D., Werner, C.: A systematic mapping literature of immersive learning from svr publications. In: Symposium on Virtual and Augmented Reality, SVR 2021, pp. 1–13. Association for Computing Machinery, New York (2022). https://doi.org/10.1145/3488162.3488163
8. Forte, J.L.B., Vela, F.L.G., Rodríguez, P.P.: User experience problems in immersive virtual environments. In: Proceedings of the XX International Conference on Human Computer Interaction, Interacción 2019. Association for Computing Machinery, New York (2019). https://doi.org/10.1145/3335595.3336288
9. Fromm, J.: More than experience? - on the unique opportunities of virtual reality to afford a holistic experiential learning cycle. Internet High. Educ. **50**, 100804 (2021). https://doi.org/10.1016/j.iheduc.2021.100804
10. Hagler, J., Lankes, M., Gallist, N.: Behind the curtains: comparing mozilla hubs with microsoft teams in a guided virtual theatre experience. In: 2022 IEEE Conference on Virtual Reality and 3D User Interfaces Abstracts and Workshops (VRW), pp. 19–22. IEEE, Christchurch (2022). https://doi.org/10.1109/VRW55335.2022.00011
11. Hassenzahl, M.: The effect of perceived hedonic quality on product appealingness. Int. J. Human-Comput. Interact. **13**(4), 481–499 (2001). https://doi.org/10.1207/S15327590IJHC1304_07

12. Holt, E.A., Heim, A.B., Tessens, E., Walker, R.: Thanks for inviting me to the party: virtual poster sessions as a way to connect in a time of disconnection. Ecol. Evol. **10**(22), 12423–12430 (2020). https://doi.org/10.1002/ece3.6756
13. Inglehart, R.: Mapping global values. Comp. Sociol. **5**(2–3), 115–136 (2006). https://doi.org/10.1163/156913306778667401
14. Jonas, M., Said, S., Yu, D., Aiello, C., Furlo, N., Zytko, D.: Towards a taxonomy of social VR application design. In: Extended Abstracts of the Annual Symposium on Computer-Human Interaction in Play Companion Extended Abstracts, CHI PLAY 2019 Extended Abstracts, pp. 437-444. Association for Computing Machinery, New York (2019). https://doi.org/10.1145/3341215.3356271
15. Laugwitz, B., Held, T., Schrepp, M.: Construction and evaluation of a user experience questionnaire. In: Holzinger, A. (ed.) HCI and Usability for Education and Work, pp. 63–76. Springer, Heidelberg (2008). https://doi.org/10.1007/978-3-540-89350-9_6
16. Le, D.A., MacIntyre, B., Outlaw, J.: Enhancing the experience of virtual conferences in social virtual environments. In: 2020 IEEE Conference on Virtual Reality and 3D User Interfaces Abstracts and Workshops (VRW), pp. 485–494. IEEE, Atlanta (2020). https://doi.org/10.1109/VRW50115.2020.00101
17. Masrom, M.: Technology acceptance model and e-learning. In: Proceedings of the 12th International Conference on Education, pp. 1–10. Universiti Brunei Darussalam, Brunei (2007)
18. Mulders, M.: Investigating learners' motivation towards a virtual reality learning environment: a pilot study in vehicle painting. In: 2020 IEEE International Conference on Artificial Intelligence and Virtual Reality (AIVR), pp. 390–393. IEEE, Utrecht (2020). https://doi.org/10.1109/AIVR50618.2020.00081
19. Niemiec, C.P., Ryan, R.M.: Autonomy, competence, and relatedness in the classroom: applying self-determination theory to educational practice. Theory Res. Educ. **7**(2), 133–144 (2009). https://doi.org/10.1177/1477878509104318
20. Pangestu, H., Karsen, M.: Evaluation of usability in online learning. In: 2016 International Conference on Information Management and Technology (ICIMTech), pp. 267–271 (2016). https://doi.org/10.1109/ICIMTech.2016.7930342
21. Peng, Z., Shi, C., Ma, X.: Exploring user experience and design opportunities of desktop social virtual reality for group learning activities. In: The Ninth International Symposium of Chinese CHI, pp. 105–111. ACM, Online Hong Kong (2021). https://doi.org/10.1145/3490355.3490367
22. Petersen, G.B., Stenberdt, V., Mayer, R.E., Makransky, G.: Collaborative generative learning activities in immersive virtual reality increase learning. Comput. Educ. **207**, 104931 (2023). https://doi.org/10.1016/j.compedu.2023
23. Sulaiman, H., Suid, N., Bin Idris, M.A.: Usability evaluation of confirm-a learning tool towards education 4.0. In: 2018 IEEE Conference on e-Learning, e-Management and e-Services (IC3e), pp. 73–78 (2018). https://doi.org/10.1109/IC3e.2018.8632637
24. Vertesi, A., Dogan, H., Stefanidis, A.: Usability evaluation of virtual learning environments: a university case study. In: Isaias, P., Sampson, D.G., Ifenthaler, D. (eds.) Online Teaching and Learning in Higher Education, pp. 161–183. Springer, Cham (2020). https://doi.org/10.1007/978-3-030-48190-2_9
25. Yin, X., Li, G., Deng, X., Luo, H.: Enhancing k-16 science education with augmented reality: a systematic review of literature from 2001 to 2020. In: 2022 8th International Conference of the Immersive Learning Research Network (iLRN), pp. 1–5 (2022).https://doi.org/10.23919/iLRN55037.2022.9815958

Training Development in Dance: Enhancing Precision Through Motion Capture and a Virtual Environment for Injury Prevention

Leonie Laskowitz[(⊠)] [iD] and Nicholas Müller[iD]

Technical University Würzburg-Schweinfurt, Sanderheinrichsleitenweg 20,
97074 Würzburg, Germany
leonie.laskowitz@thws.de

Abstract. Traditional training methods in dance, especially competitive ballet, face challenges due to the intricate movements and high injury risk associated with joints. Young athletes, aged 10–19, undergo intense physical training leading to overuse injuries, mainly in the foot and ankle. Intrinsic factors like skeletal development and extrinsic factors like incorrect techniques contribute to these injuries. To address this, extended warm-up and cool-down phases are crucial. The field of dance biomechanics and joint kinematics has been limited by traditional methods, prompting a shift towards 3D motion capture systems. These technologies, derived from the film industry, precisely analyze dance movements and prevent injuries. However, traditional methods often lack precision and objective assessment. Integration of motion capture allows for accurate evaluation, ensuring training aligns with international dance sport competition standards. This study analyzes how ballet training can be improved using motion capture to optimize the execution of ballet positions. It explains why dancers, especially ballet dancers, are often susceptible to injuries and how these can be better prevented through angle measurements. A preliminary test demonstrates how ballet movements can be measured and improved. Additionally, some examples from the literature are cited, where similar analyses have been conducted. It turns out that both rotational angles and joint angles are measures that can enhance the execution of the positions. Future research should expand on this training method by incorporating the use of Virtual Reality.

Keywords: Motion Capture · Training Development · Angle Measurement

1 Introduction

1.1 Background and Motivation

In the realm of dance sports, numerous training methods are continually evolving through the utilization of various technical and non-technical aids. This study delves into the realm of technological support, shedding light on the emerging possibilities in this field. Initially, we address the motivations and fundamentals of this study, defining precise goals to emphasize the significance of the subject area. Subsequently, possibilities for analyzing movement execution based on a preliminary study are introduced, along with an explanation of the use of motion capture technology in dance sports. Finally, future research avenues in the realm of training expansion through Virtual Reality are outlined.

Dance sports involve complex movements that regularly strain the joints of dancers. A study analyzed foot and ankle biomechanics, concluding that there is a lack of research on evaluating extreme foot and ankle mobility during dance movements using 3D motion capture. Foot biomechanics during dance remain relatively underexplored. By employing 3D motion capture systems, joint kinematics in dancers can be studied more accurately, aiding in the prevention of potential injury risks [1]. A diverse array of technologies, including Motion Capture, are utilized in the fields of motion analysis and sports training, originating from the film and animation industry. Motion Capture involves equipment that determines the position of various points on a body or object at a specific moment. A suit, often equipped with markers, is worn by a person. These markers are captured by multiple cameras to recreate the person's body, and the recorded movements can later be transformed into a digital 3D model [2]. Different technologies allow the capture, digital recording, and subsequent analysis of movements. By providing precise motion data, Motion Capture aids in analyzing dance posture and understanding human dance movements, identifying novel training methods. In the education sector, this technology can enhance dance instruction through real-time demonstrations, individual feedback, and efficient problem correction. The resulting Motion Capture data can then be transferred to 3D models and animations, opening further research avenues within Virtual Reality [3].

1.2 Objective of the Study

The aim of this study is to investigate how ballet training can be enhanced through precise angle measurements using Motion Capture. This approach is intended not only to identify injuries early but also to facilitate the optimization of movements in various ballet positions. Additionally, a theoretical analysis of the effective design of potential virtual training scenarios through the integration of Virtual Reality will be conducted. This lays the foundation for further research to create an optimal training environment and to more precisely examine the impacts on ballet training.

2 Theoretical Background

2.1 Ballett Training

In ballet, young athletes between the ages of 10 and 19 undergo intensive physical training. Risk factors for overuse injuries in the foot and ankle encompass intrinsic and extrinsic influences. Skeletal development, excessive hip rotation, and extreme ankle movement represent intrinsic risk factors, while incorrect dance techniques and excessive training pose external dangers. To prevent injuries, extended warm-up and cooldown phases are essential [4]. Basic ballet training is the longest and most scientifically grounded foundational course in history, which trains muscles, skills, and abilities. Therefore, ballet training is considered one of the compulsory foundational courses for all dancers [5, 6].

Advances in Dance Training. Dance training is still considered a young sport with plenty of room for improvement. Training sessions should be individualized, taking into account the athletes' physical abilities, and appropriate supplementary training can enhance performance [7]. Training plans should be specifically tailored to training cycles. This means that competitions and recovery periods should be integral parts of quality training, and both small and large training cycles should be combined effectively [8]. A study confirmed that the technical level of modern ballet is divided into dynamic and static techniques. In sports dance, a distinction is made between dynamic movements, which require agility and coordination, and static movements [9].

When assessing dynamic posture, gait analysis is used. This involves analyzing the behavior of different regions, joints, or segments during a specific phase of the gait cycle. However, the collection of quantitative data is essential [10]. Most studies focus on examining static postures. The analysis of motor functions can be obtained using technological tools such as dynamic electromyography [11]. To achieve perfection in the execution of the steps, years of study are required. To meet the complexity of classical techniques, it is necessary for the body to be adapted to specific requirements from childhood. Elasticity, linearity, lightness, muscle strength, and balance are crucial factors. Static posture assessments are usually used to evaluate posture, allowing visual comparisons to an ideal position. Sagittal, frontal, and dorsal planes are observed [12].

Trainers should always stay up-to-date with the latest developments in dance movement and tailor their training accordingly. This includes addressing common issues in dance sport and aligning training with the rules of international dance movement competitions to promote further development [13].

Navigating Optimization and Injury Prevention. However, it is not only about optimization but also about preventing and avoiding injuries at the same time. All forms of dance involve highly demanding movements, with an injury rate that can reach up to 95% over a dancer's lifetime [14–17]. Ballet dancers have a higher injury rate compared to other dancers. The injury rate ranges from 67% to 95% [18]. Dance companies are compelled to continuously improve their dancers' technique to maintain high technical standards and competitiveness. Due to the high injury rate, rehabilitation costs for ballet companies are consistently high [19]. Joint injuries are often induced in ballet because dancers must maintain full ankle plantarflexion during their movements. Such excessive loading is not within the normal capacity of foot joints and ligaments. For example, during the en pointe position, excessive dorsiflexion is caused in an outward turned position [20–23].

When examining the kinematics in ballet, it becomes apparent that dancers perform movements in both open and closed kinematic chains. Open chains involve movements where the foot is not engaged in any weight bearing activity as it moves freely in the air, whereas closed chains involve loading the foot during the movement, engaging all the joints [24, 25]. To prevent chronic and acute injuries, there are biomechanical rules and laws. Injury status can be identified through kinematic analyses using musculoskeletal models [26].

It is important to explore the use of technology in ballet training to enhance the performance of dancers, prevent injuries, develop a deeper understanding of biomechanics, and elevate the overall level of dance sport.

2.2 Motion Capture Technology in Sports and Immersive Training

In previous studies, various methods for evaluating sports performance using new technologies have been explored. Motion Capture technology has shown promising results in providing more objective assessments compared to subjective judgments or less precise measurement methods. As a result, a research team developed an algorithm to analyze the patterns of correct motion capture data by comparing Euclidean distances and recorded trajectories of amateur athletes with the baseline model of professional athletes. This research focused on the techniques of historical European swordsmanship. However, the study examined only a limited number of marker positions and did not account for execution speeds. Furthermore, closely spaced markers were omitted [27]. Another study analyzed the body posture and execution of movements of a professional climber to later use them for realistic 3D climbing animations. A climbing cycle was divided into four phases for separate assessment. RGB videos and depth data of posture and movement were captured using two Kinects and an iPi Recorder. This data was processed further using iPi Mocap Studio software, and then the 3D skeletal data was exported as BVH. The animations created from the MoCap data were intended for use in training beginners [28].

Virtual Reality can be used as a support for evaluating athletes or as a training method. Moreover, VR expands the training environment across various dimensions and enriches the training with an immersive experience.

The former was examined in a 2019 study that investigated the reliability, construct validity, and ecological validity of 360° VR and game footage in the decision-making of Australian football referees. Both professional and amateur referees participated in the study, in which 360° clips were developed to influence decision-making assessment. If the results of the VR tests correlate with the actual referee decisions, it strengthens the construct validity of the method. Ecological validity refers to the extent to which VR tests reflect real game situations and decision scenarios in football. If VR tests closely resemble actual field conditions, it is a positive aspect that enhances their utility. The fact that the 360° VR test showed high reliability suggests that the method yields consistent results. The results indicating that professional referees performed better in decision accuracy than amateur referees may suggest that experienced referees are better able to effectively utilize VR information to make informed decisions. It could also point to a need for training for amateur referees to fully harness the benefits of VR technology. Following section relates past studies and current experiments to the theoretical construct. The model referenced in the study [29]. There are numerous studies on how Virtual Reality contributes to improving athletes' skills, but it is rarely explored whether athletes accept technological devices for performance enhancement. One study employed the Technology Acceptance Model (TAM) to determine if perceived usefulness, perceived ease of use, perceived enjoyment, and subjective norms (i.e., social influence) are positive predictors of the intention to use a particular technology. Another study examined the validity of TAM and used a VR-Head-Mounted Display (VR-HMD) to test the enhancement of athletic performance. They also investigated the extent to which training level and the practiced sport influence the preceding TAM variables. The results indicated that athletes of all sports and skill levels had the intention to use VR, and they found it to be useful and user-friendly [30].

3   Method

In this study, a pre-test was conducted, serving as the basis for the main experiment involving numerous ballet dancers. The experiment examines the extent to which Motion Capture, as a supplementary or alternative training method, contributes to optimizing the movements of ballet dancers. Additionally, a measurement approach is applied to various classical ballet positions, with a particular focus on angle measurement. After evaluating the collected data, the discussion explores how the developed training approach could be expanded with the integration of Virtual Reality. A brief overview of the main advantages and disadvantages is also provided.

3.1   Participants in the Pre-test

The pre-test was conducted with an experienced ballet dancer who had previously only followed conventional training concepts. She is familiar with classical ballet training and had never trained with technological support before. She is knowledgeable about her level of proficiency in the ballet positions used. She is in excellent physical condition and has no limitations. She trained with the Motion Capture system once a week for two months.

3.2   Experimental Design and Measurement Instruments

The training took place in a laboratory where the Motion Capture System was assembled and installed. It was equipped with 28 OptiTrack cameras, which have a measurement accuracy of less than 0.1 mm, making them highly precise and particularly suitable for the sports and motion science field. The room was darkened during the recordings to avoid unwanted reflections. The test subject had prior ballet experience and was introduced to the technique through a demonstration video after warming up. Following the warm-up and practice phase, the individual put on an OptiTrack Motion-Capture suit, which had already been prepared with markers before the training session. It is crucial that the markers are placed according to the selected Marker Set in Motive:Body to ensure accurate data and successful recording.

To capture the Motion Capture data, the Motive software was used for real-time transmission. Since the ballet dancer's movements required control over the entire upper and lower body, as well as the feet and fingers, a full-body marker set with a total of 49 markers was selected. Once the system recognized all markers in their designated positions on the suit and the subject was in the calibration pose, an asset, in this case, a skeleton, could be created. Before actual recording, checks were performed to identify calibration errors, such as incorrect bone assignments, which could be rectified by having the subject return to the calibration pose. Ensuring not only the correct position but also the secure attachment of the markers to the suit is essential. Dynamic movements, as well as factors like hair, oils, or sweat on the skin, can cause markers to shift during recording. Therefore, the markers were fastened to the suit using Velcro straps, ensuring they remained in place. After creation, a final check was performed to verify that both markers and the skeleton were correctly calibrated. If this was not the case, markers were repositioned, and the skeleton was recreated. After each recording, takes were reviewed to identify any erroneous marker or skeleton representations. During the recording, the dancer saw her MoCap Avatar from behind on the monitor, as shown in Fig. 1.

Fig. 1. The ballet dancer is wearing the Motion Capture suit and is in the ballet position "Plie." Both arms are positioned above the head, with the palms facing towards the head. She observes herself in the frontal view within the program, which records her movements for a specific sequence.

3.3 Procedure

The ballet dancer trained in three fundamental ballet positions or movements during the experimental period. These included the Arabesque, the Plié, and the battement tendu, which forms the basis for the grand battement. The following section will delve into the specifics and injury risks of these techniques. Subsequently, it will explain why angle measurement is particularly well-suited for ballet movements and how the data were evaluated.

The following briefly explains the steps of the three ballet techniques.

Arabesque. Arabesque represents a fundamental pose in ballet. While the arms are held in a harmonious position to create the longest possible line along the body, the ballet dancer stands on one leg, with the other leg extended backward at a right angle to the supporting leg. The body position is in profile [31].

The ballet position Arabesque is a challenging ballet position often used in variations.

The postural control system plays a crucial role in integrating information from the vestibular (balance), somatosensory (touch), and visual systems. These diverse sensory inputs are of paramount importance for dancers to maintain their stability, especially when assuming complex postures and movements during ballet performances. The coordination of these sensory inputs enables dancers to precisely adjust their body posture while maintaining a high level of aesthetic expression. This integrative approach in the postural control system plays a key role in the artistic and technical execution of dance movements, as particularly evident in the Arabesque performance in classical ballet [32].

The Arabesque is a challenging movement in ballet, requiring precision in alignment, body posture, concentration, and technical execution. In contrast, in modern and contemporary dance, the Arabesque is considered a fundamental movement that diverges from the rigid lines of classical ballet. In modern dance, dancers enjoy greater technical freedom and have more room for creative interpretations. Here, the Arabesque can be varied with different angles, a flexed foot, an inward-turned position, or a lateral tilt of the body [33].

There are five different variations of it: In the first variation, the supporting leg stands upright, and the other leg is extended straight backward in line with the body. The extended leg should be parallel to the ground and lifted as high as possible behind the body. The upper body remains upright, and the arms can be held in various positions, depending on the specific style or choreography. In the second variation, the supporting leg also stands upright while the other leg is extended straight backward in line with the body. In this variation, the extended leg is angled sideways and does not remain parallel to the ground. The upper body stays upright, and the arms can assume different positions. In the third variation, the supporting leg is slightly bent, while the other leg is extended straight backward. The extended leg is in line with the body but not as high as in the previous two positions. The upper body may be slightly inclined forward, and the arms can take various positions. Similar to the third variation, in the fourth variation, the supporting leg is slightly bent, and the extended leg is lifted backward. The extended leg is not as high as in the first two positions, and it is slightly angled to the side. The upper body leans forward, and the arms can be positioned as desired. In the fifth and most complex position, the supporting leg is slightly bent, and the extended leg is lifted backward in line with the body. The extended leg is raised as high as possible and remains parallel to the ground. The upper body stays upright, and the arms can be positioned as desired. Arabesque is a graceful and challenging ballet position used to highlight the beauty and grace of the dancer, often incorporated into variations and choreography.

Pliè. Plié can be performed in various positions of classical ballet (1st position, 2nd position, etc.) and results from the flexion of the ankle, knee, and hip. Once the flexion of the ankle, knee, and hip causes the heel (unintentionally) to lift from the floor, it is referred to as a Grand Plié. Often, a plié is executed as en-dehors, where the lower limbs are turned outward, initiated by the hip. In this rotation, ballet dancers often injure themselves as the turn is frequently not executed technically correctly. This leads to muscle-tendon pathologies [34, 35].

During plié, the act of bending is trained. The training aims to make the muscles and tendons flexible and elastic through the bending of the knees [31].

Correct hip position, leg rotation without overrotation of the knee, the frontal plane of the knee, and the constant contact of the heel with the ground contribute to the correct execution of plié [36]. In the plié, you start with the first position, the Première Position, where the heels are together, and the toes are turned outward. Keep the feet in a straight line. The next position is the Deuxième Position, where there is a foot's distance between the feet, and the toes remain turned outward. The feet are shoulder-width apart. In the Troisième Position, the third position, one foot is placed in front of the other, with the heel of the front foot touching the arch of the back foot. The toes of both feet should be turned outward. In the fourth position, also called Quatrième Position, one foot starts in front of the other. The distance between the feet is wider, and the heel of the front foot should be aligned with the arch of the back foot. In the fifth position, the Cinquième Position, it is the most complex position. One foot is in front of the other, with the heel of the front foot touching the toe of the back foot. The toes are turned outward, and the legs are close together. In addition to the Demi-Plié, where a half bend of the knee occurs while the body is lowered halfway down, there is also the Grand Plié, where a full bend of the knee occurs, and the body is lowered as far as possible. In both positions, the heels are kept on the ground.

Battement Tendu. Battement tendu, like the other two ballet positions, is one of the fundamental ballet positions and signifies stretching. The working leg is stretched forward, to the side, or backward along the floor until the tip of the toe touches the ground [31].

In this ballet movement, the flexibility of the ankle is promoted, and the principles of alignment, posture, turnout, weight distribution, weight transfer, and squareness are deepened. The movement begins in the first position. The working foot is brushed along the floor and the metatarsals, ending in a fully pointed position achieved through an arch. In this position, the heel is lifted forward, and the first three toes rest on the floor. To close, on the return path, the ballet dancer first flexes the foot through the toes and then through the metatarsals, the arch, and back to the full-foot position [37].

In Battement tendu, postural control and balance play a prominent role. While postural control must be maintained to ensure precision of the limbs, maintaining balance with the load on one leg is particularly practiced in the center of a room and away from the barre. The traditional teaching method involves the trainer demonstrating and the ballet dancer imitating. During repetition, visual, verbal, and auditory cues from the trainer must be considered and applied, promoting neural coordination [37].

Data Collection and Evaluation. To analyze and control the kinematic movements of the three ballet positions, the measurement of joint angles is suitable. Using joint angles allows tracking the precise movements of body segments such as arms, legs, feet, and the overall posture during a ballet movement. The measurement of joint angles is done using the Blender software. Initially, motion capture recordings are imported, as shown in Fig. 2.

Subsequently, a measurement tool is used to analyze the relevant measurable angles between two body segments and compare them with the optimal value. In Fig. 3, the ballet position "Pliè" is depicted with four annotated angles between pairs of bones. The angles include the angle of the foot position between both feet, the angle of the knee pit between the lower leg and calf, the angle between the back and neck, and the angle between the cervical vertebrae and shoulder. Each angle has an optimal value for comparison.

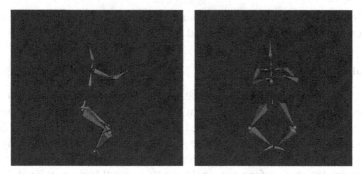

Fig. 2. Import the motion capture recordings into the blender software to evaluate the positional data based on the example of Plié at a specific measurement time

1. The foot position corresponds to an angle of 133°, resulting in a deviation of 32° and a percentage deviation of 21.48%, as the optimal value is 165°.
2. The knee bend corresponds to an angle of 103°, resulting in a deviation of 13° and a percentage deviation of 13.47%, as the optimal value is 90°.
3. The torso posture corresponds to an angle of 168°, resulting in a deviation of 12° and a percentage deviation of 6.90%, as the optimal value is 180°.
4. The shoulder posture corresponds to an angle of 103°, resulting in a deviation of 13° and a percentage deviation of 13.47%, as the optimal value is 90°.

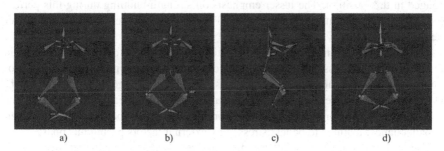

a)   b)   c)   d)

Fig. 3. The ballet position Plié with the annotated segment angles for analyzing the current position and as a basis for improving the positions.

The Optimal Values Were Taken from the Literature. Throughout the entire period, the three ballet positions were dissected into their main components to measure multiple sub-techniques. Only one angle per joint and per sub-technique was evaluated. After determining the deviation from the ideal value, this difference value could be used as the basis for training. The goal was to minimize this difference value during training to get closer to the ideal value.

During the demonstration within the training, the ballet dancer now sees how much she needs to bend or stretch her body segments to achieve the exact ballet position.

Instead of relying solely on verbal cues from the trainer, she can independently optimize her position based on numerical values and see her avatar in real-time.

3.4 Results and Discussion

The ballet dancer completed eight training sessions with the Motion Capture System for the preliminary study, abstaining from her regular training during this period. In each of these sessions, the three mentioned ballet positions were practiced. The initial three measurement points revealed a stable performance level, albeit without significant improvements in all three disciplines. Between the fourth and sixth sessions, the dancer managed to enhance her performance in the Arabesque and Battement Tendu positions more than in the Plié. The last two training sessions again demonstrated stability in performance. Over the entire period, the ballet dancer improved by 26% in the Arabesque, 21% in the Battement Tendu, and 8% in the Plié compared to the beginning. Several potential reasons for this development were discussed with the ballet dancer.

The initial consistency suggests that training with the Motion Capture System, as mentioned earlier, represented an entirely new form of training that the dancer had to acclimate to initially. After one month, significant improvements were observed, particularly in the Battement Tendu and Arabesque movements. However, progress in the Plié was comparatively modest. This could be attributed to the position placing a greater emphasis on knee flexion and the fundamental stability of the entire body. The Plié requires precise alignment of the entire body, with the knees consistently kept over the toes and the hips under tension. Notably, the quadriceps and thigh muscles are heavily engaged in this position. The lesser emphasis on strength building during this period, especially in a demanding movement like the Plié, could be another reason for the slower rate of improvement.

Fatigue and overtraining might be potential reasons for the constancy observed in the last two training sessions. Athletes often experience plateau phases in training programs, indicating a temporary halt in progress. This might suggest a need to diversify the training program, perhaps incorporating aspects of virtual reality, to introduce new stimuli. Demotivation or personal stress factors can also impact performance. However, the ballet dancer claimed to be less stressed by external factors during this phase.

The study also aimed to conduct an initial theoretical analysis on the effective design of potential virtual training scenarios through the integration of Virtual Reality (VR). For this purpose, we discussed possible extensions of the Motion Capture system with the ballet dancer. Initially, we examined the technological feasibility and its suitability for integration into ballet training sessions. In the laboratory, we had access to the wireless VR Meta Quest 3, which operates without cables and with technical specifications. Given that ballet involves many rotations and jumps, generally requiring more space, a wireless VR headset is more suitable than wired VR headsets, as confirmed by the dancer. Through the use of the Unity software and the corresponding Motive plugin, both technologies can be seamlessly integrated. The next question that arose concerned maximizing effectiveness and increasing motivation through Virtual Reality. Since the creation of a virtual ballet environment or the implementation of real-time feedback via the VR headset is still being developed in further research, the ballet dancer tested other virtual environments to get a sense of potential immersion. She confirmed that a certain gamification approach and the visual effects could enhance fun and, consequently, motivation. However, the ballet dancer came to the conclusion that there could be not only advantages. The financial hurdles and limited access to VR technology could lead to uneven availability of VR training, restricting access for ballet schools with limited resources. Potential physical limitations, such as discomfort from using the VR headset or health concerns, could create reservations among some ballet dancers about the use of VR in training. Traditionally oriented ballet teachers might have concerns regarding the distraction from proven methods and direct trainer observation through the integration of VR into training, as this could be seen as a deviation from the fundamental principles of classical ballet.

4 Conclusion

The results demonstrate an improvement in the ballet positions of the ballet dancer during the research period. However, it should be noted that the dancer trained for the first time with a motion-capture suit, the training period was limited to only two months, and there was no parallel strength, endurance, or traditional ballet training. These measures were intentionally avoided to clearly attribute the achieved progress to the motion-capture-assisted training. As this was a preliminary study, it was conducted with only one ballet dancer. The next phase of the study is planned to expand this training approach to a group of ballet participants.

Future Research. In the further study, it would be interesting to measure not only segment angles or joint angles but also rotational angles. For this purpose, a professional dancer could be recorded using motion capture and used as a reference for optimal values. As indicated in the discussion, it is recommended to further enhance the Virtual Reality (VR) setup. This involves implementing a virtual ballet studio and providing real-time feedback in the form of gamification elements. With such a setup, a group of dancers could train over an extended period to develop a well-founded argument for or against the integration of Virtual Reality in ballet training based on concrete numbers and facts.

While the subjective opinion of ballet dancers remains relevant, it can be better supported and strengthened by using solid data. Testing with a larger sample could also evaluate user-friendliness and assess the learning effort and satisfaction of the dancers more precisely. The mentioned pros and cons could be further substantiated or refuted through a comprehensive group study.

References

1. Veirs, K.P., et al.: Applications of biomechanical foot models to evaluate dance movements using three-dimensional motion capture: a review of the literature. J. Dance Med. Sci. Official Publ. Int. Assoc. Dance Med. Sci. **26**(2), 69–86 (2022)
2. Silva, F.: Motion capture-introdução à tecnologia. Laboratório de Computação Gráfica, LCG. COPPE, Universidade Federal do Rio de Janeiro, UFRJ (1997)
3. Sun, K.: Research on dance motion capture technology for visualization requirements. Sci. Program. **2022**, 8 (2022)

4. Zhou, Z.: Overuse Injuries of Foot and Ankle and Healthy Training in Young Female Ballet Dancers (2021)
5. Gu, R., Wang, G., Jiang, Z., Hwang, J.N.: Multi-person hierarchical 3D pose estimation in natural videos. IEEE Trans. Circuits Syst. Video Technol. **30**(11), 4245–4257 (2020)
6. Hua, G., Li, L., Liu, S.: Multipath affinage stacked - hourglass networks for human pose estimation. Front. Comput. Sci. **14**, 144701 (2020)
7. Nasr, M., Osama, R., Ayman, H., Mosaad, N., Ebrahim, N., Mounir, A.: Realtime multi-person 2D pose estimation. **11**, 4501–4508 (2022). https://doi.org/10.35444/IJANA.2020.11069
8. Petrov, I., Shakhuro, V., Konushin, A.: Deep probabilistic human pose estimation. IET Comput. Vis. **12** (2018). https://doi.org/10.1049/iet-cvi.2017.0382
9. Ershadi Nasab, S., Noury, E., Kasaei, S., Sanaei, E.: Multiple human 3D pose estimation from multiview images. Multimed. Tools Appl. **77** (2018). https://doi.org/10.1007/s11042-017-5133-8
10. Andriacchi, T., Alexander, E.: Studies of human locomotion: past, present and future. J. Biomech. **33**, 1217–1224 (2000). https://doi.org/10.1016/S0021-9290(00)00061-0
11. Vastola, R., Coppola, S., Sibilio, M.: Motion analysis technologies for biomechanical gait and postural analysis in ballet. J. Sports Sci. **4** (2016). https://doi.org/10.17265/2332-7839/2016.04.008
12. Magee, D.J., Manske, R.C.: Orthopedic Physical Assessment. Saunders, Philadelphia (2022)
13. McNally, W., Wong, A., McPhee, J.: Action Recognition Using Deep Convolutional Neural Networks and Compressed Spatio-Temporal Pose Encodings (2018)
14. Bronner, S., Ojofeitimi, S., Rose, D.: Injuries in a modern dance company effect of comprehensive management on injury incidence and time loss. Am. J. Sports Med. **31**, 365–373 (2003). https://doi.org/10.1177/03635465030310030701
15. Byhring, S., Bø, K.: Musculoskeletal injuries in the Norwegian National Ballet: a prospective cohort study. Scand. J. Med. Sci. Sports **12**(6), 365–370 (2002)
16. Garrick, J.G.: Early identification of musculoskeletal complaints and injuries among female ballet students. J. Dance Med. Sci. **3**(2), 80–83 (1999)
17. Nilsson, C., Leanderson, J., Wykman, A., Strender, L.E.: The injury panorama in a Swedish professional ballet company. Knee Surg. Sports Traumatol. Arthroscopy: Official J. ESSKA **9**, 242–246 (2001). https://doi.org/10.1007/s001670100195
18. Wiesler, E.R., Hunter, D.M., Martin, D.F., Curl, W.W., Hoen, H.: Ankle flexibility and injury patterns in dancers. Am. J. Sports Med. **24**(6), 754–757 (1996)
19. Ramkumar, P., Farber, J., Arnouk, J., Varner, K., McCulloch, P.: Injuries in a professional ballet dance company: a 10-year retrospective study. J. Dance Med. Sci. **20**, 30–37 (2016). https://doi.org/10.12678/1089-313X.20.1.30
20. Allen, N., Nevill, A., Brooks, J., Koutedakis, Y., Wyon, M.: Ballet injuries: injury incidence and severity over 1 year. J. Orthop. Sports Phys. Ther. **42**, 781–790 (2012). https://doi.org/10.2519/jospt.2012.3893
21. Hedrick, M.R., McBryde, A.M.: Posterior ankle impingement. Foot Ankle Int. **15**(1), 2–8 (1994)
22. Li, F., Adrien, N., He, Y.: Biomechanical risks associated with foot and ankle injuries in ballet dancers: a systematic review. Int. J. Environ. Res. Public Health **19**(8), 4916 (2022). https://doi.org/10.3390/ijerph19084916
23. Wąsik, J., Shan, G.: Target effect on the kinematics of Taekwondo Roundhouse Kick - is the presence of a physical target a stimulus, influencing muscle-power generation? Acta Bioeng. Biomech. **17**(4), 115–120 (2015)
24. Ahonen, J.: Biomechanics of the foot in dance: a literature review. J. Dance Med. Sci.: Official Publ. Int. Assoc. Dance Med. Sci. **12**(3), 99–108 (2008)
25. Barnett, C.H., Napier, J.R.: The axis of rotation at the ankle joint in man; its influence upon the form of the talus and the mobility of the fibula. J. Anat. **86**(1), 1–9 (1952)

26. Xu, D., Jiang, X., Cen, X., Baker, J., Gu, Y.: Single-leg landings following a volleyball spike may increase the risk of anterior cruciate ligament injury more than landing on both-legs. Appl. Sci. **11**, 130 (2020). https://doi.org/10.3390/app11010130

27. Grontman, A., Horyza, Ł., Koczan, K., Marzec, M., Śmiertka, M., Trybała, M.: Analysis of sword fencing training evaluation possibilities using Motion Capture techniques. In: 2020 IEEE 15th International Conference of System of Systems Engineering (SoSE), Budapest, Hungary, pp. 325–330 (2020)

28. Cha, K., Lee, E.Y., Myeong-Hyeon, H., Shin, K.C., Son, J., Kim, D.: Analysis of climbing postures and movements in sport climbing for realistic 3D climbing animations. Procedia Eng. **112**, 52–57 (2015). https://doi.org/10.1016/j.proeng.2015.07.175

29. Kittel, A., Larkin, P., Elsworthy, N., Spittle, M.: Using 360° virtual reality as a decision-making assessment tool in sport. J. Sci. Med. Sport **22**(9), 1049–1053 (2019)

30. Mascret, N., Montagne, G., Devrièse-Sence, A., Vu, A., Kulpa, R.: Acceptance by athletes of a virtual reality head-mounted display intended to enhance sport performance. Psychol. Sport Exerc. **61** (2022). https://doi.org/10.1016/j.psychsport.2022.102201

31. King, S.: Fundamentals of Ballett, 10AB, Dance (2023)

32. Aquino, J., Amasay, T., Shapiro, S., Kuo, Y., Ambegaonkar, J.: Lower extremity biomechanics and muscle activity differ between 'new' and 'dead' pointe shoes in professional ballet dancers. Sports Biomech. **20**(4), 469–480 (2021)

33. Zafeiroudi, A.: Analyzing and discussing the evolution of arabesque movement according to dance elements and aesthetics. Acade. J. Interdisc. Stud. **12**, 41 (2023). https://doi.org/10.36941/ajis-2023-0152

34. Gontijo, K.N., Candotti, C.T., Feijó, G.D., Ribeiro, L.P., Loss, J.F.: Kinematic evaluation of the classical ballet step "Plié." J. Dance Med. Sci. **19**, 70–76 (2015)

35. Swain, C.T.V., et al.: Multi-segment spine kinematics: relationship with dance training and low back pain. Gait Posture **68**, 274–279 (2019)

36. Paloschi, D., Cigada, M., Ballone, S., De Bartolomeo, O., Cigada, A., Saccomandi, P.: Analysis on the plié and grand plié in classical ballet with magneto-inertial measurement units. In: 2022 IEEE International Workshop on Metrology for Industry 4.0 & IoT (MetroInd4.0&IoT), pp. 44–48. IEEE (2022)

37. Kassing, G.: Beginning Ballet, Interactive Dance Series. Human Kinetics, Champaign (2013). 978-1-4504-0249-1, 85-90

Augmented Reality in Language Learning: Practical Implications for Researchers and Practitioners

Antigoni Parmaxi[1] (ID), Anke Berns[2] (ID), Lina Adinolfi[3] (ID), Alice Gruber[4] (ID), Mikhail Fominykh[5] (ID), Angeliki Voreopoulou[6], Fridolin Wild[3] (ID), Paraskevi Vassiliou[1] (ID), Eirini Christou[1](✉) (ID), Concepción Valero-Franco[2] (ID), Tormod Aagaard[5], and Stella Hadjistassou[7]

[1] Cyprus University of Technology, Limassol, Cyprus
eirini.christou@cyprusinteractionlab.com
[2] Universidad de Cadiz, Cadiz, Spain
[3] The Open University, Milton Keynes, UK
[4] Augsburg Technical University of Applied Sciences, Augsburg, Germany
[5] Norwegian University of Science and Technology, Trondheim, Norway
[6] 15th Primary School of Evosmos, Nemeas and Thalias, 56224 Thessaloniki, Greece
[7] University of Cyprus, Nicosia, Cyprus

Abstract. The use of Augmented Reality (AR) holds significant promise for language learning. AR enriches the learning experience by overlaying virtual elements onto the real environment, offering versatile resources for language learning. Various AR technology platforms, including headsets, glasses and mobile devices can be used to enhance language competencies such as listening, speaking, reading, writing, and linguistic components like grammar and vocabulary. The most commonly reported benefits of AR are increased learner motivation, engagement, enjoyment, reduced anxiety, elevated confidence levels and enhanced cultural awareness. In addition, well-designed AR resources may help develop 21st-century skills such as critical thinking, collaboration and creativity. Despite the rapid development of AR technology and the growth of its adoption, a literature gap exists in terms of practical guidelines for designing and implementing AR activities in language learning classrooms. This paper addresses this gap by showcasing AR activities for different languages, proficiency levels, and educational stages while providing practical guidelines for designing and implementing AR activities in language learning classrooms.

Keywords: Augmented Reality · Language Learning · Practical Guidelines

1 Introduction

Augmented reality (AR) superimposes virtual elements onto the real environment, enriching the user's perception of and interaction with the physical world. In the context of language learning, AR provides learners with new learning contexts composed of highly visual and versatile resources. This enhancement is facilitated through various AR technologies, including headsets, glasses or mobile devices that overlay computer-generated content onto the real-world view [1]. In language teaching, AR can be used to develop specific language competencies, including listening, reading, speaking, writing and cultural awareness, and linguistic components such as grammar, vocabulary and pronunciation. Amongst the most commonly cited benefits of AR for language learning are its positive effects on learner motivation, enjoyment and engagement (see [2–6]). In addition, the use of AR may reduce feelings of learner anxiety [3], increase confidence levels [7], and enhance cultural awareness [8].

Today, AR technology has become widely accessible, user-friendly, and no longer requires expensive hardware or sophisticated equipment [4]. Despite the promising potential of AR for language learning, there is a notable gap in the literature regarding learning experience design with the use of AR. Addressing this gap is essential for developing effective, engaging, and pedagogically-sound AR-based educational experiences that can foster language learning. This paper showcases examples of AR activities for different age groups across different learning environments. Moreover, it provides practical guidelines for designing and implementing AR activities in language classrooms. With a focus on practical application, it aims to inform practitioners and researchers of the potential challenges and advantages of designing and implementing AR activities for different language components and competencies.

2 Literature Review

Augmented Reality (AR), Virtual Reality (VR), Mixed Reality (MR), Extended Reality (XR) and the Metaverse refer to a technology that affects all aspects of daily life, providing new ways of interacting and learning, while potentially making learning processes more accessible, dynamic and versatile [9]. On the reality-virtuality continuum [10], applications of these technologies can vary along a single dimension, which encompasses different levels or points representing varying degrees of reality and virtuality. At one end of the virtuality continuum lies a fully real environment (the real world), and at the other is a fully virtual environment, i.e. VR (see Fig. 1).

In addition, technologies cater to either individual or multi-users experiences, offering varying degrees of synchronicity. Although Milgram and Kishino's [10] original concept of MR has evolved over time, AR is commonly defined as an augmented form of reality in which computer-generated content is superimposed on the user's view of the real world. What therefore distinguishes AR from other technologies like VR or MR is its ability to blend virtual content with the real world in real-time [1]. In AR, virtual content can be presented in either two-dimensional (2D) or three-dimensional (3D) forms, depending on the desired experience.

AR applications can be categorized into three groups based on their purpose, location, and usability: marker-based AR, markerless AR, and location-based AR [12–14]:

- **Marker-based** AR applications rely on specific visual markers, such as image targets or QR codes, to anchor virtual content in the real world.

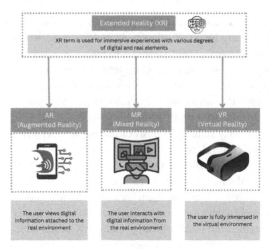

Fig. 1. Representation of the XR concept [11]

- **Markerless AR** applications do not require pre-defined markers and instead use computer vision or object recognition technologies to recognize and interact with real-world objects or surfaces.
- **Location-based AR** applications take advantage of the user's geographic location and use Global Positioning System (GPS) or other location-based technologies to provide context-aware virtual content or experiences tied to specific locations or areas.

Although different types of devices are capable of running AR applications, including mobile phones, smart glasses or dedicated AR devices, the most widely used devices today are mobile phones and tablets. In fact, these two devices provide all the necessary features, such as cameras, displays and processing power to support AR interactions [15].

2.1 AR and its Application in Language Learning and Teaching

Despite the widespread adoption of AR across various sectors, including science, arts, advertising, and education, its integration into instructed language learning has been limited to date. This is evidenced by the scarcity of language learning AR apps on commercial platforms such as Google Play- or App-Store and by the challenge to locate robust comparative and longitudinal implementation studies in the field [2].

2.2 Benefits and Challenges of Using AR in Instructed Language Learning

While research on language learning and AR is still in its early stages, several studies have shown that AR holds great promise for language learning [3]. Frequently cited key benefits of AR in instructed language learning include enhanced learner motivation and engagement, satisfaction and enjoyment, improved learning in terms of various language components and competencies, ample opportunities for authentic language tasks and reinforcement of language use [2, 3, 16, 17]. AR has also been shown to reduce learner anxiety and boost confidence [3, 18]. These favorable outcomes are often attributed to the immersive and interactive characteristics of AR, which simulate real-life learning experiences [2, 17]. Additional assertions regarding AR include its potential to contribute to improved cultural awareness and the development of essential 21st-century skills [19, 20].

2.3   The Challenges of Applying AR to Instructed Language Learning

Notwithstanding the potential benefits of AR technologies, their application to instructed language learning poses several challenges mainly related to technical issues, cognitive load, and lack of AR skills [3, 16].

Technical Issues. Both the complexity and usability of AR technology are often cited as the main challenges to their adoption, which may discourage teachers and learners from using such technologies for teaching and learning purposes [3, 21]. For example, technical issues have been reported in location-based AR applications where a GPS error may be caused by an AR application misinterpreting a location or a direction [16, 22]. Challenges to implementing AR in the classroom include the limited screen size of the mobile device used or the need for internet connectivity, which may not always be available [18].

Cognitive Load. Another challenge is cognitive load (CL) which occurs when the information to be learned exceeds the capacity of working memory [23]. Cognitive load is caused by the cognitive demands of the learning task and consists of intrinsic and extraneous load. Intrinsic load is influenced by the number of elements processed simultaneously and the learner's expertise, while extraneous load depends on the design of the learning task [23, 24]. In the context of AR, cognitive load pertains to the mental effort and resources needed by learners to process information while participating in AR tasks.

Some AR tasks have been observed to be overly demanding and complex, placing a heavy burden on learners' cognitive capacities. When tasks are too complex, learners may find it challenging to effectively process and integrate the augmented information presented to them. Heavy cognitive load can have negative consequences on both the learning experience and learner motivation [25]. Suzuki et al. (2023) describe how cognitive load in AR has been evaluated using performance metrics and subjective reports, but advocate for the addition of physiological measures like eye-tracking with biometric sensors for a more direct and objective assessment. Essentially, if the demands of an AR task surpass a learner's cognitive capacity, it can lead to frustration, decreased motivation, and potentially hinder the overall effectiveness of the educational experience. Therefore, it is crucial for educators to carefully design AR activities, ensuring that they strike a balance between providing a meaningful learning experience and avoiding excessive cognitive load. This involves considering the complexity of the AR content, the learners' prior knowledge, and the overall learning objectives to optimize engagement and facilitate effective learning [3, 17].

Lack of AR Skills. Other challenges include teachers' lack of AR skills and teaching expertise in AR [1, 21]. To overcome such challenges, comprehensive training programs are needed to equip teachers with the necessary skills and knowledge to integrate already available AR resources as well as to develop their own AR resources in line with their teaching needs [17].

3 Methodology

In the following sections we will explore the topic of AR and language learning and teaching as a relatively new field to gain some valuable insights. For this purpose, we have adopted a narrative review that aims to showcase AR activities for different languages and proficiency levels, while providing practical guidelines for designing and implementing AR activities in language classrooms.

Our review was compiled through extensive consultations with a range of experts, encompassing instructional designers, researchers and experienced practitioners in the field. The experts came together in the context of the funded European project ARIDLL (Augmented Reality Instructional Design for Language Learning). By engaging with these experts, we sought to harness a comprehensive understanding of the multifaceted landscape surrounding the application of AR in language learning. Through focused discussions, we elicited insights ranging from theoretical underpinnings to practical implementation strategies. These discussions led to a detailed narrative that blends a review of the literature with real-classroom insights and experiences and aimed to offer a comprehensive look at the prospects of AR with regard to language teaching and learning.

4 Educational Applications of AR

By seamlessly integrating digital content into the real-world environment, AR offers innovative and engaging ways to enhance learning experiences - from interactive 3D models that dissect complex biological structures to historical re-enactments that transport learners to bygone eras [26, 27]. AR has opened up new ways for educators to capture learners' attention and deepen their understanding. In the following, we will focus on how AR might be used in language learning and teaching to enhance different language components and competences.

5 Language Components and Competencies that May Be Enhanced with AR-Mediated Instructional Materials

Language is a complex communicative system consisting of various components and competencies. For the purposes of this paper, we will distinguish the following components and competencies (Table 1):

While it can be helpful to focus on language components and competencies separately in language lessons and learning resources, they rarely occur in isolation in real-life communication. We therefore recommend that language learning tasks, whether conventional or AR-mediated, should be designed to mimic authentic or meaningful

Table 1. Language components and competencies that may be enhanced with AR-mediated instructional materials.

Language components	Language competencies
Vocabulary	Listening
Pronunciation	Speaking
Morphology	Reading
Grammar	Writing
Phraseology	Cultural awareness

communication involving multiple language components and competencies wherever possible. In the following subsections, we describe each of the above language components and competencies in turn, with reference to existing studies of the use of AR in different educational settings. We are aware, however, of the limited number and scale of the studies conducted in this area to date. Further evidence is, therefore, needed to substantiate any claims made about the benefits of using AR in language learning over and above those achieved using the multiple instructional resources and approaches already available to teachers and learners.

5.1 Language Components

Vocabulary. To date, vocabulary received the most attention in terms of incorporating AR material into language learning and teaching. This is most likely because shifting attention to tangible objects and using AR to enrich them with interactivity and, at the same time, situate them in real-life context can be achieved through multiple software applications (e.g. ARTutor, CoSpaces, etc.) that often do not require demanding and complex programming skills on the part of the teachers who develop these materials. AR games, AR-based flashcards and AR activities are often employed to design sound, text, images and animations to teach new vocabulary items that relate to real objects in the environment. One of the best-known applications of AR for enhancing vocabulary is in the form of AR textbooks, which generally use marker-based and markerless AR applications. AR textbooks typically combine printed text and illustrations with digital elements (e.g. 3D models and characters, video clips, audio recordings etc.). The intention is to create interactive learning experiences that make the learning content more comprehensive and engaging. Textbook users can use AR-enabled devices to scan pages and unlock supplementary content such as animations (see Fig. 2), 3D models, videos, interactive games or additional explanations.

Previous studies using the Cognitive Theory of Multimedia Learning (CTML) have shown that, when unknown words were annotated with both text (translations) and pictures (images or videos), the latter are retained better than words annotated with text alone. This is illustrated, for example, in a study conducted by Scrivner et al. [28] in a beginner-level Spanish course. For their study, the authors used photos as triggers, each of which was accompanied by a video of a mini-dialogue or video, which helped students retain new vocabulary and its associated pronunciation in context. Similarly, in

Fig. 2. Different augmentations enriching a textbook (developed with ARTutor4 https://artutor.ihu.gr/index_el/)

a lab-based study, Ibrahim et al. [29] displayed label annotations on objects and voice commands mediated by AR smart glasses, Microsoft HoloLens, to examine productive recall compared to the use of traditional flashcards. The authors of the study observed that learners perceived the AR experience to be more constructive and enjoyable than the use of conventional flashcards. AR-enhanced flashcards are also used as part of the language instruction platform MARVL (https://marvllanguage.com/), an AR-mediated instructional tool that uses marker-based AR to enable kindergarten and pre-kindergarten learners to scan flashcards and interact with avatars while building new vocabulary (see [30]). The cognitive effect underlying this is called 'dual coding' [31]. Despite initial findings suggesting promise in vocabulary retention [32, 33] and increased motivation [34, 35], further and more longitudinal studies are needed to draw stronger conclusions about the added value of AR for vocabulary learning compared to more traditional learning resources.

Pronunciation. Teaching pronunciation involves creating perceptual and articulatory awareness and providing opportunities for the extended practice of perceptual and motor skills. It is also common to include training in how speech sounds are represented in writing. For languages with alphabetic writing systems, this process typically involves phoneme-grapheme mapping. Although little attention has been paid to exploring aspects of pronunciation in the context of AR at the phoneme level, AR could help to increase articulatory awareness by drawing learners' attention to the shape of the mouth when producing certain sounds. Mirrors, despite their simplicity and low-tech nature, have been effectively utilized for this purpose. Using a dedicated app, Zhu et al. [36] demonstrated how using the mobile phone as a high-tech mirror could draw learners' attention to their lips and tongue, when producing English phonemes (see Fig. 3). By focusing on the mouth rather than the whole face, learners may also feel less self-conscious, especially if they are required to make an accompanying video recording.

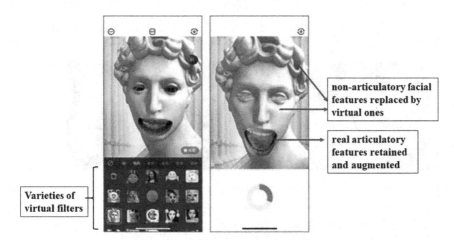

Fig. 3. Screenshot from the app used to support the production of English phonemes [36].

In addition, AR could be used to introduce different accents and dialects into language learning. By further integrating Artificial Intelligence (AI) into AR to design an active feedback system, it could be possible to detect errors and show the learner how to change the position of their lips or tongue to more accurately produce the desired sound.

The live image of the learner could be superimposed on a target mouth shape. Visual linguistic input is known to have a strong influence on auditory processing. For example, the McGurk effect shows that visual input in the form of lip movements can override the acoustic signal [37]. While processing information from lip movements seems to come naturally to speakers, results from tongue visualization experiments suggest that people do not benefit as much from such information, at least without training, and the impact of training on enhancing this ability remains uncertain [38]. For training to be effective, it should focus on form-meaning mapping from the outset, and using multiple senses increases its effectiveness. In the case of phonemes, virtual objects could be used to provide examples or 'anchor points' with a strong semantic basis for each sound.

Morphology. Although AR technology lends itself well to the development of morphology-focused applications and game-based experiences for instructional language learning, there is currently little research in this area. The ARETE project developed 3D phoneme glyphs to help with literacy development (ARETE [39]), see Fig. 4. The UNBODY art installation for spatial poetry included a word composer, engaging the audience in composing novel words out of prefix, stem, and suffix offered to then unveil a definition [40], ditto. However, modern imaging techniques such as photogrammetry could be used to develop 3D models by scanning real-world contexts in which learners could be guided to explore and interact with prefixes, suffixes, and other word formation patterns [41]. Existing AR-mediated language learning games, which typically focus on vocabulary building, could be transformed by incorporating the contextual morphological properties of the target language. These experiences could be made even richer by using AI technology to provide support and personalized feedback.

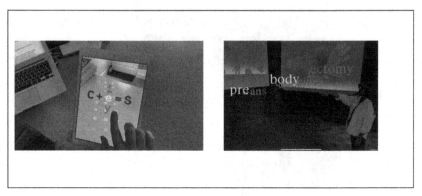

Fig. 4. Words Worth Learning app of the ARETE project for English literacy development (ARETE, [39], left); UNBODY word composer (Wild et al. [40], right).

Grammar. Studies exploring the use of AR-mediated grammar-focused tasks include Valle[42], who describes its deployment to teach the verbs 'ser' versus 'estar' and the subjunctive in Spanish – among other linguistic elements. Another interesting study in this area is that of Draxler et al. [43], who describe an AR app designed to generate quizzes to improve grammar and vocabulary learning. The participants were twenty-five learners of German, mostly undergraduates or postgraduates in various fields (e.g. medicine, business administration and linguistics). The participants' self-assessed level of German on the Common European Framework of Reference (CEFR) ranged from A1 (beginner) to C1 (advanced).

Although the game-based nature of AR-mediated environments has yet to be explored to examine the role of structured AR-mediated game-like activities in improving students' declarative grammatical knowledge, retention and active production of newly acquired grammatical structures, AR technology clearly offers interesting opportunities for creating interactive learning environments. In this sense, AR technology could be used to create applications that allow learners to engage in socially situated environments where learners build and apply new grammatical knowledge in specific contexts. The development of these applications could also consider the use of AI to provide learners with feedback and activities tailored to their language level and learning needs.

Phraseology. In recent decades, the use of corpus technology has greatly contributed to highlighting the prevalence of frequently occurring word combinations – also known as lexical chunks or formulaic sequences – in authentic communication [44]. Corresponding to up to 80% of everyday speech and writing, these may take the form of fixed units (e.g., little by little; as a matter of fact; global warming; all the best) or flexible frames with slots for a limited range of alternatives (e.g. Yours (-, truly, sincerely, faithfully). Commonly found in all languages, the use of conventionalized 'ready-made' word combinations is increasingly acknowledged as the default mode of communication among competent speakers. However, they are often neglected by teachers and textbooks [45–48].

In AR settings, contextually appropriate lexical chunks could be introduced and practiced through the use of meaningful authentic scenarios in which the learner selects from a range of appropriate recorded utterances, modifying them where they offer flexibility. After repeating the utterances, the learner could then engage in dialogues with the avatar interlocutor – or possibly several interlocutors.

Pragmatics. Pragmatics refers to the multiple ways in which language is used to convey particular meanings in specific real-life spoken and written communicative contexts. While some scholars question whether language learners can build pragmatic competence through formal instruction alone [49, 50], others (e.g. [51]) believe it is possible. Opportunities to interact with members of the target culture and exposure to the socially situated beliefs of those communities are nevertheless likely to enhance this process. While the effectiveness of AR-mediated activities in teaching and developing pragmatic competence is still underexplored, their potential to promote interaction, collaboration and incorporate intercultural awareness and understanding is promising.

In their study on pragmatic comprehension development, Shakouri et al. [52] explored how Non-Computer Mediated Instruction (NCMI), Computer Mediated Instruction (CMI), Multi User Virtual Environments (MUVE), and Mobile Augmented Reality Games (MARG) differently impact the understanding of English speech acts among Iranian EFL students. The authors showed that virtual environments such as OpenSim can be more effective than MARGs in building pragmatic comprehension in the target language. Holden and Sykes [53] designed game-based AR activities with the app MENTIRA that enable students to interact with non-playing characters and explore the consequences of framing requests to obtain information from the characters in order to solve a mystery. MENTIRA (see Fig. 5) brings the topic of pragmatics to the forefront, and conversations about social niceties in the game naturally lead to discussions about pragmatics, both in educational settings and in student interactions [54].

5.2 Language Competencies

Complementing the different components of language identified above are the different language competencies involved in real-life communication. Teachers and textbooks have traditionally concentrated on what are commonly referred to as the 'four skills': listening, speaking, reading, and writing. We use the term 'language competencies' or 'communicative modes' to more accurately describe these complex activities – which involve decoding or producing a flow of multiple linguistic elements at the same time.

The following subsections explore the possibilities for developing these different modes through the use of AR and provide several examples of AR applications created for such purposes.

Listening and Speaking. Despite the potential of AR technologies in strengthening listening skills when learning a Foreign Language (FL), this area remains another underexplored in research. In an early study, Liu [55] examined HELLO, an AR learning environment that was implemented to complete various game-based learning activities

Fig. 5. MENTIRA AR-mediated game (https://localgameslababq.wordpress.com/projects/men tira/)

including a collaborative story which was recorded. The study, which was conducted with high school junior students from Taipei studying English, demonstrated that AR is beneficial for providing immersive learning experiences tailored to the context of language learning, using game-based learning and more precisely Matching Objects and Words (MOW). Another study in this context is that of Barreira et al. [56], who studied Portuguese and English primary school learners, who received audiovisual cues to guide their pronunciation and writing skills. The study concluded that AR games positively benefit young children's learning processes, particularly in developing oral recognition of words and concepts and their written forms.

Taskiran [57], on the other hand, explored the role of an AR platform in guiding learners to practice listening and speaking skills in game-based experiences in which learners were asked to follow instructions to place artefacts in a cluttered room. The author concluded that these AR game-based activities have the potential to promote collaboration among learners and facilitate the development of speaking skills. However, in addition to marker-based, location-based or projection-based AR, a combination of AR and AI could be used to further explore the potential of these technologies for enhancing listening skills. There is also potential around holographic AIs and how they can provide an engaging form for dialogic language learning [58].

Reading. In terms of reading, AR games can be a good option for young language learners. For example, Tobar-Muñoz et al. [59] designed a game in the form of an augmented book adapted from a real storybook, with different scenes and challenges on each page for the player to engage with. The results show that, while there is no difference in reading comprehension outcomes between the game and traditional methods, children show great enthusiasm and curiosity for the activity. Furthermore, the activity gains added value by encouraging problem-solving, exploration, and social interaction behaviors [59].

Writing. The design and use of AR applications to improve language learners' writing skills, including sentence construction and orthography, has been the focus of a number of studies. For example, Wang [60] discussed the development and implementation of an AR-mediated writing system and compared the results with a control group that relied on traditional writing materials. A total of 30 female twelfth graders (aged from 16 to 17) from a girls' senior high school learning Chinese in Taiwan participated in this study. The students were divided into two groups according to their writing grades. Students were categorized as low achievers, intermediate achievers, and high achievers. The intermediate achievers benefited most from the AR techniques in terms of their writing performance in terms of content control, structure and phrasing. It is argued that the use of AR was particularly beneficial for low-achieving learners, who reported that the system guided them in composing their introductory paragraph more quickly than traditional paper-based techniques and helped them improve their ideas. On the other hand, Lin et al. [61] investigated how a recently developed ubiquitous application can improve participants' writing development in EFL by enhancing long-term memory, motivation and self-regulated cognition. The authors compared the results of a group of EFL university learners who used the AR-mediated application for their writing (ARCAUW) and a control group who used the mobile-mediated in-class writing mode. The writing proficiency levels for both groups ranged from intermediate to high-intermediate on the Taiwanese national General English Proficiency Test, which were equivalent to the B2 + and C1 + benchmarks on the CEFR: Learning, Teaching, and Assessment. The authors reported that while both methods resulted in notable enhancements in writing the process analysis essay, ARCAUW was particularly beneficial in fostering the formation of task schema in long-term memory, motivation, and self-regulation in writing. However, they found that further cognitive processing that occurred during the use of AR-mediated activities produced mixed results. Liu and Tsai [62] also examined the role of AR-mediated materials in supporting learners to build new knowledge about buildings, areas, and views and the role of this newly acquired knowledge in their writing in the target language. The authors described the students' engagement in the learning scenario as high, including the use of language (see Fig. 6).

Despite claims that AR-mediated tasks can support 'long-term memory, motivation, and self-regulation of cognitive processes in writing' [61], its role in the development and enhancement of writing skills remains unclear and requires further examination.

Cultural Awareness. Cultural awareness is often considered the fifth language competence. Through AR, learners may experience significant historical events, explore ancient structures and interact with historical figures, fostering a deeper connection to the past and a more nuanced understanding of specific historical contexts [26, 63] of the target language. For example, in Liestoel [26], the learner has to locate the approximate position of a historical monument in the real space and receive the overlaid augmentation with visual information on the screen. The information is constantly updated as the learner moves around the site and observes historical events.

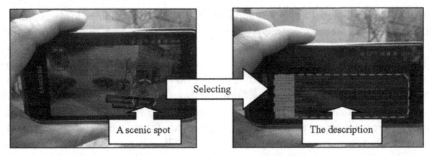

Fig. 6. A demonstration of how an EFL learner engages with AR mobile learning content on campus. When the learner utilizes their mobile phone to point in a particular direction, the device rapidly identifies their location, and the built-in camera automatically captures peripheral images. Simultaneously, the AR-based mobile learning material generates relevant information, such as names and descriptions of nearby buildings. The captured images and generated information are then displayed on the mobile phone screen. If the learner wishes to delve deeper into details about a specific building or scenic spot, they can click on specific information displayed on the screen, leading to the presentation of more comprehensive information [62].

6 Discussion – Conclusion

The integration of AR in language learning materials can have many benefits if it is implemented correctly, i.e. if it is used by incorporating resources that facilitate communication and support language components and competencies necessary for language acquisition. In this sense, the use of AR can facilitate multimodal learning by integrating different media such as video, images, 3D objects and audio files, in line with cognitive theories that suggest that the combination of words and visuals can improve learning outcomes.

As our analysis and description above shows, AR offers the potential to create rich learning resources that provide valuable opportunities to practice the target language through practice in immersive and realistic environments, offering interesting ways to make learning more visual and dynamic, as well as more interactive and engaging. These learning resources combine interesting activities such as augmented textbooks and worksheets or other digital resources such as photographs of historical sites, monuments, paintings, etc., which allow, among others, the learner to travel back in time through the augmentation of historical narratives.

Consequently, we can conclude that AR has the potential to enhance both different language components (e.g. vocabulary, grammar, pronunciation) and competencies (e.g. listening, reading, writing, cultural understanding).

However, our analysis and description also highlight several challenges that the language learning field still faces in order to successfully implement and make the most of AR technology in the language learning process. These challenges include the need for increased teacher training and the development of both accessible AR resources and user-friendly tools for developing AR resources that meet teachers' needs, as well as the use of AI to create more personalized learning environments.

Acknowledgements. This work has received funding from the European Union's Erasmus Plus programme, grant agreement 2022-1-NO01-KA220-HED-000088034 (ARIDLL project). The European Commission's support for the production of this publication does not constitute an endorsement of the contents, which reflect the views only of the authors, and the Commission cannot be held responsible for any use which may be made of the information contained therein.

Disclosure of Interests. The authors have no competing interests to declare that are relevant to the content of this article.

References

1. Kaplan-Rakowski, R., Papin, K., Hartwick, P.: Language teachers' perceptions and use of extended reality. CALICO J. **40**, 1–23 (2023). https://doi.org/10.1558/cj.22759
2. Parmaxi, A., Demetriou, A.A.: Augmented reality in language learning: a state-of-the-art review of 2014–2019. J. Comput. Assist. Learn. **36**(6), 861–875 (2020). https://doi.org/10.1111/jcal.12486
3. Panagiotidis, P.: Augmented and mixed reality in language learning. Eur. J. Educ. **4**, 28 (2021). https://doi.org/10.26417/501ibq23c
4. Valero-Franco, C., Berns, A.: Development of virtual and augmented reality apps for language teaching: A case study [Desarrollo de apps de realidad virtual y aumentada para enseñanza de idiomas: Un estudio de caso]. RIED-Revista Iberoam Educ a Distancia 27:163–185 (2024). https://doi.org/10.5944/ried.27.1.37668
5. Wang, L., Parmaxi, A., Nicolaou, A.: Teaching the ba-construction with augmented reality in online learning environments. In: Auer, M.E., Tsiatsos, T. (eds.) IMCL 2023. LNNS, vol. 936, pp. 115–126. Springer, Cham (2024). https://doi.org/10.1007/978-3-031-54327-2_12
6. Cai, Y., Pan, Z., Liu, M.: Augmented reality technology in language learning: a meta-analysis. J. Comput. Assist. Learn. **38**, 929–945 (2022). https://doi.org/10.1111/jcal.12661
7. Lin, Y., Yu, Z.: A meta-analysis of the effects of augmented reality technologies in interactive learning environments (2012–2022). Comput. Appl. Eng. Educ. **31**(4), 1111–1131 (2023). https://doi.org/10.1002/cae.22628
8. Chen, C.C., Kang, X., Li, X.Z., Kang, J.: Design and evaluation for improving lantern culture learning experience with augmented reality. Int. J. Hum. Comput. Interact. **40**(6), 1465-1478 (2024). https://doi.org/10.1080/10447318.2023.2193513
9. Yuen, SC-Y., Yaoyuneyong, G., Johnson, E.: Augmented reality: an overview and five directions for AR in education. J. Educ. Technol. Dev. Exch. **4**, 11 (2011). https://doi.org/10.18785/jetde.0401.10
10. Milgram, P., Kishino, F.: A taxonomy of mixed reality visual displays. IEICE Trans. Inf. Syst. E77-D, 1321–1329 (1994)
11. Nextias (2023) Extended Reality (XR) Startup Program - Current Affairs. https://www.nextias.com/ca/current-affairs/04-02-2023/extended-reality-xr-startup-program. Accessed 5 Mar 2024
12. Belda-Medina, J., Calvo-Ferrer, J.R.: Integrating augmented reality in language learning: pre-service teachers' digital competence and attitudes through the TPACK framework. Educ. Inf. Technol. **27**, 12123–12146 (2022). https://doi.org/10.1007/s10639-022-11123-3
13. Terzopoulos, G., Tsinakos, A.: O1.1 A review of augmented reality tools for building educational experiences (2020)
14. Gayevska, O., Gayevska, O.V., Kravtsov, H.M.: Approaches on the augmented reality application in Japanese language learning for future language teachers. Educ. Technol. Q. **2022**, 105–114 (2022). https://doi.org/10.55056/etq.7

15. Pusalabhuvansaikrishna (2023) Hardware for Augmented Reality. https://medium.com/@pus alabhuvansaikrishna/hardware-for-augmented-reality-7dc4db76f230. Accessed 10 Feb 2024
16. Akçayır, M., Akçayır, G.: Advantages and challenges associated with augmented reality for education: a systematic review of the literature. Educ. Res. Rev. **20**, 1–11 (2017). https://doi.org/10.1016/j.edurev.2016.11.002
17. Punar Özçelik, N., Yangin Eksi, G., Baturay, M.H.: Augmented reality (AR) in language learning: a principled review of 2017–2021. Particip. Educ. Res. **9**, 131–152 (2022)
18. Pegrum, M.: Augmented Reality Learning: Education in Real-World Contexts. Research-publishing.net (2021)
19. Boboc, R.G., Băutu, E., Gîrbacia, F., et al.: Augmented Reality in cultural heritage: an overview of the last decade of applications. Appl. Sci. **12**, 9859 (2022)
20. Papanastasiou, G., Drigas, A., Skianis, C., et al.: Virtual and augmented reality effects on K-12, higher and tertiary education students' twenty-first century skills. Virtual Reality **23**, 425–436 (2019). https://doi.org/10.1007/s10055-018-0363-2
21. Romano, M., Díaz, P., Aedo, I.: Empowering teachers to create augmented reality experiences: the effects on the educational experience. Interact. Learn. Environ. **31**, 1546–1563 (2020). https://doi.org/10.1080/10494820.2020.1851727
22. Chiang, T.H.C., Yang, S.J.H., Hwang, G.J.: An augmented reality-based mobile learning system to improve students' learning achievements and motivations in natural science inquiry activities. Educ. Technol. Soc. **17**, 352–365 (2014)
23. Sweller, J., Ayres, P., Kalyuga, S.: Cognitive Load Theory. Springer (2011)
24. Sweller, J.: Element interactivity and intrinsic, extraneous, and Germane cognitive load. Educ. Psychol. Rev. **22**, 123–138 (2010). https://doi.org/10.1007/s10648-010-9128-5
25. Suzuki, Y., Wild, F., Scanlon, E.: Measuring cognitive load in augmented reality with physiological methods: a systematic review. J. Comput. Assist. Learn. **40**(2), 375–393 (2024). https://doi.org/10.1111/jcal.12882
26. Liestoel, G.: Augmented Reality Storytelling – Narrative Design and Reconstruction of a Historical Event in situ (2019)
27. Yapici, İ.Ü., Karakoyun, F.: Using augmented reality in biology teaching. Malays. Online J. Educ. Technol. **9**, 40–51 (2021). https://doi.org/10.52380/mojet.2021.9.3.286
28. Scrivner, O., Madewell, J., Buckley, C., Perez, N.: Augmented reality digital technologies (ARDT) for foreign language teaching and learning. In: 2016 Future Technologies Conference (FTC), pp. 395–398 (2016)
29. Ibrahim, A., Huynh, B., Downey, J., et al.: ARbis Pictus: a study of vocabulary learning with augmented reality. IEEE Trans. Vis. Comput. Graph. **24**, 2867–2874 (2018). https://doi.org/10.1109/TVCG.2018.2868568
30. Smith, S.A., Carlo, M.S., Park, S., Kaplan, H.: Exploring the promise of augmented reality for dual language vocabulary learning among bilingual children: a case study. CALICO J. **40**, 91–112 (2023). https://doi.org/10.1558/cj.22757
31. Paivio, A.: A dual coding approach to perception and cognition. In: Modes of perceiving and processing information, pp. 39–51. Psychology Press (1978)
32. Perry, B., Perry, B.: ARIS: a tool to promote language learning through AR gaming. CALICO J. **35**, 333–342 (2018). https://doi.org/10.1558/cj.36318
33. Santos, M.E.C., et al.: Augmented reality as multimedia: the case for situated vocabulary learning. Res. Pract. Technol. Enhanc. Learn. **11**(4), 1–23 (2016). https://doi.org/10.1186/s41039-016-0028-2
34. Hadid, A., Mannion, P., Khoshnevisan, B.: Augmented reality to the rescue of language learners. Florida J. Educ. Res. **57**, 2019 (2019)
35. Karacan, C.G., Akoglu, K.: Educational augmented reality technology for language learning and teaching: a comprehensive review. Shanlax Int. J. Educ. **9**, 68–79 (2021)

36. Zhu, J., Zhang, X., Li, J.: Using AR filters in L2 pronunciation training: practice, perfection, and willingness to share Comput. Assist. Lang. Learn (2022).https://doi.org/10.1080/095 88221.2022.2080716
37. Mitterer, H., Cutler, A.: Speech Perception. In: Second, E. (ed.) Brown KBT-E of L& L, pp. 770–782. Elsevier, Oxford (2006)
38. Tiippana, K.: What is the McGurk effect? Front. Psychol. (2014). https://doi.org/10.3389/fpsyg.2014.00725
39. ARETE. D3.3 Interactive collaborative ARETE mobile app for Pilot 1. Zenodo (2021). https://doi.org/10.5281/zenodo.5060355
40. Wild, F., Marshall, L., Bernard, J., et al.: UNBODY: a poetry escape room in augmented reality. Information **12**(8), 295 (2021). https://doi.org/10.3390/INFO12080295
41. Cieri RL, Turner ML, Carney RM, et al (2021) Virtual and augmented reality: New tools for visualizing, analyzing, and communicating complex morphology. J Morphol 282:1785–1800. https://doi.org/10.1002/jmor.21421
42. Valle, R.: Teaching with Augmented Reality: It's Here – EdTechReview (2014). https://www.edtechreview.in/trends-insights/insights/teaching-with-augmented-reality-it-s-here/. Accessed 6 Mar 2024
43. Draxler, F., Labrie, A., Schmidt, A., Chuang, L.L.: Augmented reality to enable users in learning case grammar from their real-world interactions. In: Conference Human Factors Computing System Proceedings, pp. 1–12(2020).https://doi.org/10.1145/3313831.3376537
44. Sinclair, J.: Corpus, Concordance, Collocation. Oxford University Press, Oxford vol. 2, pp. 1–10 (1991)
45. Howarth, P.: Phraseology and second language proficiency. Appl. Linguist. **19**, 24–44 (1998). https://doi.org/10.1093/applin/19.1.24
46. Lewis, M.: The Lexical Approach. Language Teaching Publications, Hove (1993)
47. Wray, A.: Formulaic sequences in second language teaching: principle and practice. Appl. Linguist. **21**, 463–489 (2000). https://doi.org/10.1093/applin/21.4.463
48. Lindstromberg, S., Boers, F.: Optimizing a Lexical Approach to Instructed Second Language Acquisition. Basingstone (2009)
49. Kondo, S.: Effects on pragmatic development through awareness-raising instruction: Refusals by Japanese EFL learners. Investig. Pragmat. Foreign Lang. Learn. Teach. Test, 153–177 (2008)
50. Nikula, T.: Learning Pragmatics in Content-Based Classrooms. Investig Pragmat foreign Lang Learn Teach Test 94–113 (2008)
51. Rose, K.R., Kasper, G.: Pragmatics in Language Teaching. Cambridge University Press, Cambridge (2001)
52. Shakouri, A., Malmir, A., Esfandiari, R.: Cultivating L2 pragmatic comprehension through computerized vs. non-computerized instruction, multiuser virtual environments (MUVEs) and mobile augmented reality games (MARGs). Issues Lang. Teach. **11**, 313–358 (2022)
53. Holden, C.L., Sykes, J.M.: Leveraging mobile games for place-based language learning. Int. J. Game-Based Learn. **1**, 1–18 (2011)
54. Holden, C., Sykes, J.: Mentira: prototyping language-based locative gameplay. In: Mobile Media Learning: Amazing Uses of Mobile Devices for Learning, pp. 111–130 (2012)
55. Liu, T.-Y.: A context-aware ubiquitous learning environment for language listening and speaking. J. Comput. Assist. Learn. **25**, 515–527 (2009). https://doi.org/10.1111/j.1365-2729.2009.00329.x
56. Barreira, J., Bessa, M., Pereira, L.C., et al.: MOW: augmented reality game to learn words in different languages: case study: learning English names of animals in elementary school. In: 7th Iberian Conference on Information Systems and Technologies (CISTI 2012), pp. 1–6 (2012)

57. Taskiran, A.: Augmented reality games and motivation in language learning. In: Bastiaens, T., Braak, J Van., Brown, M., et al. (eds.) Proceedings of EdMedia + Innovate Learning 2018. Association for the Advancement of Computing in Education (AACE), Amsterdam, Netherlands, pp. 892–898 (2018)

58. Huang, X.: Development of Human-Computer Interaction for Holographic AIs (2024). https://doi.org/10.21954/OU.RO.000176D2

59. Tobar-Muñoz, H., Baldiris, S., Fabregat, R.: Augmented reality game-based learning: enriching students' experience during reading comprehension activities. J. Educ. Comput. Res. **55**, 901–936 (2017). https://doi.org/10.1177/0735633116689789

60. Wang, Y.-H.: Exploring the effectiveness of integrating augmented reality-based materials to support writing activities. Comput. Educ. **113**, 162–176 (2017). https://doi.org/10.1016/j.compedu.2017.04.013

61. Lin, V., Liu, G.Z., Chen, N.S.: The effects of an augmented-reality ubiquitous writing application: a comparative pilot project for enhancing EFL writing instruction. Comput. Assist. Lang. Learn. **35**, 989–1030 (2022). https://doi.org/10.1080/09588221.2020.1770291

62. Liu, P.H.E., Tsai, M.K.: Using augmented-reality-based mobile learning material in EFL English composition: an exploratory case study. Br. J. Educ. Technol. **44**, 1–4 (2013). https://doi.org/10.1111/j.1467-8535.2012.01302.x

63. Spierling, U., Winzer, P., Massarczyk, E.: Experiencing the presence of historical stories with location-based augmented reality BT - interactive storytelling. In: Oakley, I., Nisi, V. (eds.) Nunes N, pp. 49–62. Springer, Cham (2017). https://doi.org/10.1007/978-3-319-71027-3_5

Augmented Reality Labs: Immersive Learning in Chemistry

Hogea Razvan Ioan, Tracy Olin, Bayazit Karaman, and Doga Demirel$^{(\boxtimes)}$ (iD)

Florida Polytechnic University, Lakeland, FL, USA
ddemirel@floridapoly.edu

Abstract. Physical hands-on labs can be costly and time-consuming. Due to the advancements in hardware and computer vision technologies, virtual labs are being implemented to cut costs and save time. As augmented reality becomes more popular, the goal is to bring this technology into the education system by implementing a platform that can be accessed through common devices, such as phones and internet browsers. We developed a phone application to bring augmented reality to classes, with a focus on the field of chemistry. In addition to the mobile application, we developed a companion web application that enables professors to create classes, 3D objects for student interaction, and manage assignments, including grading, for the chemistry class. Finally, three laboratories were introduced for the chemistry class to execute a case study on the effectiveness of augmented reality in education. These laboratories are designed to instruct students on constructing 3D compounds through an assignment-based system, creating neutrally charged ionic bonds, and observing their ratios using an ionic table. Additionally, the labs aim to foster teamwork by providing a shared augmented reality experience, enabling students to collaboratively interact with the periodic table within the same virtual space. The overall feedback of the sixty students who interacted with the application was positive, with 53% strongly agreeing that augmented reality is more engaging than a standard lecture and a good learning tool in chemistry and other fields. Additionally, 39% of students strongly agree that a shared augmented reality experience promotes teamwork in the lab.

Keywords: Augmented Reality · Chemistry Lab · Immersive Learning

1 Introduction

Theory supported by hands-on practice is one of the principal keys to learning in several fields, such as electrical engineering [1]. Students can process and retain information more efficiently by visualizing the theory via hands-on practice during labs. However, physical hands-on labs can be costly due to the fast and ever-changing technology. It can also be time-consuming to assemble and disassemble various tools and objects. Thus, a remote and digital approach to hands-on labs can be taken to keep up with technology and cut costs. Even so, research papers [2, 3] showed that students consider virtual labs as effective as physical labs, if not more effective. Even though already

P. Zaphiris and A. Ioannou (Eds.): HCII 2024, LNCS 14724, pp. 155–172, 2024.
https://doi.org/10.1007/978-3-031-61691-4_11

proposed computer-based interactive laboratories focus on engineering [1, 4], the same proposed architecture and approach can be applied in different fields, such as Chemistry [5–7]. Also, with cost efficiency and hands-on practice in mind, as well as safety by removing hazardous materials from the Chemistry lab, the ARChem application [5] uses augmented reality to implement an interactive lab. In short, the application aims to teach students how to create chemical reactions using various substances' pH levels and assess students with a final quiz. Our platform aims to focus on the field of chemistry and solve the issues of cost and time efficiency that come with a physical hands-on lab. Thus, creating a platform that places virtually atoms on the table eliminates the need to acquire numerous plastic atoms for each student and eliminates the need to disassemble and repack after each class, eliminating the possibility of losing objects. Moreover, it bridges the gap of being limited to the school lab to interact with such objects and allows students to have hands-on interactions outside faculty premises. Finally, being a digital and remote lab, students can get useful information, such as molecule name, ion charge, and ratio, directly from the platform as they place and build objects without asking a professor.

Studies show that students tend to focus more on their laptops, thus eliminating the potential for collaboration [8, 9]. During the Chemistry class, the students would interact more and develop their social skills by focusing on a single object around a table, such as a 3D molecule. Previous collaborative Augmented Reality (AR) implementations in education include a mathematics lab that allowed students to draw shapes, such as cones, learn to build via pre-recorded tutorials, and even take exams [10]. However, implementing such software should not require additional equipment, like AR glasses, but instead use a more common device: the smartphone. Anatomy is perhaps one of the most targeted subjects for AR learning. A study showed how students performed better when they studied the parts of the skull while using AR, compared to just paper or VR [11].

Our platform aims to offer versatility and freedom to the professor to add any class with its corresponding models. The web platform will give access to the professor through their Florida Polytechnic e-mail account to create classes to which they can add, remove, and edit classes. Moreover, to each class, they will be able to add students and 3D objects, which will then be available to the students to interact with via the mobile application, which can download the objects from the cloud without constantly having them saved locally. Also, each 3D model will have a reference image, which, as an example, can be used to anchor 3D objects to the reference image in books. Thus, this offers versatility in the number of classes and 3D objects that can be added by not having a memory limit or by not needing any additional developing time to add the objects. The application's primary focus is to shift the focus from anatomy classes to Chemistry labs to help students understand concepts such as ion charges and compound elements. Thus, two custom labs are implemented for the Chemistry class to support the students' further understanding of complex chemistry topics such as compounds and ions. This will be made by creating an "assignment" based system, allowing the professor to create tasks in which the student has to build a compound or an ion using the available 3D models. The compound assignments can be added automatically by using an API or manually created by the professor as a fallback for the API via the web platform. The students can view a 2D image alongside general information about the compound and build it in 3D using the already available periodic table.

Moreover, after the building phase is done, the student will be able to take a picture and submit the assignment to the professor while also receiving a partial grade for placing the correct molecules and, later, a full grade updated by the professor based on the connections the student made between the molecules. A similar approach will also be available for the ion charge assignments, guiding the students into creating neutrally charged ions. Each ion will be selectable from a menu and, on tap, will be displayed in front of the student with a name, the current formula, and the charge. By having more tangible and visual cues, the goal is to provide a more engaging way of learning previously mentioned subjects in the chemistry domain.

Furthermore, previous iterations of applications that aim to teach chemistry using AR [5] have limited AR models due to a lack of database connectivity. By connecting the application to a database that supports the hosting of 3D models, such as Firebase, the application aims to break the barrier of having a limited number of models with which the students can interact. Additionally, the connection to a database will allow the students to interact with the professor to receive feedback on their work and interact with other students. Ultimately, students who join their AR session via their iPhone will be able to use the periodic table to build compounds together, thus being encouraged to socialize, collaborate, and not think individually. Moreover, as mentioned previously, one of the application's main features is the ability to go through books and interact with them on a multi-dimensional level via the 3D models attached to their reference images by the professors via the web platform. This will encourage the students to look more through the class-assigned books and not default to videos as often. Previous implementations of AR applications used marker tracking for their image tracking features [12, 13], which comes with various issues: the number of markers or generated QR codes can be limited and obstruct the image presented to the user.

Moreover, if the professor would like to allow students to track images from a book, it would mean that each student would have to attach the corresponding marker to their textbook, which is time-consuming and counterintuitive. Like more recent papers [14], by using the new technologies offered by frameworks such as ARKit, the application aims to eliminate the need for markers and automatically associate the uploaded image with the uploaded 3D model while also getting the data from the cloud instead of the local storage. This approach is possible due to the advancement of modern phones in computer vision and image processing, as well as at computing levels via very efficient and powerful chips built-in. Moreover, the project's scope is to provide a platform that is easily accessible to students via common devices that they already own, such as iPhones and iPads. This will result in the university or the student not purchasing additional devices, such as AR glasses, to interact with the application. However, due to the flexibility of the Swift programming language, the application will be able to run natively on the "Apple Vision Pro" AR glasses once they become available in early 2024. Additionally, the web application through which the professors will be able to add, remove, and edit 3D objects, as well as assignments, will not require any software installation from the user part since it will be available via any web browser, thus eliminating the need for a powerful machine, memory allocation or any knowledge of software installation.

To restate, augmented reality is the enhancement of the real world with virtually generated information [15], and has seen complex advancements in modern technology due to the higher processing power of phones and the improvement of their computer vision capability. While previous applications in AR [16] tend to focus on medical education and are limited to a number of 3D models [5], the main goal of this application is to provide the versatility and capability of adding any number of 3D models via a cloud database, while also focusing on a Chemistry lab with assignments which offer a more interactive and intuitive understanding of building compounds and Ions. What is more, the previously mentioned database will manage to connect both the web application and the mobile application for a seamless and cost-effective solution.

2 Methods

Our platform is divided into two sections: i) Web platform and ii) Mobile application. The mobile application is aimed at the professor to add, remove, and edit classes and create and grade assignments for a custom chemistry lab. The mobile application allows students to log in and interact with the 3D objects provided by the professor, build compounds, and learn about ion charges in the Chemistry Lab section. The two applications are connected by a shared database that stores user information, such as e-mail and password, student assignment submissions, and class data. The web platform is built in Dart, using the Flutter framework provided by Google. Flutter was chosen due to its simple learning curve and the option to build for Mac and Windows in case the professors require a standalone application. ARKit uses the device sensors to understand the scene and track the world and motion [17], while RealityKit seamlessly processes the data to render 3D objects in space [18]. Thus, being native frameworks provided by Apple, the two frameworks work hand-in-hand and can access all the native device features of the phone, such as true-depth cameras and LiDAR sensors. Lastly, we used Firebase, a NoSQL database provided by Google. The database is hosted on Google servers and lets the connection between iOS, web, and Android applications, thus being ideal for this project's scope. The connection between the two applications and the database can be seen in Fig. 1.

2.1 Designing and Connecting to the Database

Firebase is a service that Google offers a NoSQL database, web hosting, and cloud storage, which integrates with Swift and Flutter. The FireStore service is used to store raw data produced by both the mobile and the web app, such as class names, students enrolled in each class, and information processed by APIs to be sent to students. For example, when the professor adds a class, it will be added as a document to the class collection. Furthermore, for the chemistry class, an assignment collection is referenced to which several assignment documents are added, each containing specific data regarding each assignment. The structure continues and is respected for submissions for each assignment and books for each class.

When a professor adds a class via the web platform, it updates automatically on the mobile application without the user having to reload or sign in again. Files such as

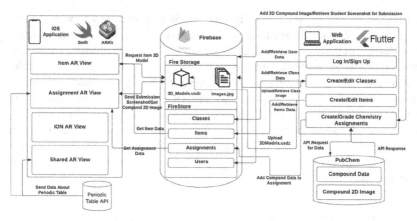

Fig. 1. Application Architecture Diagram

reference images and 3D objects are saved in a bucket in the Firebase Cloud Storage, thus eliminating the limit for 3D models which can be displayed in the application. The professor can add 3D models to each class via the web interface, while students can access and interact with them via the mobile iOS application. The interface section, which allows professors to add items to a class, can be observed in Fig. 2.

Fig. 2. Add Items via Web Interface

Often, data does not come instantly to the application and requires time to be retrieved from the database, and this is especially true for files. During data retrieval from the database, the UI should not freeze and display an indication that something is currently downloading to not give the impression to the user that the application has crashed or that their interaction with the UI elements was not registered. This process of retrieving data from the database and updating it on the main thread after completion is achieved via asynchronous operations. With the interaction of async await in Swift, the async processes can be written synchronously via tasks. Whenever a view appears, a task containing an async function is called, and on completion, the UI is updated correspondingly. Our platform uses the async-await feature of SwiftUI while downloading the 3D models from Cloud Storage. When the item view is presented, an async function is called to download the corresponding 3D model into memory. While the model downloads into the local storage, the placement buttons for the AR view are disabled, indicating to the user that the model has not been downloaded yet. When the task is completed, the buttons are enabled, indicating to the user that they can now interact with them. Similarly, Dart has an async-await feature that allows writing asynchronous functions, also known as a "Future." Our platform allows us to present a loading indicator while the files are uploaded to the cloud.

2.2 Conforming to Design Principles

Interface design is a critical factor in quality software. An interface with a simple yet expressive design can help the user interact with it much more manageable. For example, having a big title and expressive icons are some approaches to having an expressive UI.

Platform-Specific Design Principles. Since the application is multi-platform, the color pallet, shape design, and general components should be developed similarly, mainly in case the professor wants to interact with the app's mobile version. This helps the application's learning curve, as the professor does not have to learn two different UIs'. However, platform-specific elements should also be respected, precisely the difference in screen real estate between a web application and a mobile phone. Thus, our platform has the same color pallet for both applications and components, such as "class" icons, which are identical on both platforms.

In contrast, each device's layout is created to take advantage of the entire real estate of the screen. For example, on the iPhone, the application presents the list of classes in a scrollable list format, while on the web application, it displays a scrollable grid format, which adapts to the screen's width. Moreover, each application uses intuitive icons and labels, while the iOS version also respects the built-in native icons. Furthermore, the iOS application also adapts to the user's environment, considering the device theme, dark or light mode, and automatically changing the color pallet. The similarity in design, colors, and platform-specific adaptability can be seen in Fig. 3.

AR Interface Design Principles. While developing an AR application interface guidelines must be implemented. Firstly, the iOS application uses as much screen real estate as possible by even taking advantage of the safe area of the phone. Secondly, only necessary buttons are placed on the AR View so the user can close the view, open the menu for adding objects, and take a screenshot in the assignment section. Furthermore, it is also a good practice to display only relevant text, thus, we display only the molecular formula for both chemistry labs. In contrast, for the ion lab, we also display the charge, ratio, and molecule name above each placed object. This results in the screen not being too cluttered and displaying only essential information to the user so that he will not get overwhelmed. Additionally, object movement is enabled, which allows users to move, resize, and delete each object. Figure 4 depicts the good practices of human interfaces

Fig. 3. Class Menu on both Web and iOS

presented above. Guiding the user in an AR View experience via a coaching overlay is a good practice for guiding the user to move the phone to analyze their surroundings, as seen in Fig. 5.

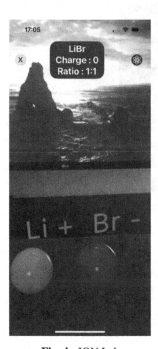

Fig. 4. ION Lab   **Fig. 5.** Coaching overlay

2.3 Case Study: Implementing Chemistry Labs

Our platform aims to have an interdisciplinary approach by giving professors access to add any type of class and relevant 3D models, whether it is a physics class, robotics, or even space engineering. While the platform has this versatility, it also focuses on Chemistry by having two labs for students to interact with and learn two key aspects: chemical compounds and ion charges. The application also has a shared AR experience to promote teamwork during the labs. This section will discuss the implementation and data collection for the labs.

Application Programming Interface (API). APIs act as a translator between two or more software programs. It is usually used to obtain a JSON or XML response, which developers use to decode data in their applications. Our application uses external APIs to obtain essential information in the field of Chemistry.

Firstly, the "periodic table" API is used to obtain data in JSON format about all the elements in the periodic table so that the students can visualize and add the 3D models of it via the ARView. The data parsed from the previously mentioned API includes element name, symbol, atomic mass, and group block. After the data is obtained, it is processed by the application and displayed to the user in a visual format, as seen in Fig. 6.

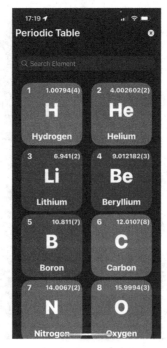

Fig. 6. Periodic Table

Secondly, the web application uses the PubChem API, which accesses the PubChem database [19], an open-source chemistry database provided by the National Institute of Health, to provide essential information for chemical compounds. The application requests information regarding compounds, which the professors can add as an assignment to students so that they can build the compound in 3D. The received information includes a 2D image of the compound, the molecular formula, a description, molecular weight, and SMILES of the compound. After the response data is parsed, it is presented on the web platform to the professor, as seen in Fig. 7, and if agreed, can be saved to the Firebase database and presented to the student in the assignment format, as seen in Fig. 8. The retrieved API information is essential in guiding the student to complete the assignment by presenting a 2D image of what they should build, hinting at how the molecular formula should look like, and expanding the student's knowledge of each compound by describing it. Thus, this aligns with the application's goal to teach students different subjects in a more interactive and spatially engaging way, with a focus on chemistry.

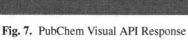

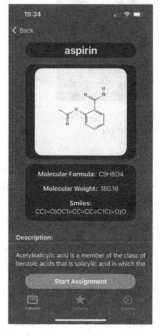

Fig. 7. PubChem Visual API Response   **Fig. 8.** Mobile Assignment View

Assignment-Based Lab for Building Compounds. The compound lab uses an assignment approach to teach students the structure of a specific compound by making them build it in a 3D format based on a 2D image. This hands-on lab allows students to visualize a chemical compound further beyond the boundaries of a 2D image by bringing it into their environment, allowing them to interact with it, and receiving a grade based on their accuracy. After the students are familiarized with the 2D image of the compound, as well as gained knowledge about it, such as the molecular formula and a description, they can proceed to start the assignment and build the 3D model of the compound. Upon starting the assignment, the platform displays an AR view, allowing the students to place molecules from the given periodic table and form connections between the placed molecules. After the student is satisfied with the model he built for the given assignment, he can take a screenshot of the model and send it to the professor to grade it via the web platform. The screenshot and submit button can be seen in Fig. 9, while the professor's view can be seen in Fig. 10.

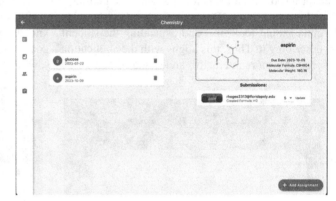

Fig. 9. Compound Submission

Fig. 10. Submissions List

Additionally, upon completing the assignment, the student receives a partial grade based on the molecular formula he built. The application achieves this by comparing the student's formula with the formula provided by the API response. Subsequently, the professor will update the grade based on the correctness of the connections via the web platform. Furthermore, the student can see the status, current grade, and overall assignment submission via the iOS application. The submission view in its final state, after the professor also assigned a grade, can be seen in Fig. 11.

Ion Lab. The second Chemistry lab aims to teach students how different ions combine to have a neutral charge. From an algorithmic point of view, this lab respects several chemistry rules: no more than two different molecules can be added, the positively charged ion always comes first in the formula, and the ratio is always reduced to its lowest value. The ratio is reduced using the most significant common devisor of both molecules. For example, if the user adds two molecules of lithium (Li^+) and two molecules of bromine (Br^-), the formula is LiBr, having a ratio of 1:1 instead of Li_2Br_2 and a ratio of 2:2, thus respecting the laws of chemistry. The charge in the previously mentioned example is 0, indicating to the user that what they built so far is correct, and when they try to add a different molecule, they will be prompted with an alert that it is incorrect. The mentioned example is shown in Fig. 12.

Creating a Shared AR Experience. ARKit uses the device camera to gather and process the user's environment, and by enabling collaboration, the data can be sent to nearby devices connected to the same network, thus offering a multi-user AR experience. The

Fig. 11. Submission View   **Fig. 12.** LiBr example in the ion lab

framework uses multipeer connectivity by importing the "MultipeerConnectivity" package to transfer data from an advertiser to a receiver and vice versa. The package uses an MCNAdvertiser and MCNBrowser to create, advertise, and look for an available via network and offers the template for sending and receiving data. After the package creates the connected session, it delegates the session to the AR session created by AR Kit, which enables anchor data transfers via the model's implemented methods for sending and receiving data to and from the connected peers.

In short, when the AR View for shared experience is enabled, the application notifies all nearby devices that a session is available to join. After two devices are connected by being close to each other, the advertiser sends all the AR anchors placed and their respective IDs. After the receiver gets the anchors, it places them in their allocated space and, based on their ID (i.e., "Bromine"), assigns a 3D entity to each anchor. The advertiser also assigns 3D entities to its anchors based on their ID, which in turn is assigned when a user selects an element from the periodic table. The interaction between an advertiser and a receiver can be seen in Fig. 13. For our application, collaboration is essential for the chemistry lab, such that students can interact with the elements of the periodic table together, thus encouraging social interaction and teamwork. Each student with an iOS device can join a session with a different iOS device and, via the provided periodic table, can place molecules in the environment of both users. The collaborative session can be seen in Fig. 14.

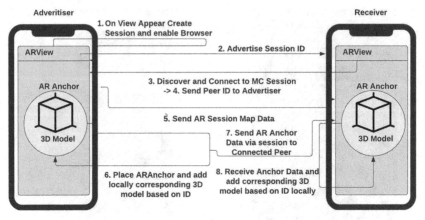

Fig. 13. Adveritiser – Receiver Workflow Diagram

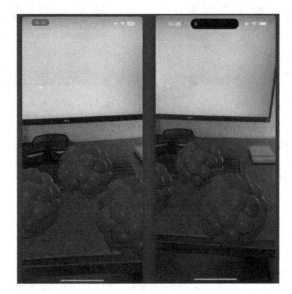

Fig. 14. Collaborative AR Experience

Data Collection. To accurately collect data and feedback for the mobile application, two questionnaires, video demos, and a hands-on experience of the application were conducted in five chemistry labs at Florida Polytechnic University to a total of sixty students. Before the students interacted with the application, a pre-demo questionnaire consisting of fourteen questions was provided. The questions consisted of nine Likert-like multiple-choice questions related to the student's prior experience with chemistry, their reasoning for taking a chemistry course, and their interest in chemistry. The remaining questions were also multiple-choice and related to the demographics of each user.

After each student completed the pre-demo questionnaire, a video demo of each lab was presented to the students. Next, they moved on with testing the application. Each student tested the application in three stages. At first, each student entered the ion lab and tried to create a neutral ion bond. Next, an assignment was created for each student, and they had to build the water compound using the periodic table. Some submissions made by students during testing can be seen in Fig. 15. Lastly, students were paired in two teams and asked to collaborate on a shared AR experience by interacting with different elements of the periodic table together.

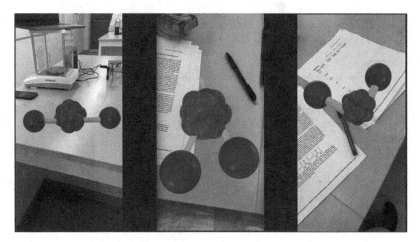

Fig. 15. Student Submissions of the Water Compound

Finally, after the hands-on tests, each student was asked to complete a post-test questionnaire formed by Likert-like multiple-choice questions. The Likert-like multiple choice questions were related to the likelihood of each student to prefer an AR lab rather than a real lab, how engaging the experience was, and their opinion on shared AR experiences.

3   Results

The study was conducted in five different chemistry labs at Florida Polytechnic, and as a result, 60 students responded to the post-questionnaire. Based on the results, over 70% of students consider AR an alternative to compound learning, with 60% considering it a tool that will help them understand the subject better. These results are reflected in Figs. 16 and 17.

Similar results were obtained regarding the ion lab, with 40% of students strongly agreeing that AR can be an alternative to learning ions and 28.3% strongly agreeing that it would help them understand the subject better. The results can be seen in Figs. 18 and 19.

Although the labs with which the students interacted were focused on the field of chemistry, the application has multiple purposes, and the students were asked if they would consider AR as an alternative to a standard lecture. To the question, "I think

I think learning compounds through AR will help me learn the subject better.

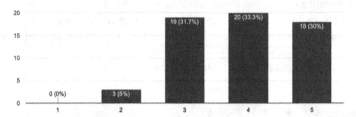

Fig. 16. Learning the Compounds Subject Better Through AR Questionnaire Results

I think Augmented Reality (AR) environment can be an alternative to learning compounds.

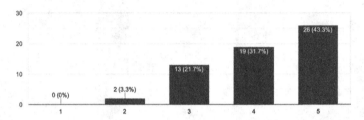

Fig. 17. AR as an Alternative for Learning Compounds Questionnaire Results

I think Augmented Reality (AR) environment can be an alternative to learning Ionic bonds.

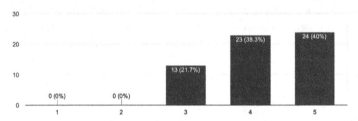

Fig. 18. AR as an Alternative for Learning Ionic Bonds Questionnaire Results

learning through AR will be more engaging than a standard lecture," 53% of students strongly agreed that AR would make a standard lecture more engaging. Similarly, 40% of students agree, and 30% of students strongly agree that they would prefer the immersive AR learning experience to the learning experience of a standard lecture. These results can be seen in Figs. 20 and 21.

The shared AR experience was implemented with the promotion of teamwork in mind, and it is an essential feature of the application. Thus, to get feedback regarding the importance of the experience for the platform, the following questions were asked: "I think learning in a shared AR experience is more engaging than an individual AR assignment experience" and "I think a shared AR experience is more engaging than an individual AR assignment experience". As a result, 44.1% of students agreed that

I think learning Ionic bonds through AR will help me learn the subject better.

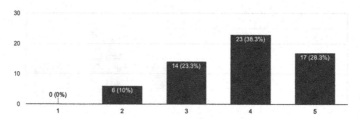

Fig. 19. Learning the Ionic Bonds Subject Better Through AR Questionnaire Results

I will prefer the immersive AR learning experience to the learning experience from a standard lecture.

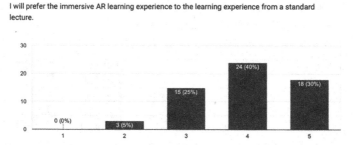

Fig. 20. Results for students who preferred an AR lecture to a standard lecture.

I think learning through AR will be more engaging than a standard lecture.

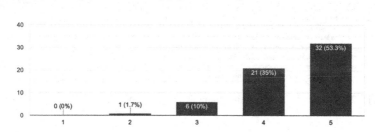

Fig. 21. Student's results for considering an AR lecture more engaging than a standard lecture.

a shared AR experience is more engaging than an individual AR experience, and an additional 25.4% strongly agreed with the statement. Moreover, 39% of students agreed, and 37.3% strongly agreed that a shared AR experience would promote teamwork in a lab environment. These results can be seen in Figs. 22 and 23.

To further test the results of our data and the credibility of our application, we performed a Spearman's analysis on all the combinations of the questions from both the post-questionnaire and the pre-questionnaire. After that, we extracted all the significant large positive and negative relationships by picking the correlations with a Spearman's coefficient value larger than 0.5 and a p-value < .001. A sample of the correlations can be seen in Figs. 24 and 25.

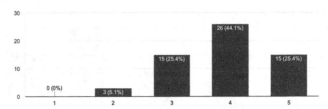

Fig. 22. Students Result on the engagement of a shared AR experience.

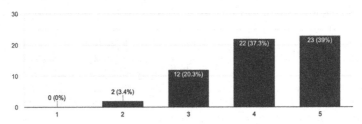

Fig. 23. Student's results on the promotion of teamwork in a lab via a shared AR experience.

Question	Spearman's Coefficient	p-value
AR as an alternative to learning compounds vs. AR as an alternative to learning ionic bonds	0.767	9.09E-13
AR as an alternative to learning compounds vs. Learning compounds better with AR	0.539	8.72E-06
AR as an alternative to learning compounds vs. AR being more engaging than a standard lecture	0.581	1.12E-06
AR as an alternative to learning compounds vs. Prefering immtersive AR to a standard lecture	0.541	8.25E-06
AR as an alternative to learning compounds vs. Being open to learning with AR	0.51	3.09E-05
AR as an alternative to learning ionic compounds vs. AR being more engaging than a standard lecture	0.581	1.15E-06
AR as an alternative to learning ionic compounds vs. Prefering immtersive AR to a standard lecture	0.555	4.16E-06
AR as an alternative to learning ionic compounds vs. Being open to learning with AR	0.526	1.61E-05

Fig. 24. Spearman's Correlation Sample results for post-questionnaire questions.

Question	Spearman's Coefficient	p-value
Interested in learning chemistry vs. Enjoying learning through standard lectures	0.533	1.20E-05
Comfortable working in a chemistry lab vs. Being anxious about working in a chemistry lab	-0.547	6.10E-06
Enjoy learning through standard lectures vs. Liking their chemistry course	0.56	3.30E-06
Open to learning with AR vs. Considering AR as an alternative to learning ionic bonds	0.53	1.60E-05
Open to learning with AR vs. Considering AR as an alternative to learning compounds	0.51	3.10E-05
Liking their chemistry course vs Liking their chemistry lab	0.602	3.65E-07

Fig. 25. Spearman's Correlation results for pre-questionnaire questions.

We can conclude that AR is a good alternative to learning compounds to the same degree that AR is an excellent alternative to learning ionic bonds. Also, there is a significant positive correlation between the learning of compounds or ionic bonds and the engagement and immersion of an AR lab compared to a standard lecture. Additionally, students who consider that learning compounds or ionic bonds through AR is better, also consider an AR lab more engaging than a standard lecture. The students who consider the learning of compounds or ionic bonds through AR, also prefer the immersive shared AR experience, and agree that a shared AR experience will promote teamwork in the lab. The only negative significant relationship is between the students who feel anxious about working in a chemistry lab and the students who feel comfortable working in a chemistry lab. Overall, it can be concluded that students who are open to learning with AR also consider AR as an alternative to learning ionic bonds or compounds.

4 Conclusions

With the advancement of computer vision and phone hardware, AR became more accessible to the public. Having an impact on commercial use, gaming, and education, AR is being used more and more daily. In this study, we implemented an AR platform for your iPhone, with a companion web application, to demonstrate the potential use case and impact of AR in education. Although the web application allows the professors to add AR objects to any class, a more detailed implementation was applied for the chemistry lab to be able to perform a case study. In this study, we implemented three different AR chemistry labs for students to interact with and provide feedback via a questionnaire. Sixty students had to complete a compound assignment in which the goal was to build the water compound in AR, then build a neutrally charged ion bond, and finally place atoms in a shared AR experience.

In conclusion, for the chemistry case study, the general feedback on the application was positive overall, with an average of 29% of students strongly agreeing and 36% agreeing that they would use AR to learn compounds or ionic bonds to understand the subjects better. On average, 40% of students would strongly consider, and 35% would consider AR an alternative to a standard lecture to learn ionic bonds and compounds. To further conclude the study and the versatility of the application, 53% of students strongly agreed that AR would make a standard lecture more engaging, with 30% of students strongly agreeing that they would prefer an AR lecture over a standard lecture. Additionally, the application intends to promote teamwork, and the results conform with this idea, with 39% of students strongly agreeing that a shared AR experience would promote teamwork in a lab, and an additional 37% also agreeing to that statement. While 25% of students also strongly consider a shared AR experience more engaging than an individual AR experience, an additional 44% agree. Moreover, a large set of questions resulted in being highly correlated, thus proving the relevance of this case study.

Disclosure of Interests. The authors have no competing interests to declare that are relevant to the content of this article.

References

1. Ertugrul, N.: New era in engineering experiments: an integrated and interactive teaching/learning approach, and real-time visualisations. Int. J. Eng. Educ. **14**(5), 344–355 (1998)

2. Corter, J.E., Nickerson, J.V., Esche, S.K., Chassapis, C.: Remote versus hands-on labs: a comparative study. In: 34th Annual Frontiers in Education, 2004. FIE 2004, IEEE, pp. F1G-17 (2004)

3. Demirel, D., Hamam, A., Scott, C., Karaman, B., Toker, O., Pena, L.: Towards a new chemistry learning platform with virtual reality and haptics. In: Zaphiris, P., Ioannou, A. (eds.) HCII 2021. LNCS, vol. 12785, pp. 253–267. Springer, Cham (2021). https://doi.org/10.1007/978-3-030-77943-6_16

4. Esche, S.K., Chassapis, C., Nazalewicz, J.W., Hromin, D.J.: An architecture for multi-user remote laboratories. Dyn. Typ. Cl. Size 20 Stud., vol. 5, no. 6 (2003)

5. Dinc, F., De, A., Goins, A., Halic, T., Massey, M., Yarberry, F.: Archem: augmented reality based chemistry lab simulation for teaching and assessment. In: 2021 19th International Conference on Information Technology Based Higher Education and Training (ITHET), pp. 1–7. IEEE (2021)

6. Ben-Zaken, D., Hamam, A., Demirel, D.: User movement for safety training in a virtual chemistry lab. In: Chen, J.Y.C., Fragomeni, G. (eds.) HCII 2022. LNCS, vol. 13318, pp. 3–13. Springer, Cham (2022). https://doi.org/10.1007/978-3-031-06015-1_1

7. Demirel, D., Hamam, A.: Design of a virtual reality based pedagogical framework. In: Zaphiris, P., Ioannou, A. (eds.) HCII 2022. LNCS, vol. 13329, pp. 38–47. Springer, Cham (2022). https://doi.org/10.1007/978-3-031-05675-8_4

8. Billinghurst, M.: Augmented reality in education. New Horiz. Learn. 12(5), 1–5 (2002)

9. Kesim, M., Ozarslan, Y.: Augmented reality in education: current technologies and the potential for education. Procedia-Soc. Behav. Sci. 47, 297–302 (2012)

10. Kaufmann, H.: Collaborative augmented reality in education. Inst. Softw. Technol. Interact. Syst. Vienna Univ. Technol. 2–4 (2003)

11. Chien, C.-H., Chen, C.-H., Jeng, T.-S.: An interactive augmented reality system for learning anatomy structure. In: Proceedings of the International Multiconference of Engineers and Computer Scientists, International Association of Engineers Hong Kong, China, pp. 17–19 (2010)

12. Nechypurenko, P.P., et al.: Development and implementation of educational resources in chemistry with elements of augmented reality (2020)

13. Nassar, M.A., Meawad, F.: An augmented reality exhibition guide for the iPhone. In: 2010 International Conference on User Science and Engineering (i-USEr), pp. 157–162 (2010). https://doi.org/10.1109/IUSER.2010.5716742

14. Abdinejad, M., Ferrag, C., Qorbani, H.S., Dalili, S.: Developing a Simple and Cost-Effective Markerless Augmented Reality Tool for Chemistry Education. ACS Publications, 2021

15. Furht, B.: Handbook of Augmented Reality. Springer, New York (2011)

16. Kamphuis, C., Barsom, E., Schijven, M., Christoph, N.: Augmented reality in medical education? Perspect. Med. Educ. 3, 300–311 (2014)

17. Oufqir, Z., El Abderrahmani, A., Satori, K.: ARKit and ARCore in serve to augmented reality. In: 2020 International Conference on Intelligent Systems and Computer Vision (ISCV), pp. 1–7. IEEE (2020)

18. Asaad, R.R.: Virtual reality and augmented reality technologies: a closer look. Int. Res. J. Sci. Technol. Educ. Manag. IRJSTEM, 1(2) (2021)

19. Kim, S., et al.: PubChem 2023 update. Nucleic Acids Res. 51(D1), D1373–D1380 (2023)

Bridging Theory into Practice: An Investigation of the Opportunities and Challenges to the Implementation of Metaverse-Based Teaching in Higher Education Institutions

Abhishek Sharma[1]([✉]) [iD], Lakshmi Sharma[2], and Joanna Krezel[3]

[1] Institute of Health and Management, Melbourne, Australia
sharmaabhishek570@gmail.com
[2] Amity University, Noida, India
lakshmisharma9891@gmail.com
[3] Victoria University, Melbourne, Australia
joanna.krezel@vu.edu.au

Abstract. Due to the recent COVID-19 pandemic, there has been a shift in how education is delivered from face-to-face environments to virtual learning platforms. Moreover, virtual learning platforms are becoming increasingly popular in higher education institutions as they provide immersive experiences that improve student experience. Nevertheless, there are concerns about the large-scale implications of Metaverse-based learning systems within higher education institutions. With the increasing opportunities and challenges associated with Metaverse-based learning systems, this scoping review investigates the key opportunities and challenges associated with implementing Metaverse-based teaching in higher education institutions. In doing so, the study also showcases how theoretical notions of the technology acceptance model (i.e., TAM) and unified theory of acceptance and use of technology (i.e., UTAUT) are linked with user acceptance towards Metaverse-based teaching in higher education institutions. Additionally, keyword searches are carried out on Scopus, ProQuest, and Web of Science databases to screen out studies that meet the selection criteria of the analysis. In doing so, the study's findings are depicted with the help of VOSviewer, which showcases the key clusters and studies related to opportunities and challenges of Metaverse-based teaching in higher education institutions. The findings showcase that most of the studies are published on Metaverse and its related technologies, such as AR, and how it creates an immersive learning experience through the help of gamification. Finally, the paper concludes with future directions related to the large-scale implementation of Metaverse-based teaching in higher education institutions.

Keywords: Metaverse · Virtual Worlds · Virtual Learning Platforms · Higher Education Institutions · Technology Acceptance Model (TAM) · Unified Theory of Acceptance and Use of Technology (UTAUT)

P. Zaphiris and A. Ioannou (Eds.): HCII 2024, LNCS 14724, pp. 173–189, 2024.
https://doi.org/10.1007/978-3-031-61691-4_12

1 Introduction

With the gradual advancements in technology, there has been an increase in the way individuals use technologies such as Augmented Reality (i.e., AR)/Virtual Reality (i.e., VR)/Extended Reality (i.e., XR)/Mixed Reality (i.e., MR) and Metaverse (See Fig. 1) (Duan et al., 2021; Mystakidis, 2022). Moreover, studies also contend that Metaverse is one of the most debated topics as it provides immersive experiences for its users and allows them to interact within the virtual worlds. However, Metaverse and its wide range of implementations in various fields remain a contentious issue in existing literature (Rojas et al., 2023; Zhang et al., 2022). In general, Metaverse is a shared virtual space where individuals can interact in real-time with other users via digital avatars (De Felice et al., 2023; Mystakidis, 2022). From a technological viewpoint, Metaverse is a 3D virtual space that combines both technologies, such as AR (i.e., augmented reality) and VR (i.e., virtual reality) (De Felice et al., 2023; Gao et al., 2023). Several platforms, including Second Life, Sandbox, and Decentraland, allow users access to the Metaverse systems, where they can create realistic avatars that can attend conferences and concerts and interact with other users (De Felice et al., 2023; Trunfio & Rossi, 2022). Moreover, Metaverse provides the opportunity for users to interact via immersive internet platforms where users are not only seen to have higher levels of engagement but also are seen to have practical learning experiences (Beck et al., 2023; Onu et al., 2023; Sin et al., 2023; Suh et al., 2023; Villalonga-Gómez et al., 2023). Currently, Metaverse continues to gain popularity, with reports indicating that the user base for Metaverse systems is expected to reach approximately 5 billion by around 2030 (Morris, 2022; Sharma et al., 2023).

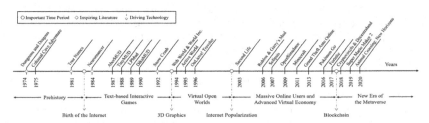

Fig. 1. Timeline for Gradual Advancements in Technology Source-(Duan et al., 2021)

In particular, Metaverse has gained immense attention of academics and researchers on how it can be implemented within the domains of entertainment (Chakraborty et al., 2023; Evans et al., 2022a; Niu & Feng, 2022; Sahoo et al. 2023), healthcare systems (Kim et al., 2023; Musamih et al., 2022; Petrigna & Musumeci, 2022; Tan et al., 2022; G. Wang et al., 2022), education (Kye et al., 2021; Mystakidis, 2022; Sharma et al., 2023; Tlili et al., 2022; Zhang et al., 2022), banking (Mozumder et al., 2023; Ooi et al., 2023; Sahoo & Ray, 2023; Zainurin et al., 2023), manufacturing (Z. Lin et al., 2022; Mourtzis et al., 2023a; Yao et al., 2022), advertising (Dwivedi et al., 2022; Eyada, 2023; Kim, 2021; Ozkaynar, 2023; Park & Kim, 2023), tourism (Buhalis et al., 2023; Koo et al., 2023; Tsai, 2022; Yang & Wang, 2023), retail (CHA, 2022; Gadalla et al., 2013; Hudson, 2022; Jenkins, 2022; Popescu et al., 2022), gaming (Evans et al., 2022b; Oliveira & Cruz,

2023; Onu et al., 2023) and real estate (Aharon et al., 2022; Kennedy, 2023; Yoo, 2022). The majority of these studies have either shed light on the varying opinions regarding the possibility of employing Metaverse in various sectors or on the determinants that will allow for Metaverse's adoption in a wide range of technological settings (Alfaisal et al., 2022; Dwivedi et al., 2022; Gao et al., 2023; Wu & Hao, 2023).

Within higher education institutions, Metaverse-based learning systems are mostly centred towards the development of captivating virtual environments that allow students to have higher knowledge retention (Akour et al., 2022; Lee & Kim, 2022; Rojas et al., 2023). Moreover, these studies also highlight various frameworks that would enable the implementation of Metaverse-based teaching in higher education institutions. However, only a few studies have unearthed the linkages of theoretical underpinnings of user acceptance towards the Metaverse platforms. Hence, the purpose of this study remains to (a) investigate the existing literature and related theories (i.e., Technology Acceptance Model, Unified Theory of Acceptance and Use of Technology) to understand the user acceptance towards Metaverse-based learning systems; (b) identify the key opportunities and challenges that are associated with the implementation of Metaverse-based teaching in higher education institutions.

To meet the objectives mentioned above of this study, a keyword search is conducted across three major databases, including Scopus, ProQuest, and Web of Science, to identify studies that elucidate theoretical notions as well as the key opportunities and challenges associated with the implementation of Metaverse-based teaching in higher education institutions. Additionally, to understand the trends within Metaverse-based teaching in higher education institutions, a co-occurrence analysis of keywords is conducted with the help of VOSviewer. The size of the labels within the figure denotes the number of occurrences of keywords within the extracted papers gathered from the Scopus database.

2 Background of the Study

Metaverse is an immersive platform that has the potential to reshape how education is delivered in HEIs by offering immersive experiences and enabling students to explore digital reality across various educational disciplines (Lin et al., 2022) (See Fig. 2). In detail, some of the positive impacts of Metaverse within higher education include (a) providing an immersive learning experience for students (Beck et al., 2023; Hwang et al., 2023; Sharma et al., 2023; Sin et al., 2023; Wei & Yuan, 2023); (b) Enhancing the visual experience for students (Di Natale et al., 2024; Han et al., 2022; Ng et al., 2023); (c) Creating hands-off experience for students which are of low-risk but of higher learning experience (Gómez-Cambronero et al., 2023; H. Lin et al., 2022; Sihna et al., 2023); (d) Personalised experiences (De Felice et al., 2023; Salloum et al., 2023; Sharma et al., 2023); (d) Fostering game based learning environments (Ng et al., 2023; Sihna et al., 2023); (e) collaborative experiences for development of new knowledge (Joshi & Pramod, 2023; Mourtzis et al., 2023b; Sharma et al., 2023).

Metaverse is in its infancy, and its potential is yet to be discovered in this technological age. However, it is vital to understand the prospective developments that existed as the building blocks of the Metaverse systems. To begin with, Second Life has been a

Fig. 2. Applications of Metaverse in Higher Education Institutions Source-(H. Lin et al., 2022)

driving force behind the Metaverse revolution, which was released in 2003 as a platform for multiplayer online gaming in virtual worlds through avatars (Onu et al., 2023). Following that, technological applications such as Unity, Roblox, Unreal Engine, Nvidia Omniverse, Hololens 2, and Oculus Quest 2 have been recognised as practical tools for implementing Metaverse systems (See Fig. 3).

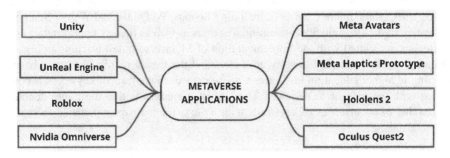

Fig. 3. Applications Related to Metaverse Systems Source- (Onu et al., 2023; Xu et al., 2022)

3 Theoretical Linkages in the Implementation of Metaverse-Based Teaching in Higher Education Institutions

3.1 Technology Acceptance Model (TAM)

With the rapid advancements in technology, it is crucial to understand the user acceptance towards a particular technology. From a theoretical standpoint, the technology acceptance model (i.e., TAM) is one of the critical frameworks that uncover the acceptance level of human behaviour, explaining the potential approval or disapproval of technology. In detail, TAM predicts the acceptance level of a user by understanding the perceived usefulness, perceived ease of use and attitude towards the use of technology. Moreover, TAM is also one of the prominent theories widely applied to various technologies ranging from mobile learning technologies to Metaverse technologies. The majority of studies conducted on the acceptance of a particular technology can be visualised to be taken by learners, educators, and stakeholders (Al-Adwan & Al-Debei, 2023; Al-Adwan et al., 2023; Alkhwaldi, 2023). As a result, it is essential to understand how Metaverse-based teaching in higher education institutions might be accepted by students and educators in the current technological age. Hence, Table 1 showcases the studies that are relevant to the technology acceptance model (TAM) and the adoption of Metaverse-based learning systems in higher education institutions as follows: -

Table 1. Studies Pertaining to TAM & Metaverse-Based Learning Systems

Relevant Studies	Type of Study	Findings
Al-Adwan et al. (2023)	**Quantitative Study**	According to the study's findings, perceived usefulness, personal innovativeness in IT, and perceived enjoyment are essential enablers of students' behavioural intentions towards adopting metaverse-based learning systems in higher education institutions
İbili et al. (2023)	**Quantitative Study**	The study's findings show that students' behavioural intentions towards adopting metaverse-based learning systems in higher education institutions are significantly influenced by perceived usefulness and hedonic motivation
Salloum et al. (2023)	**Quantitative Study**	According to the study's findings, innovativeness's moderating impact is crucial as it contributes to users' pervasive perceptions of adopting metaverse-based learning systems in higher education institutions
Alkhwaldi (2023)	**Quantitative Study**	The study's findings show that user satisfaction, performance expectancy, facilitating conditions, and hedonic gratification all have a significant impact on students' behavioural intentions towards adopting metaverse-based learning systems in higher education institutions
Al-Adwan & Al-Debei (2023)	**Quantitative Study**	According to the study's findings, apart from social influence, all other included determinants (e.g., personnel innovativeness) significantly and positively impact students' adoption intentions for the metaverse in higher education learning environments

(continued)

Table 1. (*continued*)

Relevant Studies	Type of Study	Findings
Akour et al. (2022)	**Quantitative Study**	The study's findings show that students' perceptions of trialability, compatibility, observability, and complexity are positively associated with adopting metaverse-based learning systems in higher education institutions
Wang & Shin (2022)	**Quantitative Study**	The study's findings show that personalised learning, perceived ease of use, social needs, and social impact play a positive influence on the willingness to adopt Metaverse education systems

3.2   Unified Theory of Acceptance and Use of Technology (UTAUT)

In addition to TAM, UTAUT remains a key theory that provides a robust framework that explains the key factors behind a user's behaviour and their acceptance level of a particular technology. According to the UTAUT, the four independent factors contributing to user's behaviour and acceptance level are performance expectation, expected effort, social impact, and facilitating conditions (Lee & Kim, 2022). In light of these discussions, Venkatesh et al. (2012) also proposed the UTAUT2 model, which includes additional factors such as hedonic motivation, price value, and habit that would provide a deeper understanding towards the acceptance level of users towards a particular technology. Moreover, most studies have adopted the theoretical lenses of the UTAUT model to explain Metaverse-based teaching in higher education institutions. As a result, it is essential to understand how metaverse-based teaching in higher education institutions might be accepted by students and educators in the current technological age. Hence, studies relevant to the Unified Theory of Acceptance and Use of Technology (UTAUT) and the adoption of Metaverse-based teaching in higher education institutions are showcased in Table 2.

4   Methodology

Based on the data extracted from the Scopus database, metaverse-based learning systems have gained enormous attention in countries such as South Korea, China, and India due to their current technological revolution (See Fig. 4).

Also, the database results showcase that Metaverse-based learning systems have been implemented effectively in various educational fields, including computer science, social sciences, and engineering-related fields in higher education institutions (See Fig. 5).

Table 2. Studies Pertaining to UTAUT & Metaverse-Based Learning Systems

Relevant Studies	Type of Study	Findings
Kalınkara & Özdemir (2023)	**Quantitative Study**	According to the study's findings, social influence, habit variables, and facilitating conditions affect the behavioural intentions of students to adopt metaverse-based learning systems in higher education institutions. Furthermore, the study discovered that students had an elevated level of participation in hedonic motivation
Alkhwaldi (2023)	**Quantitative Study**	The study's findings revealed that an individual's behavioural intentions regarding the usage of Metaverse-based learning systems are influenced by their satisfaction, performance expectancy, and facilitating conditions
Wiangkham & Vongvit (2023)	**Quantitative Study**	The study's findings revealed that cyber security, performance expectancy, social influence, and hedonic motivation all significantly affect the intention to use metaverse-based learning systems in higher education institutions
Lee & Kim (2022)	**Quantitative Study**	Based on the study's findings, it was determined that students' satisfaction levels and intentions to use metaverse-based learning technologies are increased when they have higher expectations regarding their performance, their level of effort, and the social influence of these technologies

Besides this, to address the critical purpose of this study, a rigorous approach is taken, where a keyword search is conducted on various designated databases such as Scopus, ProQuest, and the Web of Science platforms to showcase the key opportunities and challenges that are associated with the implementation of Metaverse-based learning systems in higher education institutions (See Table 3). VOSviewer is implemented to analyse the cluster analysis of Metaverse and its implementation in higher education institutions based on the search results gathered from the Scopus database.

Documents by country or territory
Compare the document counts for up to 15 countries/territories.

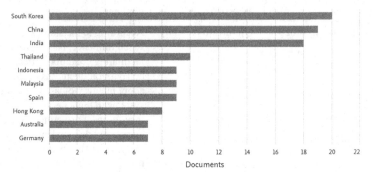

Fig. 4. Studies on Metaverse Learning Systems Published by Different Countries Source-(Scopus)

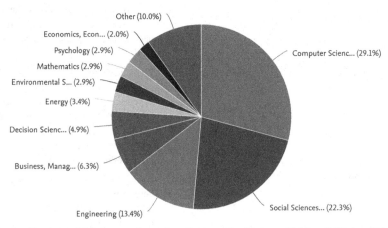

Fig. 5. Application of Metaverse Learning Systems in Various Fields of Higher Education Institutions Source-(Scopus)

More precisely, the co-occurrence analysis is undertaken in VOSviewer, which explores that there exist three major clusters (i.e., Red, Green, and Blue) that provide ideas on the implementation of Metaverse-based teaching in higher education institutions (See Fig. 6). Firstly, the red cluster signifies the concepts such as Metaverse and its related technologies, such as AR and how it creates immersive learning experiences through the help of gamification. Secondly, the blue clusters showcase the notions and studies linked to virtual reality, e-learning and higher education. Finally, the green clusters depict the studies related to virtual worlds, avatars, and extended reality.

Table 3. Keyword and Search Results from Designated Databases

Keywords	ProQuest	Scopus	Web of Science
("Metaverse") AND ("Opportunities" OR "Barriers") AND ("Higher Education") AND ("Teaching")	219	–	–
("Metaverse") AND ("Opportunities" OR "Barriers") AND ("Higher Education") AND ("Teaching") AND PUBYEAR > 2019 AND PUBYEAR < 2025 AND (LIMIT-TO (LANGUAGE, "English")) AND (LIMIT-TO (EXACTKEYWORD, "Metaverse"))	–	156	–
("Metaverse") AND ("Opportunities" OR "Barriers") AND ("Higher Education") AND ("Teaching")	–	–	2

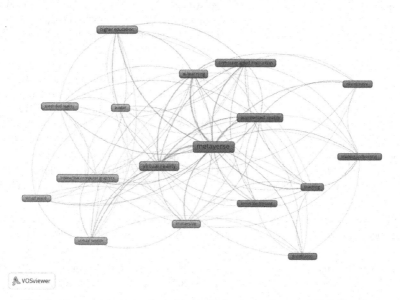

Fig. 6. Co-occurrence Analysis Through Vosviewer Source-(VOSviewer)

5   Key Opportunities and Challenges of Metaverse Technologies

With the growing popularity of Metaverse-based learning systems, it is critical to identify the opportunities and challenges associated with the implementation of Metaverse
systems in higher education institutions (See Table 4 and Table 5). In detail, the key
benefits of Metaverse systems in higher education institutions can be summarised as
their ability to provide students with immersive and interactive experiences (Park &
Kim, 2023; Richter & Richter, 2023; Said, 2023). Furthermore, some studies also state
that metaverse-based learning systems not only provide personalised learning experiences for students but also provide students with an opportunity to learn skills through a

game-based approach to learning (Akour et al., 2022; Al-Adwan et al., 2023). Furthermore, Metaverse-based learning systems are thought to provide collaborative learning experiences for students, fostering a constructivist approach to learning among them (Kryvenko & Chalyy, 2023; Onu et al., 2023). Lastly, it is also assumed that the implementation of Metaverse-based learning systems will boost the digital literacy level of both students and teachers, allowing them to have an enhanced experience while using Metaverse systems (Farias-Gaytan et al., 2023; Simbaqueba-Uribe et al., 2024).

Table 4. Key Opportunities of Metaverse Systems

Key Opportunities of Metaverse Systems	Related Studies
Immersive & Interactive Learning Experience	AbuKhousa et al. (2023); Akour et al. (2022); Al-Adwan et al. (2023); Asiksoy (2023); Beck et al. (2023); Camilleri (2023); De Felice et al. (2023); George-Reyes et al. (2023); Hwang et al. (2023); JosephNg et al. (2023); Kaur et al. (2023); Li & Yu (2023); Maheswari et al. (2022); Mourtzis et al. (2023b); Onu et al. (2023); Park & Kim (2022); Richter & Richter (2023); Said (2023); Samarnggoon et al. (2023); Sin et al. (2023); Siyaev & Jo (2021); Villalonga-Gómez et al. (2023); Wei & Yuan (2023); Yilmaz et al. (2023)
Personalised Learning Experiences/Skill-Practising Environment/Game-Based Learning	AbuKhousa et al. (2023); Arantes (2023); George-Reyes et al. (2023); Kryvenko & Chalyy (2023); Mourtzis et al. (2023b); Onu et al. (2023); Samarnggoon et al. (2023)
Collaborative & Social Learning Experiences	De Felice et al. (2023); George-Reyes et al. (2023); Onu et al. (2023); Said (2023); Sharma et al. (2023); Sin et al. (2023); Tlili et al. (2022)
Constructivist Learning	Camacho & Esteve, (2015); Ng et al. (2023); Onu et al. (2023); Sin et al. (2023); Suh & Ahn (2022)
Digital Literacy	Farias-Gaytan et al. (2023); George-Reyes et al. (2023); Guzzo et al. (2023); Li & Yu (2023); Mohsin et al. (2023); Simbaqueba-Uribe et al. (2024); Sin et al. (2023); Villalonga-Gómez et al. (2023)

Table 5. Key Challenges of Metaverse Systems

Critical Challenges in Implementation of Metaverse Systems	Related Studies
Technical Limitations	De Felice et al. (2023); Mosco (2023); Onu et al. (2023); Yaqoob et al. (2023)
Privacy Breaches & Security Concerns/Cybersecurity Concerns	Al-Ghaili et al. (2022); Onu et al. (2023); Park & Kim (2022); Said (2023)
Health Concerns	Benrimoh et al. (2022); Song & Qin (2022); Wylde et al. (2023)
Ensuring Strong Governance on Metaverse Systems and User Behaviour	Mosco (2023); Ølnes et al. (2017); Said (2023); Wylde et al. (2023); Yaqoob et al. (2023)
Lack of Interconnectedness Among Various Metaverse Platforms	Al-Ghaili et al. (2022); Y. Wang et al. (2022); Zyda (2022)
Copyright & Intellectual Property Challenges	(Nanobashvili (2021); Ramos, (2022); Yaqoob et al. (2023)
Content Moderation Across Metaverse Platforms & Ethical Use of Avatar Integrity	Commission (2022); Hu et al. (2021); Lake (2019); Lau (2022); Lin & Latoschik (2022); Wylde et al. (2023)
Data Protection Frameworks	Lau (2022); Milmo (2023); Rahman (2022); Wylde et al. (2023)
Cost Associated with Metaverse Learning Systems Implementation	Koohang et al. (2023); Onu et al. (2023); Simbaqueba-Uribe et al. (2024); Zhang et al. (2023)
Lack of Resources for Content Creation in Metaverse Learning Systems	Onu et al. (2023); Velev et al. (2023); Zhang et al. (2023)
Addiction to Using Metaverse Systems	H. Lin et al. (2022); Mohammed et al. (2024); Pal & Arpnikanondt (2024); Yaqoob et al. (2023)

6   Conclusion and Future Research Directions

Following the COVID-19 pandemic, one of the most hotly debated topics is the Metaverse and its potential applications across various domains, including higher education. Furthermore, reflecting the arguments presented in the paper, it can be concluded that Metaverse not only provides an enhanced immersive experience for students but also comes with an array of challenges related to wide-scale implementations in higher education institutions. As a result, it is suggested that stakeholders, regulators, and government bodies need necessary actions to make substantial refinements in terms of privacy and governance of Metaverse systems.

References

AbuKhousa, E., El-Tahawy, M.S., Atif, Y.: Envisioning architecture of metaverse intensive learning experience (MiLEx): career readiness in the 21st century and collective intelligence development scenario. Future Internet 15(2), 53 (2023)

Aharon, D.Y., Demir, E., Siev, S.: Real returns from unreal world? Market reaction to metaverse disclosures. Res. Int. Bus. Financ. 63, 101778 (2022)

Akour, I.A., Al-Maroof, R.S., Alfaisal, R., Salloum, S.A.: A conceptual framework for determining metaverse adoption in higher institutions of gulf area: an empirical study using hybrid SEM-ANN approach. Comput. Educ.: Artif. Intell. 3, 100052 (2022)

Al-Adwan, A.S., Al-Debei, M.M.: The determinants of Gen Z's metaverse adoption decisions in higher education: Integrating UTAUT2 with personal innovativeness in IT. Educ. Inf. Technol. 1–33 (2023)

Al-Adwan, A.S., Li, N., Al-Adwan, A., Abbasi, G.A., Albelbisi, N.A., Habibi, A.: Extending the technology acceptance model (TAM) to Predict University Students' intentions to use metaverse-based learning platforms. Educ. Inf. Technol. 28(11), 15381–15413 (2023)

Al-Ghaili, A.M., et al.: A Review of Metaverse's Definitions, Architecture, Applications, Challenges, Issues, Solutions, and Future Trends. IEEE Access (2022)

Alfaisal, R., Hashim, H., Azizan, U.H.: Metaverse system adoption in education: a systematic literature review. J. Comput. Educ. 1–45 (2022)

Alkhwaldi, A.F.: Understanding learners' intention toward Metaverse in higher education institutions from a developing country perspective: UTAUT and ISS integrated model. Kybernetes (2023)

Arantes, J.: Digital twins and the terminology of "personalization" or "personalized learning" in educational policy: a discussion paper. Policy Futures Educ. 14782103231176357 (2023)

Asiksoy, G.: Empirical studies on the metaverse-based education: a systematic review. Int. J. Eng. Pedagogy 13(3), 120–133 (2023)

Beck, D., Morgado, L., O'Shea, P.: Educational practices and strategies with immersive learning environments: mapping of reviews for using the metaverse. IEEE Trans. Learn. Technol. (2023)

Benrimoh, D., Chheda, F.D., Margolese, H.C.: The best predictor of the future—the metaverse, mental health, and lessons learned from current technologies. JMIR Mental Health 9(10), e40410 (2022)

Buhalis, D., Leung, D., Lin, M.: Metaverse as a disruptive technology revolutionising tourism management and marketing. Tour. Manage. 97, 104724 (2023)

Camacho, M., Esteve, V.: Moving beyond learning: the potential of inmmersive environmesnts in education. Teach. Learn. Digit. World: Strateg. Issues High. Educ. 70, 109 (2015)

Camilleri, M.A.: Metaverse applications in education: a systematic review and a cost-benefit analysis. Interact. Technol. Smart Educ. (2023)

Cha, S.-S.: Metaverse and the evolution of food and retail industry. Korean J. Food Health Converg. 8(2), 1–6 (2022)

Chakraborty, D., Patre, S., Tiwari, D.: Metaverse mingle: discovering dating intentions in metaverse. J. Retail. Consum. Serv. 75, 103509 (2023)

Commission, E.: Shaping Europe's digital future: a European strategy for a better internet for kids (2022). https://digital-strategy.ec.europa.eu/en/policies/strategy-better-internet-kids

De Felice, F., Petrillo, A., Iovine, G., Salzano, C., Baffo, I.: How does the metaverse shape education? A systematic literature review. Appl. Sci. 13(9), 5682 (2023)

Di Natale, A.F., Repetto, C., Costantini, G., Riva, G., Bricolo, E., Villani, D.: Learning in the metaverse: are university students willing to learn in immersive virtual reality? Cyberpsychol. Behav. Soc. Netw. 27(1), 28–36 (2024)

Duan, H., Li, J., Fan, S., Lin, Z., Wu, X., Cai, W.: Metaverse for social good: a university campus prototype. In: Proceedings of the 29th ACM International Conference on Multimedia (2021)

Dwivedi, Y.K., et al.: Metaverse beyond the hype: multidisciplinary perspectives on emerging challenges, opportunities, and agenda for research, practice and policy. Int. J. Inf. Manage. **66**, 102542 (2022)

Evans, L., Frith, J., Saker, M.: Entertainment worlds. In: From Microverse to Metaverse, pp. 65–73. Emerald Publishing Limited (2022a)

Evans, L., Frith, J., Saker, M.: Gaming worlds. In: From Microverse to Metaverse: Modelling the Future through Today's Virtual Worlds, pp. 33–40. Emerald Publishing Limited (2022b)

Eyada, B.: Advertising in the metaverse: opportunities and challenges. Int. J. Market. Stud. **15**(1) (2023)

Farias-Gaytan, S., Aguaded, I., Ramirez-Montoya, M.-S.: Digital transformation and digital literacy in the context of complexity within higher education institutions: a systematic literature review. Human. Soc. Sci. Commun. **10**(1), 1–11 (2023)

Gadalla, E., Keeling, K., Abosag, I.: Metaverse-retail service quality: a future framework for retail service quality in the 3D internet. J. Mark. Manag. **29**(13–14), 1493–1517 (2013)

Gao, H., Chong, A.Y.L., Bao, H.: Metaverse: literature review, synthesis and future research agenda. J. Comput. Inf. Syst. 1–21 (2023)

George-Reyes, C.E., Peláez Sánchez, I.C., Glasserman-Morales, L.D., López-Caudana, E.O.: The Metaverse and complex thinking: opportunities, experiences, and future lines of research. Front. Educ. (2023)

Gómez-Cambronero, Á., Miralles, I., Tonda, A., Remolar, I.: Immersive virtual-reality system for aircraft maintenance education: a case study. Appl. Sci. **13**(8), 5043 (2023)

Guzzo, T., Ferri, F., Grifoni, P.: Lessons learned during COVID-19 and future perspectives for emerging technology. Sustainability **15**(14), 10747 (2023)

Han, D.-I.D., Bergs, Y., Moorhouse, N.: Virtual reality consumer experience escapes: preparing for the metaverse. Virtual Reality **26**(4), 1443–1458 (2022)

Hu, J., Iosifescu, A., LiKamWa, R.: Lenscap: split-process framework for fine-grained visual privacy control for augmented reality apps. In: Proceedings of the 19th Annual International Conference on Mobile Systems, Applications, and Services (2021)

Hudson, J.: Virtual immersive shopping experiences in metaverse environments: predictive customer analytics, data visualization algorithms, and smart retailing technologies. Linguist. Philos. Investigat. **21**, 236–251 (2022)

Hwang, Y., Shin, D., Lee, H.: Students' perception on immersive learning through 2D and 3D metaverse platforms. Educ. Technol. Res. Developm. **71**(4), 1687–1708 (2023)

İbili, E., et al.: Investigation of learners' behavioral intentions to use metaverse learning environment in higher education: a virtual computer laboratory. Interact. Learn.. Environ. 1–26 (2023)

Jenkins, T.: Immersive virtual shopping experiences in the retail metaverse: consumer-driven E-commerce, blockchain-based digital assets, and data visualization tools. Linguist. Philos. Investigat. **21**, 154–169 (2022)

JosephNg, P.S., Gong, X., Singh, N., Sam, T.H., Liu, H., Phan, K.Y.: Beyond your sight using metaverse immersive vision with technology behaviour model. J. Cases Inf. Technol. **25**(1), 1–34 (2023)

Joshi, S., Pramod, P.: A collaborative metaverse based a-la-carte framework for tertiary education (CO-MATE). Heliyon **9**(2), e13424 (2023)

Kalınkara, Y., Özdemir, O.: Anatomy in the metaverse: exploring student technology acceptance through the UTAUT2 model. Anatom. Sci. Educ. (2023)

Kaur, N., Singh, V., Mahajan, N., Garg, N.: Game based learning-immersive teaching and learning platform through metaverse. In: 2023 3rd International Conference on Innovative Practices in Technology and Management (ICIPTM) (2023)

Kennedy, J.: Metaverse property: advocating for the regulation of metaverse land and property through a real estate legal regime. Ohio St. Bus. LJ **17**, 323 (2023)

Kim, J.: Advertising in the metaverse: research agenda. J. Interact. Advert. **21**(3), 141–144 (2021)

Kim, K., Yang, H., Lee, J., Lee, W.G.: Metaverse wearables for immersive digital healthcare: a review. Adv. Sci. **10**(31), 2303234 (2023)

Koo, C., Kwon, J., Chung, N., Kim, J.: Metaverse tourism: conceptual framework and research propositions. Curr. Issue Tour. **26**(20), 3268–3274 (2023)

Koohang, A., et al.: Shaping the metaverse into reality: a holistic multidisciplinary understanding of opportunities, challenges, and avenues for future investigation. J. Comput. Inf. Syst. **63**(3), 735–765 (2023)

Kryvenko, I., Chalyy, K.: Phenomenological toolkit of the metaverse for medical informatics' adaptive learning. Educ. Méd. **24**(5), 100854 (2023)

Kye, B., Han, N., Kim, E., Park, Y., Jo, S.: Educational applications of metaverse: possibilities and limitations. J. Educ. Eval. Health Profess. **18**, 32 (2021)

Lake, J.: Hey, you stole my avatar!: virtual reality and its risks to identity protection. Emory LJ **69**, 833 (2019)

Lau, P.L.: The metaverse: three legal issues we need to address (2022). https://theconversation.com/the-metaverse-three-legal-issues-we-need-to-address-175891

Lee, U.-K., Kim, H.: UTAUT in Metaverse: an "Ifland" case. J. Theor. Appl. Electron. Commer. Res. **17**(2), 613–635 (2022)

Li, M., Yu, Z.: A systematic review on the metaverse-based blended English learning. Front. Psychol. **13**, 1087508 (2023)

Lin, H., Wan, S., Gan, W., Chen, J., Chao, H.-C.: Metaverse in education: vision, opportunities, and challenges. In: 2022 IEEE International Conference on Big Data (Big Data) (2022)

Lin, J., Latoschik, M.E.: Digital body, identity and privacy in social virtual reality: a systematic review. Front. Virtual Reality **3**, 974652 (2022)

Lin, Z., Xiangli, P., Li, Z., Liang, F., Li, A.: Towards metaverse manufacturing: a blockchain-based trusted collaborative governance system. In: The 2022 4th International Conference on Blockchain Technology (2022)

Maheswari, D., Ndruru, F.B.F., Rejeki, D.S., Moniaga, J.V., Jabar, B.A.: Systematic literature review on the usage of iot in the metaverse to support the education system. In: 2022 5th International Conference on Information and Communications Technology (ICOIACT) (2022)

Milmo, D.: Meta dealt blow by EU ruling that could result in data use 'opt-in' (2023). https://www.theguardian.com/technology/2023/jan/04/meta-dealt-blow-eu-ruling-data-opt-in-facebook-instagram-ads

Mohammed, S.Y., Aljanabi, M., Gadekallu, T.R.: Navigating the nexus: a systematic review of the symbiotic relationship between the metaverse and gaming. Int. J. Cognit. Comput. Eng. **5**, 88–103 (2024)

Mohsin, A.N., Mohammed, M.A., Al-Maatoq, M.: Employing metaverse technologies to improve the quality of the educational process. In: International Multi-disciplinary Conference-Integrated Sciences and Technologies (2023)

Morris, C.: Citi says metaverse economy could be worth $13 trillion by 2030. Fortune (2022). https://fortune.com/2022/04/01/citi-metaverse-economy-13-trillion-2030/

Mosco, V.: Into the metaverse: technical challenges, social problems, utopian visions, and policy principles. Javnost-The Public **30**(1), 161–173 (2023)

Mourtzis, D., Angelopoulos, J., Panopoulos, N.: Blockchain integration in the era of industrial metaverse. Appl. Sci. **13**(3), 1353 (2023)

Mourtzis, D., Angelopoulos, J., Panopoulos, N.: Metaverse and blockchain in education for collaborative product-service system (PSS) design towards University 5.0. Procedia CIRP **119**, 456–461 (2023)

Mozumder, M.A.I., Theodore, A.T.P., Athar, A., Kim, H.-C.: The metaverse applications for the finance industry, its challenges, and an approach for the metaverse finance industry. In: 2023 25th International Conference on Advanced Communication Technology (ICACT) (2023)

Musamih, A., et al.: Metaverse in healthcare: applications, challenges, and future directions. IEEE Consum. Electron. Magaz. (2022)

Mystakidis, S.: Metaverse. Encyclopedia 2(1), 486–497 (2022)

Nanobashvili, L.: If the metaverse is built, will copyright challenges come? UIC Rev. Intell. Prop. L. 21, i (2021)

Ng, P.H., et al.: From classroom to metaverse: a study on gamified constructivist teaching in higher education. Int. Conf. Web-Based Learn. (2023)

Niu, X., Feng, W.: Immersive entertainment environments-from theme parks to metaverse. Int. Conf. Hum.-Comput. Interact. (2022)

Oliveira, A., Cruz, M.: Virtually connected in a multiverse of madness?—perceptions of gaming, animation, and metaverse. Appl. Sci. 13(15), 8573 (2023)

Ølnes, S., Ubacht, J., Janssen, M.: Blockchain in Government: Benefits and Implications of Distributed Ledger Technology for Information Sharing, vol. 34, pp. 355–364. Elsevier (2017)

Onu, P., Pradhan, A., Mbohwa, C.: Potential to use metaverse for future teaching and learning. Educ. Inf. Technol. 1–32 (2023)

Ooi, K.-B., et al.: Banking in the metaverse: a new frontier for financial institutions. Int. J. Bank Market. 41(7), 1829–1846 (2023)

Ozkaynar, K.: Consumer behavior, marketing approach, branding, advertising, and new opportunities in the metaverse areas. In: Metaverse: Technologies, Opportunities and Threats, pp. 151–159. Springer (2023)

Pal, D., Arpnikanondt, C.: The sweet escape to metaverse: exploring escapism, anxiety, and virtual place attachment. Comput. Hum. Behav. 150, 107998 (2024)

Park, J., Kim, N.: Examining self-congruence between user and avatar in purchasing behavior from the metaverse to the real world. J. Glob. Fashion Market. 1–16 (2023)

Park, S.-M., Kim, Y.-G.: A metaverse: taxonomy, components, applications, and open challenges. IEEE Access 10, 4209–4251 (2022)

Petrigna, L., Musumeci, G.: The metaverse: a new challenge for the healthcare system: a scoping review. J. Funct. Morphol. Kinesiol. 7(3), 63 (2022)

Popescu, G.H., Valaskova, K., Horak, J.: Augmented reality shopping experiences, retail business analytics, and machine vision algorithms in the virtual economy of the metaverse. J. Self-Gov. Manag. Econ. 10(2), 67–81 (2022)

Rahman, M.: The Metaverse – What Does It Mean for Data Privacy and Information Security? (2022). https://www.jdsupra.com/legalnews/the-metaverse-what-does-it-mean-for-2751284/

Ramos, A.: The metaverse, NFTs and IP rights: to regulate or not to regulate? Intellectual property forum. J. Intellect. Indust. Property Soc. Australia New Zealand (2022)

Richter, S., Richter, A.: What is novel about the metaverse? Int. J. Inf. Manage. 73, 102684 (2023)

Rojas, E., Hülsmann, X., Estriegana, R., Rückert, F., Garcia-Esteban, S.: Students' perception of metaverses for online learning in higher education: hype or hope? Electronics 12(8), 1867 (2023)

Sahoo, D., Ray, S.: Metaverse in banking: an initiative for banking transformation from emerging country prospective. Acad. Market. Stud. J. 27(S4) (2023)

Sahoo, N., Gupta, D., Sen, K.: Metaverse: the pursuit to keep the human element intact in the media and entertainment industry. In: The Business of the Metaverse, pp. 156–167. Productivity Press (2023)

Said, G.R.E.: Metaverse-based learning opportunities and challenges: a phenomenological metaverse human-computer interaction study. Electronics 12(6), 1379 (2023)

Salloum, S., et al.: Sustainability model for the continuous intention to use metaverse technology in higher education: a case study from Oman. Sustainability 15(6), 5257 (2023)

Samarnggoon, K., Grudpan, S., Wongta, N., Klaynak, K.: Developing a virtual world for an open-house event: a metaverse approach. Future Internet **15**(4), 124 (2023)

Sharma, A., Sharma, L., Krezel, J.: Exploring the use of metaverse for collaborative learning in higher education: a scoping review. Int. Conf. Hum.-Comput. Interact. (2023)

Sihna, A., Raj, H., Das, R., Bandyopadhyay, A., Swain, S., Chakrborty, S.: Medical education system based on metaverse platform: a game theoretic approach. In: 2023 4th International Conference on Intelligent Engineering and Management (ICIEM) (2023)

Simbaqueba-Uribe, J., Alvarez-Risco, A., Del-Aguila-Arcentales, S., Rojas-Osorio, M., Mejia, C.R., Yañez, J.A.: Training courses by metaverse: intention of consumers in Colombia. Developm. Stud. Res. **11**(1), 2292474 (2024)

Sin, Z.P., et al.: Towards an edu-metaverse of knowledge: immersive exploration of university courses. IEEE Trans. Learn. Technol. (2023)

Siyaev, A., Jo, G.-S.: Towards aircraft maintenance metaverse using speech interactions with virtual objects in mixed reality. Sensors **21**(6), 2066 (2021)

Song, Y.-T., Qin, J.: Metaverse and personal healthcare. Procedia Comput. Sci. **210**, 189–197 (2022)

Suh, I., McKinney, T., Siu, K.-C.: Current Perspective of Metaverse Application in Medical Education, Research and Patient Care. Virtual Worlds (2023)

Suh, W., Ahn, S.: Utilizing the metaverse for learner-centered constructivist education in the post-pandemic era: an analysis of elementary school students. J. Intelligence **10**(1), 17 (2022)

Tan, T.F., et al.: Metaverse and virtual health care in ophthalmology: opportunities and challenges. Asia-Pacific J. Ophthalmol. **11**(3), 237–246 (2022)

Tlili, A., et al.: Is metaverse in education a blessing or a curse: a combined content and bibliometric analysis. Smart Learn. Environ. **9**(1), 1–31 (2022)

Trunfio, M., Rossi, S.: Advances in metaverse investigation: streams of research and future agenda. Virtual Worlds **1**(2), 103–129 (2022)

Tsai, S.-P.: Investigating metaverse marketing for travel and tourism. J. Vacat. Market. 13567667221145715 (2022)

Velev, D., Dimitrov, D., Zlateva, P.: Challenges of metaverse in education digitalization. In: Digitalization and Management Innovation II, pp. 43–51. IOS Press (2023)

Venkatesh, V., Thong, J.Y., Xu, X.: Consumer acceptance and use of information technology: extending the unified theory of acceptance and use of technology. MIS Quart. **36**(1), 157–178 (2012)

Villalonga-Gómez, C., Ortega-Fernández, E., Borau-Boira, E.: Fifteen years of metaverse in higher education: a systematic literature review. IEEE Trans. Learn. Technol. **16**(6), 1057–1070 (2023)

Wang, G., et al.: Development of metaverse for intelligent healthcare. Nat. Mach. Intell. **4**(11), 922–929 (2022)

Wang, G., Shin, C.: Influencing factors of usage intention of metaverse education application platform: empirical evidence based on PPM and TAM models. Sustainability **14**(24), 17037 (2022)

Wang, Y., et al.: A survey on metaverse: fundamentals, security, and privacy. IEEE Commun. Surv. Tutor. (2022)

Wei, Z., Yuan, M.: Research on the current situation and future development trend of immersive virtual reality in the field of education. Sustainability **15**(9), 7531 (2023)

Wiangkham, A., Vongvit, R.: Exploring the Drivers for the Adoption of Metaverse Technology in Engineering Education using PLS-SEM and ANFIS. Educ. Inf. Technol. 1–28 (2023)

Wu, T., Hao, F.: Edu-metaverse: concept, architecture, and applications. Interact. Learn. Environ. 1–28 (2023)

Wylde, V., Prakash, E., Hewage, C., Platts, J.: Post-covid-19 metaverse cybersecurity and data privacy: present and future challenges. In: Data Protection in a Post-Pandemic Society: Laws, Regulations, Best Practices and Recent Solutions, pp. 1–48. Springer (2023)

Xu, M., et al.: A full dive into realizing the edge-enabled metaverse: visions, enabling technologies, and challenges. IEEE Commun. Surv. Tutor. **25**(1), 656–700 (2022)

Yang, F.X., Wang, Y.: Rethinking metaverse tourism: a taxonomy and an agenda for future research. J. Hosp. Tourism Res. 10963480231163509 (2023)

Yao, X., Ma, N., Zhang, J., Wang, K., Yang, E., Faccio, M.: Enhancing wisdom manufacturing as industrial metaverse for industry and society 5.0. J. Intell. Manuf. 1–21 (2022)

Yaqoob, I., Salah, K., Jayaraman, R., Omar, M.: Metaverse applications in smart cities: enabling technologies, opportunities, challenges, and future directions. Internet Things **23**, 100884 (2023)

Yilmaz, M., O'farrell, E., Clarke, P.: Examining the training and education potential of the metaverse: results from an empirical study of next generation SAFe training. J. Softw. Evolut. Process e2531 (2023)

Yoo, J.: A study on transaction service of virtual real estate based on metaverse. J. Inst. Internet Broadcast. Commun. **22**(2), 83–88 (2022)

Zainurin, M.Z.L., Haji Masri, M., Besar, M.H.A., Anshari, M.: Towards an understanding of metaverse banking: a conceptual paper. J. Financ. Report. Account. **21**(1), 178–190 (2023)

Zhang, K., Shao, Z., Lu, Y., Yu, Y., Sun, W., Wang, Z.: Introducing massive open metaverse course (MOMC) and its enabling technology. IEEE Trans. Learn. Technol. **16**(6), 1154 (2023)

Zhang, X., Chen, Y., Hu, L., Wang, Y.: The metaverse in education: definition, framework, features, potential applications, challenges, and future research topics. Front. Psychol. **13**, 6063 (2022)

Zyda, M.: Let's rename everything "the metaverse!" Computer **55**(3), 124–129 (2022)

Amplifying Language Learning Effects with Olfactory-Enhanced Virtual Reality: An Empirical Study

Lei Xia[1] , Yulong Qin[2]([⊠]) , and Jixiang Fan[3]

[1] College of Design and Innovation, Tongji University, Shanghai, China
2210908@tongji.edu.cn
[2] School of Design, Shanghai Jiaotong University, Shanghai, China
Yulongqin86@gmail.com
[3] Department of Computer Science, Virginia Tech, Blacksburg, VA 24061, USA
jfan12@vt.edu

Abstract. Language learning, intrinsic to human cognitive development, has historically been rooted in conventional methodologies. Nevertheless, the technological renaissance introduces novel avenues, with Virtual Reality (VR) standing out as a revolutionary medium for immersive linguistic experiences. However, the expansive sensory potential of VR, significantly beyond visual and auditory stimuli, still needs to be explored. This research breaks new ground by integrating the olfactory dimension into VR-based language learning, centering on German vocabulary acquisition. The study embarks on a journey to unveil the latent potential of olfactory-enhanced VR in language pedagogy, offering insights into the cognitive intricacies of learners. Recognizing the profound influence of multisensory experiences on retention, the research introduces a novel categorization of learning methodologies: conventional learning, traditional VR, and VR + Olfactory. Each modality's distinct attributes are meticulously detailed, reflecting the diverse use case of learners. The research's paramount contribution lies in its pioneering approach to multisensory learning. By championing the olfactory dimension, it underscores the need for holistic learning experiences that cater to all human senses. Furthermore, the study sets a precedent for future research, advocating for the seamless integration of technology and pedagogy. This research work confronts established paradigms in language learning and sheds light on future advancements at the intersection of education and human-computer interaction, particularly focusing on the integration of olfactory interfaces.

Keywords: Virtual Reality (VR) · Olfactory Interface · Language Learning · Technology in Education

1 Introduction

Language acquisition, a pivotal aspect of human cognitive evolution, has traditionally relied on conventional pedagogical methods. The emergence of Vir-

P. Zaphiris and A. Ioannou (Eds.): HCII 2024, LNCS 14724, pp. 190–204, 2024.
https://doi.org/10.1007/978-3-031-61691-4_13

tual Reality (VR) technology, however, is revolutionizing educational paradigms, particularly in language learning. VR offers an immersive and interactive platform, significantly enriching the learning experience by simulating realistic environments and scenarios [1]. This technological advancement allows learners to engage with languages in contexts that closely mirror real-life situations, thereby enhancing comprehension and retention of linguistic nuances and fostering a deeper understanding of the language. While VR's impact on language learning is increasingly recognized, this study seeks to extend its application by integrating an often-overlooked sensory dimension: olfactory. The olfactory sense, intrinsically linked to memory and emotional responses, presents a novel avenue to augment language acquisition. This paper hypothesizes that incorporating scent cues into VR environments can lead to more holistic, multisensory engagement, thereby enhancing vocabulary retention and accelerating language proficiency [2]. This paper aims to provide a novel perspective on language learning by merging cutting-edge VR technology with the sensory experience of smell, potentially reshaping educational practices and offering deeper insights into the multisensory nature of language acquisition [3].

The main purposes of this study are threefold:

(1) We want to examine whether the combination of VR and olfactory stimulation leads to superior language learning outcomes compared to traditional methods.
(2) We try to explore the significance of multisensory teaching approaches in enhancing memory retention and overall learning effectiveness.
(3) We hope to offer practical case studies and actionable recommendations for designing and developing future multisensory education models.

The paper is structured as follows: First, we provide a comprehensive review of existing literature on multisensory learning and the role of VR in language education. Next, we delve into the theoretical underpinnings of olfactory learning and its potential synergies with VR-based language acquisition. Subsequent to this introductory phase, we proceed to elucidate the conceptualization and execution of our experimental study, which ingeniously integrates the realms of Virtual Reality (VR) and olfactory stimuli, thereby offering a novel and innovative dimension to the domain of language acquisition and learning. Finally, we discuss the implications of our findings for future educational models and propose recommendations for integrating multisensory elements into language learning curricula.

2   Literature Review

Virtual Reality in Language Learning. Virtual Reality (VR) technology has emerged as a transformative tool in the realm of language learning, offering unparalleled opportunities for immersive learning experiences. This technology stands out for its ability to create simulated environments that closely mimic real-world contexts, thus providing learners with authentic language use scenarios [4]. Such immersive simulations are instrumental in fostering a sense of presence, a psychological state where the learner feels 'transported' into the virtual environment, facilitating deeper engagement with the language learning process [5]. One of the critical advantages of VR in language education is its capacity to facilitate interaction with native speakers within these simulated environments. This interaction is not merely limited to verbal communication but also extends to non-verbal cues like gestures and facial expressions, which are integral components of effective language learning. Such interactions in a VR setting provide learners with a safe, controlled environment to practice and hone their language skills without the fear of real-world repercussions, thereby enhancing learner motivation and reducing anxiety associated with language acquisition [6]. The multisensory nature of VR environments plays a pivotal role in stimulating cognitive processes essential for language learning. VR's ability to engage multiple senses simultaneously – sight, sound, and sometimes touch – ensures a more holistic learning experience. This multisensory engagement is known to aid in attention retention, enhance memory recall, and bolster problem-solving skills, all of which are critical in acquiring a new language [7]. Empirical research in the field of language education has begun to underscore the effectiveness of VR technology. Studies have demonstrated notable improvements in various language competencies among learners using VR, including vocabulary acquisition, listening comprehension, and speaking skills. VR's interactive and immersive nature appears to facilitate better retention of new vocabulary as opposed to traditional rote memorization methods. Similarly, listening comprehension is enhanced as learners are exposed to authentic language usage in contextually rich settings, which traditional audio-only methods may not provide. As for speaking skills, the simulated immersive environments offer a conducive platform for practicing spoken language in a variety of contexts, ranging from everyday conversations to more formal scenarios [8]. Virtual Reality represents a significant advancement in language education, offering an immersive, interactive, and multisensory learning experience. Its capacity to simulate real-world contexts and foster genuine interactions with native speakers establishes a new paradigm in language acquisition. As the technology continues to evolve and become more accessible, it is poised to play an increasingly vital role in language education, offering promising avenues for research and practice in this field.

Olfactory Stimuli in Learning. The olfactory system's profound influence on learning and memory has been a subject of increasing interest in educational research. Olfactory stimuli are unique in their ability to evoke emotional responses and directly impact cognitive functions such as attention and memory consolidation. A growing body of empirical evidence suggests that exposure to certain scents, including lavender, peppermint, and cinnamon, can significantly enhance cognitive performance, reduce stress levels, and improve mood in learning environments [9]. These findings point towards the potential of integrating olfactory interfaces in educational settings, particularly as a means to aid memory encoding and retrieval. The presence of specific scents can provide sensory cues that strengthen the associations between the learned material and its contextual elements, thereby enhancing the learning experience. However, despite these advancements in understanding the role of olfactory stimuli in learning, there remains a substantial gap in their integration within Virtual Reality (VR)-based language learning environments. Present research in the field of VR for education has primarily concentrated on visual and auditory modalities. There is a conspicuous lack of exploration into how olfactory cues can be effectively synergized with VR technologies to augment language learning experiences [10]. This oversight represents a significant opportunity for future research, particularly in investigating how multisensory experiences – combining VR and olfactory stimuli – can lead to more effective and engaging language learning environments [11]. The integration of olfactory stimuli in VR-based language learning could revolutionize the way languages are taught and learned. The multi-modal sensory engagement could potentially enhance memory retention and facilitate deeper language proficiency. This approach could mimic real-life experiences more closely by incorporating the sense of smell, which is a critical element of human perception and memory. The challenge lies in identifying the most effective ways to integrate these olfactory cues within VR environments without overwhelming the learner or detracting from the educational content. To fully understand the impact of this integration, rigorous empirical research is needed. Such research should aim to investigate the specific effects of various scents on language learning processes in VR environments, explore the optimal balance between olfactory and other sensory inputs, and assess the long-term benefits on language retention and proficiency. Furthermore, this research could expand into examining the differential impacts of various scents on diverse language learning tasks, such as vocabulary acquisition, grammar comprehension, and conversational fluency. The potential for integrating olfactory stimuli in VR-based language learning environments opens up new frontiers in educational technology. It presents a novel approach to creating comprehensive multisensory educational models that could significantly enhance the effectiveness of language learning. Future research in this area not only promises to deepen our understanding of multisensory learning processes but also holds the potential to transform language education practices.

Challenges of Cutting-Edge Technology in Education. The integration of cutting-edge technology in education, such as Virtual Reality (VR) and olfactory interfaces, presents a set of complex challenges. Technical complexity and integration issues are at the forefront, requiring significant investment in resources, time, and training for effective implementation [12]. Additionally, the high cost of these technologies raises concerns about accessibility and equity, potentially widening the digital divide in educational settings [13]. Cognitive overload and distraction are also notable challenges, as the immersive and multisensory nature of these technologies might overwhelm learners or divert attention from educational content [14]. Pedagogical integration poses another hurdle, demanding educators to adeptly incorporate these tools into curricula without overshadowing traditional learning methods [15]. Furthermore, there is a pressing need for more empirical research to validate the effectiveness of these technologies in educational outcomes, ensuring that the investment in these advanced tools yields tangible benefits in learning.

Identifying the Gap. The literature reviews above highlight a significant gap in the integration and utilization of multisensory technologies, particularly Virtual Reality (VR) and olfactory stimuli, in educational settings. Despite the recognized potential of these technologies to enhance learning experiences, their application remains largely confined to visual and auditory modalities, with a notable underutilization of olfactory cues in VR-based learning environments. This gap suggests a substantial opportunity for research and development in creating more immersive and effective educational tools that leverage the full spectrum of sensory engagement [16]. Additionally, challenges such as technical complexity, accessibility, cognitive overload, and the need for pedagogical integration underscore the necessity for comprehensive strategies to effectively incorporate these advanced technologies in educational contexts [17]. Addressing these issues is crucial for the development of holistic and inclusive educational models that harness the benefits of multisensory learning experiences. The gap also indicates a need for further empirical research to assess the impact of integrating multisensory technologies on educational outcomes, ensuring that their adoption contributes meaningfully to enhancing student learning and proficiency [18].

3   Research Hypotheses

This study presents two hypotheses regarding language acquisition through Virtual Reality (VR) and olfactory integration:

Hypothesis 1 (H1): The integration of olfactory stimuli with VR is hypothesized to enhance word retention more effectively than VR alone. This hypothesis suggests that learners in VR environments with olfactory cues will show higher retention rates and less word loss compared to those using only VR.

Hypothesis 2 (H2): VR-based language learning is expected to surpass traditional non-VR methods in memory retention. This is based on the immersive and interactive qualities of VR, which are anticipated to facilitate better language retention.

4   Methodology and Experimental Design

Participant Selection and Grouping. In the study investigating the impact of multisensory technologies on language acquisition, all participants underwent a preliminary assessment to ascertain their baseline knowledge, specifically their unfamiliarity with the German vocabulary intended for the study. This initial

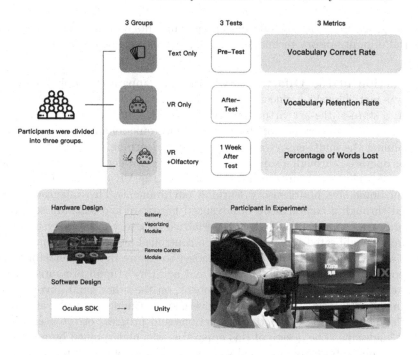

Fig. 1. Olfactory System Design & Test Design

evaluation was crucial to ensure that any observed learning outcomes could be attributed to the intervention rather than prior knowledge. To guarantee a comprehensive representation of diverse learning backgrounds and cognitive styles, the participant cohort was deliberately diversified. This diversity encompassed various demographic factors, including age, gender, majors in university, and prior exposure to language learning methodologies. Such a stratified approach was instrumental in enhancing the generalizability of the study findings across a broader population. Following the initial assessment, participants were systematically stratified into three distinct groups: a traditional learning group, a VR learning group, and a VR + Olfactory learning group. The traditional learning group served as a control, engaging in conventional language learning methods without the aid of advanced technological tools. The VR learning group was exposed to language learning in a fully immersive virtual environment, leveraging the visual and auditory capabilities of VR technology. The VR + Olfactory group, however, experienced an augmented version of this environment, where olfactory cues were integrated into the VR experience, aiming to investigate the additive effects of multisensory inputs on language acquisition. This stratification was designed to meticulously evaluate the differential impacts of these varied learning environments. By comparing the outcomes across these groups, the study aimed to isolate the specific contributions of VR and olfactory stimuli to language learning, thereby offering valuable insights into the effectiveness and potential of multisensory technologies in educational settings (Fig. 1).

Introduction of the Olfactory System. The apparatus employed in this study was meticulously engineered to seamlessly interface with the Meta Oculus headset, a state-of-the-art virtual reality device. This integration was pivotal in facilitating the incorporation of olfactory interface functionalities, a key element in examining the multisensory aspect of language learning. The olfactory interface was operated through a sophisticated remote controller, which was designed to release specific scents in synchronization with the VR content, thereby creating an immersive multisensory learning environment. This integration was achieved through a combination of advanced hardware and software solutions. The hardware component included a specialized olfactory delivery system that was carefully calibrated to emit scents in a controlled and precise manner. This system was synchronized with the VR headset to ensure that the olfactory cues corresponded accurately with the visual and auditory stimuli presented in the virtual environment. The software component, on the other hand, involved the development of custom algorithms that governed the timing, intensity, and duration of scent release based on the interactions and progress of the user within the VR landscape. The design of this apparatus was underpinned by a rigorous understanding of both the technical aspects of VR and olfactory technology, as well as the pedagogical principles guiding their application in an educational context. The aim was to create a seamless and intuitive user experience, where the integration of olfactory stimuli would enhance, rather than complicate, the language learning process. The sophisticated engineering of this apparatus represents a significant advancement in the field of educational technology, offering a novel approach to creating engaging and effective learning experiences through the integration of multisensory stimuli.

Test Procedure. The participant pool for this experiment comprised 40 college students, aged between 21 and 28 years. This age range was chosen to represent a demographic typically engaged in higher education and likely to be receptive to innovative learning methodologies. These participants were randomly assigned to one of three groups to ensure a balanced distribution across different learning modalities. Each group experienced a distinct approach to language learning: text-only, Virtual Reality (VR) with olfactory cues (VR+Olfactory), and VR without olfactory cues (VR Only). Random assignment was critical in minimizing pre-existing biases and variations among participants, thereby enhancing the validity of the study results.

The test design of this research was structured as a three-stage experimental process: a pre-test, an immediate post-test, and a one-week follow-up test. This design was meticulously planned to evaluate both the immediate and sustained impacts of the different learning modalities on language acquisition.

Pre-Test: Conducted at the outset, this test aimed to assess the participants' baseline knowledge of the German vocabulary used in the study. Participants

Classroom in VR made in Unity

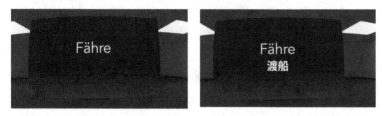

1st Step: 10s German Words   2nd Step: 10s Chinese Meaning

Fig. 2. Classroom Environment in VR

were asked to guess the meanings of specific German words, providing a clear measure of their initial familiarity with the language material.

Learning Session: Subsequent to the pre-test, participants partook in a structured learning session employing their designated methodologies. Each German word was presented for a duration of 20 s, a temporal interval chosen to maximize memory retention while avoiding cognitive overload. The German word was initially displayed for 10 s, followed by the presentation of its corresponding Chinese meaning at the bottom for an additional 10 s (Fig. 2).

Immediate Post-Test: This test was administered immediately after the learning session to evaluate the short-term learning outcomes. It aimed to assess the immediate effectiveness of each learning modality in facilitating vocabulary acquisition.

One-Week Follow-Up Test: Conducted one week after the immediate post-test, this stage was crucial in assessing the long-term retention of the learned vocabulary. This follow-up test provided valuable insights into the enduring impact of each learning modality on memory retention.

In all testing stages, the order of the German words was kept constant to ensure consistency and fairness in testing conditions. Participants completed the tests without any time constraints, allowing for an accurate assessment of their learning outcomes. The tests were designed to evaluate various metrics such as the correct rate of responses, retention rate of the learned words, and the percentage of word loss, across the different learning modalities. This comprehensive testing approach was instrumental in providing a holistic understanding of the effectiveness of each learning modality in enhancing language acquisition (Fig. 3).

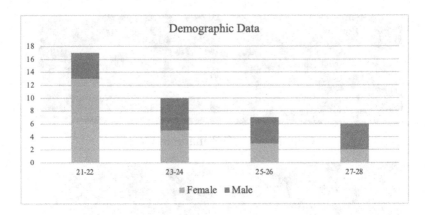

Fig. 3. Demographic Data

5   Results, Findings and Discussion

In the present analysis, we scrutinize the outcomes of our experimental study, as delineated in Fig. 4, meticulously examining each phase to ascertain the efficacy of different learning modalities on vocabulary retention. The empirical data from the Immediate and Delayed Post-Tests shed light on the retention dynamics across the traditional, VR, and VR+Olfactory groups, with a particular emphasis on the retention capabilities fostered by the multisensory VR+Olfactory experience.

Pre-Test Scores: Participants across all experimental groups exhibited notably low scores on the pre-test assessment. With Text-only group (M = 0.25, SD = 0.55), VR (M = 0, SD = 0) and VR+Olfactory (M = 0, SD = 0) groups score low on the test indicating a limited pre-existing acquaintance with the words under investigation before the initiation of the experiment.

Immediate Post-Test Observations: The findings from the Immediate Post-Test are intriguing. The traditional text-only approach (M = 13.46, SD = 5.11) yielded the similar high immediate recall scores compared to VR (M = 13.77, SD = 5.01) and VR+Olfactory (M = 13.62, SD = 5.03), indicating a robust initial grasp of vocabulary. However, the substantial standard deviation observed within this cohort signals a wide disparity in individual participant outcomes, suggesting that while some learners thrived with the text-only method, others found it less conducive to immediate retention.

Delayed Post-Test Insights: The Delayed Post-Test, conducted one week subsequent to the learning session, revealed a compelling trend: the performances of the VR (M = 8.54, SD = 2.62) and VR+Olfactory (M = 9.15, SD = 3.35) groups converged, with both groups displaying similar rates of correct responses. This convergence might imply that the addition of olfactory cues does not significantly enhance immediate recall but may influence long-term retention. Conversely, the traditional learning group (M = 6.54, SD = 4.48) exhibited a marked decrement in performance, indicating a potential erosion of the initial learning advantage over time as shown in Fig. 4.

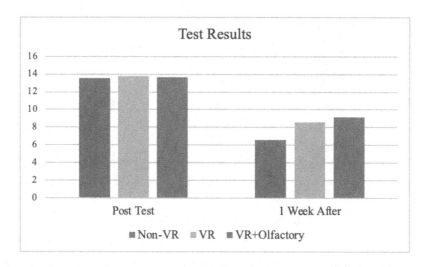

Fig. 4. Test Results

Retention Rate Analysis: A more nuanced analysis of retention, juxtaposing the Immediate with the Delayed Post-Test results, intimates a superior retention rate within the VR+Olfactory group. This assertion is bolstered by the relatively diminished word loss percentage in this group compared to their counterparts. Such an observation posits that the integration of olfactory stimuli within VR learning environments may fortify the retention of linguistic material over extended periods. In Table 1, it is evident that the VR+Olfactory group demonstrated the lowest percentage of word loss, thereby indicating the highest degree of word retention one week following the experimental procedure, as illustrated in Fig. 5.

Table 1. Percentage of Words Lost

	Non-VR	VR	VR+Olfactory
Percentage of Words Lost	0.52	0.38	0.33

The constellation of data harvested from this study calls into question the long-held tenets of traditional learning paradigms, particularly when juxtaposed with the accumulating body of evidence favoring multisensory learning environments. Traditional text-centric pedagogies, while not deficient in facilitating immediate recall, appear to pale in comparison when it comes to the sustainability of knowledge retention over time. The conjunction of Virtual Reality (VR)

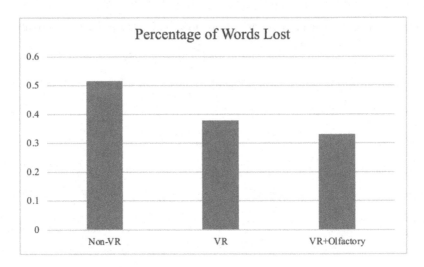

Fig. 5. Percentage of Words Lost

with olfactory cues has emerged as a crucial element in bolstering the consolidation and longevity of memory. This is not a trivial enhancement but a fundamental shift in the cognitive engagement with educational material, implicating the olfactory sense as an anchor for recollection [9]. The observed diminution in recall ability within the VR Only group is particularly telling, underscoring the significance of a multimodal sensory strategy in learning environments. It appears that the solitary reliance on visual and auditory stimuli within VR, though initially engaging, may not suffice for the deeper encoding of information necessary for long-term retention [19].

In contrast, the integration of olfactory stimuli may serve as a potent mnemonic device, effectively cementing the learned material in the learner's memory through the unique and direct connections the olfactory system has with the brain's limbic system, a nexus crucial for memory and learning [20]. The implications of these findings are profound, suggesting that the immersive VR learning experiences, when augmented with olfactory cues, could substantially surpass traditional learning methods in long-term educational outcomes. Such a multisensory approach could revolutionize the pedagogical strategies employed across educational sectors [21]. Additionally, the evidence supports the cognitive theory of multimedia learning, suggesting that learning is optimized when complementary sensory modalities are engaged, allowing for more substantial cognitive processing [22].

Building upon these insights, the future inclusion of kinesthetic elements alongside olfactory stimulation within VR environments heralds a new frontier for language learning, where the embodiment and physicality of interaction are just as crucial as the sensory inputs [23]. Kinesthetic learning, or tactile engagement, involves the use of muscle memory to reinforce cognitive tasks, such as writing or speaking a new language [24]. When merged with the evocative power of scent and the immersive visual and auditory stimuli of VR, the learning experience becomes deeply immersive and multi-dimensional [11]. This synergy of sensory and motor inputs could harness the full spectrum of neuroscience interventions, aligning with the principles of embodied cognition which posit that learning is more profound when it engages the whole body [25].

The potential benefits for language acquisition are substantial. By engaging multiple senses and motor responses, learners can experience a more holistic grasp of the language context, including cultural nuances and situational appropriateness [26]. This multimodal approach could facilitate not just the memorization of vocabulary, but also the intuitive understanding of syntax, grammar, and usage. The enriched sensory environment of VR, combined with kinesthetic and olfactory cues, could emulate real-life experiences, allowing learners to practice language skills in simulated scenarios that feel authentic, thereby enhancing both acquisition and retention [27]. Future research in this domain could very well redefine the landscape of language education, transforming how we understand and facilitate the learning process in an increasingly digital world.

6   Conclusion

This investigation has shed light on the considerable promise held by the integration of olfactory cues with Virtual Reality (VR) for the advancement of language learning among college-aged individuals. The evidence amassed calls for an essential reevaluation of entrenched educational paradigms, particularly in the wake of a growing body of evidence that endorses multisensory learning environments. Our findings suggest that while traditional text-based instruction may suffice for immediate vocabulary recall, the assimilation of olfactory stimuli within a VR framework profoundly amplifies long-term memory retention.

The research demonstrates that VR environments enriched with olfactory cues offer a more robust framework for memory consolidation than those utilizing solely visual and auditory stimuli. The observed decline in the VR-only group's performance accentuates the importance of integrating multiple sensory inputs to bolster the effectiveness of virtual learning platforms.

As the trajectory of educational technology arcs towards the future, it is clear that an experiential learning model, marked by multisensory engagement, is indispensable. This study champions educational strategies that extend beyond traditional auditory and visual stimuli, advocating for a more immersive and comprehensive approach to learning that includes the olfactory dimension. The ramifications of these findings extend significantly, with the potential to redefine language education and influence the development of VR applications in diverse domains.

In advocating for ongoing progress in education, this paper underscores the necessity of expanding research into multisensory learning and applying such pedagogical models to a broader demographic. The confluence of VR and olfactory stimuli stands as a promising domain for future research, with the expectation that continued interdisciplinary study will reinforce and broaden the encouraging outcomes of this study. Through such pioneering educational research, we may enhance the sensory fabric of learning, offering more profound and efficacious educational experiences to learners across the globe.

The present study, therefore, signifies a preliminary step toward a future where language education is not confined to the visual and auditory realms but is enriched by the olfactory, providing a richer, more immersive learning experience. The path ahead is abundant with opportunities for inquiry and innovation in the field of multisensory VR-enhanced learning, inviting further scholarly engagement and creativity.

7   Limitation and Future Works

The research presented here is not without its limitations, which in turn lay the groundwork for future explorations. A significant challenge encountered was the stability and consistency of the olfactory stimuli. Participants reported variability in their perception of the smells, which suggests that the method of delivering the olfactory stimuli needs refinement to ensure a standardized experience across different users and sessions. Additionally, the correlation between thematic words and the corresponding olfactory stimuli faced obstacles, as personal and cultural differences led to divergent interpretations of how certain concepts, such as "the sea," should smell. This variability in olfactory perception highlights the subjective nature of smell and its associative memories.

Future work in this domain should prioritize the development of consistent olfactory stimuli, focusing on the design and engineering perspectives to create more reliable scent delivery mechanisms. This could involve the advancement of technology to control the intensity and duration of scent release, or the development of standardized scent profiles for commonly referenced themes. Moreover, addressing these challenges is of significant consequence, as the relationship between olfactory stimuli and word memory has far-reaching implications, particularly in the realm of language learning. Enhancing the consistency of olfactory cues could greatly benefit educational strategies, leveraging the potent mnemonic influence of smell to reinforce memory retention and recall in language acquisition. The work of Hubbard et al. in 2017 on enhancing learning through virtual reality and neurofeedback provides insights into how these technologies can be integrated for educational purposes [28]. Additionally, Bouzid et al. in 2015 discuss the design of educational technology for specific learning needs, which can be relevant for incorporating olfactory elements into language learning tools [29]. Thus, while the current research provides valuable insights, it also paves the way for transformative advancements in the integration of olfactory elements into cognitive and educational tools.

References

1. Kalunga, R., Elshobosky, F.: Using immersive technologies to enhance student learning outcomes in clinical sciences education and training (2023). https://doi.org/10.36315/2023v2end123

2. Shukla, T., Duthade, A., Deshbhratar, N.: Improving kids English vocabulary through immersive mobile games (2023). https://doi.org/10.55041/ijsrem26473
3. Herdiawan, R.D., Afrianto, A., Nurhidayat, E., Nurhidayah, Y., Rofi'i, A.: Folklore-based virtual reality as a teaching media in the secondary school viewed from its implication and multimodal aspects (2023). https://doi.org/10.21009/ijlecr.v9i1.37646
4. Colibaba, A., Gheorghiu, I., Ursa, O., Croitoru, I., Antoniță, C., Colibaba, A.: The VR@School project: redefining the teaching/learning process (2019). https://doi.org/10.21125/EDULEARN.2019.0583
5. Deng, X., Yu, Z.: A systematic review on the influence of virtual reality on language learning outcomes (2022). https://doi.org/10.4018/ijopcd.302083
6. Cai, Y.: A review of virtual reality technology in EFL teaching (2022). https://doi.org/10.54097/ehss.v4i.2783
7. Rudnik, Y.: The use of augmented reality and virtual reality technologies in teaching foreign languages (2023)
8. Lin, V., Barrett, N., Liu, G.Z., Chen, N.S., Jong, M.: Supporting dyadic learning of English for tourism purposes with scenery-based virtual reality (2021). https://doi.org/10.1080/09588221.2021.1954663
9. Andonova, V., Reinoso-Carvalho, F., Jimenez Ramirez, M.A., Carrasquilla, D.: Does multisensory stimulation with virtual reality (VR) and smell improve learning? An educational experience in recall and creativity (2023). https://doi.org/10.3389/fpsyg.2023.1176697
10. Kaimal, G., Carroll-Haskins, K., Ramakrishnan, A., Magsamen, S.H., Arslanbek, A., Herres, J.: Outcomes of visual self-expression in virtual reality on psychosocial well-being with the inclusion of a fragrance stimulus: a pilot mixed-methods study (2020). https://doi.org/10.3389/fpsyg.2020.589461
11. Repetto, C.: The use of virtual reality for language investigation and learning (2014). https://doi.org/10.3389/fpsyg.2014.01280
12. Carpenter, R.E., McWhorter, R.R., Stone, K., Coyne, L.: Adopting virtual reality for education: exploring teachers' perspectives on readiness, opportunities, and challenges (2023). https://doi.org/10.5121/ijite.2023.12303
13. Soliman, M., Pesyridis, A., Dalaymani-Zad, D., Gronfula, M., Kourmpetis, M.: The application of virtual reality in engineering education (2021). https://doi.org/10.3390/APP11062879
14. Williams, J., Orooji, F., Aly, S.J.: Integration of Virtual Reality (VR) in architectural design education: exploring student experience (2019). https://doi.org/10.18260/1-2-32999
15. Alnagrat, A.J., Ismail, R.C., Idrus, S.Z.S.: The Opportunities and challenges in virtual reality for virtual laboratories (2023). https://doi.org/10.11113/itlj.v6.91
16. Ferrise, F., Dozio, N., Spadoni, E., Rossoni, M., Carulli, M., Bordegoni, M.: Adding a novel olfactory dimension to multisensory experience in virtual reality training (2023). https://doi.org/10.1115/detc2023-116561
17. Papanastasiou, G.P., Drigas, A., Skianis, C., Lytras, M.D., Papanastasiou, E.: Virtual and augmented reality effects on K-12, higher and tertiary education students' twenty-first century skills (2018). https://doi.org/10.1007/s10055-018-0363-2
18. Ferdig, R., Schottke, K., Rivera-Gutierrez, D.J., Lok, B.C.: Assessing past, present, and future interactions with virtual patients (2012). https://doi.org/10.4018/jgcms.2012070102
19. Dozio, N., Maggioni, E., Pittera, D., Gallace, A., Obrist, M.: May i smell your attention: exploration of smell and sound for visuospatial attention in virtual reality (2021). https://doi.org/10.3389/fpsyg.2021.671470

20. Covaci, A., Ghinea, G., Lin, C.H., Huang, S.H., Shih, J.L.: Multisensory games-based learning - lessons learnt from olfactory enhancement of a digital board game (2018). https://doi.org/10.1007/s11042-017-5459-2

21. Obregon, R., Hall, K.: Web based visualization: an innovative approach to providing technical instruction (2005). https://doi.org/10.18260/1-2-14280

22. Vázquez, C., Xia, L., Aikawa, T., Maes, P.: Words in motion: kinesthetic language learning in virtual reality, July 2018. https://doi.org/10.1109/ICALT.2018.00069

23. Autrey, M.: The Interaction of Cyberaggression and Self-Efficacy within the Virtual World and the Real World (n.d.)

24. Schildkrout, B., Niu, K., Cooper, J.J.: Clinical neuroscience continuing education for psychiatrists (2023). https://doi.org/10.1007/s40596-023-01776-8

25. Chun, D.M., Karimi, H., Sañosa, D.J.: Traveling by headset (2022). https://doi.org/10.1558/cj.21306

26. Li, H.: The effect of VR on learners' engagement and motivation in K12 English education (2023). https://doi.org/10.54097/ehss.v22i.12291

27. Fazio, A., Isidori, E.: Technology-enhanced learning and CLIL for physical education (2021). https://doi.org/10.12753/2066-026x-21-144

28. Hubbard, R.J., Sipolins, A., Zhou, L.: Enhancing learning through virtual reality and neurofeedback: a first step (2017). https://doi.org/10.1145/3027385.3027390

29. Bouzid, Y., Khenissi, M.A., Jemni, M.: Designing a game generator as an educational technology for the deaf learners (2015). https://doi.org/10.1109/ICTA.2015.7426914

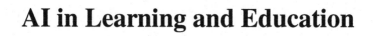

AI in Learning and Education

The Impact of ChatGPT on Students' Learning Programming Languages

Itzhak Aviv$^{(\boxtimes)}$, Moshe Leiba, Havana Rika, and Yogev Shani

The Academic College of Tel Aviv–Yaffo, Tel Aviv–Yaffo, Israel
itzhakav@mta.ac.il

Abstract. This study addresses the gap in understanding the impact of Chat-GPT, on Java programming language education. We examined ChatGPT's afinity on undergraduate Information Systems students learning Java through a mixed-methods approach. Quantitatively, we assessed constructs like ChatGPT Prompting Skills, Trust, Objective Values, and their relationship with student satisfaction, revealing mixed effectiveness. Qualitatively, we explored students' perspectives, uncovering insights into ChatGPT's role in coding support and the nuances of its educational impact. Our findings indicate that while ChatGPT can enhance certain aspects of learning, its effectiveness varies with context and task complexity. Key positive findings from the regression analysis indicated that ChatGPT's prompting skills positively impacted both Objective and Subjective Values, suggesting a significant role in enhancing students' understanding and engagement with programming concepts. This positive influence extends to the relationship between Subjective Value and Student Satisfaction, highlighting the importance of students' subjective experiences in their overall satisfaction with learning programming languages. The study contributes to the evolving discourse on AI in education, highlighting the need to integrate LLMs carefully in educational settings. It underscores the importance of aligning AI tools with specific learning objectives and outlines implications for educators and AI developers in optimizing these tools for educational purposes.

Keywords: ChatGPT · Large Language Models · LLM · software development

1 Introduction

Artificial Intelligence (AI) is oriented to comprehend, model, and replicate human Intelligence and cognitive processes into artificial systems. AI covers a wide range of subfields, such as machine learning, perception, natural language processing, knowledge representation and reasoning, and computer vision, among many others [1].

ChatGPT has gained popularity since its release in November 2022. This Artificial Intelligence (AI) Large Language Models (LLM) is designed to generate human-like text based on patterns found in massive amounts of data scraped from the internet. The increasing integration of AI and machine learning technologies in education has become an important issue [2]. LLM literacy can be defined as a set of skills that enable

© The Author(s), under exclusive license to Springer Nature Switzerland AG 2024
P. Zaphiris and A. Ioannou (Eds.): HCII 2024, LNCS 14724, pp. 207–219, 2024.
https://doi.org/10.1007/978-3-031-61691-4_14

effective use, such as prompt engineering. Furthermore, as an emerging educational goal, LLM literacy refers to understanding and interacting effectively with LMM systems in three aspects: learning about AI, learning how artificial intelligence works, and lifelong learning with artificial Intelligence [3, 4].

ChatGPT, a generative AI model, has demonstrated significant potential in aiding students' problem-solving, knowledge acquisition, and content generation, raising concerns such as cheating, misinformation, bias, abuse and misuse, and privacy and safety [5]. Prompting skills and trust in AI systems are critical factors influencing the effectiveness of AI-based educational tools [6]. Prompting training is a form of instruction designed to enhance the skills and trust in using AI tools, which holds promise in enhancing students' LLM literacy. Exposure to LMM technologies and prompting engineer skills are essential for improving students' LMM literacy and preparing them for the demands of the 21st-century job market [7].

Technology Acceptance Model (TAM) pinpoints technology adoption factors, while Information Systems Success Model (ISSM) evaluates information system successes [8, 9]. As we constructed in this research, the combined model of TAM and ISSM provides insights into LLM literacy and its impact on learning and education (see Fig. 1).

This research focuses on the intersection of AI and education, specifically examining the impact of ChatGPT on undergraduate students learning Java programming language. The importance of understanding how AI tools can be integrated into educational settings, particularly in disciplines like Information Systems, where programming is a core skill, cannot be overstated. The study employs a mixed-methods approach, combining quantitative assessments with qualitative insights, to provide a comprehensive evaluation of ChatGPT's role in the learning process. By focusing on Java programming, the research offers insights into how emerging technologies can augment traditional learning methodologies. The research revealed that ChatGPT's prompting skills positively impact Objective and Subjective Values, enhancing understanding and engagement with programming concepts. A significant correlation was found between Subjective Value and Student Satisfaction, highlighting the importance of students' subjective experiences in their learning satisfaction. Qualitatively, students' experiences with ChatGPT varied, providing insights into the practical application of such AI tools in education.

This study contributes to the growing body of knowledge on AI in education. It provides empirical evidence on the benefits and challenges of integrating AI tools like ChatGPT in learning environments. It offers valuable guidance for educators and AI developers in optimizing these tools for educational purposes. The findings underscore the necessity of aligning AI with specific learning objectives to enhance student learning experiences effectively.

2   Literature Review

2.1   Large Language Models in Education: Benefits and Concerns

Contemporary research elucidates several benefits of LLMs in the educational sector. One benefit is personalized learning, where LLMs custom-tailor learning materials and pedagogical approaches to individual learners augment student engagement and comprehension. This bespoke learning is enabled via adaptive learning platforms that exploit

LLMs to modulate difficulty levels, dispense targeted feedback, and devise individualized learning trajectories [10]. Moreover, LLMs significantly bolster language acquisition by providing instantaneous feedback on writing and grammar, enhancing vocabulary development, and facilitating conversational exercises in foreign languages [11].

Regarding operational efficiency, LLMs expedite routine tasks such as essay grading and feedback provision, freeing educators to concentrate more on bespoke instruction and student support [12]. They also facilitate accessibility by translating texts into myriad languages, vocalizing content for visually impaired learners, and offering varied formats for educational materials, thus democratizing education for a diverse learner population [2, 10]. Additionally, LLMs contribute to content generation, including quizzes, study guides, and interactive lessons, furnishing educators with supplementary resources to enrich their pedagogical repertoire [13].

Conversely, applying LLMs in educational contexts is not devoid of concerns and potential risks. A predominant issue is the potential for bias and unfairness, as LLMs trained on prejudiced data may perpetuate stereotypes or favor certain viewpoints, possibly leading to disparities in educational outcomes [14]. Excessive reliance on LLMs for educational purposes might also hinder the development critical analytical, problem-solving, and research skills. Hence, promoting a balanced use of technology and fostering independent learning habits is imperative [15].

The ease of text generation with LLMs introduces challenges concerning academic integrity, particularly plagiarism and academic dishonesty. Educators are thus compelled to devise strategies for detecting and mitigating the misuse of these tools [16]. Furthermore, LLMs' opacity and lack of explainability can impede educators' ability to assess student understanding and provide constructive feedback [15]. LLMs' limitations in handling complex or nuanced concepts and their lack of adaptability to unforeseen scenarios necessitate continual human oversight and intervention in the learning process [13].

2.2 Large Language Models Literacy During Software Development

Contemporary studies in software development, especially concerning Artificial Intelligence (AI) and emerging technologies, reveal a significant trend toward adopting the TAM. This adaptation incorporates critical elements such as perceived skills and trust, recognized as crucial in influencing technology adoption. A recent advancement in this area is the proposition of an extended TAM model, which integrates perceived skills and trust with factors like individual differences and the learning context. This model mainly focuses on determining the acceptance of learning applications [2].

Further research delves into the realm of AI-powered recommendation systems, examining the influence of perceived trust on user satisfaction and engagement. This study introduces a model that synergizes perceived trust with traditional TAM constructs, including perceived ease of use and usefulness, thereby offering a more holistic understanding of user interaction with AI technologies [17]. The intricate relationship between AI skills, the appropriateness of technology for specific tasks, and learning performance in AI-based learning tools is another focal point of recent research. This investigation underscores the necessity to tailor TAM to address the distinct characteristics of AI technologies, thereby providing a nuanced understanding of technology acceptance in

AI-based learning [18]. Additional study presents a framework that encapsulates perceived skills, trust, and other considerations such as perceived security and privacy to provide a more in-depth understanding of the factors influencing user acceptance of AI services, highlighting the multifaceted nature of technology adoption [19].

The adapted version of TAM posits two primary factors influencing technology adoption in the context of software development: 1) Perceived Skills, referring to the extent to which users believe they possess the necessary competencies to utilize technology effectively, and 2) Perceived Trust, indicating the degree to which users feel confident in the reliability and integrity of the technology in question. These factors are pivotal in shaping the development and acceptance of new software models, particularly those involving AI and LLM technologies.

2.3 Students Experience with Large Language Models During Software Development

Recent studies have introduced a modified version of ISSM, integrating perceived objective and subjective values derived from AI and LLMs. This adaptation seeks to encapsulate a holistic view of quantifiable benefits and experiential gains from user interactions with these systems. Investigations into LLM applications for automated feedback in education revealed how perceptions of the feedback's precision and utility (objective value) impact learning outcomes [12]. In language learning, research focused on how LLMs enhance vocabulary acquisition and writing skills, with findings indicating that user perceptions of these improvements are crucial for overall system satisfaction [20]. Additionally, studies have explored LLMs' role in providing socioemotional support to students, noting that perceptions of reduced stress and increased confidence lead to heightened knowledge of the system [14]. The significance of building trust in LLMs within educational settings has also been emphasized, suggesting that such trust contributes to both objective and subjective values experienced by users [13]. Furthermore, a recent study has studied how users' acceptance and use of LLMs are influenced by their skills in system prompting and perceptions of the system's effectiveness and efficiency [15].

These collective research efforts highlight the value of adapting the ISSM to the distinctive context of AI and LLM systems. Emphasizing perceived objective and subjective values offers a more comprehensive understanding of user experiences and benefits from these technologies. Focusing on system efficiency, skill enhancement, error detection, desired output generation, and interaction length aligns well with this approach. These elements are potential metrics for assessing perceived objective and subjective values in software development tasks. They provide insights into how LLM systems can be optimally designed and deployed to maximize their beneficial impact on users' experiences and outcomes.

3   Research Model and Hypothesis Development

Scholarly works have explicitly referenced the application of TAM and ISSM constructs in their analyses of Large Language Models (LLMs). For instance, Tsai [21] correlates prompting skills with TAM's fundamental constructs of perceived ease of use and perceived usefulness. Similarly, recent study establishes a link between user trust in LLMs and TAM's perceived usefulness and ISSM's system quality metrics [14]. Further research delves into how elements like explainability, transparency, and trust in AI systems bear upon user acceptance and their perceived efficacy, employing TAM and ISSM frameworks in their analysis [14, 22]. Moreover, other research assesses the influence of social interaction capabilities, content sharing, and community building on user satisfaction and engagement in AI-based platforms [23]. While some studies do not directly cite TAM or ISSM, they explore concepts intimately associated with these models. For example, Bubaš [24] investigates the impact of prompting skills on user satisfaction, an aspect that resonates with the user satisfaction construct of ISSM.

Although research explicitly addressing the interplay of LLM prompting skills and user trust within the TAM and ISSM frameworks is in a nascent stage, several studies offer insightful perspectives on the relationships between these variables. These studies posit that prompting skills and user trust are instrumental in shaping users' acceptance, experiences, and satisfaction with LLMs, echoing the foundational principles of TAM and ISSM. In identifying the research gap, our study integrates adapted versions of TAM and ISSM to examine the nexus between ChatGPT literacy, students' experiences in learning Java, and their satisfaction, focusing on the role of prompting skills as a pivotal factor. The conceptual framework is presented in Fig. 1.

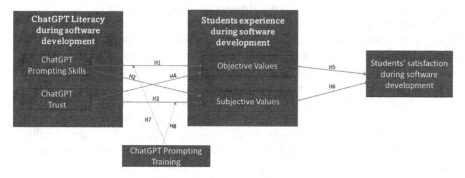

Fig. 1. The conceptual framework

Eight hypotheses were formulated for this study, each grounded in relevant literature:

H1: Impact of ChatGPT Prompting Skills on Objective Values

Hypothesis 1 posits that ChatGPT Prompting Skills positively affect the objective values of students' experiences in software development. This hypothesis is supported by Prather [25], who observed enhanced learning outcomes with LLMs in programming education compared to traditional methods. Additionally, Hou [23] suggests that the automation capabilities of LLMs, such as code review, lead to improved objective learning outcomes through more personalized feedback and guidance.

H2: Impact of ChatGPT Prompting Skills on Subjective Values

Hypothesis 2 suggests that ChatGPT Prompting Skills positively affect the subjective values of students' experiences in software development. This hypothesis is based on findings by Essel [27], who found that LLMs in language learning enhanced students' confidence and enjoyment. Carlsson [28] reported improvements in students' self-efficacy and perceived learning gains due to real-time feedback provided by LLMs.

H3: Influence of Trust in ChatGPT on Subjective Values

Hypothesis 3 posits that trust in ChatGPT positively affects the subjective values of a student's experience in software development. This hypothesis is informed by Huang [14], who found that trust in AI tutors positively influences emotional engagement and learning outcomes. Chan [13] also underscores the significance of user trust in AI educational tools for fostering positive perceptions and engagement.

H4: Influence of Trust in ChatGPT on Objective Values.

Hypothesis 4 proposes that trust in ChatGPT positively affects the objective values of a student's experience in software development. Supporting this hypothesis, Darvishi [12] suggests that trust in AI-powered feedback systems can lead to higher motivation and adherence to feedback, potentially enhancing performance.

H5 & H6: Effect of Perceived Values on Student Satisfaction

Hypothesis 5 and Hypothesis 6 assert that perceived objective and subjective values positively affect students' satisfaction with ChatGPT in software development. This notion is backed by recent studies, who identified a positive correlation between students' perceived learning gains and their satisfaction with AI tools in language learning [29, 30].

H7: Moderating Role of Prompting Training on Objective Values

Hypothesis 7 posits that Prompting Training positively moderates the impacts of ChatGPT prompting skills on students' software development experience objective values. Bernabei [15] suggests that training in effective prompting strategies enhances LLMs' effectiveness in learning support. Huang [14] also indicates that guidance on interacting with AI systems can improve learning outcomes.

H8: Moderating Role of Prompting Training on Subjective Values

Hypothesis 8 suggests that Prompting Training positively moderates the impacts of ChatGPT trust on students' software development experience subjective values. Although research in this area is limited, Ciampa [16] highlights the importance of developing critical thinking skills alongside trust in LLMs to avoid overreliance.

4   Research Method

This study employed a mixed-methods research design to investigate the relationships between various educational constructs. Our primary aim was to explore how TAM and ISSM constructs correlates to each other and contribute to the LLM-driven educational experience during the software development course. All participants were informed about the purpose of the research, the voluntary nature of their participation, and their right to withdraw at any time without any consequences. Consent was obtained before participation.

Participants and Data Collection. The quantitative phase involves the administration of surveys to the 78 undergraduate students in the School of Information Systems. The qualitative phase involves an analysis of students' answers to open-ended questions to gain a deeper understanding of the subjective values of their Java studying experiences, their trust and satisfaction with ChatGPT, and their prompting skills. Participants were invited to complete an online survey. The survey ensured anonymity and confidentiality to encourage honest and accurate responses.

Measurement Instrument. The survey consisted of multiple-item scales for each construct. Items were designed based on existing literature and tailored to fit the context of our study. Before the primary survey, a pilot test was conducted with a small group of students to ensure the clarity and relevance of the survey items. Adjustments were made based on feedback.

Statistical Analysis Plan. We initially performed Exploratory Factor Analysis (EFA) to explore the survey items' underlying factor structure and assess each construct's dimensionality. Items with factor loadings above 0.3 were retained for further analysis. Following EFA, Confirmatory Factor Analysis (CFA) was conducted to test the hypothesized measurement model. This step involved evaluating the model's fit and refining the scales based on various fit indices and item loadings. We performed multiple regression analyses to test the hypotheses related to the relationships between constructs. It included testing direct effects and moderation effects where applicable. In addition to the quantitative analyses, qualitative data was collected and analyzed to understand better the constructs, especially where quantitative measures indicated limitations. Qualitative data from the open-ended items are analyzed using content analysis techniques.

5 Research Results

In the initial phase of our statistical analysis, an Exploratory Factor Analysis (EFA) was conducted to unveil the latent structure of the observed variables derived from questionnaire responses. Table 1 provides EFA for loadings above 0.3.

In the exploratory investigation, it was observed that ObjVal_Q1 did not load significantly on any factor. This lack of statistical alignment with the underlying construct of Objective Value prompted its removal from subsequent analyses. The decision was reinforced by the need to improve the scale's reliability and validity. However, despite ObjVal_Q3 exhibiting a loading below the accepted threshold and a high uniqueness value, it was retained in the CFA (Table 2). This decision was underpinned by its theoretical importance, as it captured a critical aspect of the Objective Value construct.

The subsequent CFA (Table 2) provided a more stringent test of our hypothesized measurement model. It was observed that certain items like PrmtSkl_Q2 and ObjVal_Q3 exhibited lower-than-expected factor loadings. Nonetheless, they were retained in the model due to their theoretical relevance. PrmtSkl_Q2, though with a lower loading, was deemed essential for a comprehensive understanding of the Promoter Skill construct. The quantitative analysis indicated a need for improvement in the internal consistency of the ChatGPT Prompting Skills (PrmtSkl) construct. It was echoed in the qualitative feedback, where students noted specific instances of using ChatGPT. For example, one student mentioned, "I used ChatGPT for debugging when my code wasn't running correctly." This targeted application of ChatGPT in coding challenges illustrates its utility in specific contexts and explains the variability in PrmtSkl's effectiveness, emphasizing the context-specific nature of ChatGPT's educational impact.

Table 1. Exploratory Factor Analysis (EFA) Results.

Factor Loading	Factor 1	Factor 2	Factor 3	Uniqueness
PrmtSkl_Q1		0.596		0.694
PrmtSkl_Q2	−0.332	0.591		0.694
ObjVal_Q2		0.434		0.816
ObjVal_Q3		0.333		0.892
PrmtSkl_Q4	0.416		−0/332	0.623
SubVal_Q1	0.475			0.640
SubVal_Q2	0.497			0.739
PrmtSkl_Q3	0.326	0.367		0.625
ObjVal_Q1				0.883
Trst_Q1		0.364	0.738	0.274
Trst_Q2			0.674	0.547
Trst_Q3	0.370		0.668	0.355
StuSat_Q1	0.699			0.573
StuSat_Q2	0.694			0.541
StuSat_Q3	0.659			0.627
PrmtTrn_Q1		0.585		0.596
PrmtTrn_Q2	0.434	0.381		0.522
PrmtTrn_Q3	0.589			0.595

Similarly, despite its marginal loading, ObjVal_Q3 was considered vital for ensuring the breadth of the Objective Value construct. The mixed-methods approach of the study, integrating quantitative results with qualitative insights, was particularly relevant for the Objective Values construct. The qualitative responses clarified the significant lack of internal consistency in the Objective Values constructs found in the quantitative analysis. Students reported instances where ChatGPT's advice was misaligned with their coursework requirements. As the student noted, "ChatGPT sometimes missed the mark on our assignment guidelines," indicating a mismatch between ChatGPT's responses and the specific objectives of programming tasks. This feedback is pivotal in understanding the quantitative results, suggesting that the effectiveness of ChatGPT in achieving objective learning outcomes is contingent on its alignment with the educational objectives and constraints of the task.

While the CFA showed reasonable trust in ChatGPT, the qualitative insights revealed a spectrum of experiences. A student's comment: "Sometimes ChatGPT was helpful, especially in explaining tough concepts," contrasts with another's experience: "There were times when the guidance was not entirely relevant to my specific task." These diverse experiences likely contributed to the overall trust ratings and satisfaction levels, highlighting the nuanced role of ChatGPT in student learning and the importance of

Table 2. Confirmatory Factor Analysis (CFA) Results.

Indicator	CFA Factor Loading	Cronbach's Alpha	Composite Reliability	AVE
ChatGPT Prompting Skills		0.4947	0.4269	0.1676
PrmtSkl_Q1	0.38			
PrmtSkl_Q2	0.252			
PrmtSkl_Q3	0.566			
PrmtSkl_Q4	0.377			
ChatGPT Trust		0.7454	0.5829	0.3355
Trst_Q1	0.686			
Trst_Q2	0.329			
Trst_Q3	0.654			
Objective Values		0.1737	0.1563	0.0922
ObjVal_Q2	0.38			
ObjVal_Q3	0.2			
Subjective Values		0.6587	0.5506	0.3817
SubVal_Q1	0.669			
SubVal_Q2	0.562			
Students' satisfaction		0.6991	0.7414	0.4906
StuSat_Q1	0.751			
StuSat_Q2	0.731			
StuSat_Q3	0.611			
Prompting Training		0.6309	0.6319	0.3687
PrmtTrn_Q1	0.512			
PrmtTrn_Q2	0.718			
PrmtTrn_Q3	0.573			

aligning its use with the learners' specific needs. The CFA results also shed light on the psychometric properties of the measurement scales. The ChatGPT Prompting Skills (PrmtSkl) construct, measured by four indicators, indicated a need for improvement in internal consistency, with a Cronbach's Alpha of 0.4947 and a Composite Reliability (CR) of 0.4269. The Trust construct showed better internal consistency with a Cronbach's Alpha of 0.7454. However, the Objective Values construct displayed a significant lack of internal consistency, with Cronbach's Alpha of 0.1737, suggesting issues with the operationalization of this construct. Subjective Values and Students' Satisfaction constructs showed satisfactory internal consistency, with Cronbach's Alphas of 0.6587 and 0.6991, respectively. The Prompting Training construct also demonstrated good internal consistency with a Cronbach's Alpha of 0.6309.

Finally, we conducted a regression analysis, as presented in Table 3.

Table 3. Regression Analysis (EFA) Results

Hypothesis	Path Coefficient	R-squared	P-value	t-statistic	Results
H1: PrmtSkl → ObjVal	0.585	0.101	0.004	2.986	Supported
H2: PrmtSkl → SubVal	0.382	0.060	0.027	2.249	Supported
H3: Trst → ObjVal	0.194	0.040	0.074	1.810	Not Supported
H4: Trst → SubVal	0.228	0.076	0.013	2.554	Supported
H5: ObjVal → StuSat	−0.002	0.099	0.982	0.023	Not Supported
H6: SubVal → StuSat	0.257	0.099	0.005	2.916	Supported
H7: PrmtTrn moderates PrmtSkl → ObjVal	−0.328	0.144	0.287	1.071	Not Supported
H8: PrmtTrn moderates Trst → SubVal	−0.110	0.262	0.336	0.968	Not Supported

The regression analysis of the study (Table 3) tested seven hypotheses to explore the relationships between the educational constructs. The results supported the positive influence of Prompting Skill (PrmtSkl) on both Objective Value (ObjVal) and Subjective Value (SubVal).

Regarding H1, students often cited instances where ChatGPT's prompting skills were beneficial. For example, one student stated, "ChatGPT was great for quick clarifications on Java concepts." It aligns with the positive relationship observed in the regression analysis, indicating that practical prompting skills can enhance objective learning outcomes. In the context of H2, several students expressed how ChatGPT made learning more engaging. A student mentioned, "Using ChatGPT made the learning process more interactive and less monotonous." This positive sentiment supports the regression analysis findings, suggesting that ChatGPT's prompting skills can increase the subjective value of the learning experience.

Trust was found to have a significant positive effect on Subjective Value (H4) but not on Objective Value (H3). The mixed effectiveness of ChatGPT, as reported by students, provides context here. In the H3 context, a student noted, "While I trusted ChatGPT for basic questions, it sometimes fell short on more complex problems." This variability in trust could explain why the regression analysis did not find a significant effect of trust on objective learning outcomes. On the other hand, regarding H3, students often referenced trust concerning their comfort and satisfaction with the learning process. "I felt more confident asking ChatGPT questions I was too shy to ask in class," said one student. This increased comfort level aligns with the positive influence of trust on subjective value, as found in the regression analysis.

Surprisingly, Objective Value did not significantly influence Student Satisfaction (H5), while Subjective Value did (H6). The qualitative data of H5 highlights the complexity of factors influencing student satisfaction. A student remarked, "Even when the information was helpful, sometimes I didn't feel delighted due to the lack of personalized context." It indicates that objective value alone might not be a strong predictor of overall student satisfaction, reflecting the findings from the regression analysis. Regarding H6, students expressed that their satisfaction was closely tied to how subjectively valuable they found the learning experience. For instance, one student said, "When I felt engaged and interested, I was more satisfied with my learning." This positive correlation between subjective value and satisfaction aligns with the regression analysis, highlighting the importance of subjective experiences in educational satisfaction.

The data did not support the anticipated moderating effects of Prompting Training. Students' experiences did not distinctly highlight the role of prompting training in enhancing the effectiveness of prompting skills (H7). One student mentioned, "I used ChatGPT the same way regardless of the training." Similar to H7, students did not clearly articulate a difference in their trust or subjective value based on the level of prompting training (H8). "My trust in ChatGPT was more about its accuracy, not how well I was trained to use it," a student expressed. This sentiment suggests that the moderation effect of prompting training did not significantly impact the relationship between trust and subjective value, aligning with the quantitative findings.

6 Discussion and Conclusion

This research represents a significant contribution to the evolving field of AI in education and LLM literacy by examining the afinity of the usage of LLM on students' experience and satisfaction with Java learning. The study aims to provide actionable insights for educators and curriculum designers, enhance the understanding of LLM's role in education, and promote LLM literacy among students.

This study explored the impact of ChatGPT on programming language education among undergraduate Information Systems students. The quantitative results revealed mixed effectiveness in ChatGPT Prompting Skills, Trust, Objective Values, and their influence on student satisfaction. Qualitative insights enriched these findings, offering a deeper understanding of students' experiences and perceptions. The qualitative data highlighted ChatGPT's role as a supplemental learning tool, handy for coding support and debugging. It aligns with the positive impact of Prompting Skills on Objective and Subjective Values but also explains the variability in its effectiveness. Students' varied experiences, as expressed in their own words, underscore the importance of context in utilizing ChatGPT for educational purposes.

The moderate levels of trust in ChatGPT, as indicated by the quantitative data, were echoed in the qualitative responses. Students expressed confidence in using ChatGPT for basic queries but reported limitations in more complex scenarios. This nuanced view of trust is critical in shaping students' satisfaction with their learning experience. As noted in some student responses, a significant revelation was the mismatch between ChatGPT's guidance and specific coursework requirements. It highlights a crucial limitation in the current application of ChatGPT in educational settings and points to the need for more tailored approaches in integrating AI tools into the curriculum. The study's findings suggest that while ChatGPT can be a valuable educational tool, its integration into programming education should be done thoughtfully, considering the specific needs and contexts of the learning objectives. Educators are encouraged to guide students effectively using such tools and to remain aware of their limitations.

Further research is recommended to explore more refined ways of integrating AI tools like ChatGPT in educational contexts. Investigations into how these tools can be better tailored to align with specific educational objectives and learning outcomes would be particularly valuable.

References

1. Khan, W., Daud, A., Khan, K., Muhammad, S., Haq, R.: Exploring the frontiers of deep learning and natural language processing: a comprehensive overview of key challenges and emerging trends. Nat. Lang. Process. J. **4**, 100026 (2023)
2. Dogan, M.E., Goru Dogan, T., Bozkurt, A.: The use of artificial intelligence (AI) in online learning and distance education processes: a systematic review of empirical studies. Appl. Sci. **13**(5), 3056 (2023)
3. Casal-Otero, L., Catala, A., Fernández-Morante, C., Taboada, M., Cebreiro, B., Barro, S.: AI literacy in K-12: a systematic literature review. Int. J. STEM Educ. **10**(1), 29 (2023)
4. Miao, F., Holmes, W., Huang, R., Zhang, H.: AI and Education: A Guidance for Policymakers. UNESCO Publishing (2021)
5. Grassini, S.: Shaping the future of education: exploring the potential and consequences of AI and ChatGPT in educational settings. Educ. Sci. **13**(7), 692 (2023)
6. Nazaretsky, T., Cukurova, M., Alexandron, G.: An instrument for measuring teachers' trust in AI-based educational technology. In: LAK22: 12th International Learning Analytics and Knowledge Conference, pp. 56–66 (2022)
7. Masoura, M., Malefaki, S.: Evolution of the digital economy and society index in the European Union: α socioeconomic perspective. TalTech J. Eur. Stud. **13**(2), 177–203 (2023)
8. Davis, F.D.: Perceived usefulness, perceived ease of use, and user acceptance of information technology. MIS Quart. **13**, 319–340 (1989)
9. DeLone, W.H., McLean, E.R.: Information systems success: the quest for the dependent variable. Inf. Syst. Res. **3**(1), 60–95 (1992)
10. Mazzullo, E., Bulut, O., Wongvorachan, T., Tan, B.: Learning analytics in the era of large language models. Analytics **2**(4), 877–898 (2023)
11. Zou, B., Guan, X., Shao, Y., Chen, P.: Supporting speaking practice by social network-based interaction in Artificial Intelligence (AI)-assisted language learning. Sustainability **15**(4), 2872 (2023)
12. Darvishi, A., Khosravi, H., Sadiq, S., Gašević, D., Siemens, G.: Impact of AI assistance on student agency. Comput. Educ. **210**, 104967 (2024)
13. Chan, C.K.Y.: A comprehensive AI policy education framework for university teaching and learning. Int. J. Educ. Technol. High. Educ. **20**(1), 38 (2023)
14. Huang, A.Y., Lu, O.H., Yang, S.J.: Effects of artificial Intelligence-Enabled personalized recommendations on learners' learning engagement, motivation, and outcomes in a flipped classroom. Comput. Educ. **194**, 104684 (2023)
15. Bernabei, M., Colabianchi, S., Falegnami, A., Costantino, F.: Students' use of large language models in engineering education: a case study on technology acceptance, perceptions, efficacy, and detection chances. Comput. Educ. Artif. Intell. **5**, 100172 (2023)
16. Ciampa, K., Wolfe, Z.M., Bronstein, B.: ChatGPT in education: transforming digital literacy practices. J. Adolesc. Health. **67**(3), 186–195 (2023)
17. Saif, N., Khan, S.U., Shaheen, I., Alotaibi, A., Alnfiai, M.M., Arif, M.: Chat-GPT; validating Technology Acceptance Model (TAM) in education sector via ubiquitous learning mechanism. Comput. Hum. Behav. 108097 (2023)

18. Na, S., Heo, S., Choi, W., Kim, C., Whang, S.W.: Artificial Intelligence (AI)-based technology adoption in the construction industry: a cross national perspective using the technology acceptance model. Buildings **13**(10), 2518 (2023)
19. Mogaji, E., Viglia, G., Srivastava, P., Dwivedi, Y.K.: Is it the end of the technology acceptance model in the era of generative artificial intelligence? Int. J. Contemp. Hosp. Manag. (2024)
20. Calafato, R.: Charting the motivation, self-efficacy beliefs, language learning strategies, and achievement of multilingual university students learning Arabic as a foreign language. Asian-Pacific J. Second Foreign Lang. Educ. **8**(1), 20 (2023)
21. Tsai, M.L., Ong, C.W., Chen, C.L.: Exploring the use of large language models (LLMs) in chemical engineering education: building core course problem models with Chat-GPT. Educ. Chem. Eng. **44**, 71–95 (2023)
22. Miron, O.A., Wai, K.N.H.: Sentiment Analysis on Generative Large Language Models based on Social Media Commentary of Industry Participants (2023)
23. Saqr, R.R., Al-Somali, S.A., Sarhan, M.Y.: Exploring the acceptance and user satisfaction of AI-driven e-learning platforms (Blackboard, Moodle, Edmodo, Coursera and edX): an integrated technology model. Sustainability **16**(1), 204 (2023)
24. Bubaš, G., Čižmešija, A., Kovačić, A.: Development of an assessment scale for measurement of usability and user experience characteristics of Bing chat conversational AI. Future Internet **16**(1), 4 (2023)
25. Prather, J., et al.: The robots are here: navigating the generative AI revolution in computing education. In: Proceedings of the 2023 Working Group Reports on Innovation and Technology in Computer Science Education, pp. 108–159 (2023)
26. Hou, X., et al.: Large language models for software engineering: a systematic literature review. arXiv preprint arXiv:2308.10620 (2023)
27. Essel, H.B., Vlachopoulos, D., Essuman, A.B., Amankwa, J.O.: ChatGPT effects on cognitive skills of undergraduate students: Receiving instant responses from AI-based conversational large language models (LLMs). Comput. Educ. Artif. Intell. 100198 (2023)
28. Carlsson, S.V., Esteves, S.C., Grobet-Jeandin, E., Masone, M.C., Ribal, M.J., Zhu, Y.: Being a non-native English speaker in science and medicine. Nat. Rev. Urol. 1–6 (2024)
29. Zheng, L., Niu, J., Zhong, L., Gyasi, J.F.: The effectiveness of artificial intelligence on learning achievement and learning perception: a meta-analysis. Interact. Learn. Environ. **31**(9), 5650–5664 (2023)
30. Aviv, I., Gafni, R., Sherman, S., Aviv, B., Sterkin, A., Bega, E.: Cloud infrastructure from python code–breaking the barriers of cloud deployment. In: European Conference on Software Architecture, ECSA 2023 (2023)

Quantum Course Prophet: Quantum Machine Learning for Predicting Course Failures: A Case Study on Numerical Methods

Isaac Caicedo-Castro[(✉)] [ID]

SOCRATES Research Team, University of Córdoba, Montería 230002, Colombia
isacaic@correo.unicordoba.edu.co

Abstract. This study delves into the application of Quantum Machine Learning to predict student course failures based on their performance in prerequisite courses. Specifically, we adopt Quantum-enhanced Support Vector Machines to develop an intelligent system called "Quantum Course Prophet" to forecast whether a student might fail the numerical methods course. We used a dataset comprising 103 examples from the academic histories of students enrolled in the Systems Engineering bachelor's degree program at the University of Córdoba in Colombia. Notably, the Numerical Methods course involves 10 prerequisite courses in the latest version of the curriculum. For each course, we included in every student's example the highest final grade, the lowest one, and the number of times the student has enrolled in the prerequisite course. Consequently, each student is represented by 33 independent variables, with the target variable indicating whether the student is likely to fail the Numerical Methods course. To deal with memory constraints, Non-Negative Matrix Factorization is employed to reduce the dimensions of each example. Following dimension reduction, each variable is rescaled to standardize the maximum value to 1. The dimension of the input space is determined through 10-fold cross-validation, resulting in a seven-dimensional input space. This approach yields a mean accuracy of 73.82%, precision of 70%, recall of 61.5%, and a harmonic mean of 64.44%. This study underscores the potential of quantum machine learning as a viable alternative for addressing real-world problems in the future.

Keywords: Quantum computing · Machine learning · Quantum machine learning · Matrix factorization · Educational data mining

1 Introduction

Forecasting whether students might fail courses in undergraduate programs is an active research subject in educational data mining. In this context, failing means either dropping out or not passing the course. Several studies have widely focused on online courses [9, 13, 15, 18, 19], such as computer networking and web design [13], mathematics [19], and STEM (science, technology, engineering, and mathematics) courses in general [18]. In these previous studies, the endeavor has been centered on forecasting during the course development phase, instead of predicting students' failure before they start their courses. Therefore, the course failure forecast is based on students' coursework and learning behavior, which is evidenced in the number of course views, downloads of content, grades, and so forth.

Despite predicting course failure throughout the course development being important, an anticipatory forecast aids stakeholders and policymakers in making decisions by providing them with the insights required to elaborate strategies and precautions to prevent students' failure in a given course. Thus, there are studies whose goal is to forecast whether a student might fail before the course begins, based on their grades in prerequisite courses. To this end, admission test outcomes are used to predict whether a student might fail courses in mathematics and physics in the first term [2], while admission test outcomes, along with grades from prerequisite courses, are utilized as input variables for forecasting if a given student might fail the course of numerical methods [3]. However, improved results are achieved using only grades and additional information from prerequisite courses as input variables for the forecasting method [4].

In prior research on predicting the possibility of failing a course given previous prerequisite course performance, several machine learning methods for classification have been adopted, including artificial neural networks or multilayer perceptron [3,4,9,13,15,18,22], support vector machines [3,4,9,13,24], logistic regression [3,9,19,24], decision trees [3,4,9,19,24], ensemble methods with different classification methods [13,15], random forest [3,4,9,15,22], gradient boosting [22], extreme gradient boosting (XGBoost) [3,4,15,22], variants of gradient boosting [22,24], such as CatBoost [7] and LightGBM [10], and Gaussian processes for classification [3,4].

Although quantum machine learning has been used for predicting if a student might fail courses during the first term based on the admission test results [2], to our knowledge, this method has not been adopted when the input variables are based on the prerequisite course history. Our study is part of a broader project called Course Prophet [3,4], whose goal is to design an intelligent system that early alerts policymakers and stakeholders to students at risk of failing the Numerical Methods course in the bachelor's degree in Systems Engineering at the University of Córdoba in Colombia. Thus, in our study, we ponder the following question: Might the intelligent system based on quantum machine learning be more accurate at detecting students at risk than the one studied in [4]?

To answer the above-mentioned question, we adopted the same data representation proposed in [4], where the input variables used for each prerequisite course are as follows: the variables $x_{i,j}$ and $x_{i,j+2}$ represent the highest and lowest final grades obtained by the ith student in the jth course, while $x_{i,j+1}$ denotes the number of semesters the ith student has enrolled in the jth course. If the ith student passes the jth course upon the first enrollment, $x_{i,j}$ and $x_{i,j+2}$ will have the same value, and $x_{i,j+1}$ is equal to one. We assume that there are 11 prerequisite courses required for succeeding in the numerical methods course, namely, linear algebra, calculus I, II, III, physics I, II, III, introduction to computer programming, computer programming I, II, and III. There are three variables for each prerequisite course, resulting in 33 variables representing the student's prerequisite course history.

On the other hand, we shall denote the target variable as y_i, where it takes the value of one if the ith student has either failed or dropped out of the numerical course the first time it is enrolled (i.e., a positive example, or $y_i = 1$), or minus one otherwise (i.e., a negative example, or $y_i = -1$). To formalize the problem, let $\mathcal{D}$ be the dataset that represents the academic history of several students, or the training dataset, i.e., $\mathcal{D} = \{(\mathbf{x}_i, y_i) | \mathbf{x}_i \in \mathcal{X} \wedge y_i \in -1, 1\}$, where $\mathcal{X} \subset \mathbb{R}^D$. Regarding the previous example, the variables $x_{i,j}, x_{i,j+2} \in [0, 5]$ are constrained according to the Colombian grade conventions, i.e., 5 is the highest possible grade, whereas 0 is the lowest possible one. Moreover, $x_{i,j+1} \in \mathbb{Z}^+ \cup 0$ is a positive integer number or zero if the student has never enrolled in the jth course. Therefore, the problem is finding a function $g : \mathcal{X} \to \mathbb{R}$ such that it maps the input variables, corresponding to the academic histories, to the aforementioned target variable, based on the training dataset. Hence, $g(\mathbf{x}_i)$ is positive as long as the ith student is classified as at-risk of failing the numerical methods course; otherwise, $g(\mathbf{x}_i)$ is negative.

The contribution of this study is twofold: firstly, we propose the design of a hybrid intelligent system called Quantum Course Prophet, based on quantum and classical machine learning, that predicts whether a student might fail the numerical methods course based on their performance in prerequisite courses. Secondly, the results of an experimental validation reveal that quantum-enhanced support vector machines yield a mean accuracy of 73.82%, mean precision of 70%, mean recall of 61.5%, and an average harmonic mean of 64.44%.

The remainder of this paper is outlined as follows: the architecture of Quantum Course Prophet is presented in Sect. 2. Each input variable is encoded into a quantum bit (qubit), requiring 33 qubits for all input variables. However, we employ Non-Negative Matrix Factorization to reduce the dimensions of each example due to memory constraints; thus, this method is explained in Sect. 3. The quantum machine learning method used in our study, quantum-enhanced support vector machines, is described in Sect. 4. The validation process conducted to test the methods used in our study is presented in Sect. 5. We present and analyze the results of the study in Sects. 6 and 7, respectively. In Sect. 8, we conclude the discussion about the results, present the novelty of our study, and discuss perspectives for future research.

2 Nuts and Bolts of Quantum Course Prophet

In this section, we present the key components of the Quantum Course Prophet system. These components are depicted in Fig. 1, with each one explained as follows:

– Repository of students' academic history: This is the set of records that stores the final grades achieved by each student in every enrolled course.
– Preprocessor: This component retrieves the dataset from the repository and formats it, as explained in the introductory section. Subsequently, it reduces the dimensionality of the input vector space. Finally, it rescales every variable, ensuring that the maximum value for each one is standardized to 1.
– Quantum Machine Learning Classifier: This component classifies each student in the repository as either at-risk of failing the numerical methods course or not. Every student at risk is included in the output of this component.

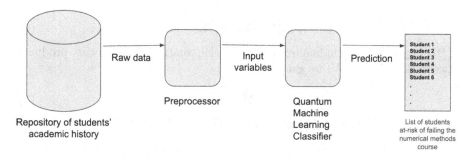

Fig. 1. The architecture of Quantum Course Prophets: The academic history is used to predict whether a student might fail the numerical methods course. The output of the intelligent system is a list of those students at-risk.

3   Dimensionality Reduction Method

In order to explain this method, we represent the independent variables in matrix form. Each column corresponds to the original D-dimensional vector from the dataset. Let $\mathbf{X} \in \mathbb{R}^{D \times n}$ be a $D \times n$-dimensional matrix such that $\mathbf{X} = [\mathbf{x}_1 \ \ldots \ \mathbf{x}_n]$, where each $\mathbf{x}_i$ denotes the ith vector in the dataset.

Non-negative matrix factorization is a method used to decompose a non-negative matrix into two non-negative matrices of lower rank, which are referred to as factor matrices [11]. Given the matrix $\mathbf{X}$, the objective is to find two non-negative factor matrices $\mathbf{W}$ and $\mathbf{Z}$ such that their product approximates the non-negative matrix $\mathbf{X}$ as closely as possible. Therefore, we seek $\mathbf{W} \in \mathbb{R}^{D \times d}$ and $\mathbf{Z} \in \mathbb{R}^{d \times n}$, where d represents a lower-dimensional space for the independent variables (i.e., $d < D$), such that $\mathbf{X} \approx \mathbf{W}\mathbf{Z}$. The objective function for this task is defined as follows:

$$\min_{\mathbf{W},\mathbf{Z}} J(\mathbf{W}, \mathbf{Z}) = \frac{1}{2}\|\mathbf{W}\mathbf{Z} - \mathbf{X}\|_F^2, \tag{1}$$

subject to the constraints $\mathbf{W}, \mathbf{Z} \geq 0$, where the factor of $1/2$ is included for later convenience. Therefore, the Lagrangian is defined as follows:

$$\mathcal{L}(\mathbf{W}, \mathbf{Z}, \boldsymbol{\Theta}, \boldsymbol{\Omega}) = J(\mathbf{W}, \mathbf{Z}) + \mathrm{Tr}(\boldsymbol{\Theta} \mathbf{W}^T) + \mathrm{Tr}(\boldsymbol{\Omega} \mathbf{Z}^T), \qquad (2)$$

where the entries of both matrices $\boldsymbol{\Theta} \in \mathbb{R}^{D \times d}$ and $\boldsymbol{\Omega} \in \mathbb{R}^{d \times n}$ are Lagrange multipliers.

So, in order to calculate the factor matrix $\mathbf{W}$, we set the derivative of Eq. (2) with respect to $\mathbf{W}$ equal to zero as follows:

$$\nabla_{\mathbf{W}} \mathcal{L}(\mathbf{W}, \mathbf{Z}, \boldsymbol{\Theta}, \boldsymbol{\Omega}) = (\mathbf{W}\mathbf{Z} - \mathbf{X})\mathbf{Z}^T + \boldsymbol{\Theta} = 0 \qquad (3)$$

Because of the distributive property of addition over multiplication, we obtain:

$$\mathbf{W}\mathbf{Z}\mathbf{Z}^T - \mathbf{X}\mathbf{Z}^T + \boldsymbol{\Theta} = 0 \qquad (4)$$

By applying the Hadamard product (aka, matrix element-wise product) between Eq. (4) and $\mathbf{W}$, we get:

$$(\mathbf{W}\mathbf{Z}\mathbf{Z}^T - \mathbf{X}\mathbf{Z}^T + \boldsymbol{\Theta}) \odot \mathbf{W} = 0 \qquad (5)$$

Regarding the Karush-Kuhn-Tucker condition $\boldsymbol{\Theta} \odot \mathbf{W} = 0$, we obtain the following result:

$$(\mathbf{W}\mathbf{Z}\mathbf{Z}^T)_{ij} W_{ij} - (\mathbf{X}\mathbf{Z}^T)_{ij} W_{ij} = 0, \forall i = 1, \ldots, D, \text{ and } \forall j = 1, \ldots, d \qquad (6)$$

From the latter equation, the updating rule for calculating $\mathbf{W}$ is as follows:

$$W_{ij} = W_{ij} \frac{(\mathbf{X}\mathbf{Z}^T)_{ij}}{(\mathbf{W}\mathbf{Z}\mathbf{Z}^T)_{ij}}, \forall i = 1, \ldots, D, \text{ and } \forall j = 1, \ldots, d \qquad (7)$$

On the other hand, to calculate $\mathbf{Z}$, we set the derivative of Eq. (2) with respect to $\mathbf{Z}$ equal to zero as follows:

$$\nabla_{\mathbf{Z}} \mathcal{L}(\mathbf{W}, \mathbf{Z}, \boldsymbol{\Theta}, \boldsymbol{\Omega}) = \mathbf{W}^T(\mathbf{W}\mathbf{Z} - \mathbf{X}) + \boldsymbol{\Omega} = 0 \qquad (8)$$

By applying the distributive property of addition over multiplication, we arrive at the following equation:

$$\mathbf{W}^T\mathbf{W}\mathbf{Z} - \mathbf{W}^T\mathbf{X} + \boldsymbol{\Omega} = 0 \qquad (9)$$

Next, we apply the Hadamard product between the matrix $\mathbf{Z}$ and Eq. (9), yielding:

$$(\mathbf{W}^T\mathbf{W}\mathbf{Z} - \mathbf{W}^T\mathbf{X} + \boldsymbol{\Omega}) \odot \mathbf{Z} = 0 \qquad (10)$$

$\boldsymbol{\Omega} \odot \mathbf{Z} = 0$ due to the Karush-Kuhn-Tucker condition; therefore:

$$(\mathbf{W}^T\mathbf{W}\mathbf{Z})_{ij} Z_{ij} - (\mathbf{W}^T\mathbf{X})_{ij} Z_{ij} = 0, \forall i = 1, \ldots, d, \text{ and } \forall j = 1, \ldots, n \qquad (11)$$

From Eq. (11), we obtain the following updating rule to calculate $\mathbf{Z}$:

$$Z_{ij} = Z_{ij} \frac{(\mathbf{W}^T\mathbf{X})_{ij}}{(\mathbf{W}^T\mathbf{W}\mathbf{Z})_{ij}}, \forall i = 1,\ldots,d, \text{ and } \forall j = 1,\ldots,n \tag{12}$$

The factorization algorithm consists of minimizing Eq. (2). The first step is initializing $\mathbf{W}$ to small and positive random values. Then, it starts a loop, where $\mathbf{Z}$ is updated using Eq. (12). In the next step, $\mathbf{W}$ is updated given the values of $\mathbf{Z}$ and $\mathbf{X}$ by using Eq. (7). The algorithm ends when it converges to the solution. Further details about Non-Negative Matrix Factorization algorithms and their implementation have been broadly discussed in the literature [5,11,12].

Thus, from the original dataset $\mathcal{D}$, the resulting one, denoted as $\mathcal{D}^d$, has a lower dimensionality and is defined as follows: $\mathcal{D}^d = \{(\mathbf{z}_i, y_i) | \mathbf{z}_i \in \mathcal{Z} \wedge y_i \in \{-1,1\}\}$

Finally, in order to calculate the lower dimensional representation $\mathbf{z}' \in \mathcal{Z}$ of a new example $\mathbf{x}' \in \mathcal{X}$, given the factor matrix $\mathbf{W}$, we must find a vector $\mathbf{z}'$ such that $\mathbf{W}\mathbf{z}' = \mathbf{x}'$. Isolating the vector $\mathbf{z}'$ yields:

$$\mathbf{z}' = (\mathbf{W}^T\mathbf{W})^{-1}\mathbf{W}^T\mathbf{x}' \tag{13}$$

4   Classification Method

Once the vector representation of the ith student's prerequisite performance is calculated in a lower-dimensional space, i.e., $\mathbf{z}_i$, the goal is to find the prediction function $g : \mathcal{Z} \rightarrow \mathbb{R}$ such that $g(\mathbf{z}_i)$ is positive if the ith student is at-risk; otherwise, $g(\mathbf{z}_i)$ is negative. The method adopted in our study to determine this function is known as Quantum-enhanced Support Vector Machines (QSVMs). This method is based on the theoretically well-motivated and state-of-the-art classifier called Support Vector Machines (SVMs), proposed in 1995 by Cortes and Vapnik [6].

SVMs is a margin-based classification method, as illustrated in Fig. 2, where the goal is to find a decision boundary hyperplane that separates positive examples (denoted as $\oplus$ in the figure) from negative ones (represented as $\ominus$). The decision boundary is the continuous straight line between the dashed lines in the figure, which is defined as $g(\mathbf{z}) = 0$, while the right and left margins are defined as $g(\mathbf{z}) = 1$ and $g(\mathbf{z}) = -1$, respectively. Thus, the prediction function is defined as follows:

$$g(\mathbf{z}) = \beta^T\mathbf{z} + \beta_0, \tag{14}$$

where β is a d-dimensional vector in the same space as $\mathbf{z}$, i.e., $\beta \in \mathcal{Z}$, and β_0 is a scalar, i.e., $\beta_0 \in \mathbb{R}$. Above the decision boundary, the prediction function is positive, i.e., $g(\mathbf{z}) > 0$, whereas below the decision boundary, the prediction function is negative, i.e., $g(\mathbf{z}) < 0$.

Finding the prediction function in (14) involves calculating β and β_0. To this end, the margin size ρ is maximized while ensuring that the prediction function classifies every vector properly, i.e., $g(\mathbf{z}_i)y_i \geq 1$ for $i = 1,\ldots,n$. The margin is maximized because there is an inversely proportional relationship between the margin size and the norm of the vector β. The larger the margin, the smaller the norm of β, as we shall see later.

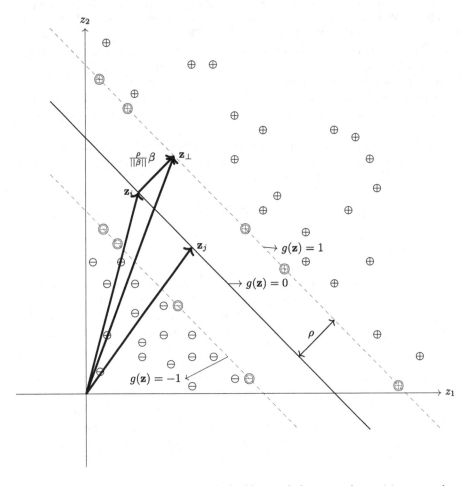

Fig. 2. The vectors on the upper green dashed line and above are the positive examples, i.e., students who have failed the numerical methods course, while those ones below the lower green dashed line are negative examples. In this figure, green dashed lines are margins, whereas the continuous thick line is the decision boundary. Those vectors along the green dashed line, represented through double-circled green examples, are the support vectors. (Color figure online)

In order to understand the aforementioned relationship, let us notice that the vector β is orthogonal to the decision boundary. This can be observed in Fig. 2, where β is perpendicular to the vector $\mathbf{z}_j - \mathbf{z}_i$, which is parallel to the decision boundary, and the inner product between both vectors is zero, i.e., $g(\mathbf{z}_j) - g(\mathbf{z}_i) = \beta^T(\mathbf{z}_j - \mathbf{z}_i) = 0$. Therefore, $\mathbf{z}_\perp = \mathbf{z}_i + \frac{\rho}{||\beta||}\beta$. Subtracting $\mathbf{z}_i$ from both sides and multiplying the equation by $\frac{1}{||\beta||}\beta^T$, we obtain:

$$\rho = \frac{\beta^T \mathbf{z}_\perp + \beta_0}{||\beta||} = \frac{1}{||\beta||} \tag{15}$$

So, we minimize $||\beta||$ in lieu of maximizing the margin size ρ, as follows:

$$\min_\beta \frac{||\beta||^2}{2} \text{ subject to } g(\mathbf{z}_i)y_i \geq 1 \forall i = 1,\ldots,n \tag{16}$$

Where the factor $1/2$ is used for later convenience, and the squared Euclidean norm of β (i.e., $||\beta||^2$) is convex. Thus, using Lagrange multipliers $\alpha_1,\ldots,\alpha_n$, the objective function is defined as follows:

$$\min_\beta \mathcal{L} = \frac{||\beta||^2}{2} - \sum_{i=1}^{n} \alpha_i [y_i(\beta^T \mathbf{z}_i + \beta_0) - 1] \tag{17}$$

By setting the derivative of the objective function in (17) with respect to β and β_0 equal to zero, we obtain:

$$\beta = \sum_{i=1}^{n} \alpha_i y_i \mathbf{z}_i \tag{18}$$

$$\sum_{i=1}^{n} \alpha_i y_i = 0 \tag{19}$$

Substituting (18) and (19) into (17), we obtain the dual form of the objective function:

$$\max_{\alpha_1,\ldots,\alpha_n} \mathcal{L}_D = \sum_{i=1}^{n} \alpha_i - \frac{1}{2} \sum_{i=1}^{n} \sum_{j=1}^{n} \alpha_i \alpha_j y_i y_j \mathbf{z}_i^T \mathbf{z}_j \tag{20}$$

subject to the constraints $\alpha_i \geq 0$, for $i = 1,\ldots,n$, and $\sum_{i=1}^{n} \alpha_i y_i = 0$. The latter is a quadratic programming problem that satisfies the Karush-Kuhn-Tucker conditions, namely:

$$\alpha_i \geq 0 \tag{21}$$

$$y_i g(\mathbf{z}_i) \geq 0 \tag{22}$$

$$\alpha_i [y_i g(\mathbf{z}_i) - 1] = 0. \tag{23}$$

Regarding the latter condition, for every vector, either α_i is zero or the product $y_i g(\mathbf{z}_i) = 1$. Thus, those vectors in the margin that satisfy $y_i g(\mathbf{z}_i) = 1$

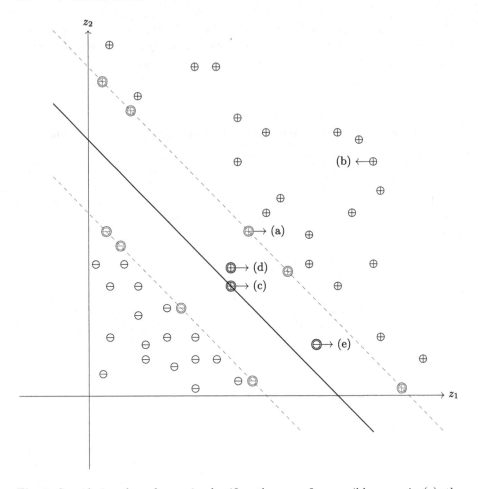

Fig. 3. Considering the soft-margin classifier, there are five possible cases: in (a), the vector is positive example on the right side and on the margin, so $\xi_i = 0$. In (b), the vector is a positive example on the correct side above the right margin, whose case $y_i g(\mathbf{z}) \geq 1$ and $\xi_i = 0$. In (c), the vector is a positive example on the decision boundary, thereby, $\xi_i = 1$. In (d), the vector is a positive example on the right side, between the margin and the decision boundary, where $\xi_i = 1 - g(\mathbf{z}_i)$, hence, $0 \leq \xi_i \leq 1$. Finally, in (e), the vector is a negative example on the wrong side above the decision boundary, above the decision boundary instead of below of it, where $\xi_i = 1 + g(\mathbf{z}_i)$, hence, $\xi_i \geq 1$. The latter case corresponds to students with a poor performance during their academic history (e.g., failed prerequisite courses several times), yet they passed the numerical methods course.

are called support vectors, giving the name to the classification method, and correspond to those Lagrange multipliers that are not equal to zero, i.e., $\alpha_i \neq 0$.

Nevertheless, in the real-world context, there are exceptions, or students that succeed in the numerical methods course despite their poor performance during prerequisite courses. So far, we assumed that the vectors can be linearly separable; however, because of the exceptions, an exact separation might lead to poor generalization. To face this problem, henceforth, we assume that some vectors can be on the wrong side of the margins, i.e., the vector is misclassified, although including a penalty ξ_i, which is a slack variable, where $i = 1, \ldots, n$, and there is a slack variable per training vector. Thus, the further the distance between the wrongly classified vector and the decision boundary is, the larger the penalty is. Figure 3 illustrates the possible values of the slack variable depending on the aforementioned distance. As a consequence, the constraint in the optimization problem expressed in (16) is relaxed using the slack variable as follows:

$$y_i g(\mathbf{z}_i) \geq 1 - \xi_i, \tag{24}$$

where $i = 1, \ldots, n$, $\xi_i = 0$ as long as the vector $\mathbf{z}_i$ has been correctly classified; otherwise, either the vector is also on the right side of the decision boundary but inside the margin, i.e., $0 \leq \xi_i \leq 1$, or the vector is wrongly classified, i.e., $\xi_i > 1$. So, the soft error is the sum of the slack variables ($\sum_i^n \xi_i$), and the goal is maximizing the margin while each slack variable penalizes every vector that lies on the wrong side of the margins as follows:

$$\min_{\beta} \frac{||\beta||^2}{2} + C \sum_{i=1}^{n} \xi_i \text{ subject to } g(\mathbf{z}_i)y_i \geq 1 - \xi_i, \forall i = 1, \ldots, n \tag{25}$$

where $C > 0$ is the regularization parameter, that controls the trade-off between the soft error minimization and margin maximization (or model complexity). The larger C is, the higher the penalty is for non-separable vectors. Indeed, if C is too large (e.g., $C \to \infty$), there will be a vast amount of support vectors, and the classifier might overfit. This hyper-parameter is chosen using cross-validation.

So now, we aim to minimize (25) subject to the constraints in (24) and $\xi_i \geq 0$. Hence, the objective function using Lagrange multipliers is defined as follows:

$$\min_{\beta} \mathcal{L} = \frac{||\beta||^2}{2} + C \sum_{i=1}^{n} \xi_i - \sum_{i=1}^{n} \alpha_i[y_i(\beta^T \mathbf{z}_i + \beta_0) - 1 + \xi_i] - \sum_{i=1}^{n} \mu_i \xi_i \tag{26}$$

where Lagrange multipliers are either positive or equal to zero, i.e., $\alpha_i \geq 0$ and $\mu_i \geq 0$ for $i = 1, \ldots, n$. Moreover, the following Karush-Kuhn-Tucker conditions hold in the later quadratic programming problem:

$$\alpha_i \geq 0 \tag{27}$$

$$y_i g(\mathbf{z}_i) - 1 + \xi_i \geq 0 \tag{28}$$

$$\alpha_i[y_i g(\mathbf{z}_i) - 1 + \xi_i] = 0 \tag{29}$$

$$\mu_i \geq 0 \tag{30}$$

$$\xi_i \geq 0 \tag{31}$$

$$\mu_i \xi_i = 0 \tag{32}$$

where $i = 1, \ldots, n$. Thus, setting the derivative of (26) equal to zero with respect to β, β_0, and ξ_i yields:

$$\beta = \sum_{i=1}^{n} \alpha_i y_i \mathbf{z}_i \tag{33}$$

$$\sum_{i=1}^{n} \alpha_i y_i = 0 \tag{34}$$

$$\alpha_i = C - \mu_i \tag{35}$$

By substituting (33), (34), and (35) into (26), we obtain:

$$\max_{\alpha_1, \ldots, \alpha_n} \mathcal{L}_D = \sum_{i=1}^{n} \alpha_i - \frac{1}{2} \sum_{i=1}^{n} \sum_{j=1}^{n} \alpha_i \alpha_j y_i y_j \mathbf{z}_i^T \mathbf{z}_j, \tag{36}$$

which is the dual objective function that we aim to maximize subject to the constraints $0 \leq \alpha_i \leq C$, for $i = 1, \ldots, n$, and $\sum_{i=1}^{n} \alpha_i y_i = 0$. Here, $\alpha_i \geq 0$ because of (35) and $\mu_i \geq 0$. This forms a constrained quadratic programming problem that may be solved through algorithms such as sequential minimal optimization. For further details about SVMs, see [14].

On the other hand, when vectors in the input space ($\mathcal{Z}$) are not linearly separable by any possible decision boundary, we may cope with this problem by harnessing the kernel trick. Thus, in (36), let us focus on the inner product between vectors $\mathbf{z}_i$ and $\mathbf{z}_j$, for $i, j = 1, \ldots, n$. This is noteworthy because it allows us to use the kernel trick, which consists of replacing the inner product with a kernel function to map input variables into a higher dimensional space, where the problem might be linearly separable, hence, easier to solve. Therefore, this is the part where we adopt quantum kernels rather than classical kernel functions to accomplish the goal of our study (e.g., radial basis function, sigmoid, polynomial, or a combination of these kernels).

The quantum kernel consists of mapping the classical input space $\mathcal{Z}$, obtained from the matrix factorization method, to a Hilbert space using the quantum feature mapping function $\phi(\mathbf{z})$, resulting in the following kernel function:

$$k(\mathbf{z}_i, \mathbf{z}_j) = |\langle \phi(\mathbf{z}_i) | \phi(\mathbf{z}_j) \rangle|^2 \tag{37}$$

where ϕ represents the quantum feature map, $\langle \phi(\mathbf{z}_i) |$ denotes the quantum state produced by the vector $\mathbf{z}_i$, and $\langle \phi(\mathbf{z}_i) | \phi(\mathbf{z}_j) \rangle$ measures the overlap between two quantum states, $\langle \phi(\mathbf{z}_i) |$ and $\langle \phi(\mathbf{z}_j) |$, reflecting the inner product between both vectors and indicating their similarity or correlation. Each component in the input vector corresponds to a qubit, and quantum circuits, such as the one depicted in Fig. 4, are employed to map the input vector into a higher-dimensional space. Thus, this approach focuses on leveraging a quantum state space for the independent variables. For further details, refer to [8]. To implement this, we utilized the ZZ feature mapping, a well-established feature mapping in Qiskit, a prominent open-source software development kit. This mapping enables the encoding of d components of the input vector across d qubits. Qiskit offers a comprehensive toolkit with a diverse range of quantum gates and circuits designed for various computational tasks [20]. For additional information about the ZZ feature mapping, please consult the documentation available on the Qiskit website [21]. In the context of representing qubits as normalized complex-value space vectors, we individually rescaled each component of every input vector to ensure that the maximum value for each variable was standardized to 1, as qubits are unit vectors in a two-dimensional complex-valued Hilbert space.

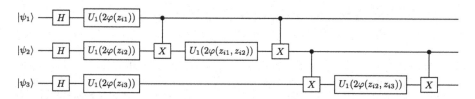

Fig. 4. Quantum circuit for the kernel, that includes three qubits, one repetition, and a linear entanglement strategy. Here φ is a classical non-linear function, where $\varphi(a) = a$ and $\varphi(a, b) = (\pi - a)(\pi - b)$.

5   Validation Method and Experimental Setting

In our study, we validated the methods described in the preceding sections using a dataset gathered by Caicedo-Castro [4]. This dataset was collected through a survey conducted among students of systems engineering at the University of Córdoba in Colombia. To safeguard the privacy of participants, the dataset has been anonymized, with only students' grades being retained. Personal information, such as identification numbers, names, gender, and economic stratum, has been omitted.

The dataset consists of 103 instances, each with 33 input variables along with their corresponding target variable. In Fig. 5, the proportion of positive instances (students who failed the numerical methods course) and negative instances (students who passed the course) is depicted through a pie chart. The chart illustrates that the dataset is reasonably balanced, albeit with a slightly higher number of negative examples. This suggests that more students successfully passed the course compared to those who failed.

We used this dataset to validate the methods described in Sects. 3 and 4. To achieve this, we adopted the K-fold cross-validation (KFCV) technique, which systematically tests the quantum classifier K times using K different datasets for training and validation. This involved splitting the dataset Z^d into K equal

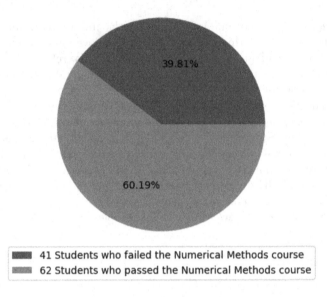

Fig. 5. Distribution of student outcomes in the numerical methods course dataset. The chart pie illustrates that 41 out of 103 students who participated in the study failed the numerical methods course (39.81% of the surveyed students), whereas 62 out of 103 students passed the course (60.19% of the sample).

parts, denoted as $\mathcal{Z}_k^d$, where k ranges from 1 to K. During each iteration, one of the K parts was set aside as the validation set, while the remaining $K - 1$ parts were used for training the classifier.

$$\mathcal{V}_1 = \mathcal{Z}_1^d \text{ and } \mathcal{T}_1 = \mathcal{Z}_2^d \cup \mathcal{Z}_3^d \cup \cdots \cup \mathcal{Z}_K^d$$
$$\mathcal{V}_2 = \mathcal{Z}_2^d \text{ and } \mathcal{T}_2 = \mathcal{Z}_1^d \cup \mathcal{Z}_3^d \cup \cdots \cup \mathcal{Z}_K^d$$

$$\vdots$$

$$\mathcal{V}_K = \mathcal{Z}_2^d \text{ and } \mathcal{T}_K = \mathcal{Z}_1^d \cup \mathcal{Z}_2^d \cup \cdots \cup \mathcal{Z}_{K-1}^d$$

Here, $\mathcal{V}_k$ and $\mathcal{T}_k$ denote the validation set and training set, respectively, for each iteration where k ranges from 1 to K. Following K tests, accuracy, precision, recall, and harmonic mean are computed, and the mean of each measure is subsequently determined.

In our study, we selected for K to be 10, aligned with the choice made in [3,4]. This setting facilitates direct comparison with the results obtained in [4].

During the validation, we also seek to identify the most effective hyperparameters, including the number of dimensions, the regularization parameter, and the entanglement strategy. Specifically, six entanglement strategies were examined::

– Full Entanglement: All qubits are entangled with each other.
– Linear Entanglement: The ith qubit is entangled with the $i + 1$th qubit for all $i \in \{1, 2, \ldots, d - 2\}$, where d represents the number of qubits.

- Reverse Linear Entanglement: Similar to linear entanglement, but the entanglement order is reversed.
- Pairwise Entanglement: This involves two layers of entanglement. In the first layer, even-indexed qubits are entangled with their successive qubits, while odd-indexed qubits are entangled in the second layer.
- Circular Entanglement: Similar to linear entanglement, but the first and last qubits are also entangled.
- Shifted-Circular-Alternating: This strategy, based on a circuit proposed in [23], involves circular entanglement with shifting entanglement connections between the first and last qubits and alternating control and target qubits in each block.

We used Python to write the source code of the test bed and experiments. Besides, we used Scikit-Learn Scikit-Learn library [16], Google Colaboratory [1], Qskit library, and the quantum computing simulator known as Aer [20].

6 Results

The results of the experiments are shown in Table 1, where the best outcomes are achieved with a regularization parameter (C) greater than one. This result is consistent with the context of the problem, where some students passed the numerical methods course despite their poor performance during their academic history, and vice versa.

An increase in the regularization parameter C from 4 to 8 resulted in improved accuracy but a decrease in recall and, consequently, the harmonic mean (F_1 score). This trade-off suggests that higher values of C prioritize accuracy at the expense of correctly identifying positive instances, which impacts the overall model performance. These observations were consistent across our validation experiments.

The linear entanglement strategy performed better than the others, hence, the results shown in Table 1 correspond to this setting. Other hyper-parameter configurations were omitted from the results due to their comparatively poorer performance across various metrics.

The Quantum-enhanced Support Vector Machines (QSVMs) exhibited higher precision and accuracy compared to recall, which is reflected in the lower harmonic mean across most hyper-parameter settings. This discrepancy is further elucidated by the confusion matrix presented in Table 2, where a notable number of false negative examples contributed to the decrease in recall. Specifically, 16 out of 41 students were incorrectly classified as negative examples, indicating that 39% of students at risk of failing the numerical course were not accurately identified during the 10-fold Cross-Validation. The confusion matrix was generated using the hyper-parameter setting that yielded the highest harmonic mean, corresponding to $C = 4$ and $d = 7$. This setting was chosen as it strikes a balance between precision and recall, as reflected by the harmonic mean.

The results in both tables also demonstrate consistency regarding precision, as indicated by the lower number of false positive examples compared to false

Table 1. Performance of quantum-enhanced support vector machines.

d	C	MA (%)	MP (%)	MR (%)	AF$_1$ (%)
2	0.125	66.09	65	17	27
2	0.25	67	66.67	20	29.71
2	0.25	67	66.67	20	29.71
2	1	67	66.67	20	29.71
2	2	65	56.67	20	28.38
2	4	66.82	66.67	27	36.05
2	8	69.73	77.5	34.50	44.5
2	16	69.82	77.5	34.5	44.5
2	32	69.73	75.83	34.5	45.02
3	1	67.73	66.67	28.5	37.95
3	2	68.73	75	32	42.48
3	4	67.73	80	29.5	40.48
3	8	68.73	**80.83**	32	43.02
3	16	67.73	70.83	29.5	39.02
4	1	67.91	70.83	31.5	41.4
4	2	67	67.5	31.5	40.69
4	4	66	64.17	36.5	45.07
4	8	62.18	55.83	31.5	38.88
4	16	64.09	64.33	34	42.05
7	0.5	60.91	15	10	11.9
7	1	71.73	71.67	45.5	56.62
7	2	72.73	71	56.5	61.67
7	4	73.82	70	**61.5**	**64.44**
7	8	**74**	71.79	59	63.19
7	16	73.91	70.95	**61.5**	64.42
7	32	73.91	70.95	**61.5**	64.42
8	1	70.09	63	52	54.32
8	2	67.09	56.5	57	55.2
8	4	64.27	51.33	57	53.1
8	8	67.18	53.17	59.5	55.27
8	16	67.18	53.17	59.5	55.27
9	1	70	72.5	32.5	41.83
9	2	73	75.83	51.5	60.36
9	4	71	70.83	51.5	58.69
9	8	71.91	68.33	56.5	61.43
9	16	71.91	68.33	56.5	61.43

MA stands for Mean Accuracy
MP stands for Mean Precision
MR stands for Mean Recall
AF$_1$ is the Average Harmonic Mean (**F$_1$**)
d represents the dimensionality size of the input space $\mathcal{Z}$
C is the regularization parameter

Table 2. Confusion matrix illustrating the performance of Quantum-enhanced Support Vector Machines.

True Class	Forecasted Class		Total
	Student without Risk	Student at Risk	
Student without risk	51	11	62
Student at risk	16	25	41
Total	67	36	103

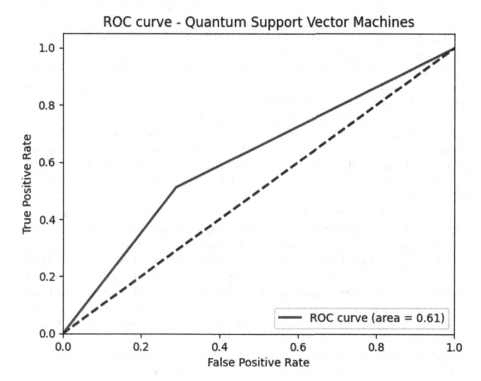

Fig. 6. Receiver Operating Characteristics (ROC) curve for the Quantum-enhanced Support Vector Machines (QSVMs). The ROC curve above the diagonal dashed line illustrates that the QSVMs method outperforms guessing at random.

negative instances. It is noteworthy that during the 10 validations, the system incorrectly classified 11 out of 61 students as being at risk, despite them not being so. This indicates that approximately 17% of students without risk were incorrectly identified as potentially failing the numerical methods course.

Thus, with the above-mentioned hyper-parameter setting, we obtained the Receiver Operating Characteristics (ROC) curve for the QSVMs, depicted in Fig. 6. The area of the curve exceeds 0.5, which implies that QSVMs predictions are better than guessing at random.

7   Discussion

In our study, we opted for the hyper-parameter setting that maximizes the highest harmonic mean (F_1) when designing the Quantum Course Prophet to keep the trade-off between precision and recall. While other settings yield higher precision or accuracy, reaching values of 80.83% and 74%, respectively. It is essential to consider that a system with high precision but poor recall might overlook students at risk who need support. Whereas, a system with poor recall but high precision may flag students as at-risk who are not truly facing academic challenges.

The Quantum Course Prophet prototype achieved lower accuracy and harmonic mean compared to its classical counterpart, as proposed by Caicedo-Castro [4]. Despite these figures, using the same validation scheme and dataset, there is no solid statistical evidence indicating significant differences among the measures in both systems (see Table 3).

In the configuration with fewer components in the input space ($d = 3$), the system achieved higher precision at the expense of accuracy, recall, and consequently, the harmonic mean. Besides, Table 3 presents statistical evidence indicating that the classical system outperforms the quantum system in terms of accuracy, recall, and harmonic mean, while there are no significant differences in precision.

In Table 3, the configuration corresponding to a relaxed regularization (i.e., $C = 8$) and seven dimensions in the input space enables the system to achieve slightly greater accuracy compared to the configuration with stronger regularization (i.e., $C = 4$), albeit at the cost of recall and the harmonic mean. However, there are no statistically significant differences in the performance of both systems. It is noteworthy that relaxed regularization might lead to overfitting, potentially causing the system to fail at accurately predicting new input data. Therefore, we opted for the stronger regularization setting for Quantum Course Prophet.

Additionally, the reduction in the dimensionality of the input space may have a detrimental effect on the accuracy and other characteristics of the Quantum Course Prophet. This is because valuable information may be lost during the process, despite the removal of noise from the original input data. Therefore, the only way to make a fair comparison between models is to use the original input space during validation. However, this approach is computationally costly and unfeasible when using an emulator, such as the one utilized in our study. Unfortunately, using two or three dimensions for visualizing the decision boundary to analyze latent factors may be constrained by the accuracy of such settings, as demonstrated in Table 1, potentially leading decision-makers to incorrect conclusions.

Furthermore, the Course Prophet prototype proposed in [4] is based on Gaussian Processes (GP), providing users with information about the probability of failing the course. This feature aids decision-making. In contrast, the prototype of its quantum counterpart, proposed in our study, relies on Quantum-enhanced Support Vector Machines (QSVMs), which are not inherently probabilistic machine learning methods. As a result, the Quantum Course Prophet prototype cannot provide users with information regarding the probability of a student failing the numerical methods course. However, this limitation is mitigated by leveraging Platt scaling [17] to estimate probabilities from the decision values of the QSVMs, as it is internally implemented in the Scikit-Learn library.

Adopting QSVMs for implementing Quantum Course Prophet offers two significant advantages. Firstly, QSVMs leverage quantum parallelism, potentially accelerating both the training and forecasting processes. This inherent quantum advantage can lead to significant time savings compared to classical methods. Secondly, QSVMs hold promise for scalability in quantum computation. As error correction techniques advance, the scalability of quantum computers is expected to improve, allowing QSVMs to handle larger datasets more effectively. This scalability is particularly crucial as GP face challenges with the construction of the Gram matrix, limiting the scalability. Finally, ongoing research in quantum machine learning suggests that QSVMs will continue to improve in performance, paving the way for even greater advancements in the foreseeable future.

Table 3. Results of the t-test on Mean Accuracy (MA), Mean Precision (MP), Mean Recall (MR), Average Harmonic Mean (AF$_1$) to compare the Gaussian Processes for Classification (GP) adopted in [4] with Quantum-enhanced Support Vector Machines (QSVM).

Metric	Classifiers		p-value	Is it statistically significant?
	GP	QSVMs		
		$C = 4, d = 7$		
MA (%)	80.45	73.82	0.33	No
MP (%)	81.33	70	0.18	No
MR (%)	66.5	61.5	0.63	No
AF$_1$ (%)	72.52	64.44	0.39	No
		$C = 4, d = 3$		
MA (%)	80.45	68.73	0.03	Yes
MP (%)	81.33	80.83	0.84	No
MR (%)	66.5	32	1.94×10^{-3}	Yes
AF$_1$ (%)	72.52	43.02	3.44×10^{-3}	Yes
		$C = 8, d = 7$		
MA (%)	80.45	74	0.31	No
MP (%)	81.33	71.79	0.21	No
MR (%)	66.5	59	0.48	No
AF$_1$ (%)	72.52	63.19	0.31	No

8   Conclusions

In our study, we have designed an intelligent system called Quantum Course Prophet, leveraging Quantum-enhanced Support Vector Machines (QSVMs), to address a real-world issue in education. Specifically, our system predicts whether a student is at risk of failing the numerical methods course based on their performance in prerequisite courses. To our knowledge, the adoption of quantum machine learning for this specific problem in the field of educational data mining has not been explored previously.

Our study indicates that the differences in accuracy, precision, recall, and harmonic mean between QSVM and Gaussian Processes (GP) are not statistically significant. While previous research by Caicedo-Castro [4] suggests that GP classifiers outperform various machine learning methods for the problem at hand, QSVM presents a viable alternative due to its potential scalability benefits with quantum computing. Despite not conclusively demonstrating superior accuracy in this domain compared to classical machine learning, our findings highlight the need for further investigation to draw more definitive conclusions.

In future research endeavors, it would be valuable to conduct empirical validations utilizing alternative techniques for reducing the dimensionality of input spaces. This could involve exploring methods such as Principal Component Analysis (PCA), kernel PCA, autoassociative neural networks, among others, to assess their efficacy in improving model performance.

Additionally, there is merit in validating QSVMs on actual quantum computers, as opposed to relying solely on emulators. Leveraging the inherent parallelism of quantum computing could significantly accelerate both training and prediction processes, offering valuable insights into the practical benefits of quantum approaches.

Exploring novel quantum kernels represents another promising avenue for future investigation. By designing and evaluating new quantum circuit-based kernels, researchers can assess the potential for these novel approaches to outperform classical machine learning methods, thereby pushing the boundaries of quantum-enhanced learning.

Expanding the size of the dataset used in evaluations could provide further insights into the scalability and generalizability of QSVMs. A larger dataset would enable a more comprehensive evaluation across various scenarios, yielding deeper insights into the robustness and performance of these models.

Lastly, there is scope for exploring hybrid quantum-classical machine learning methods in future research. This could involve integrating quantum techniques, such as parameterized quantum circuits, into classical neural networks. Such hybrid models offer probabilistic outputs, which are invaluable for risk assessment tasks such as predicting the likelihood of failing the numerical methods course.

Acknowledgments. Caicedo-Castro thanks the Lord Jesus Christ for blessing this project and the Universidad de Córdoba in Colombia for supporting the Course Prophet

Research Project (grant FI-01-22). Finally, the author thanks the anonymous referees for their comments, that improved the quality of this article.

Disclosure of Interests. The author has no competing interests to declare.

References

1. Google Colaboratory (2004). https://colab.research.google.com/. Accessed Feb 2024
2. Caicedo-Castro, I., Macea-Anaya, M., Castaño-Rivera, S.: Forecasting failure risk in early mathematics and physical science courses in the bachelor's degree in engineering. In: IARIA Congress 2023: International Conference on Technical Advances and Human Consequences, pp. 177–187. International Academy, Research, and Industry Association (2022)
3. Caicedo-Castro, I., Macea-Anaya, M., Rivera-Castaño, S.: Early forecasting of at-risk students of failing or dropping out of a bachelor's course given their academic history - the case study of numerical methods. In: PATTERNS 2023: The Fifteenth International Conference on Pervasive Patterns and Applications, pp. 40–51. International Conferences on Pervasive Patterns and Applications, IARIA: International Academy, Research, and Industry Association (2023)
4. Caicedo-Castro, I.: Course prophet: a system for predicting course failures with machine learning: a numerical methods case study. Sustainability **15**(18) (2023). https://doi.org/10.3390/su151813950
5. Cichocki, A., Zdunek, R., Phan, A.H., Amari, S.i.: Fast local algorithms for large scale nonnegative matrix and tensor factorizations. IEICE Trans. Fund. Electron. Commun. Comput. Sci. **92**(3), 708–721 (2009)
6. Cortes, C., Vapnik, V.: Support vector networks. Mach. Learn. **20**, 273–297 (1995)
7. Dorogush, A.V., Ershov, V., Gulin, A.: CatBoost: gradient boosting with categorical features support. CoRR **abs/1810.11363** (2018)
8. Havlíček, V., et al.: Supervised learning with quantum-enhanced feature spaces. Nature **567**(7747), 209–212 (2019). https://doi.org/10.1038/s41586-019-0980-2
9. Kabathova, J., Drlik, M.: Towards predicting student's dropout in university courses using different machine learning techniques. Appl. Sci. **11**, 3130 (2021). https://doi.org/10.3390/app11073130
10. Ke, G., et al.: LightGBM: a highly efficient gradient boosting decision tree. In: Guyon, I., et al. (eds.) Advances in Neural Information Processing Systems, vol. 30. Curran Associates, Inc. (2017)
11. Lee, D.D., Seung, H.S.: Learning the parts of objects by non-negative matrix factorization. Nature **401**(6755), 788–791 (1999)
12. Lin, C.J.: Algorithms for nonnegative matrix factorization with the beta-divergence. Neural Comput. **19**(9), 2505–2529 (2007)
13. Lykourentzou, I., Giannoukos, I., Nikolopoulos, V., Mpardis, G., Loumos, V.: Dropout prediction in e-learning courses through the combination of machine learning techniques. Comput. Educ. **53**(3), 950–965 (2009). https://doi.org/10.1016/j.compedu.2009.05.010
14. Mohri, M., Rostamizadeh, A., Talwalkar, A.: Foundations of Machine Learning, 2nd edn. The MIT Press, Cambridge (2018)

15. Niyogisubizo, J., Liao, L., Nziyumva, E., Murwanashyaka, E., Nshimyumukiza, P.C.: Predicting student's dropout in university classes using two-layer ensemble machine learning approach: a novel stacked generalization. Comput. Educ. Artif. Intell. **3**, 100066 (2022). https://doi.org/10.1016/j.caeai.2022.100066

16. Pedregosa, F., et al.: Scikit-learn: machine learning in Python. J. Mach. Learn. Res. **12**, 2825–2830 (2011)

17. Platt, J.C.: probabilistic outputs for support vector machines and comparisons to regularized likelihood methods. In: Advances in Large Margin Classifiers, pp. 61–74. MIT Press (1999)

18. Čotić Poturić, V., Bašić-Šiško, A., Lulić, I.: Artificial neural network model for forecasting student failure in math course. In: ICERI2022 Proceedings, pp. 5872–5878. 15th Annual International Conference of Education, Research and Innovation, IATED (2022). https://doi.org/10.21125/iceri.2022.1448

19. Čotić Poturić, V., Dražić, I., Čandrlić, S.: Identification of Predictive Factors for Student Failure in STEM Oriented Course. In: ICERI2022 Proceedings, pp. 5831–5837. 15th Annual International Conference of Education, Research and Innovation, IATED (2022). https://doi.org/10.21125/iceri.2022.1441

20. Qiskit Development Team: Qskit Development Kit (2017). https://qiskit.org/. Accessed Feb 2024

21. Qiskit Development Team: ZZ Feature Mapping Library Documentation (2017). https://qiskit.org/documentation/stubs/qiskit.circuit.library.ZZFeatureMap. html. Accessed Feb 2024

22. da Silva, D.E.M., Pires, E.J.S., Reis, A., de Moura Oliveira, P.B., Barroso, J.: Forecasting students dropout: a UTAD university study. Future Internet **14**(3), 1–14 (2022)

23. Sim, S., Johnson, P.D., Aspuru-Guzik, A.: Expressibility and entangling capability of parameterized quantum circuits for hybrid quantum-classical algorithms. Adv. Quant. Technol. **2**(12) (2019). https://doi.org/10.1002/qute.201900070. http://dx. doi.org/10.1002/qute.201900070

24. Zihan, S., Sung, S.H., Park, D.M., Park, B.K.: All-year dropout prediction modeling and analysis for university students. Appl. Sci. **13**, 1143 (2023). https://doi. org/10.3390/app13021143

Do Engineering Students Know How to Use Generative Artificial Intelligence? A Case Study

Miguel Á. Conde[1]([✉]) [iD] and Jesús-Ángel Román-Gallego[2] [iD]

[1] Department of Mechanics, Computer Science and Aerospace Engineering, Robotics Group, Universidad de León, Campus de Vegazana S/N, 24071 León, Spain
mcong@unileon.es
[2] Department of Computer Science and Automatic, EPS of Zamora, Universidad de Salamanca, Avda. Cardenal Cisneros, 34, 49022 Zamora, Spain
zjarg@usal.es

Abstract. In the context of engineering education, the utilization of generative artificial intelligence (AI) holds significant promise for enhancing learning experiences. This article presents a compelling case study designed to assess the proficiency of engineering students in employing generative AI, particularly focusing on ChatGPT. Students from diverse engineering disciplines and academic levels engage in a knowledge questionnaire, with one group utilizing ChatGPT and the other leveraging unrestricted internet resources. The study not only investigates the effectiveness of generative AI as a learning tool but also explores its impact on problem-solving skills. Towards the end of the questionnaire, students are surveyed using a validated instrument to gauge their perceptions and experiences regarding the use of ChatGPT and generative AI in the realm of engineering education. This research contributes valuable insights into the integration of generative AI as a pedagogical tool, shedding light on its potential to shape the future of engineering instruction.

Keywords: Artificial Intelligence · AI · Generative · Engineering Education

1 Introduction

In today's rapidly evolving society, the methods and tools utilized in teaching and learning must also progress accordingly. Information and Communication Technologies (ICTs) have played a pivotal role in various domains, with education being no exception. Internet and web-based platforms, such as Learning Management Systems (LMS), have notably shaped the educational landscape. However, one of the most disruptive technologies in recent times is Artificial Intelligence (AI). While AI is not a novel concept [1] and has been applied across diverse sectors such agriculture [2], healthcare [3], law [4], transportation [5] or education [6, 7] for many years, its recent advancements have led to unprecedented opportunities and challenges.

The application of AI aims to support individuals in their tasks, saving time, energy, facilitating access to information, etc. [8]. In education specifically, AI has

© The Author(s), under exclusive license to Springer Nature Switzerland AG 2024
P. Zaphiris and A. Ioannou (Eds.): HCII 2024, LNCS 14724, pp. 241–254, 2024.
https://doi.org/10.1007/978-3-031-61691-4_16

been employed over the past three decades for personalized learning, skill development, collaborative learning, student engagement, learning support, and decision-making processes [1, 7] through intelligent tutoring systems, teaching robots, learning analytics dashboards, adaptive learning systems, and more [9]. Numerous systematic reviews have explored various facets of AI in education [8, 10–12].

However, the definitive disruption in the realm of AI stems from the emergence of Generative AI and its implications for education [13]. The pivotal moment came with the release of ChatGPT in November 2023, a freely accessible chatbot based on a Large Language Model (LLM) capable of responding to natural language queries. Its exponential impact was evident, with 5 million users in its first 5 days of life, 100 millions in about a month and 180 million users in January of 2024 [14]. This marked the beginning of a new era, with other Generative AI applications such as Bard and Copilot swiftly following suit, along with advancements in image, video, and sound generation [14].

The integration of Generative AI in education has sparked debates [15, 16], with proponents touting it as the future cornerstone of education, while skeptics perceive it as a potential threat [13, 17]. However, irrespective of these views [18], the reality is that students will inevitably encounter Generative AI beyond educational institutions. Therefore, it becomes imperative to equip them with the requisite knowledge and skills to effectively utilize such technologies, including the ability to ask pertinent questions [16].

While recent research has explored students' perceptions and usage of ChatGPT [19], there remains a gap in understanding how it is applied in specific engineering tasks or activities. This paper aims to address this gap by presenting a case study examining how students leverage Generative AI, specifically ChatGPT 3.5, to answer knowledge questions in engineering scenarios. The study seeks to ascertain whether students possess sufficient know-how to effectively utilize Generative AI in education or if specific training is required.

The rest of the paper is structured as follows first the theoretical context about AI and Generative AI in Education is presented. Third section describes the case study carried out in an engineering context. Forth section shows the produced results and a discussion about them is carried out in section fifth. Finally, some conclusions are posed.

2 Theoretical Context

This section briefly introduces some key concepts to aid in the understanding of the paper. Firstly, it outlines the concepts of AI and Generative AI, followed by an exploration of their applications in education.

2.1 Definitions of AI and Generative AI

Although AI is currently experiencing a disruptive moment, the term itself was coined approximately 70 years ago [1]. The initial inquiry into AI was sparked by Turing's contemplation of whether machines could exhibit human-like thought processes [20], with John McCarthy later defining it as "The science and engineering of making intelligent machines" [21]. However, defining AI in a singular manner proves challenging due to its diverse approaches and development paths [22]. Various categories of AI have been described [23]:

- Artificial narrow intelligence (ANI). A kind of AI which possesses a limited range of abilities and represents the only achievement thus far.
- Artificial general intelligence (AGI). A kind of AI which aims to emulate human-like capabilities.
- Artificial superintelligence (ASI). A kind of AI which surpasses human intelligence.
- Also some authors consider different types of AI such as [24]:
- Artificial Intelligence. A type which enables machines to replicate human cognition.
- Machine Learning. A subset focused on learning from data examples primarily through statistical methods like linear regressions and decision trees, requiring less data and computation power but more human intervention.
- Deep Learning. A subset of Machine Learning relying on neural networks, complex algorithms that demand more data and computing power while involving less human intervention.

Once the concept of AI is defined, it becomes essential to comprehend the current landscape, particularly with the emergence of a phenomenon that has gained significant popularity, known as Generative AI. Generative AI can be defined as "… a technology that (i) leverages deep learning models to (ii) generate human-like content (e.g., images, words) in response to (iii) complex and varied prompts (e.g., languages, instructions, questions)" [17]. Other possible definition could be "production of previously unseen synthetic content, in any form and to support any task, through generative modeling" [25].

AI can be classified based on the type of generative algorithms, as outlined by Jovanovic and Campbell, who differentiate between Generative Adversarial Networks (GAN), Generative Pre-trained Transformers, Generative Diffusion Models (GDM), or Geometric Deep Learning (GDL) [26]. Alternatively, García-Peñalvo and Vázquez-Ingelmo categorize algorithms and techniques into GAN, Encoder-Decoder Networks, Neural Networks, Transformers, and others [25]. However, the most notable approach in the past year has been the development of Large Language Models (LLMs).

Large language models, crucial in Natural Language Processing (NLP), are "models are trained on massive amounts of text data and are able to generate human-like text, answer questions, and complete other language-related tasks with high accuracy" [27]. They can be understood as "a statistical language model that assigns a probability to a sequence of m tokens $P(w1,…,wm)$ using a probability distribution" [28], widely applied in various tasks such as speech recognition, machine translation, part-of-speech tagging, parsing, handwriting recognition, and information retrieval. These models serve as the foundation for current Generative AI chatbots and other AI applications. However, maintaining them is challenging, requiring substantial investment and months of training, while accessing training data poses additional difficulties [29].

2.2 AI and Generative AI in Education

In the realm of AI applications, numerous studies have explored its potential and associated successes [30]. Various categorizations of potential applications exist, such as those outlined by Dahwan & Batra [1] or the one proposed by Holmes et al. [31]. However, for the purpose of this research, we will consider two categorizations: one defined by Hwang et al. [7] focusing on application roles, and another by Ouyang [10], focusing on paradigms.

Regarding the former categorization by Hwang et al. [7], the authors delineated distinct roles for AI applications in education:

- Intelligent tutor: Encompassing systems aimed at personalizing and adapting learning to students' needs, including intelligent tutoring systems, adaptive/personalized learning systems, and recommendation systems.
- Intelligent tutee: Although less common, this role involves learners engaging with others to provide assistance.
- Intelligent learning tool/partner: Providing intelligent data gathering and analysis to identify critical focal points for learning.
- Policy Making Advisor: Implementing AI techniques to aid decision-makers by considering evidence generated within educational institutions.

As for the latter categorization by Ouyang [10], three possible paradigms are defined:

- AI-directed, learner-as-recipient: AI directs learning processes and defines suitable learning pathways, with intelligent tutoring systems serving as an example.
- AI-supported, learner-as-collaborator: AI serves as a supportive tool for students in their learning journey, assisting them in focusing on relevant issues.
- AI-empowered, learner-as-leader: AI functions as a tool to enhance human intelligence, aiding both learners and teachers in improving teaching and learning performance.

The utilization of a chatbot like ChatGPT could fall under the intelligent learning tool category of the former classification, as it assists students in avoiding mechanical tasks and finding solutions to facilitate their learning progression. Regarding the latter classification, it could be considered as part of AI-supported, learner-as-collaborator and AI-empowered learner paradigms, as it aids students in their work following interaction with AI technology and provides them with knowledge they may not have initially possessed.

Regarding the use of generative AI, it has gained significant popularity since its emergence in November 2023. Reactions to its potential applications have varied widely, with some authors describing its arrival as a "calculator moment" in digital writing classrooms—a transformative technology that necessitates a shift in educational goals [32].

However, as with any disruptive technology, there are also negative reactions, viewing the new technology as undermining scientific pursuits and moral principles by fostering a flawed understanding of language and knowledge [33].

Nevertheless, Generative AI is readily available, and understanding its potential applications is imperative. Authors such as Baidoo-Anu & Owusu have outlined several possible applications, including [16]:

- Personalized tutoring and feedback tailored to students' individual learning needs and progress.

- Automated Essay Grading to support teachers and streamline their workload.
- Language translation of texts into different languages following appropriate training.
- Interactive learning through virtual tutors that engage students in conversational interactions.
- Adaptive learning, which personalizes teaching methods based on student progress and performance.

This classification represents only a portion of the diverse range of tools provided by Generative AI. They can be categorized based on the outcomes they produce into various domains, including text generation (such as chatbots, content creation, exams generation, and language teaching), image generation (including graph and presentation generation), video generation, 3D objects generation, audio generation (including voice modulation and transcription), source code generation (including debugging and generation), and AI-generated text detection (including anti-plagiarism tools) [34].

The possibilities offered by the use of generative AI are vast. For instance, the work by Nerantzi et al. [35] gathers 101 potential ideas for using AI in education. However, it is crucial to acknowledge that generative AI comes with associated advantages, drawbacks, and challenges. Importantly, students across different educational levels are already using AI, highlighting the necessity for them to understand how to use it and develop critical thinking skills when interpreting the feedback they receive from AI-generated content [34].

3 The Case Study

3.1 Description of the Activity

The case study conducted entails an optional activity offered at the conclusion of the subject, which is completed online via an online form. The primary objective of this activity is to discern the disparity in answering knowledge questions, pertinent to the subjects covered, through the use of Generative AI versus other potential tools and sources. Therefore, the case study seeks to evaluate the following hypothesis:

- The utilization of Generative AI by students for answering knowledge questions is correlated with improved outcomes.

To examine this hypothesis, participating students will be divided into an experimental group and a control group. Students in the experimental group will utilize ChatGPT 3.5, whereas those in the control group will have the liberty to employ any other resources available on the internet. The responses provided will be evaluated and analyzed by the teachers.

This distribution enables us to explore the average means of the subgroups within the subjects, assess correlations with the manner in which ChatGPT was utilized, examine the most frequently utilized alternative tools, and ascertain students' use/perception of ChatGPT. Feedback will be gathered through a questionnaire concerning AI usage, adapted from [19].

3.2 Description of the Involved Subjects

In order to understand the background of the students involved in case study it is necessary to describe the courses in which they are enrolled. These are three:

- Computer Systems Administration (CSA). This is a fourth-year subject in the Bachelor's Degree in Computer Sciences. The subject is proposed in the final year of the degree as a journey through the public and private environment regarding their workflows, resources, data storage, data transmission, security, and optimization of these processes, among others. It is a subject that has both theoretical and practical aspects, so all concept explanations must be implemented in practice so that students further consolidate their knowledge and better acquire the necessary skills to pass this subject. The main interest of the subject is to show students the possibility that they themselves manage the information systems of an organization, as well as the ability to administer them. It is also intended for students to acquire the ability to carry out an analysis of the needs of any organization, public or private, in this area, and the subsequent implementation of these information systems, satisfying the anticipated needs optimally at the resource and economic levels. In this subject, the experiment is proposed as an optional activity with no impact on the student's final grade.
- Service Oriented Architectures (SOA). This is a fourth-year subject in the Bachelor's Degree in Computer Sciences. Currently, new computing models require Service-Oriented Architectures (SOA). These approaches make clients and providers pivotal actors in providing or consuming applications, which are generally accessible through services. The subject consists of three interconnected blocks aimed at enabling students to perform analysis, design, implementation, and deployment of service-oriented architectures. To achieve this, they must use the proposed standards in each case and follow a methodology based on Service-Oriented Engineering, thereby optimizing resources and the solution lifecycle. Additionally, various enterprise solutions based on Business Intelligence (BI) are proposed for analysis and subsequent deployment. As in the previous subject the activity carried out is not mandatory.
- Informatics (INF). A first-year subject shared by the Bachelor's Degree in Mechanical Engineering and the Bachelor's Degree in Agri-Food Engineering. The subject aims to provide students with the basic concepts of computer science, enabling them to expand their knowledge in this field in the future and allowing them to handle computers proficiently. This will facilitate their future academic and professional activities, enabling them to successfully meet the requirements of other subjects that involve the use of computer applications throughout their education. Specifically, fundamental concepts in computer science are taught, such as: basic computing, microprocessors, memory, peripherals, programming languages, operating systems, data structures, etc. When it comes to the case study, the proposed activity is optional but carries an additional weight of 10 points out of 100 in the final grade of the subject. These points will be added only if the subject is passed by successfully completing the mandatory activities.

3.3 Materials and Methods

This research adopts a mixed-methods approach [36], integrating quantitative and qualitative analysis. The quantitative analysis involves comparing the scores assigned to students' knowledge questions when utilizing ChatGPT versus other resources. On the other hand, qualitative analysis centers on students' perceptions regarding the use of ChatGPT and is currently in progress, with potential conclusions to be outlined in future research.

Initially, we provide an overview of the student sample, followed by an examination of the questionnaires.

The Sample. The sample is summarized by the Table 1. On it is possible to see the sample size, divided by gender and by subject and how many of the students are in the experimental and in the control group. This division was done following a systematic sampling, however some of the students did not understand properly the instructions and used the GenerativeAI option when they should not and vice versa, so it was necessary to change their groups to maintain coherence in average study. The activity involved 88 students. It is necessary to point out that there is an unbalance from the experimental and control group (specially in SOA subject) motivated by the fact the activity was elective, and the subject classes have ended when the activity was carried out. In addition, it is necessary to mention the clear lower number of female students in engineering (about a 26% in the case study) something common and already pointed out by several authors [37]. For the case study it is more relevant in Computer Science Degrees than in other engineering (between a 1,5%–1,7% in computer science subjects vs a 33% in the others engineering degrees involved in the case study).

Participation in the study was voluntary, and participating students had to explicitly accept and sign a consent form, by which they allowed instructors and the research team to access and analyze their data. For research purposes, data is anonymized. Students could cancel this agreement at any given moment. Participants were also informed that there were not risks associated with the study, nor any payment due for participation.

Table 1. Sample distribution.

	CSA	SOA	INF	Totals
N	20	17	51	88
Female	3	3	17	23
Male	17	14	34	65
Exp. Group	8	10	28	46
Female	1	2	12	14
Male	7	8	16	28
Cont. Group	12	7	23	42
Female	2	1	5	8
Male	10	6	18	34

The Knowledge Questionnaire. The knowledge questionnaire comprised two knowledge questions for each subject, along with common procedure questions for both experimental and control groups across all subjects.

For the CSA subject, the knowledge questions were:

- K1. Describe the differences between SCRUM and Extreme Programming.
- K2. Describe the differences between and ERP and a CRM.

For the SOA subject:

- K1. What is the protocol XMPP and what is its purpose?
- K2. What is the Enterprise Service Bus?

For the INF subject:

- K1. What are the functions of the arithmetic logical unit of a computer?
- K2. What does it mean that the Operating Systems acts as a Extended Virtual Machine?

The procedure questions for the experimental group, which utilized ChatGPT, were as follows:

- Experimental Group (same questions for knowledge questions 1 and 2):

    - EP1. Have you used the ChatGPT to answer question X? (Yes/No/I have edited it)
    - EP2. How many prompts did you use for question X?

- Control Group

    - CP1. List the tools you used to answer the questions.
    - CP2. Among all of them, which do you consider the best for answering?

The ChatGPT Questionnaire. Another interesting aspect is understanding the students' knowledge about using ChatGPT. To assess this, we utilized part of the questionnaire proposed by Amo-Filvà et al. [19]. Specifically, the following questions were included:

- CQ1. I know what Generative AI is and how to use it (measured on a 5-point Likert scale).
- CQ2. I am familiar with the tool ChatGPT (measured on a 5-point Likert scale).
- CQ3. I have a ChatGPT account (Yes/No).
- CQ4. I use ChatGPT (participants select one or more options from "No", "for learning", "in my personal life", "at work", "other").

Additionally, there are other questions answered by the students that are not included in this study as they are still under analysis.

4   Results

To present the results, it is crucial to analyze the students' responses. The initial analysis focuses on the average grades obtained by students when completing the activity. To achieve this, a descriptive analysis of the samples is necessary, followed by a comparison of the means. Table 2 presents the descriptive statistics of each group and subject, including the ratio of students who completed the activity compared to those enrolled in the subject.

Table 2. Descriptive statistics and ratio of completion

Subject	N	Avg. Mean (Std. Dev)	Var
CSA	20	6,65 (2,53)	6,42
Exp	12	7,92 (0,51)	3,08
Control	8	4,75 (0,84)	5,71
SOA	17	7,35 (2,88)	8,30
Exp	10	8,25 (0,66)	4,40
Control	7	6,07 (1,32)	12,29
INF	51	8,21 (1,99)	3,97
Exp	28	9,82 (0,10)	0,30
Control	23	6,26 (0,24)	1,38
Ratio of completion vs Enrolment			
		Enrolled	Percentage
CSA	20	25	80%
SOA	17	24	71%
INF	51	85	60%

After conducting the descriptive analysis, it is essential to compare whether there are significant differences between the experimental and control groups, i.e., between students who used ChatGPT and those who used other tools. The null hypothesis assumes that there is no difference between the groups. Table 3 presents the values for the difference tests.

CSA satisfies the normality and homoscedasticity test criteria, allowing for the application of a Student's t-test. However, for the other two subjects, the sample distribution is not normal, necessitating the application of non-parametric tests such as the Mann-Whitney U test.

Table 3. Mean Differences Tests

Student T Test					
Subject	Avg. Exp	Avg. Cont	t	df	p-value
CSA	7,92	4,75	3,42	18,00	0.0030
MannWhitney U Test					
Subject		U	W	Std Error	p-value
SOA		18,50	46,50	10,06	0,1090
INF		17,50	293,50	48,79	0,0000

On the other hand, another potential issue to explore is the correlation between the grades in the experimental group and the number of prompts used in ChatGPT, as well as between the grades and whether students used the answer directly or edited it. Table 4 presents these correlations. If the sample is normally distributed, the Pearson correlation test is employed; otherwise, Kendall's Tau is used. Additionally, the table includes the number of prompts per student and the percentage of students who edited their answers.

Table 4. Correlations between average mean, prompts and edits

Pearson Correlation Test						
Subject	Pearson Corr. Prompts	Sign. Prompts	Pearson Correlation Edits	Sign. Edits	Prompts Per Student	Percentage Edits
CSA	−0,714	0,009	0,075	0,817	1,29	50%
Kendall's Tau Test						
Subject	Corr. Prompts	Sign. Prompts	Corr. Edits	Sign. Edits	Prompts Per Student	Percentage Edits
SOA	−0,111	0,716	−0,162	0,588	1,15	20%
INF	0,202	0,259	−0,087	0,641	1,14	21%

Regarding the questions related to ChatGPT knowledge and use, Table 5 presents some of the results categorized by subjects. The responses for CQ1 and CQ2 are described as the average mean of the answers, while for CQ3, the table provides the percentage of users with a ChatGPT account. In this case, the table does not differentiate between the results of the experimental and control groups, as all students completed these questions.

Table 5. ChatGPT Knowledge and Use Results by Subject

	CSA	SOA	INF
CQ1	3,90 (1,12)	4,00 (0,93)	3,90 (0,70)
CQ2	4,25 (1,21)	4,41 (1,00)	4,41(0,66)
CQ3	90,00%	88,23%	70%

Regarding CQ4, which assesses the students' use of ChatGPT, Fig. 1 illustrates graphs for each of the subjects.

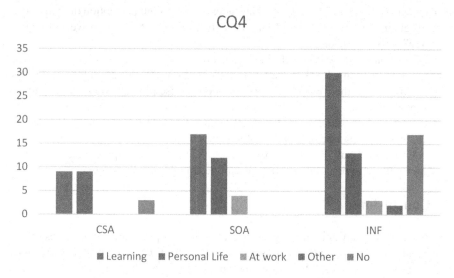

Fig. 1. Distribution of CQ4 answers per subject, considering how students use ChatGPT in chase they use it.

5 Discussion

Regarding the obtained results, several issues need to be explored:

- Table 2 reveals a significant difference in average grades across all subjects. However, techniques for average mean comparison have been applied. It is important to note that the samples for CSA and SOA may present limitations for this research.
- The participation percentage, measured as the number of students who completed the activity compared to the number of students enrolled in the subject, is quite high in all subjects, exceeding 60%. Notably, for INF, where students were awarded for completing the task, the participation percentage is the lowest. This may be attributed to the topic of the activity, as INF students come from engineering disciplines other than Computer Science.
- Average comparison indicates a significant difference in tests for both CSA and INF, leading to the rejection of the null hypothesis that stated there were no differences between experimental and control groups. Differences in grades mean that the application of ChatGPT yields different outcomes compared to other resources, with higher average grades in these cases.
- Table 4 displays correlations between the number of prompts and edits of students and their grades, along with statistics about these interactions. For CSA, there is a correlation between prompts and grades, possibly due to the higher number of prompts per student or the perceived difficulty of the questions. However, for other subjects, the correlation is not significant. Regarding edits or direct use of provided answers, no clear correlation is evident. Notably, in CSA, where more prompts are used, there are also more edits, potentially indicating question difficulty.

- CQ1 and CQ2 responses indicate that students have a high perception of their knowledge about Generative AI and ChatGPT before the activity, with answers close to "I agree" across most subjects.
- CQ3 responses show relatively high percentages of students who have or have not had an account in ChatGPT. Notably, students from INF have a lower percentage, possibly due to their enrollment in engineering disciplines unrelated to computer science.
- CQ4 reveals how students use ChatGPT, with most using it for learning. However, in INF, there is a significant number of students who do not use it. The percentage of students using ChatGPT in their personal life is higher for Computer Science students than for those in other engineering disciplines involved in the study.

6 Conclusions

The integration of artificial intelligence (AI) has already permeated various disciplines, yet the advent of generative AI marks a significant shift, necessitating a universal understanding of its principles. This pivotal moment underscores the importance of comprehending AI's nuances for individuals across all fields. For students, acquiring comprehensive education on AI, encompassing both theoretical foundations and practical applications, is essential. Moreover, cultivating an educational environment that embraces AI-driven methodologies is crucial for preparing students for the evolving technological landscape.

This study has aimed to illuminate the usage patterns of AI among engineering students, highlighting the need for deeper insights into their AI-related practices to inform educational strategies effectively. The findings indicate a robust understanding of AI among participants, affirming its suitability for educational integration. Furthermore, the analysis of the case study data suggests that the utilization of generative AI, exemplified by ChatGPT, may enhance academic performance in specific tasks. However, further research involving diverse subject areas and larger sample sizes is required to validate these findings conclusively. Additionally, targeted training initiatives focusing on generative AI, especially in non-computer science disciplines, are imperative to leverage its potential effectively for educational enhancement.

7 Disclosure of Interests.

The authors have no competing interests.

Acknowledgments. A third level heading in 9-point font size at the end of the paper is used for general acknowledgments, for example: This study was funded by X (grant number Y).

References

1. Dhawan, S., Batra, G.: Artificial intelligence in higher education: promises, perils, and perspective. Expanding Knowl. Horizon. OJAS **11**, 11–22 (2020)

2. Bannerjee, G., Sarkar, U., Das, S., Ghosh, I.: Artificial intelligence in agriculture: a literature survey. Int. J. Sci. Res. Comput. Sci. Appl. Manage. Stud. **7**, 1–6 (2018)
3. Yu, K.-H., Beam, A.L., Kohane, I.S.: Artificial intelligence in healthcare. Nat. Biomed. Eng. **2**, 719–731 (2018)
4. Surden, H.: Artificial intelligence and law: an overview. Georgia State Univ. Law Rev. **35**, 19–22 (2019)
5. Abduljabbar, R., Dia, H., Liyanage, S., Bagloee, S.A.: Applications of artificial intelligence in transport: an overview. Sustainability **11**, 189 (2019)
6. Qu, J., Zhao, Y., Xie, Y.: Artificial intelligence leads the reform of education models. Syst. Res. Behav. Sci. **39**, 581–588 (2022)
7. Hwang, G.-J., Xie, H., Wah, B.W., Gašević, D.: Vision, challenges, roles and research issues of Artificial Intelligence in Education. Comput. Educ. Artif. Intell. **1**, 100001 (2020)
8. Zafari, M., Bazargani, J.S., Sadeghi-Niaraki, A., Choi, S.-M.: Artificial intelligence applications in K-12 education: a systematic literature review. IEEE Access **10**, 61905–61921 (2022)
9. Chen, X., Xie, H., Zou, D., Hwang, G.-J.: Application and theory gaps during the rise of Artificial Intelligence in Education. Comput. Educ. Artif. Intell. **1**, 100002 (2020)
10. Ouyang, F., Jiao, P.: Artificial intelligence in education: the three paradigms. Comput. Educ. Artif. Intell. **2**, 100020 (2021)
11. Tahiru, F.: AI in education: a systematic literature review. J. Cases Inf. Technol. (JCIT) **23**, 1–20 (2021)
12. Tang, K.-Y., Chang, C.-Y., Hwang, G.-J.: Trends in artificial intelligence-supported e-learning: a systematic review and co-citation network analysis (1998–2019). Interact. Learn. Environ. **31**, 2134–2152 (2023)
13. García-Peñalvo, F.J.: La percepción de la Inteligencia Artificial en contextos educativos tras el lanzamiento de ChatGPT: disrupción o pánico. Educ. Knowl. Soc. (EKS) 24, e31279 (2023)
14. García-Peñalvo, F.J.: Generative Artificial Intelligence in Higher Education: A 360° Perspective. IFE Conference 2024, Monterrey, Mexico (2024). https://doi.org/10.5281/zenodo.104 99828
15. Qadir, J.: Engineering education in the era of ChatGPT: promise and pitfalls of generative AI for education. In: Conference Engineering Education in the Era of ChatGPT: Promise and Pitfalls of Generative AI for Education, pp. 1–9 (Year)
16. Baidoo-Anu, D., Ansah, L.O.: Education in the era of generative artificial intelligence (AI): understanding the potential benefits of ChatGPT in promoting teaching and learning. J. AI **7**, 52–62 (2023)
17. Lim, W.M., Gunasekara, A., Pallant, J.L., Pallant, J.I., Pechenkina, E.: Generative AI and the future of education: Ragnarök or reformation? A paradoxical perspective from management educators. Int. J. Manag. Educ. **21**, 100790 (2023)
18. Arboleda, A.M.: Producción y análisis de textos con ChatGPT. presentado en Evento ReCrea, México (2023)
19. Amo Filvà, D., et al.: Usos y desusos del modelo GPT-3 entre estudiantes de grados de ingeniería. In: Conference Usos y desusos del modelo GPT-3 entre estudiantes de grados de ingeniería, pp. 415–418. Universidad de Granada, (Year)
20. Turing, A.M.: Can a machine think. World Math. **4**, 2099–2123 (1956)
21. McCarthy, J., Minsky, M., Rochester, N., Shannon, C.: Dartmouth Summer Research Conference on Artificial Intelligence. Dartmouth College (1956)
22. Nilsson, N.J.: Principles of Artificial Intelligence. Springer, Heidelberg (1982). https://doi.org/10.1007/978-3-662-09438-9
23. What are the 3 types of AI? A guide to narrow, general, and super artificial intelligence, Codebots, https://codebots.com/artificial-intelligence/the-3-types-of-ai-is-the-third-even-pos sible. Accessed 02 Feb 2024

24. Therón, R.: Inteligencia Artificial en la Enseñanza de Idiomas. Herramientas y aplicaciones. presentado en Inteligencia artificial en la enseñanza de idiomas: Herramientas y aplicaciones, Salamanca, España (2023)
25. García-Peñalvo, F., Vázquez-Ingelmo, A.: What do we mean by GenAI? A systematic mapping of the evolution, trends, and techniques involved in Generative AI (2023)
26. Jovanovic, M., Campbell, M.: Generative artificial intelligence: trends and prospects. IEEE Comput. Soc. **55**, 107–112 (2022). https://doi.ieeecomputersociety.org/10.1109/MC.2022. 3192720
27. Kasneci, E., et al.: ChatGPT for good? On opportunities and challenges of large language models for education. Learn. Individ. Differ. **103**, 102274 (2023)
28. García-Peñalvo, F.J.: La integración de la inteligencia artificial generativa en la práctica docente. V Seminário Escola Digital: A Educação na Era da Inteligência Artificial, Centro de Competência TIC da Escola Superior de Educação do Instituto Politécnico de Bragança (CCTIC), Portugal (2023). https://bit.ly/3AhcCKI
29. García-Peñalvo, F.J.: Cómo se percibe la Inteligencia Artificial en la educación tras el lanzamiento de ChatGPT. Foro Internacional "La Inteligencia Artificial y la Docencia Científica". , Centro de Investigaciones Económicas, Administrativas y Sociales del Instituto Politécnico Nacional, Mexico (2023). https://bit.ly/45rtrB3
30. Chen, L., Chen, P., Lin, Z.: Artificial intelligence in education: a review. IEEE Access **8**, 75264–75278 (2020)
31. Holmes, W., Bidarra, J., Køhler Simonsen, H.: Artificial Intelligence in Higher Education: A Roadmap and Future Perspectives. SmartLearning og forfatterne (2021)
32. Johinke, R., Cummings, R., Di Lauro, F.: Reclaiming the technology of higher education for teaching digital writing in a post—pandemic world. J. University Teach. Learn. Pract. **20** (2023)
33. Chomsky, N., Roberts, I., Watumull, J.: The False Promise of ChatGPT. The New York Times, New York, USA (2023). http://bit.ly/3GycXfx
34. García-Peñalvo, F.J., Llorens Largo, F., Vidal, J.: The new reality of education in the face of advances in generative artificial intelligence. Revista Iberoamericana de Educación a Distancia **27**, 9–39 (2024)
35. Nerantzi, C., Abegglen, S., Karatsiori, M., Martínez-Arboleda, A.: 101 creative ideas to use AI in education, a crowdsourced collection. Comput. Software. Zenodo (2023). https://doi. org/10.5281/zenodo.8355454
36. Green, J.L., Camilli, G., Elmore, P.B.: Handbook of Complementary Methods in Education Research. American Educational Research Association by Lawrence Erlbaum Associates, Inc. (2006)
37. Charlesworth, T.E., Banaji, M.R.: Gender in science, technology, engineering, and mathematics: Issues, causes, solutions. J. Neurosci. **39**, 7228–7243 (2019)

Enhancing Language Learning Through Human-Computer Interaction and Generative AI: LATILL Platform

Alicia García-Holgado[(✉)] ⓘ, Andrea Vázquez-Ingelmo ⓘ, Nastaran Shoeibi ⓘ, Roberto Therón ⓘ, and Francisco José García-Peñalvo ⓘ

GRIAL Research Group, Research Institute for Educational Sciences (https://ror.org/00xnj6419), Universidad de Salamanca (https://ror.org/02f40zc51), Salamanca, Spain
{aliciagh,andreavazquez,nastaran,theron,fgarcia}@usal.es

Abstract. Reading comprehension is crucial in German as a Foreign Language (GFL) education. Despite its importance, there has been limited scholarly engagement in enhancing reading strategies and materials that align with learners' proficiency levels, as outlined by the Common European Framework of Reference for Languages (CEFR). The LATILL project aims to address this gap by providing open educational resources tailored to the CEFR levels and a platform based on AI-tools for German as a foreign and second language teachers. A user-centred approach was adopted, utilizing Human-Computer Interaction techniques to enhance usability and the user experience of the LATILL platform. The development and deployment of the LATILL platform represents significant strides in leveraging AI and HCI to support language teaching. This work outlines the efforts to enhance the use of the platform, involving secondary school teachers of German as a foreign language from Ukraine and Spain. Two phases were conducted, one phase for testing the platform following a constructive interaction approach and a second phase for collecting feedback through focus groups.

Keywords: language teaching · text-to-text · text-to-image · focus groups · German teachers · generative AI · reading skills

1 Introduction

Enhancing reading comprehension is paramount within the framework of numerous German as a Foreign Language (GFL) curricula. The importance of this educational goal cannot be overstated, yet scholarly engagement in this area has remained modest in recent years. Kienberger and Schramm [1, 2] have delineated key research domains that merit attention. Among these are inquiries into text and corpus linguistics focusing on issues of textual comprehensibility, readability, and the alignment of texts with proficiency levels as outlined by the Common European Framework of Reference for Languages (CEFR) [3]. Representative studies in this vein include the work of Niederhaus [4], Weiss and Meurers [5], and Wisniewski [6], each contributing valuable insights into readability and CEFR level adequacy as central topics.

© The Author(s), under exclusive license to Springer Nature Switzerland AG 2024
P. Zaphiris and A. Ioannou (Eds.): HCII 2024, LNCS 14724, pp. 255–265, 2024.
https://doi.org/10.1007/978-3-031-61691-4_17

Moreover, the exploration of cognitive and metacognitive processes that facilitate reading comprehension has emerged as a vital strand of research Ehlers [7] and Meireles [8]. Recent doctoral research [9–11], primarily concentrates on the reading strategies and competencies of university-level German as a Foreign Language learners from diverse linguistic backgrounds. However, given the global predominance of school-aged learners within the GFL demographic, there is a pressing need to expand research efforts to encompass this group more fully, thereby ensuring a broader and more inclusive understanding of reading comprehension challenges and strategies in the context of GFL education.

The LATILL (Level-Adequate Texts in Language Learning) project [12] aims to provide open educational resources for GFL and German as a second language (GSL) teachers that meet the need for current, authentic and, most importantly, level-appropriate reading texts and didactic materials. It is a proposal of the Erasmus + programme of the European Union (Ref. 2021-1-AT01-KA220-SCH-000029604) under the coordination of the Universität Wien (Austria) and with the participation of the University of Salamanca (Spain), Eberhard Karls Universität Tübingen (Germany), Chernivtsi National University Yuriy Fedkovych (Ukraine), and Verein Österreichisches Sprachdiplom Deutsch (Austria).

To achieve this goal, a platform for GFL and GSL teachers is being developed, the main purpose of which is to facilitate the search for authentic texts in German according to the subject, CEFR level. The platform is linked to a corpus of German texts produced as part of the project. The corpus includes text from different sources under licenses that allow modification (over 10000 texts), such as Klexikon (http://www.klexikon.de) or Das Biber (https://www.dasbiber.at); and sources that do not allow modification (over 6000 texts) such as Fluter (https://www.fluter.de). These texts are analysed using Natural Language Processing (NLP) techniques in order to determine different aspects, including subject matter and complexity according to CEFR level.

Among the functionalities of the platform, the integration of different techniques based on Artificial Intelligence (AI) to generate text bundles —sets of variations of texts, such as simplifications or illustrated texts derived from the original— that can be used in the classroom and adapted to the level of the students is noteworthy. In this sense, the platform allows the teacher to create bundles from a text located through the search tool, in such a way that a summary version of the text can be generated from it. We are also working on simplification, that is, a new text will be automatically generated with a lower CEFR level than the original one. The aim of this simplification is to facilitate the adaptation of the text to the different levels of learning that may coexist in a language teaching classroom. Other means of adaptation can be produced by generating from the original translations into different languages aimed at supporting students from different nationalities. These functionalities enrich the text search process and support an adaptive learning model.

Finally, among the features offered by the platform, the use of texts at CEFR levels A1 and A2 has been addressed. At these levels, texts are accompanied by images, so that the visual part is a fundamental element in the learning process. The search for authentic texts with associated images which are also A1 and A2 level texts is complex. To solve this problem, the LATILL platform incorporates the generation of images through AI.

The teacher can choose parts of the text and request that an image be generated to illustrate it.

Currently, the use of AI tools for the teaching context is growing, although the concept of NLP, including its advantages as a language learning medium, is not yet well known [13]. The platform developed in LATILL brings the use of these tools closer to a real-life context, supporting German as a foreign language teachers and facilitating the use of AI techniques without the need for any technical background knowledge of them [14].

The development of the LATILL platform follows a user-centred approach, applying Human-Computer Interaction techniques and methods to consider usability and user experience as key objectives. This study describes the process to improve the interaction with the generative AI tools involving secondary school teachers of German as a Foreign Language from Ukraine and Spain.

This work is organised into six sections. The next section introduces previous works related to generative AI in education. Section 3 introduces the methodology conducted to evaluate the LATILL platform based on workshops and focus groups. Sections 4 and 5 describes the main results of the focus groups and the impact in the development of the platform. Finally, last section summarizes the main conclusions.

2   Previous Works

Generative AI can create various types of content like text, images, and videos, using tools like ChatGPT for text and Midjourney for images. Therefore, its implementation in education transforms how content is created and personalized for learning, but also it can transform the teaching and assessment processes [15]. It facilitates the development of customized educational materials, interactive simulations based on the unique needs of each student [16]. In the context of foreign language teaching, there are studies focused on English as a foreign or second language [17–19]. However, there are no experiences integrating these tools in teaching German. Although there are large language models (LLM) that work in German, such as German BERT (Bidirectional Encoder Representations from Transformers), DBMDZ BERT or Multilingual BERT, most of the models that are arising rely on translating the input from German into English and vice versa for the output.

On the other hand, there is a need of improving the user experience and usability of the tools that integrates generative AI in education. HCI's focus on creating intuitive, efficient interfaces aligns with generative AI's capability to anticipate and adapt to user needs, facilitating personalized interactions. Roldan et al. [20] emphasize the importance of understanding user challenges in HCI education and the potential of project-based learning involving real users.

Combining HCI principles with generative AI gives a unique opportunity to how users interact with technology, making it more accessible, engaging, and practical, which enhances user experience and addresses educational challenges by incorporating real-world complexities into the learning process, fostering empathy and critical thinking among future designers [21].

In the literature, Jingyu Shi et al. [22] and Morris et al. [23] have significantly contributed to integrating HCI and generative AI. Shi et al. developed a comprehensive taxonomy from an analysis of 291 papers to guide future GenAI application designs, focusing on user-centric approaches. Morris et al. proposed two design spaces to understand how HCI impacts generative AI models and vice versa, aiming to enhance HCI research and practice. Another study [24] explores the potential of integrating generative AI into operating systems for more intuitive and personalized interactions, showcasing the evolving synergy between HCI and AI technologies. These works collectively emphasize the need for user feedback in GenAI development, and the potential for creating engaging digital environments.

3 Methodology

Throughout the development of the LATILL platform, a series of workshops were conducted involving educators in Spain and Ukraine. All of them are teachers of German as a foreign language in secondary schools. These workshops were instrumental in gathering direct user feedback and guiding the platform's iterative refinement. Participants included language teachers who brought invaluable insights into the platform's usability and functionality.

3.1 Study Design and Data Collection

The LATILL project includes a teacher training programme implemented from June 2023 to June 2024 focused on encouraging GFL educators to experiment with AI-based tools available in the LATILL platform and pedagogical approaches in their lesson planning. The final goal is promoting the development of reading skills in German as a foreign language.

The teacher training included a three-day workshop for teachers that was organised in June 2023 and repeated in September 2023 aimed at engaging more participants. Moreover, the training also includes four webinars spread over the 2023–24 school year, supplemented by continuous self-study and exchange through a space in the virtual campus of the Universität Wien with resources and forums. Additionally, the LATILL platform hosts a variety of resources, including video tutorials, lectures on text complexity and teaching methods, didactic videos, and extensive teaching materials designed by the partners in Czernivtsi (Ukraine) and Vienna (Austria) to support GFL/GSL educators in enhancing their instructional approaches and reading lessons.

The workshops for teachers were focused on introducing the LATILL platform and the tools and didactic materials available there. Methodological and didactic suggestions for learner-oriented GFL/GSL lessons were presented, including reading strategies and how to teach them. In particular, the main topics were:

- Search and select level-adequate reading texts for GFL lessons.
- Tools, tips and many practical examples for didactic implementation.
- Activity-oriented reading lessons and internal differentiation.

A testing session was conducted during the first day of the workshop. The teachers were divided into groups, each group was moderated by members of the LATILL consortium. The participants shared their screens in Zoom and tried out the tools available in the LATILL platform. No specific tasks were provided, the role of the moderators was taking notes and guide the constructive interaction between the participants. The testing was recorded for further analysis, and the audio was transcripted. The testing finished with a card sorting activity using the online tool Optimal Sort; it provided information to identify how different concepts used in the interface were understood.

A total of six testing groups were conducted. In June, the participants were divided into four groups, two moderated by domain experts from Universität Wien, who also designed and organised the workshop; one in Ukrainian by a domain expert from Chernivtsi National University Yuriy Fedkovych; and one in Spanish moderated by HCI experts from the University of Salamanca. They tested the first version of the LATILL platform. In September, two testing groups were conducted, one in Spanish and one in Ukrainian. They tested the second version of the LATILL platform.

After the three-day workshop, at the end of the third day, two focus groups were conducted to collect feedback from the platform and understand the challenges faced by GFL/GSL teachers. One focus group was conducted in Ukrainian by domain experts and one in Spanish by HCI experts. A total of four focus groups were conducted.

3.2 Participants

Participant selection for the teacher training was conducted using a snowball method. Specifically, invitations were extended to secondary education schools in both Spain and Ukraine where German is taught as a foreign language. The participants in the teacher training came from those centres that agreed to participate. Although it has proven challenging to engage teachers, this is attributable on one hand to the situation in Ukraine, and on the other, to the employment conditions of language teachers in Spain, who often transition between schools during the summer. Consequently, not all of them could commit to starting in June and continuing thereafter. Finally, a total of 15 teachers were involved in the teacher training, 10 from Ukraine and 5 from Spain.

Regarding the focus groups, a total of 10 teachers participated in this activity. All Ukrainian teachers participated. Seven teachers in the first focus group, four teachers of German as the first foreign and three teachers of Germans as the second foreign language; and three GFL teachers in the second focus group. From Spain, two teachers per focus groups, three teachers of German as first foreign and one of German as second foreign language at school.

3.3 Instrument

The testing phases did not include tasks or specific guidelines to use the platform. Participants follow a constructive interaction as test method to measure usability.

Regarding the focus groups, we used a semi-structured interview (Table 1), that was developed by project partners in Vienna and Spain. It is divided into two topics:

- Use of the LATILL online platform.
- Lesson preparation including text simplification (simplify), translations (translate) and pictures.

Table 1. Semi-structured interview for LATILL focus groups.

Topic	Key question	In-depth question
Use of the LATILL online platform	What problems have you encountered?	Which functions do you find useful? Which functions were not useful to you? What do you expect from the system?
	What did you use the online platform for?	Were there any ways of using the platform that surprised you? What functions do you miss in the platform that would be useful for your reading classes?
Lesson preparation	To what extent does the online platform support you in planning and preparing GFL reading lessons?	How do you plan to use the online platform … to find texts for your classes? … to produce scaffolds?
specific: text simplification (simplify)	What did you notice regarding the simplification of the text (differentiated texts)?	How appropriate were the language difficulty levels of the different text versions within a CEFR level?
specific: translations (translate)	What did you notice regarding the text translation?	Were there any deviations from the original text? How would you use the translations as scaffolds?
specific: pictures	What did you notice regarding the pictures?	How do you plan to use pictures as reading scaffolds?

4   Results

The focus groups made it possible to obtain two different types of information. On the one hand, the challenges faced by foreign language teachers of German in Spain and Ukraine. On the other hand, the participants tested the LATILL platform and provided useful information. These sessions, critical for gathering firsthand insights, involved detailed feedback mechanisms to capture participants' experiences and suggestions.

4.1   Challenges in GFL/GSL

The identified challenges regarding teaching German as a second or foreign language include the selection and adaptation of materials, student motivation, fostering reading skills, managing diversity in the classroom, and effectively integrating technology into the educational process:

- Difficulty in finding suitable texts: Teachers face challenges in finding texts that are appropriate in terms of theme and level for their students. This task is time-consuming, especially when they need to adapt and simplify these texts to make them accessible for different learning levels.
- Demotivation of students: Excessively difficult texts can quickly demotivate students, especially in a context where the reading habit is no longer as common among the youth. This poses an additional challenge for teachers trying to maintain interest and motivation in language learning.
- The Importance of reading in language learning: Participants highlight the importance of encouraging reading habits among students to improve their reading comprehension, vocabulary, grammar, and writing skills in German. However, they note that this habit has declined due to the use of technologies and applications, representing a challenge for teachers.
- Diversity of formats and contents: The need to work with a variety of formats and contents to keep students interested and address different learning styles is mentioned. This includes integrating texts with images and the ability to tailor material to the specific needs of students, which can be complex without the right resources.
- Adapting to different skill levels: There is difficulty in adapting lessons and materials to a heterogeneous group of students with different language skill levels. Teaching must find ways to support every learner in the classroom while meeting individual needs, which is a logistical and pedagogical challenge.
- Use of technology and platforms: While technology and educational platforms offer opportunities to enhance the teaching of German, issues also arise related to the effective integration of these tools into the professional habits of the teachers and the ability of these technologies to generate appropriate and specific content in the language.

4.2 Feedback from the LATILL Platform

The initial version of the LATILL platform was met with enthusiasm for its innovative approach to language learning (Fig. 1). However, participants identified several areas for improvement:

- Interface clarity: Users found navigation challenging and suggested enhancements to make the platform more intuitive.
- Functionality: Feedback highlighted the need for better text simplification, more relevant image generation, and accurate translation features.
- Content and categorization: The lack of up-to-date content and transparent categorization system for texts by level and topic was highlighted.

In response to the feedback, significant changes were made in the subsequent version of the LATILL platform (Fig. 2):

- Improved interface and usability: Adjustments were made to streamline navigation, making it easier for users to find and utilize platform features.
- Enhanced text simplification and translation: Efforts were made to improve the accuracy of translations and the quality of text simplifications, aiming to retain the original text's essence more effectively.

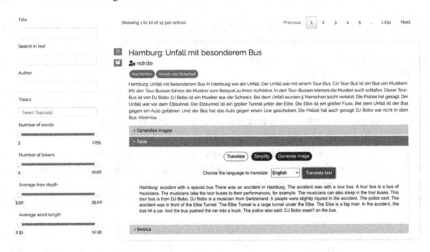

Fig. 1. First version of the platform testing in the first workshop in June 2023.

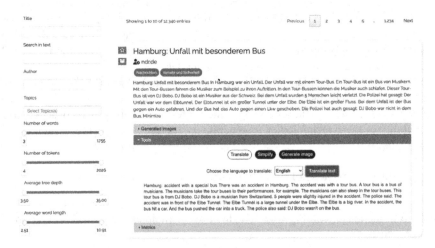

Fig. 2. Second version of the platform.

- Updated content and better categorization: The platform was updated with current topics and implemented a more precise categorization system to facilitate accessible access to texts suitable for various learning levels.

Comparing the first and second versions of the LATILL platform, the workshops revealed significant user satisfaction improvements. The modifications based on initial feedback led to a more user-friendly and effective tool for language teaching and learning. For the final version, it is crucial to continue this iterative feedback loop, focusing on:

- User interface (UI) and experience (UX): Refine the UI/UX to ensure the platform remains intuitive and accessible.

- Feature optimization: Based on user feedback, continue enhancing text simplification, translation accuracy, and image generation relevancy.
- Content expansion and categorization: Regularly update the platform's content library with engaging topics and maintain a comprehensive categorization system.

5 Impact in the Functional Prototype

Based on the user feedback and observations, here is the in-depth feature feedback on the LATILL platform:

- Use of the LATILL platform. Users appreciated the platform's concept but encountered usability challenges. Feedback highlighted the need for a more intuitive interface to facilitate easier navigation, suggesting that a more straightforward design could enhance user engagement and satisfaction.
- Lesson preparation. Educators noted the importance of efficient search functionality to find texts appropriate for different learning levels and topics quickly. A more user-friendly interface for modifying texts and creating lessons was also deemed essential, including current and engaging content.
- Text simplification. The text simplification feature received mixed reviews, with users noting it often resulted in summaries rather than simplified versions of texts. This feedback suggests the platform needs to better balance simplification with retaining the original text's essence, ensuring the simplified text remains useful for language learners.
- Text translation. While the translation feature was generally well-received, there were calls for improved translation accuracy and quality. Users noted the importance of translations that preserve the original meaning and context, highlighting a need for refinement.
- Image generation. The picture generation feature elicited mixed responses, with some users finding the generated images only sometimes relevant to the text's content. Suggestions were made for improving the algorithm to ensure images are more closely aligned with the text, allowing users to provide more context or select themes.

These detailed feedback points highlight the users' experiences and expectations, offering valuable insights for further development and refinement of the LATILL platform's features to better meet the needs of educators and learners in language teaching and learning contexts.

6 Conclusions

The LATILL platform represents a significant step forward in the application of AI in education, offering promising avenues for research and practice in language learning and teaching. The development of the platform follows a user-centered approach, involving GFL teachers from secondary schools, experts of professionalisation and further training of GFL teachers, experts of German language and HCI experts.

The findings of this study underscore the transformative potential of the LATILL platform in the realm of language education. By harnessing the power of human-computer interaction and generative AI, the LATILL tools offer a novel approach to language teaching that is both engaging and effective. The integration of text-to-text and text-to-image functionalities within the platform not only enriches the language learning experience but also provides educators with versatile tools to enhance comprehension and engagement among learners.

The teachers used the new AI-based LATILL tools in their teaching practice and continuously reflect on this process with other pairs, creating a learning community. Moreover, the challenges identified during the focus groups have provided useful information not only for improving the tested functionality, but also for providing AI-tools that solve the problems faced by GFL/GSL teachers in their daily tasks.

Acknowledgments. This research was partially funded by the Ministry of Science and Innovation through the AVisSA project grant number (PID2020-118345RB-I00). LATILL project was undertaken with the support of the Erasmus+ Programme of the European Union: "KA2 - Cooperation partnership in school education." Level-Adequate Texts in Language Learning (LATILL) (Reference number 2021–1-AT01-KA220-SCH-000029604). Views and opinions expressed are those of the author(s) only and do not necessarily reflect those of the European Union or the European Education and Culture Executive Agency (EACEA). Neither the European Union nor EACEA can be held responsible for them.

References

1. Kienberger, M., Schramm, K. (eds.): Lesedidaktik Deutsch als Fremdsprache. Aktuelle Entwicklungen und Ansätze. Peter Lang Verlag, Berlin, Germany (2023)
2. Kienberger, M., Schramm, K.: Einführung. In: Kienberger, M., Schramm, K. (eds.) Lesedidaktik Deutsch als Fremdsprache. Aktuelle Entwicklungen und Ansätze, pp. 7–12. Peter Lang Verlag, Berlin, Germany (2023)
3. Council of Europe: Common European Framework of Reference for Languages: Learning, Teaching, Assessment (CEFR). Companion Volume. Council of Europe Publishing (2020)
4. Niederhaus, C.: Fachsprachlichkeit in Lehrbüchern. Korpuslinguistische Analysen von Fachtexten der beruflichen Bildung. Waxmann, Münster (2011)
5. Weiß, Z., Meurers, D.: Modeling the Readability of German Targeting Adults and Children: An empirically broad analysis and its cross-corpus validation, pp. 303–317. Association for Computational Linguistics (Year)
6. Wisniewski, K.: Lesen im und mit dem GER. Eine kritische Auseinandersetzung - und ein Plädoyer für erweiterte (rezeptive) Referenzniveaubeschreibungen des Deutsche. In: Kienberger, M., Schramm, K. (eds.) Lesedidaktik Deutsch als Fremdsprache. Aktuelle Entwicklungen und Ansätze, pp. 13–38. Peter Lang Verlag, Berlin, Germany (2023)
7. Ehlers, S.: Lesetheorie und fremdsprachliche Lesepraxis aus der Perspektive des Deutschen als Fremdsprache. Gunter Narr, Tübingen (1998)
8. Meireles, S.M.: Leseverstehen aus der Perspektive des Nicht-Muttersprachlers. In: Hardarik, B., Eva, B., Ulrich, H.W. (eds.) Text - Verstehen, pp. 299–314. De Gruyter, Berlin, New York (2006)
9. Kienberger, M.: Das Potenzial des potenziellen Wortschatzes nutzen. Erschließungsstrategien für unbekannten Wortschatz unter DaF-Lernenden an spanischen Universitäten. Universität Wien, Wien (2020)

10. Introna, S.: Der Erwerb fremdsprachiger akademischer Lesekompetenz. Eine Educational Design Research- Studie zur Lesekompetenz in der L2 Deutsch internationaler Studierender der Geistes- und Sozialwissenschaften. Universität Bielefeld, Bielefeld (2021)
11. Herzig, K.: Multimodale Leseprozesse im mexikanischen DaF-Anfängerunterricht. In: Kienberger, M., Schramm, K. (eds.) Lesedidaktik Deutsch als Fremdsprache. Aktuelle Entwicklungen und Ansätze, pp. 193–215. Peter Lang Verlag, Berlin, Germany (2023)
12. Kienberger, M., et al.: Enhancing adaptive teaching of reading skills using digital technologies: LATILL project. In: García-Peñalvo, F.J., García-Holgado, A. (eds.) Proceedings TEEM 2022: Tenth International Conference on Technological Ecosystems for Enhancing Multiculturality. TEEM 2022, pp. 1092–1098. Springer, Singapore (2023). https://doi.org/10.1007/978-981-99-0942-1_115
13. Haristiani, N.: Artificial Intelligence (AI) chatbot as language learning medium: an inquiry. In: Journal of Physics: Conference Series, vol. 1387 (2019)
14. Schuff, H., Vanderlyn, L., Adel, H., Vu, N.T.: How to do human evaluation: a brief introduction to user studies in NLP. Nat. Lang. Eng. **29**, 1199–1222 (2023)
15. Zeb, A., Ullah, R., Karim, R.: Exploring the role of ChatGPT in higher education: opportunities, challenges and ethical considerations. Int. J. Inf. Learn. Technol. **41**, 99–111 (2024)
16. Michel-Villarreal, R., Vilalta-Perdomo, E., Salinas-Navarro, D.E., Thierry-Aguilera, R., Gerardou, F.S.: Challenges and opportunities of generative AI for higher education as explained by ChatGPT. Educ. Sci. **13**, 856 (2023)
17. Pack, A., Maloney, J.: Potential affordances of generative AI in language education: demonstrations and an evaluative framework. Teach. Engl. Technol. **23**, 4–24 (2023)
18. Lee, J.H., Shin, D., Noh, W.: Artificial intelligence-based content generator technology for young English-as-a-foreign-language learners' reading enjoyment. RELC J. **54**, 508–516 (2023)
19. Law, L.: Application of Generative Artificial Intelligence (GenAI) in Language Teaching and Learning: A Scoping Literature Review. Preprint (2024)
20. Roldan, W., et al.: Opportunities and challenges in involving users in project-based HCI education. In: CHI 2020: Proceedings of the 2020 CHI Conference on Human Factors in Computing Systems, pp. 1–15. Association for Computing Machinery (2020)
21. Mørch, A., Andersen, R.: Human-Centred AI in education in the age of generative AI tools. In: Bellucci, A., Russis, L.D., Diaz, P., Mørch, A., Fogli, D., Paternò, F. (eds.) Workshops, Work in Progress Demos and Doctoral Consortium at the IS-EUD 2023 co-located with the 9th International Symposium on End-User Development (IS-EUD 2023). CEUR Workshop Proceedings, Cagliari, Italy (2023)
22. Shi, J., Jain, R., Doh, H., Suzuki, R., Ramani, K.: An HCI-Centric Survey and Taxonomy of Human-Generative-AI Interactions. arXiv preprint arXiv:2310.07127 (2024)
23. Morris, M.R., Cai, C.J., Holbrook, J., Kulkarni, C., Terry, M.: The design space of generative models. In: 36th Conference on Neural Information Processing Systems (NeurIPS 2022) (2023)
24. Tolomei, G., Campagnano, C., Silvestri, F., Trappolini, G.: Prompt-to-OS (P2OS): Revolutionizing Operating Systems and Human-Computer Interaction with Integrated AI Generative Models. arXiv preprint arXiv:2310.04875 (2023)

Exploring Explainability and Transparency in Automated Essay Scoring Systems: A User-Centered Evaluation

Erin Hall, Mohammed Seyam[(✉)], and Daniel Dunlap[(✉)]

Virginia Polytechnic Institute and State University, Blacksburg, VA 24061, USA
{erinehall,seyam,dunlapd}@vt.edu

Abstract. In recent years, rapid advancements in computer science, including increased capabilities of machine learning models like Large Language Models (LLMs) and the accessibility of large datasets, have facilitated the widespread adoption of AI technology, underscoring the need to ethically design and evaluate these technologies with concern for their impact on students and teachers. Specifically, the rise of Automated Essay Scoring (AES) platforms have made it possible to provide real-time feedback and grades for student essays. Despite the increasing development and use of AES platforms, limited research has focused on AI explainability and algorithm transparency and their influence on the usability of these platforms. To address this gap, we conducted a qualitative study on an AI-based essay writing and grading platform, Packback Deep Dives, with a primary focus of exploring the experiences of students and graders. The study aimed to explore the system's usability related to explainability and transparency and to uncover the resulting implications for users. Participants took part in surveys, semi-structured interviews, and a focus group. The findings reveal several important considerations for evaluating AES systems, including the clarity of feedback and explanations, effectiveness and actionability of feedback and explanations, perceptions and misconceptions of the system, evolving trust in AI judgments, user concerns and fairness perceptions, system efficiency and feedback quality, user interface accessibility and design, and system enhancement design priorities. These proposed key considerations can help guide the development of effective essay feedback and grading tools that prioritize explainability and transparency to improve usability.

Keywords: usability · algorithmic transparency · explainability · machine learning · artificial intelligence · writing · feedback · automated essay scoring

1 Introduction

In recent years, the field of computer science has seen significant advancements, particularly in the capabilities of advanced machine learning (ML) models, including Large Language Models, and the increasing availability of large

P. Zaphiris and A. Ioannou (Eds.): HCII 2024, LNCS 14724, pp. 266–282, 2024.
https://doi.org/10.1007/978-3-031-61691-4_18

datasets. These advancements have resulted in the widespread availability of AI technology, including OpenAI's ChatGPT and Google's Bard. AI has also become increasingly adopted in the educational sector, which presents a new set of challenges, particularly in addressing ethical implications and understanding its impact on students and teachers.

Automated Essay Scoring (AES) and similar AI-driven systems have gained significance as valuable tools for grading and providing feedback for written content. These systems offer real-time feedback and grades, enhancing the learning experience for students while helping them to adhere to a set of foundational writing conventions and promoting a higher quality floor.

Despite the growing adoption of AES platforms, limited research has specifically focused on AI explainability and algorithm transparency and their influence on usability. Understanding the impact of AI explainability and algorithm transparency on the usability of AES platforms is crucial for their successful integration into the classroom. Exploring these factors not only enhances transparency and trust but also facilitates informed decision-making for both instructors and students, ultimately improving both their learning and teaching experiences.

In order to address this research gap, our study aims to investigate the characteristics of an effective AES-driven platform and develop a set of key evaluation considerations to assess the usability of such tools. We conducted a literature review to analyze the current state of research in this area and collected data on user experiences and perceptions of using an automated essay scoring tool, Packback Deep Dives. The primary focus of this study is to explore the system's usability related to explainability and transparency and to uncover the resulting implications for users.

The following research questions guide this study:

RQ1. How do AI explainability and algorithm transparency techniques affect the overall usability and user experience of an AI-based essay feedback system?

RQ2. How do graders perceive the integration of an AI-based essay feedback system into their grading process, and what are the factors influencing their acceptance or resistance of automated feedback?

RQ3. What are the key components that constitute an effective automated essay scoring system, and how can they inform the development and assessment of reliable grading and feedback tools?

2   Related Work

This section outlines areas of prior research that are necessary to address before describing the research methods of this paper. This includes usability for AI-driven systems, AI in the classroom, explainable AI (XAI), algorithm transparency, and an overview of Packback's Deep Dives.

2.1 Usability for AI-Driven Systems

As AI becomes more prevalent in everyday life, the integration of human-computer interaction (HCI) and human-centered design principles is key to bridge the gap between the technical complexity of AI systems and the user-friendly interfaces necessary for widespread adoption and understanding. Research in the usability of AI-driven systems involves an added layer of complexity, as it requires adapting traditional user-centered design methods to meet the dynamic nature of AI systems. This poses a challenge, as learning algorithms have a broader set of possible user outcomes, making the potential to cover all use cases in a usability evaluation a complex task. Despite this, several researchers have identified AI explainability and algorithm transparency through user interfaces (UI) as a way to mitigate some of these challenges, although there remains a gap in adequate research to support these initiatives [22]. These ideas prioritize user interaction with the system over other elements of the UI when it comes to usability, design, and the success of the system [1,5].

Building on these challenges, there are several known guidelines for human-AI interaction that can serve as a basis for addressing the usability of AI systems. One of which, developed by Amershi et al., includes the following: "make clear what the system can do, make clear how well the system can do what it can do, show contextually relevant information, support efficient correction, and make it clear why the system did what it did" [2]. These guidelines highlight the need for developing methods of usability evaluations that are tailored toward the unique characteristics of AI systems and promote improved human-AI interactions through explainability and transparency.

2.2 AI in the Classroom

The field of AI in education has seen rapid growth over the past several years [10, 26], evident with the widespread use of various educational and learning-based AI platforms, such as Duolingo, ALEKS, and Quizlet [4,9,18]. These developments have resulted in an abundance of specialized tools across various domains.

Crompton et al. described five ways AI is used in higher education, including assessment/evaluation, predicting, AI assistants, intelligent tutoring systems (ITS), and managing student learning [10]. Luckin et al. further segmented these categories of AI education software applications into intelligent personal tutors, support for collaborative learning, and virtual reality to support learning in authentic environments [16].

On top of this, AI is present in a wide range of domain applications in the educational sector, including language learning, computer science, management, engineering, science, social science, business, and math, among others [10]. In the context of writing education, despite promising developments in Natural Language Processing (NLP), the use of AI for essay grading poses several challenges, including ethical considerations, potential biases, and subjective evaluation.

AI in Writing Education. Automated Essay Scoring (AES) is a technology that uses software algorithms to grade and provide feedback on written content [23]. Historically, this has been seen in Project Essay Grader, Intelligent Essay Assessor, E-rater, IntelliMetric, and Bayesian Essay Test Scoring sYstem [23]. Each of these systems use ML algorithms and NLP techniques to analyze different characteristics of essays [23], and the use of these systems have proven to show positive impacts on student writing outcomes [17].

Machine learning is a key component of automated essay scoring systems, enabling the generation of real-time feedback and grades for student essays. ML algorithms, such as deep learning models, utilize statistical methods and pattern recognition to make predictions based on input data [14,24]. However, the complexity of ML algorithms can result in "black box" models, where it becomes challenging to understand how the algorithm arrives at its conclusions [19]. Many deep learning models consist of multiple layers of hidden units and intricate computations. This makes interpreting their decision-making processes difficult. High dimensionality of the representations, complex interactions between layers, and non-linear activation functions used in their architecture further limits their explainability and interpretability [11]. This lack of interpretability poses a challenge to improving the explainability and transparency of AES platforms, affecting their usability.

Ethical Concerns and Bias. In promoting more usable AI-driven systems, there are ethical implications of using AI systems in the classroom. A major concern with the use of ML models is that these algorithms can risk perpetuating existing biases if they are trained on historically biased datasets, whether intentionally or unintentionally [1]. As an attempt to address this concern, Amershi et al. identified a key aspect of usable AI-driven applications as to mitigate social bias and to make sure these systems do not reinforce any unfair biases [2]. The use of explainability and transparency in AI systems has the potential to mitigate this bias by providing more insights to developers and users about how decisions are made.

Perceptions of AI in the Classroom. Another primary concern regarding the integration of AI in the classroom is the acceptance of these technologies among stakeholders. There have been several recent studies that have attempted to uncover user perceptions of integrating these systems in the classroom. Research on STEM teachers utilizing an AI system for scientific writing indicated both appreciation for its support and concerns regarding its impact on the role of the teacher and AI decision transparency [12]. Comparatively, an analysis of generative artificial intelligence (GenAI) in academic writing showed minor disagreements between educators and students on the use of generative AI in the classroom, pointing towards a need for clear guidelines and improved teacher training on GenAI [3]. Another study on middle school students' views of AES systems highlighted that classroom environment and writing skills significantly influence their opinions on the technology, with stronger writers viewing these technologies as less useful [25]. These insights underscore the potential of AI in education, alongside the necessity for addressing its integration challenges to promote wider acceptance in the classroom.

2.3   Explainable AI

To address the challenge of AI explainability, current research is focused on developing techniques for opening "black box" models and providing insights into their decision-making processes [13]. XAI techniques aim to uncover the inner workings of ML algorithms and provide explanations for their predictions, bridging the gap between the technical complexity of AI models and the users' understanding [13]. In the context of AES, XAI can help students and instructors understand how the AES system evaluates their writing, fostering improved writing skills and building a deeper understanding of AI. Researchers are actively investigating methods to open the "black box" and extract meaningful explanations from such algorithms, ensuring that the feedback provided by AES systems is understandable and useful to users [13].

2.4   Algorithm Transparency

One approach in harnessing XAI techniques is to provide simple and understandable pieces of feedback that cater to users' limited attention spans and potential lack of interest in technical details [13]. By translating the mathematical concepts and prediction-making techniques of ML into human-like narratives, users can gain insights into the decision-making process of the AES system [13]. This approach is referred to as algorithmic transparency, and its value lies in its ability to empower users to make informed choices and judge the potential consequences of the system's outputs [20]. Algorithm transparency proves beneficial in helping users gain a basic understanding of AI techniques and ML driven decisions through repeated interactions. There are many current research efforts that are exploring methods to incorporate user-centered explanations, simplifying technical concepts and presenting them in a manner that is accessible to users with varying levels of AI literacy [13,15].

2.5   Packback Deep Dives

Packback Deep Dives is designed to automate the assessment and feedback process for written assignments. This section provides an overview of the platform's features.

Instructor Functionality. For instructors, the platform provides a streamlined and efficient approach to grading essays. Through a human-machine teaming approach, instructors can leverage the capabilities of AI to assist in the grading process while maintaining their expertise and control over the evaluation. The platform offers customizable rubrics, a plagiarism check, and AI-generated scores for various mechanics-related categories, including word count and depth, grammar and mechanics, flow and structure, research and citations, and formatting and presentation. These AI-suggested scores serve as a starting point for instructors, who can review and modify them as they choose. At the time of the study, the platform did not include any tools to detect AI-generated content.

Student Functionality. Deep Dives offers students a supportive and interactive environment to enhance their writing skills. Students can access features such as a writing assistant and a research assistant. The writing assistant offers real-time feedback on various aspects of their writing, while the research assistant helps students generate citations and assess the credibility of their sources.

Benefits and Pedagogical Value. For instructors, the platform streamlines the grading process, reducing the time and effort required for evaluation and leaving more time for instructors to focus on content and ideas. For students, the platform provides timely and constructive feedback that aids in the development of their writing skills. Furthermore, the platform fosters AI literacy among students by exposing them to AI-driven evaluation processes and the use of algorithms in educational settings.

3   Methods

3.1   Approach

This section outlines the methodology employed to address the three driving research questions. A study was conducted in the Fall of 2022 at a large public university in the United States. Several courses at this university utilized an AI-based essay feedback and grading platform, Packback Deep Dives, to assist with their writing assignments. All participants were part of a course that used Deep Dives, and data on their experiences and perceptions of using this platform were collected during a study over the course of the Fall 2022 semester.

The surveys were administered to only the graders, as they were geared towards the instructor version of Deep Dives. The initial survey was distributed before the first assignment using Deep Dives. It consisted of 9 core questions, with an additional set of 10 questions for participants who had prior experience in grading essays or using automated essay scoring systems. The second survey, consisting of 16 questions, was distributed after half of the semester's assignments were completed. The final survey was 17 questions and was sent after all Deep Dives assignments were completed. After the semester was completed, hour-long Zoom interviews were held with each participant. A subsequent focus group, involving a student, instructor, and teaching assistant (TA), was conducted on Zoom for about an hour. The interviews and focus group were conducted using a conversational approach, guided by talking points rather than adhering to a rigid set of questions.

3.2 Participants and Courses

Participants were recruited to provide a broad range of perspectives across different roles within the academic context. Participants in this study consisted of nine individuals at the university, including five TA's of a computer science course, one instructor of a non-computer science course, and three computer science students, all who were currently using the essay grading platform at the time of the study.

The computer science course that the participants were drawn from was aimed to help students explore the social, ethical, and professional side of computing. The course required intensive essay writing as part of the curriculum.

To ensure a diverse range of perspectives, the study also included one participant from a humanities course where essay writing played a key role in the curriculum. While their course context deviates from the main scope of the study, their inclusion offers valuable insights into the tool's application in a non-technical academic setting.

3.3 Objectives

The objectives of the study and sample questions for each of the five phases can be seen in Table 1 below:

3.4 Data Analysis and Evaluation

The System Usability Scale (SUS) was used as the primary way to obtain quantitative data on the system's usability [8]. The SUS is a survey designed to measure the usability of a system throughout a variety of contexts [8]. The survey consists of ten questions that alternate between statements of positive and negative connotations. Participants were asked to rank each statement on a five-point scale ranging from "Strongly Disagree" (0) to "Strongly Agree" (4). These values were then scaled to produce a score out of 100. A score "above a 68 would be considered above average and anything below 68 is below average" [21].

The audio recordings and transcripts of the individual interviews and focus group were evaluated using reflexive thematic analysis conducted by a single researcher [6,7]. The raw data from interview transcripts were thoroughly reviewed to develop a understanding of the content and context. We conducted a line-by-line analysis of the transcripts and extracted significant quotes from participants. These quotes were then assigned unique labels as codes that consisted of descriptive keywords or short phrases that encapsulated the key concepts and ideas expressed in the data.

To ensure consistency and rigor in the coding process, a systematic and iterative approach was followed. We repeated this process three times, comparing and refining the codes as new insights emerged. Codes were iteratively reviewed, condensed, reworded, and refined. Finally, each of these codes were organized into broader themes.

Table 1. Objectives and Sample Questions

Phase	Objectives	Sample Questions
Survey 1	- To understand participants' prior knowledge and experiences. - To understand user needs and expectations.	- Have you graded writing assignments in the past? - What do you expect to be the advantages of using this tool?
Survey 2	- To assess initial platform impressions. - To measure grading efficiency improvement. - To evaluate trust in automated scores. - To gauge understanding of Deep Dives' algorithms	- Please describe your initial impressions of using the platform. - How much do you trust the accuracy of the automated grades the platform provides?
Survey 3	- To quantify usability via System Usability Scale [21]. - To compare experiences with traditional vs. automated grading	- What part of grading Deep Dives assignments took the longest? - Did the automated grader typically grade higher, lower, or the same as you would have?
Grader Interviews	- To clarify survey responses. - To evaluate system usability. - To understand participants' mental models of system's driving algorithms. - To assess trust in automated scores	- How did the use of the AI grading platform change the way you grade writing assignments? - How well did you understand how grades were made? - Explain how you think scores were generated for each of the 5 rubric categories
Student Interviews	- To understand student experiences with platform. - To investigate student understanding of system's driving algorithms. - To analyze feedback's impact on writing process	- What was your overall experience with using the platform? - What feedback did you receive that was clear to you? Unclear?
Focus Group	- To uncover additional experiences. - To validate other evaluation methods. - To compare mental models across different users	- Was it clear to you what AI feedback different user groups were seeing? - Do you feel you had a strong understanding of how the system worked? Why or why not?

4   Results

Following the completion of the study, 182 initial codes were extracted from the survey responses, interview, and focus group transcripts. 8 broader themes emerged that captured the main findings of the data. The themes and number of codes that contributed to each theme are listed in Table 2 below:

Table 2. Number of Codes that Contributed to Each Theme

Theme	Instructor Codes	Student Codes
Clarity of Feedback and Explanations	15	25
Effectiveness and Actionability of Feedback and Explanations	5	13
Perceptions and Misconceptions of System	19	16
Evolving Trust in AI Judgements	32	5
User Concerns and Fairness Perceptions	9	14
System Efficiency and Feedback Quality	6	4
User Interface Accessibility and Design	9	4
System Advancement Design Priorities	4	2
Totals	99	83

4.1   Clarity of Feedback and Explanations

Instructors expressed concerns about the algorithm's grading decisions, unclear expectations, and inadequate explanations. Students criticized vague feedback, confusing suggestions, and lack of guidance. Both groups emphasized the importance of enhancing the system's clarity by providing specific examples, clearer expectations, and more informative explanations.

The following quote highlights these concerns:

> *If I had to associate a word with Deep Dives overall, it's probably vagueness. In this situation more information is almost certainly better.*

4.2   Effectiveness and Actionability of Feedback

Instructors valued the system for tasks like word count and plagiarism checks that saved them time. Errors in grading logic led them to double-check automated grades. Students had varied responses to feedback; many students disregarded feedback that was unclear, or that required more effort to address.

4.3   Perceptions and Misconceptions of the System

Instructors' familiarity with essay grading and AI influenced their ability to understand the system and recognize the system's ability to analyze grammar and mechanics using NLP. Misconceptions existed about student's ability to see feedback and scores. Instructors sought a deeper understanding of the algorithms driving the system and had uncertainties about how automated grades were calculated. Students relied on trial and error, discussions with peers and professors, and guess-work to understand how the system operated. Misconceptions regarding flow and structure calculations and citation credibility assessments were also apparent. Students expressed a desire for a clearer understanding of the algorithm to aid their writing process and navigate grading outcomes more effectively.

Below is a quote that highlights these concerns.

If I had a deeper understanding of exactly how the algorithm works for each subcategory, I could figure out which subcategories I trusted and which ones I don't.

4.4   Evolving Trust in AI Judgements

Instructors' trust in the system grew with familiarity. They valued double-checking scores to ensure fairness and trusted the grammar and mechanics assessment more than other rubric categories. While some instructors had disagreements with the system's grading decisions, they generally recognized its consistency with their own evaluation approach. Students generally trusted AI without extensive questioning. They learned not to solely rely on AI scores. Different perceptions of fairness and trustworthiness were associated with different individual grading categories and specific grades. Instructors occasionally overrode grades; students believed AI was fair.

The following quote highlights some of these concerns:

I didn't inherently trust it, but I also didn't inherently think it was wrong. I felt that it needed to be checked, but not necessarily that it was giving back the wrong scores.

4.5   User Concerns and Fairness Perceptions

Instructors questioned the fairness of forcing students into a specific writing style. They occasionally disagreed with system's assessment and debated whether or not to override scores. Students expressed frustration with conflicting feedback and desired more comprehensive engagement with AI. They found system to be sometimes limiting to their writing.

The following quote describes one such concern:

It kind of seems like it's trying to pigeonhole different styles of writing into a more straightforward and basic style of writing.

4.6   System Efficiency and Feedback Quality

Instructors acknowledged the system's ability to expedite the grading process, providing a second opinion that could increase confidence. They appreciated features that checked for repetitiveness and toned down flowery writing. Students also recognized the system's strengths, including the small checks that aided them in refining their writing. They found value in the word count and minimum citation requirements. Additionally, they appreciated the dynamic feedback provided during the writing process.

The following quote highlights one example of these strengths:

I kind of second guess myself a lot when I'm grading so just having that reassurance of the Packback score agreeing with me was nice.

4.7   User Interface Accessibility and Design

Some instructors generally found the UI to be easy to use and navigate, with feedback readily accessible, while others noted that the feedback could be somewhat hidden and required multiple clicks to access the flagged elements. Some instructors encountered challenges in finding explanations and found it time-consuming to manually transfer grades to the gradebook. Conversely, students reported finding everything within the UI to be easily accessible. They often left their writing unchanged due to difficulties addressing confusing feedback errors. While the UI was generally user-friendly, students noted occasional issues such as small font size and limitations in viewing more than two pieces of feedback.

4.8   System Advancement Design Priorities

Instructors expressed the desire for inline comments, allowing them to provide more specific and contextualized feedback. They also raised concerns about the system flagging grammar issues that were not actual errors and called for an enhanced plagiarism check. Additionally, instructors wished for clearer visibility into the system's prompts and instructions provided to students. Students, on the other hand, expressed the need to view all feedback at once to prioritize easier revisions. They also wished for deeper engagement with the system, with a desire for more informative feedback.

4.9   System Usability Score

Based on the interview data and survey responses, the majority of participants found the system easy to use and thought most people would learn to use it quickly. However, there were some participants who found the system unnecessarily complex or very cumbersome to use. The majority of participants were pleased with the UI.

The SUS scores, as obtained from the final survey, can be seen in Table 3. To calculate the total SUS score, the scores of the odd questions were calculated by the scale position minus 1, while the scores for the even questions were the scale position subtracted from 5. The scores were summed and multiplied by 2.5 to obtain the total score of 68.33 [8]. This indicates an average usability rating, as defined by Jeff Sauro [21]. The SUS scores can be seen in Table 3 below:

Table 3. SUS Scores of Deep Dives

Question 1	4	4	2	3	4	3	3.33
Question 2	2	2	4	2	3	4	2.83
Question 3	3	4	3	5	4	4	3.83
Question 4	1	1	3	1	2	1	1.5
Question 5	4	4	1	4	4	3	3.33
Question 6	3	3	3	1	4	2	2.67
Question 7	5	4	3	4	4	4	4
Question 8	1	2	4	2	2	2	2.17
Question 9	3	4	3	4	5	4	3.83
Question 10	2	1	2	2	2	2	1.83
Totals	75	77.5	40	80	70	67.5	68.33

5 Discussion

5.1 RQ1: How Do AI Explainability and Algorithm Transparency Techniques Affect the Overall Usability and User Experience of an AI-Based Essay Feedback System?

The findings from reflexive thematic analysis and the SUS scores provide insights into the impact of explainability and algorithm transparency techniques on the overall usability and user experience of the AI-based essay feedback platform.

Based on the theme of "Clarity of Feedback and Explanations," participants, including both graders and students, highlighted the importance of clear and specific feedback that helps them understand how essays are being evaluated. In some instances, the AI system's feedback was considered vague or contradictory, leading to confusion among students. This suggests that improvements in the clarity and specificity of feedback and explanations could enhance the overall usability and user experience of the system.

The theme of "Impact and Actionability of Feedback" was influenced by participants' trust in the AI system. Gradual familiarity with the system and understanding its underlying algorithms led to increased trust over time. However, some participants expressed concerns about certain aspects of the feedback and grading criteria, which were perceived as subjective or not aligned with their own grading criteria. This indicates that further transparency and explainability of the AI system's evaluation process could enhance users' trust and increase their willingness to act upon the provided feedback.

In terms of usability, participants' feedback highlights the importance of clear and accessible information regarding the system's features, evaluation criteria, and expectations. The need for better organization of feedback, ease of finding explanations, and the inclusion of inline comments demonstrates a desire for more transparency. By addressing these usability concerns, the system can enhance transparency and explainability. Clear organization and accessibility of feedback help users understand how their essays are being evaluated and what specific areas they need to focus on for improvement. Inline comments can provide additional context and explanations, fostering the human-machine teaming approach by making the feedback more informative and actionable. More comprehensive information about the AI's expectations contributes to a clearer understanding of how the system operates, and helps users learn AI-decision making processes.

Incorporating these enhancements in the system's usability not only addresses users' practical needs but also promotes transparency and explainability. Users can have a better grasp of the system's inner workings, the factors influencing their scores, and the rationale behind the provided feedback, thus improving their AI literacy. This fosters a sense of trust and understanding, ultimately improving the overall user experience and the effectiveness of the system.

5.2 RQ2: How Do Graders Perceive the Integration of an AI-Based Essay Feedback System into Their Grading Process, and What Are the Factors Influencing Their Acceptance or Resistance of Automated Feedback?

The survey results suggest that the incorporation of explainability and transparency techniques in an automated essay scoring system influences the way graders used the system.

The thematic analysis process identified several themes related to the impact of explainability and transparency on human grading behavior. One theme that emerged was the influence of system explanations on graders' decision-making process. Clear and detailed explanations regarding the AI's assessment criteria and the factors contributing to the assigned scores helped align human graders' evaluations with the automated system. Gradual understanding of the algorithms and familiarity with the system's functioning empowered graders to make informed judgments, increasing their confidence in the automated scores. One SUS question assessed how confident participants felt using the system. The average score for this question was 3.83 out of 5, indicating a moderately high level of confidence and leaving room for improvement.

Another theme that emerged was the influence of prior experiences and expertise on human grading behavior. Graders with previous experience with automated essay scoring systems or with a stronger writing background demonstrated a deeper understanding of how the algorithm worked. Their expertise allowed them to critically evaluate the AI-generated scores, identify system strengths and limitations, and make informed decisions when overriding scores or providing additional feedback, thus highlighting the importance of improving users' AI literacy to increase their user experience.

5.3 RQ3: What Are the Key Components that Constitute an Effective Automated Essay Scoring System, and How Can They Inform the Development and Assessment of Reliable Grading and Feedback Tools?

The SUS scores and thematic analysis provided insights into the system's usability, as well as its strengths and areas of improvement. Participants greatly appreciated the presence of small checks for specific criteria, such as word count objectives. The SUS question related to the system's ease of use received an average score of 4.6 out of 5, indicating a high level of satisfaction. This demonstrates that user-friendly features play a crucial role in enhancing the overall usability of the system.

Qualitative analysis revealed specific components that influenced user experience, such as clarity of feedback and explanations. Both graders and students expressed the need for more explicit and informative feedback. Participants desired clearer definitions, more examples, and a better understanding of how the system calculated scores for different rubric categories. This highlights the importance of providing comprehensive explanations and specific guidance to enhance the effectiveness of the feedback and grading process.

Furthermore, thematic analysis revealed the importance of trust in automated scores. Participants gradually developed trust in the system through familiarity and understanding of its functioning. However, concerns were raised with certain pieces of feedback, which were perceived as subjective or contradictory at times. This emphasizes the importance of algorithm transparency and continuous evaluation to enhance the system's reliability and foster trust among users.

In conclusion, an effective automated essay scoring system comprises of key components such as clear and informative feedback, user-friendly features, transparent algorithms, and trust between users and the system. Enhancing the clarity of feedback, addressing user concerns, ensuring algorithm transparency, and refining user-friendly features are vital steps in developing reliable grading and feedback tools that enhance the overall usability and user experience of automated essay scoring systems. To help advance the informed use of AI systems, attempts to build users' AI literacy by revealing certain algorithm decision making processes can create a more positive user experience. Continuous evaluation and user feedback are essential for iterative refinement and the development of effective tools in educational settings. During the evaluation process, specific questions should be asked about the ability to provide feedback to users, the transparency and explainability of the system, and the impact of the system on user learning and understanding.

6 Ethical Considerations and Limitations

6.1 Ethical Considerations

Before participating in the study, participants were informed of the purpose of the study, the procedures involved, and the potential risks and benefits of participating. Participant names and courses were kept anonymous. After each phase of the study, participants were given an opportunity to review and redact their comments before they were included in the findings of this study.

6.2 Limitations

Due to the small selection of classes that utilized Deep Dives, there were a limited number of participants that could participate, and resultingly, their experiences may not be generalizable to a larger population. This study took place at one institution, which may limit the applicability of the findings to other settings. The results of this study were obtained over the course of a single semester. Thus, the long term impacts of using Deep Dives are unknown. There have since been updates to Deep Dives that were not available when the study took place, so the findings presented in this study may not be reflective of the latest version of the platform. Despite these limitations, the results of this study can still serve as a valuable starting point for researchers and educators interested in considering and developing AI-driven essay grading systems in their own contexts.

7 Conclusion and Future Works

This paper has presented a set of key considerations for evaluating the usability of AI-based essay grading tools. These considerations hold significant potential for informing future research in the field of AI-based essay feedback systems and promoting design choices that improve users' technical writing while developing their knowledge of AI-driven systems. They can serve as a valuable tool for researchers seeking to investigate the impact of explainability and transparency techniques on grading behavior. Additionally, the list of considerations can be adapted and expanded to encompass different contexts and users. By applying this approach in future research, scholars can gain a deeper understanding of the effectiveness and limitations of AI-based essay feedback systems, ultimately enhancing their usability and educational value.

Disclosure of Interests. The authors have no competing interests to declare that are relevant to the content of this article.

References

1. Alshamari, M., Alsalem, T.: Usable AI: critical review of its current issues and trends. J. Comput. Sci. **19**(3), 326–333 (2023). https://doi.org/10.3844/jcssp.2023. 326.333, https://thescipub.com/abstract/jcssp.2023.326.333
2. Amershi, S., et al.: Guidelines for human-AI interaction (2019). https://doi.org/ 10.1145/3290605.3300233, https://doi-org.ezproxy.lib.vt.edu/10.1145/3290605. 3300233
3. Barrett, A., Pack, A.: Not quite eye to A.I.: student and teacher perspectives on the use of generative artificial intelligence in the writing process. Int. J. Educ. Technol. High. Educ. **20**(1), 59 (2023). https://doi.org/10.1186/s41239-023-00427-0

4. Bicknell, K., Brust, C., Settles, B.: How Duolingo's AI learns what you need to learn: the language-learning app tries to emulate a great human tutor. IEEE Spectr. **60**(3), 28–33 (2023). https://doi.org/10.1109/MSPEC.2023.10061631

5. Brand, L., Humm, B., Krajewski, A., Zender, A.: Towards Improved User Experience for Artificial Intelligence Systems (2023). https://doi.org/10.1007/978-3-031-34204-2_4

6. Braun, V., Clarke, V.: Using thematic analysis in psychology. Qual. Res. Psychol. **3**, 77–101 (2006). https://doi.org/10.1191/1478088706qp063oa

7. Braun, V., Clarke, V.: Reflecting on reflexive thematic analysis. Qual. Res. Sport Exerc. Health **11**(4), 589–597 (2019). https://doi.org/10.1080/2159676X.2019.1628806

8. Brooke, J.: SUS: a quick and dirty usability scale. Usability Eval. Ind. **189**, 4–7 (1995)

9. Craig, S.D., et al.: The impact of a technology-based mathematics after-school program using ALEKS on student's knowledge and behaviors. Comput. Educ. **68**, 495–504 (2013). https://doi.org/10.1016/j.compedu.2013.06.010, https://www.sciencedirect.com/science/article/pii/S0360131513001619

10. Crompton, H., Burke, D.: Artificial intelligence in higher education: the state of the field. Int. J. Educ. Technol. High. Educ. **20**, 22 (2023). https://doi.org/10.1186/s41239-023-00392-8

11. Devlin, J., Chang, M.W., Lee, K., Toutanova, K.: BERT: pre-training of deep bidirectional transformers for language understanding (2019). https://doi.org/10.18653/v1/n19-1423, https://aclanthology.org/N19-1423/, https://www.wikidata.org/entity/Q57267388, https://orkg.org/resource/R12209

12. Kim, N.J., Kim, M.K.: Teacher's perceptions of using an artificial intelligence-based educational tool for scientific writing. Front. Educ. **7**, 755914 (2022). https://doi.org/10.3389/feduc.2022.755914, https://www.frontiersin.org/articles/10.3389/feduc.2022.755914

13. Kumar, V., Boulanger, D.: Explainable automated essay scoring: deep learning really has pedagogical value. Front. Educ. **5**, 572367 (2020). https://doi.org/10.3389/feduc.2020.572367, https://www.frontiersin.org/article/10.3389/feduc.2020.572367

14. Lamba, S., Saini, P., Kukreja, V., Sharma, B.: Role of mathematics in machine learning. SSRN Electron. J. (2021). https://doi.org/10.2139/ssrn.3833931

15. Long, D., Magerko, B.: What is AI literacy? Competencies and design considerations, pp. 1–16. Association for Computing Machinery (2020). https://doi.org/10.1145/3313831.3376727

16. Luckin, R., Holmes, W.: Intelligence unleashed: an argument for AI in education (2016)

17. Nunes, A., Cordeiro, C., Limpo, T., Castro, S.L.: Effectiveness of automated writing evaluation systems in school settings: a systematic review of studies from 2000 to 2020. J. Comput. Assist. Learn. **38**(2), 599–620 (2022). https://doi.org/10.1111/jcal.12635

18. Parra-Santos, T., Molina-Jordá, J.M., Casanova-Pastor, G., Maiorano-Lauria, L.P.: Gamification for formative assessment in the framework of engineering learning (2018). https://doi.org/10.1145/3284179.3284193, https://doi-org.ezproxy.lib.vt.edu/10.1145/3284179.3284193

19. Petch, J., Di, S., Nelson, W.: Opening the black box: the promise and limitations of explainable machine learning in cardiology. Can. J. Cardiol. **38**(2), 204–213 (2022). https://doi.org/10.1016/j.cjca.2021.09.004, https://www.sciencedirect.com/science/article/pii/S0828282X21007030

20. Rader, E., Cotter, K., Cho, J.: Explanations as mechanisms for supporting algorithmic transparency (2018). https://doi.org/10.1145/3173574.3173677

21. Sauro, J.: Measuring usability with the system usability scale (SUS) (2011). https://measuringu.com/sus/

22. Schmidt, A., Giannotti, F., Mackay, W., Shneiderman, B., Väänänen, K.: Artificial Intelligence for Humankind: A Panel on How to Create Truly Interactive and Human-Centered AI for the Benefit of Individuals and Society (2021)

23. Semire, D.: An overview of automated scoring of essays. J. Technol. Learn. Assess. **5**(1) (2006). https://ejournals.bc.edu/index.php/jtla/article/view/1640

24. Wang, H., Ma, C., Zhou, L.: A brief review of machine learning and its application. In: 2009 International Conference on Information Engineering and Computer Science, pp. 1–4 (2009). https://doi.org/10.1109/ICIECS.2009.5362936

25. Wilson, J., et al.: Predictors of middle school students' perceptions of automated writing evaluation. Comput. Educ. **211**, 104985 (2024). https://doi.org/10.1016/j.compedu.2023.104985, https://www.sciencedirect.com/science/article/pii/S0360131523002622

26. Zawacki-Richter, O., Marín, V., Bond, M., Gouverneur, F.: Systematic review of research on artificial intelligence applications in higher education-where are the educators? Int. J. Educ. Technol. High. Educ. **16**, 1–27 (2019). https://doi.org/10.1186/s41239-019-0171-0

Exploring the Use of Generative AI in Education: Broadening the Scope

Irfan Jahić[(✉)], Martin Ebner, Sandra Schön, and Sarah Edelsbrunner

Graz University of Technology, Graz, Austria
irfan.jahic@student.tugraz.at,
{martin.ebner,sarah.edelsbrunner}@tugraz.at, mail@sandra-schoen.de

Abstract. Artificial Intelligence (AI) already plays a significant role in education and society altogether. With the rapid and largely impactful development in the field of generative AI, we must consider the potential changes and shifts of the new normal. Generative models like ChatGPT, Google Bard, Bing Chat, DALL-E, and many others, are proving to be powerful allies and assistants in practically every branch and aspect of life. Given their proficiency in language and their technical capabilities, we must acknowledge their significance and ensure they are not overlooked. In this work, we focus on their impact on education and what is the feedback from the educational community. We want to determine exactly how generative AI is used and how it can be used in education. Our goal is to review more, and new papers, to classify the papers based on the subject the paper has covered, the type of the study, the educational level it concerns, and how is generative AI generally perceived. After the analysis, we conclude that it is perceived as generally positive, with most papers focusing on higher education, and STEM subjects while mostly using qualitative research methods.

Keywords: Education · Artificial Intelligence · ChatGPT · Higher Education · Generative AI · Google Bard · Bing Chat

1 Introduction

AI is everywhere. From helping doctors make better decisions about our health to giving us song or movie suggestions, AI has become a big part of our daily lives. In the world of business, AI helps companies understand what their customers like and even predicts trends. In our homes, AI is there in the form of smart speakers that answer our questions or set reminders for us. Now, within this world of AI, there's a branch called "generative AI". Generative AI is now changing the way we think about learning, creating, and even communicating. This branch of AI, as the name suggests, generates content - it creates text, images, and music. If a certain satisfactory level of its generated results is achieved, we can speed up innovation, research, analysis and creation in general with its help. Generative AI has a lot of potential in education and already plays a significant role. With understanding and correct utilization of generative AI, we can accomplish a lot and change in education. We will build on top of our previous work [48] that focused on ChatGPT in education. We reviewed more and new papers, we focus not only on ChatGPT, but generative AI in general and we will also explore papers which address Google Bard, Bing Chat, IBM Watson and DALL-E and their role and use in education. The purpose of this research is to find out how generative AI affects teaching and learning in schools and universities as well as teaching and learning of certain subjects individually. Furthermore, we want to explore how the community perceives the usage of generative AI in education. Finally, we want to identify gaps and recommend the direction of future research. We will explain the method used in the next section. The results and main findings are also described in a separate section with their interpretation. We will finish the paper with separate sections for discussion, conclusion, and recommendations for future work.

2   Materials and Methods

In this section, we will describe the methodology we used for this research and relevant details. Our methodology is a literature review, where 100 academic articles were gathered, read, analyzed and included in the final analysis. These articles provided invaluable insights into generative AI in education, forming the foundation for the discussion and conclusions presented in this paper. The entire selection process and the number of papers included in total is represented by Fig. 1.

2.1   Objective

The objective of our literature review was to gain a comprehensive understanding of AI in education and to identify key insights, trends, and conclusions from prior research on this topic. We wanted to find out what subjects the paper focused on the most, i.e. we wanted to find out how is generative AI used in each specific subject and what are examples of that use. Furthermore, we wanted to identify which type of research was used most frequently and in which educational level was the research conducted or which educational level the research aimed to explore or explain. Finally, we wanted to use papers that are relatively new and to see if teachers and students see a positive and good impact of generative AI in education or do they see it more pessimistically.

2.2   Search Strategy and Sources

We were searching for papers on 2 different databases, using many different keywords and we aimed to get newer papers from 2023.

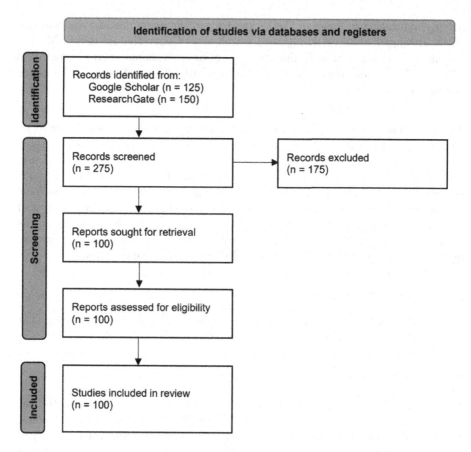

Fig. 1. Flow diagram of record selection according to PRISMA [76]

Databases Accessed:

– Google Scholar
– ResearchGate

Keywords and Phrases Used: In the end, we used a lot of keywords to search for papers, here is a list of most important ones

– Generative AI in education
– Generative AI in schools
– AI in education
– AI in schools
– ChatGPT in education

It is important to mention here that we adapted our search frequently because of the goal we wanted to achieve. We wanted to look for academic papers in different education fields, i.e. research that also focused on specific subjects and not just education in general. We looked for specific examples and applications of AI. Examples of adjusted keyword search are: "Generative AI in STEM education", "Generative AI in Humanities education", "Generative AI in geography education", "Generative AI in physics education", "Generative AI in language education", etc.

Time Period: Our focus was on including papers as new as possible, or to be more specific from April 2023 onwards. The reason for that is because in our previous paper we did not limit ourselves this strictly to the time period and we did not want to have same papers twice. Since the field is still young, our goal was also to include latest research on the subject now that 2 semesters have passed since ChatGPT has been released. We filtered results from 2023 only and we aimed to find papers no older than April 2023. Eventually, we came across interesting and relevant papers that are older and because of the significance, quality and interesting content we included those older papers as well.

2.3 Selection Criteria

We included and we found relevant all academic articles written in English that addressed how AI is used in any sphere of education.

2.4 Data Extraction

Reading and Cataloging: After reading and analyzing each paper, we noted key findings, methodologies, and conclusions. We made a separate document solely for keeping track of all papers and we wrote a short summary of the work as well as our chosen categories. Based on the information provided in the paper and to the best of our understanding, we noted down if the author considered AI to have positive, negative, neutral or mixed impact to education. In the same way we noted down whether the research was qualitative, quantitative or mixed. Additionally, we kept track of educational level, by determining if the author was focusing on primary, secondary or tertiary (university) education. Lastly, we wrote the main subject of the work, differentiating between Science, Engineering, Technology and Mathematics (STEM), or Humanities (with Social Sciences), and Arts, or if there was no clear main subject category then we consider it to be education in general (General).

2.5 Analysis Process

A small Python program was written to identify duplicates which were discarded, to extract and count relevant category information which was then plotted in Excel. This relevant info for our categories is presented in the results and findings section.

3   Results

In this section, we will present our results and provide our interpretation of all findings. Our main goal is to discover:

– How generative AI affects teaching and learning in schools and universities.
– How the community perceives the usage of generative AI in education until now.

We read and analyzed 100 papers. We found 55 papers on ResearchGate, and 45 on Google Scholar. Figure 2 illustrates the number of papers taken from the mentioned databases and sources.

PAPER SOURCES

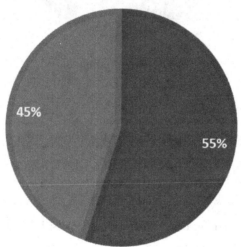

Fig. 2. Paper's sources

Since we aimed to pick preferably newer papers, it is no surprise that we found 73 papers from 2023, and only 27 papers older than 2023. Figure 3 depicts this statistic.

While reading these papers we noticed some common threads and themes which we found important for the goals we wanted to achieve. In the following subsections, we will explain each of them and we will present our results.

PAPER'S DATE OF PUBLISHING

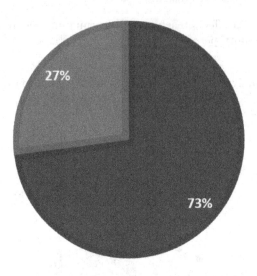

Fig. 3. Paper's publishing dates

3.1 Educational Level

We categorized the papers according to educational level and we decided to divide them into the following four choices:

– Primary (primary schools)
– Secondary (high schools)
– Tertiary (universities)
– Other (life-long learning, other educational institutions, etc.)

If the paper mentioned all educational levels we considered that it mentioned primary, secondary, and tertiary education. If the paper mentioned two categories then we increased the number for those two categories. For example, if a paper mentions primary and secondary schools only, like "K-12 education", we increased the number for primary and secondary levels only. In the end, 86 papers were relevant for tertiary education, 19 papers for secondary, 15 for primary, and only 2 were relevant for other. [71] was focusing on Vietnamese biology teaching in schools so we marked that paper for secondary educational level, while [18] wrote about architecture students at universities, so we marked that paper under tertiary educational level. Figure 4 shows how papers are distributed across educational level categories.

EDUCATIONAL LEVEL

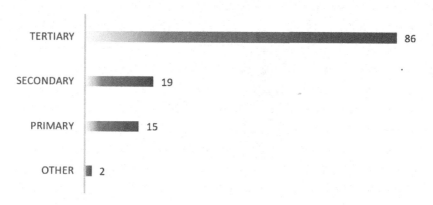

Fig. 4. Graphical depiction of the quantity of papers addressing tertiary (higher), secondary, primary and other education.

3.2 Type of Study

We categorized the work according to the type of study. We set three different choices:

- Qualitative
- Quantitative
- Mixed

We considered a study qualitative if the data types were non-numerical such as texts, audio recordings, and videos. Studies marked as quantitative were those studies that focused on numerical data that can be transformed into usable statistics. A mixed study is a study that contains both quantitative and qualitative research methods. Ultimately, 64 papers fell under qualitative studies, 16 papers used quantitative research methods while 20 were considered to use mixed research methods. [14] was using literature review methodology so we marked it under qualitative, while we consider [92] to be quantitative since it was a survey research design, with data analysis, and hypothesis testing. [98] was marked under mixed since it included interviews, data analysis, and combining questionnaires. Figure 5 illustrates the amount of papers that fall in each of the mentioned three categories.

3.3 Outcomes and Benefits

We categorized the work according to the author's perceived impact of generative AI on education. We set three different categories:

- Positive
- Negative

TYPE OF STUDY

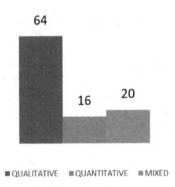

Fig. 5. In this visualization, you can see the number of papers that used qualitative, quantitative and mixed research methods.

– Neutral or Mixed

If the paper expressed rather positive remarks and positive impacts of AI in education, or generally - we marked it as positive. However, if the paper expressed rather negative remarks, talked mostly about problems and troubles caused by AI in education, or generally - we marked it as negative. However, if the paper did not bring out the positive or negative at all, or if the paper equally mentioned and explained both negative and positive then we marked it as neutral or mixed. [74] explained the potential drawbacks and concerns of using ChatGPT in programming - so we marked it with a negative perceived impact. [50] shows that teachers had a positive perspective on generative AI in education - so we marked it with a positive perceived impact. Figure 6 shows how many papers argued for positive negative or mixed feelings.

3.4 Main Subject

We made four separate categories regarding the main subject and they are:

– STEM (Science, Technology, Engineering, Mathematics)
– Humanities (Languages, Philosophy, Religion, History, Law, Geography, Social sciences, ...)
– Art
– General

We categorized the papers based on the subject or course that the paper focused on by using AI in that particular subject. [44] talked about the use of ChatGPT in chemistry, so we marked that paper for STEM. [96] discussed the social life of AI in education and the societal implications of AI, so we marked it under Humanities. Figure 7 shows the amount of papers that discussed a particular subject.

PERCEIVED IMPACT

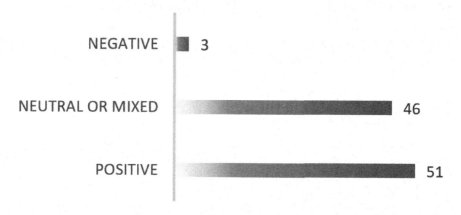

Fig. 6. In this visualization, you can see the number of papers that expressed mostly negative, neutral or mixed and positive thoughts towards generative AI usage in education.

3.5   List of Reviewed Publications

In this section, we provide a compiled overview of the literature that was carefully examined in the course of this study and the respective categories (Table 1).

Table 1. All papers and their categories

Name of the Paper	Educational Level	Main Subject	Type of Study	Perceived Impact
Incorporating AI Tools into Medical Education: Harnessing the Benefits of ChatGPT and Dall-E [10]	Tertiary	STEM	Qualitative	Positive
Challenges for higher education in the era of widespread access to Generative AI [94]	Tertiary	STEM	Mixed	Positive
What's in a text-to-image prompt? The potential of stable diffusion in visual arts education [26]	Tertiary	Art	Qualitative	Positive
Empowering learners for the age of artificial intelligence [38]	Tertiary	STEM	Mixed	Positive
The usability of Images Generated by Artificial Intelligence (AI) in Education [5]	Tertiary	STEM	Qualitative	Positive
Artificial Intelligence versus Software Engineers: An Evidence-Based Assessment Focusing on Non-Functional Requirements [67]	Other	STEM	Quantitative	Positive
The Social life of AI in Education [96]	Tertiary	Humanities	Qualitative	Neutral
AIED-Coming of Age? [42]	All	STEM	Qualitative	Neutral
Artificial Intelligence in Education: Developing Competencies and Supporting Teachers in Implementing AI in School Learning Environments [33]	Primary And Secondary	STEM	Mixed	Positive
Revolutionizing Education: The Power of Artificial Intelligence (AI) [81]	All	STEM And Humanities	Qualitative	Positive
Student Perspectives on the Role of Artificial Intelligence in Education: A Survey-Based Analysis [46]	All	STEM	Quantitative	Mixed
Potential of ChatGPT in Biology Teaching and Learning at the Vietnamese High School [71]	Secondary	STEM	Qualitative	Positive
Generative artificial intelligence (ChatGPT): Implications for management educators [80]	Tertiary	Humanities	Qualitative	Neutral
Beyond the Hype: A Cautionary Tale of ChatGPT in the Programming Classroom [74]	Tertiary	STEM	Mixed	Negative

continued

Table 1. continued

Name of the Paper	Educational Level	Main Subject	Type of Study	Perceived Impact
Generative AI and Teachers' Perspectives on Its Implementation in Education [50]	Tertiary	STEM	Quantitative	Positive
Artificial Intelligence in Education: A Review [21]	Tertiary	STEM	Qualitative	Positive
Artificial intelligence in higher education: the state of the field [24]	Tertiary	STEM	Qualitative	Neutral
ENAI Recommendations on the ethical use of Artificial Intelligence in Education [34]	All	Humanities	Qualitative	Positive
Ethical Problems of Digitalization and Artificial Intelligence in Education: a Global Perspective [51]	All	Humanities	Qualitative	Neutral
Examining Science Education in ChatGPT: An Exploratory Study of Generative Artificial Intelligence [23]	All	STEM	Qualitative	Positive
Ethical principles for artificial intelligence in K-12 education [3]	Primary And Secondary	Humanities	Qualitative	Neutral
On the Educational Impact of ChatGPT: Is Artificial Intelligence Ready to Obtain a University Degree? [63]	Tertiary	STEM	Qualitative	Mixed
Impact of Artificial Intelligence on Dental Education: A Review and Guide for Curriculum Update [88]	Tertiary	STEM	Qualitative	Mixed
The Use of Artificial Intelligence (AI) in Online Learning and Distance Education Processes: A Systematic Review of Empirical Studies [29]	Other	STEM	Mixed	Positive
Collaborating With ChatGPT: Considering the Implications of Generative Artificial Intelligence for Journalism and Media Education [77]	Tertiary	Humanities	Qualitative	Positive
A study on perceived benefits and applications of generative artificial intelligence in education [57]	Tertiary	STEM	Mixed	Neutral
Possibilities and Apprehensions in the Landscape of Artificial Intelligence in Education [6]	Tertiary	STEM	Qualitative	Neutral
Vision, challenges, roles and research issues of Artificial Intelligence in Education [45]	Tertiary	STEM	Qualitative	Positive
Artificial intelligence in education: The three paradigms [75]	Tertiary	STEM	Qualitative	Positive
Artificial Intelligence in Education - Ethical framework [37]	Tertiary	Humanities	Qualitative	Positive
Potential ChatGPT Use in Undergraduate Chemistry Laboratories [44]	Tertiary	STEM	Qualitative	Neutral
Implications of large language models such as ChatGPT for dental medicine [32]	Tertiary	STEM	Qualitative	Mixed
Students' voices on generative AI: perceptions, benefits, and challenges in higher education [20]	Tertiary	Humanities	Quantitative	Mixed
Enhancing Physics Learning with ChatGPT, Bing Chat, and Bard as Agents-to-Think-With: A Comparative Case Study [30]	Tertiary	STEM	Mixed	Mixed
Exploring the AI competencies of elementary school teachers in South Korea [54]	Primary And Secondary	Humanities	Mixed	Neutral
ChatGPT is Good but Bing Chat is Better for Vietnamese Students [97]	Secondary	STEM	Mixed	Neutral
Application of CHATGPT in Civil Engineering [9]	Tertiary	STEM	Qualitative	Positive
ChatGPT: A Revolutionary Tool for Teaching and Learning Mathematics [95]	Tertiary	STEM	Qualitative	Positive
Artificial Intelligence (AI) in the Education of Accounting and Auditing Profession [7]	Tertiary	STEM	Qualitative	Positive
Artificial Intelligence in Agriculture [40]	Tertiary	STEM	Qualitative	Positive
Role of artificial intelligence in chemistry [22]	Tertiary	STEM	Qualitative	Positive
What Are the Top 20 Questions in Sociology? A ChatGPT Reply [64]	Tertiary	Humanities	Qualitative	Neutral
ChatGPT in Higher Education: The Good, The Bad, and The University [83]	Tertiary	General	Qualitative	Neutral
Exploring the Application of ChatGPT to English Teaching in a Malaysia Primary School [62]	Primary	Languages	Qualitative	Neutral
The application of artificial intelligence technology in education influences Chinese adolescent's emotional perception [56]	Secondary	Humanities	Quantitative	Negative
Generative AI: Implications and Applications for Education [91]	Tertiary	STEM	Qualitative	Neutral

continued

Table 1. continued

Name of the Paper	Educational Level	Main Subject	Type of Study	Perceived Impact
Leveraging AI to Instruct Architecture Students on Circular Design Techniques and Life Cycle Assessment [18]	Tertiary	Art	Qualitative	Positive
Architecture Decisions in AI-based Systems Development: An Empirical Study [100]	Tertiary	STEM	Mixed	Neutral
Critical Reflections on ChatGPT in UAE Education: Navigating Equity and Governance for Safe and Effective Use [52]	Tertiary	General	Qualitative	Positive
Could an Artificial Intelligence Agent Pass an Introductory Physics Course? [55]	Tertiary	STEM	Mixed	Neutral
ChatGPT's Impact on Nursing and Health Science Education [8]	Tertiary	STEM	Qualitative	Neutral
Exploring the Future of Mathematics Teaching with ChatGPT [86]	Tertiary	STEM	Qualitative	Positive
Concerns About Using ChatGPT in Education [60]	Tertiary	General	Mixed	Neutral
Acceptance of Artificial Intelligence (ChatGPT) in Education: Trust, Innovativeness, and Psychological Needs of Students [1]	Tertiary	General	Quantitative	Neutral
An Empirical Investigation of the Impact of Artificial Intelligence on Accounting Practice in Nigeria [92]	Tertiary	Humanities	Quantitative	Positive
Exploring the Use of Artificial Intelligence in Teaching Management and Evaluation Based on Citation Space Analysis [101]	Tertiary	General	Mixed	Neutral
"AI, Concepts of Intelligence, and Chatbots: The" "Figure of Man," "the Rise of Emotion, and Future Visions of Education" [15]	Tertiary	General	Qualitative	Neutral
Integrating Artificial Intelligence into Medical Education: Lessons Learned From a Belgian Initiative [78]	Tertiary	STEM	Mixed	Positive
Artificial Intelligence and its Implications in Basic Education [11]	Primary And Secondary	General	Qualitative	Positive
Artificial Intelligence for Education and Teaching [98]	Tertiary	General	Mixed	Positive
Research on the Analysis of Classroom Teaching Behavior Based on Artificial Intelligence Technology [102]	Tertiary	General	Mixed	Positive
Artificial Intelligence and Teaching of Linear Algebra [31]	Tertiary	STEM	Qualitative	Positive
Leading teachers' perspective on teacherAI collaboration in education [53]	Primary	STEM	Qualitative	Positive
AI Language Models as Educational Allies: Enhancing Instructional Support in Higher Education [99]	Tertiary	STEM	Qualitative	Positive
Integrating Generative AI into Higher Education: Considerations [41]	Tertiary	STEM	Qualitative	Positive
Transforming Education: A Comprehensive Review of Generative Artificial Intelligence in Educational Settings through Bibliometric and Content Analysis [14]	Tertiary	STEM	Qualitative	Positive
When things go wrong: the recall of AI systems as a last resort for ethical and lawful AI [87]	Tertiary	Humanities	Qualitative	Neutral
AI and Organizational Transformation: Anthropological Insights into Higher Education [66]	Tertiary	Humanities	Qualitative	Mixed
Exploring the impact of AI on teacher leadership: regressing or expanding? [39]	All	General	Qualitative	Mixed
Artificial intelligence in intelligent tutoring systems toward sustainable education: a systematic review [59]	All	General	Mixed	Mixed
Challenges and Opportunities of Generative AI for Higher Education as Explained by ChatGPT [65]	Tertiary	General	Qualitative	Mixed
Why and how to embrace AI such as ChatGPT in your academic life [61]	Tertiary	STEM	Qualitative	Positive
Balancing: The Effects of AI Tools in Educational Context [58]	Tertiary	Humanities	Qualitative	Neutral
Do Innovative Teachers use AI-powered Tools More Interactively? A Study in the Context of Diffusion of Innovation Theory [93]	Tertiary	General	Quantitative	Positive
Analyzing Sentiments Regarding ChatGPT Using Novel BERT: A Machine Learning Approach [79]	Tertiary	STEM	Quantitative	Neutral
Exploring The Potential of Generative AI [82]	Tertiary	STEM	Qualitative	Neutral
The Intersection of AI, Information and Digital Literacy: Harnessing ChatGPT and Other Generative Tools to Enhance Teaching and Learning [84]	Tertiary	STEM	Qualitative	Positive

continued

Table 1. continued

Name of the Paper	Educational Level	Main Subject	Type of Study	Perceived Impact
How to Harness Generative AI to Accelerate Human Learning [49]	All	General	Qualitative	Positive
The use of ChatGPT as a learning tool to improve foreign language writing in a multilingual and multicultural classroom [12]	Secondary	Languages	Quantitative	Positive
A Shakespearean Experiment with ChatGPT [68]	Tertiary	Humanities	Qualitative	Neutral
An Analysis of the Suitability of Philosophy as a Core K-12 Public School Subject [16]	Tertiary	Humanities	Qualitative	Positive
Energy Consumption of AI in Education: A Case Study [19]	Tertiary	STEM	Quantitative	Positive
Building a Strategy to Harness ChatGPT in Education [35]	Tertiary	STEM	Qualitative	Positive
A Model for Integrating Generative AI into Course Content Development [28]	Tertiary	STEM	Qualitative	Positive
Field courses for dummies: can ChatGPT design a higher education field course? [90]	Tertiary	General	Quantitative	Mixed
Language Models, Plagiarism, and Legal Writing [85]	Tertiary	Humanities	Qualitative	Mixed
Can ChatGPT explain it? Use of artificial intelligence in multiple sclerosis communication [47]	Tertiary	STEM	Qualitative	Positive
Automatic assessment of text-based responses in post-secondary education: A systematic review [36]	Tertiary	STEM	Mixed	Positive
An analysis of Watson vs. BARD vs. ChatGPT: The Jeopardy! Challenge [73]	Tertiary	STEM	Mixed	Mixed
Exploring the ethical considerations of using Chat GPT in university education [43]	Tertiary	Humanities	Qualitative	Negative
AI in Education, Learner Control, and Human-AI Collaboration [17]	Tertiary	STEM	Qualitative	Mixed
AI in Education: Cracking the Code Through Challenges: A Content Analysis of one of the recent Issues of Educational Technology and Society (ET&S) Journal [25]	Tertiary	STEM	Qualitative	Neutral
War of the chatbots: Bard, Bing Chat, ChatGPT, Ernie and beyond [2]	Tertiary	STEM	Qualitative	Neutral
Performance of Large Language Models (ChatGPT, Bing Search, and Google Bard) in Solving Case Vignettes in Physiology [27]	Tertiary	STEM	Quantitative	Positive
Evaluation of Google Bard on Vietnamese High School Biology Examination [70]	Secondary	STEM	Quantitative	Mixed
Google Bard's Performance on Vietnamese High School Civic Education Examination [72]	Secondary	Humanities	Quantitative	Mixed
Google Bard Generated Literature Review: Metaverse [13]	Tertiary	STEM	Mixed	Neutral
Microsoft Bing vs Google Bard in Neurology: A Comparative Study of AI-Generated Patient Education Material [69]	Tertiary	STEM	Quantitative	Positive
Artificial intelligence and the transformation of management education [89]	Tertiary	STEM	Qualitative	Positive
AI-Supported Academic Advising: Exploring ChatGPT's Current State and Future Potential toward Student Empowerment [4]	Tertiary	STEM	Qualitative	Positive

3.6   Novelties and Other Remarks

Compared to our previous work, we now have access to papers, that were read and analyzed here, that explore not only ChatGPT but also other chatbots like Google Bard, Bing Chat, Watson, and other generative AI models like DALL-E which generates an image based on a textual description. They prove to be worthy adversaries to ChatGPT and they can also be used for educational purposes.

MAIN SUBJECT

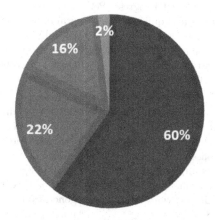

Fig. 7. In this visualization, you can see how many papers focused on either STEM subjects, Humanities subjects, Art or Education in General.

4 Answers to the Research Questions

In this section, we will revisit our research questions and give a clear answer with examples. The two questions were:

- How does generative AI affect teaching and learning in schools and universities and how does it affect teaching and learning of certain subjects individually?
- How does the community perceive the usage of generative AI in education until now?

4.1 How Does Generative AI Affect Teaching and Learning in Schools and Universities?

Table 2 explains and provides concrete examples gathered from literature about how generative AI can be used for teaching in schools and universities as well as how it can be used for learning in schools and universities.

Table 2. Generative AI in Education

	Teaching	Learning
Schools	– Lesson Planning: Tailored plans based on student metrics. Examples in [62,71,93], – Content Creation: Generation of quizzes, worksheets, etc. Examples in: [23,28] – Assessing Student Progress: Personalized tests and quizzes. [24,36, 38,80] – Feedback Generation: Detailed feedback and intervention strategies. [31,41,46,71]	– Personalized Tutoring: Real-time question answering. Examples in: [14,60,99] – Homework Assistance: Guided problem-solving. Examples in: [20, 70] – Language Learning: Practice and grammar checks. Examples in: [12, 24,62] – Interactive Learning: AI-crafted stories or scenarios. Examples in: [41,71,93]
Universities	– Research Assistance: Help with drafts, data analysis, etc. Examples in: [60,66,85] – Curriculum Development: Updates based on research and industry. Examples in: [21,88,98] – Collaboration: Suggestions for interdisciplinary work. Examples in: [45,60,86] – Administration: Help with scheduling, correspondence, grading. Examples in: [21,31,83]	– Research and Writing: Assistance with drafts and data analysis. Examples in: [20,24,46] – Study Aids: Personalized study guides or flashcards. Examples in: [11,60,86] – Specialized Learning: Content generation for complex and narrow subjects. Examples in: [12,18,88]

4.2 How Does the Community Perceive the Usage of Generative AI in Education Until Now?

Our goal is to find out what is the perceived impact of generative AI in education. We found several good points of both positive and negative impacts. Table 3 provides concrete examples of the positive impacts of generative AI according to the literature review as well as negative impacts.

5 Discussion

Our extensive literature review underscored the rapid integration of generative AI models, particularly in higher education. Notably, STEM disciplines are the main subject of the majority of papers in the research, with qualitative methodologies being the favorite research method. This preference for qualitative methods made it harder to determine whether the author considered generative AI to have a more positive, or negative impact, which is why a neutral or mixed category had to be created. It is evident from our findings that models like Chat-GPT, Google Bard, Bing Chat, and DALL-E are positively perceived within the

Table 3. Impacts of Generative AI on Teaching and Learning in Educational Context

Impact	Description and Example
Positive	**Facilitated Content Creation**: Educators can use generative AI to create tailored teaching materials. Examples in: [17,45,81]
	Continuous Learning Support: Students can access AI tutors 24/7. Examples in: [4,52,99]
	Language Barrier Reduction: AI provides real-time translations. Examples in: [12,97]
	Customized Responses: Adapts to query and context for relevant answers. Examples in: [31,67,69]
Negative	**Over-standardization of Content**: Over-reliance on popular AI platforms might lead to homogenization. Examples in: [23,28,51]
	Teacher-student Relationship Strain: Over-reliance on AI could diminish direct interaction. Examples in: [51,87,96]
	Equity Concerns: Not every institution can afford AI tools, widening the educational divide. Examples in: [15,52,86]
	Ethical Concerns in Content Generation: AI might generate biased or culturally insensitive content. Examples in: [15,66,88]

educational community. People are reacting more positively now than they did in some earlier opinions, such as one mentioned in [74], which conveyed skepticism. This change might be because of fast improvements in AI or changes in teaching methods to meet today's needs. The frequent mention of STEM in the papers, compared to the few mentions of humanities or arts, was interesting. This might be because STEM fields rely heavily on data, or because our study mostly looked at recent articles that highlight a popular trend. Still, this suggests there might be unexplored opportunities for using AI in non-STEM fields. We have found that generative AI, like ChatGPT, can be a big help in learning. As mentioned in [49], ChatGPT can accelerate learning, and for the best results, it is key to give it clear instructions and prompts. While it is a useful tool, it should not replace human judgment, especially when detailed knowledge is needed. For example, experts and teachers need to check and fix any mistakes ChatGPT might make. Generative AI is also helping in designing courses and curriculums. For example, it's been used to design school curriculums and courses on philosophy, as seen in [16]. Students can use it to study better for exams, like in a study from [70] about a biology exam in Vietnam. Teachers can also use it to make exams and come up with new questions, as shown in [23] for a quiz about renewable energy. To give more specific examples, [95] talked about math students using ChatGPT. It can help them understand basic math ideas, do simple math, and even solve complex equations and answer geometry questions. Though our review was thorough, some limitations persisted. The emphasis on contemporary papers may have overlooked seminal works from prior years. Also, the swift progress in

AI could render some of our sources outdated in terms of technical specifics, though their broader implications remain relevant. Generative AI's impact on education goes beyond the confines of classroom instruction. With these tools gaining traction, we might be on the brink of a transformative shift in pedagogical methodologies, curriculum formation, and the dynamics between educators and learners. The overwhelmingly positive reception of AI tools indicates a willingness to integrate technology, reshaping how we envision 21st-century learning. To fill the existing research gaps, future studies should probe into the potential of generative AI in the arts, humanities, and social sciences. Additionally, as the capabilities of these AI models expand, exploring their long-term influence on educational results is crucial. In summation, the role of generative AI in education is in a state of fluid evolution. The educational sphere seems poised to harness this technology judiciously. As we go through this change, it is crucial to keep discussing and researching. Given our significant findings, it is vital to remain objective. As the AI field keeps changing, it's important to thoroughly address new challenges and viewpoints. As AI becomes more integrated into our education system, how will it change the traditional teaching paradigms? How do we make sure AI is used ethically and effectively, always focusing on holistic learning?

6   Conclusion

In the ever-evolving landscape of education, the ascent of generative AI models marks a pivotal moment. Our comprehensive literature review has illuminated the profound and predominantly positive impact of these tools, especially in higher education and notably within STEM disciplines. Qualitative methodologies have helped guide researchers to explore the implications of generative AI integration. The growing enthusiasm for models like ChatGPT, Google Bard, Bing Chat, and DALL-E showcases the educational community's readiness to embrace technology that promises transformative shifts. However, it's crucial to note the tendency towards STEM, indicating a potential research void in the humanities and arts. This observation raises questions about broader applications and suggests areas mature for future investigation. As we stand at the intersection of tradition and innovation, the challenges are many. AI is advancing quickly, so we need to consistently review its use to make sure it's ethical, and meaningful, and supports well-rounded learning. The growing acceptance of AI tools reflects current trends, but we must be careful. As we move into this new area, we must protect the fundamental principles of education. In summary, AI is not only growing in education but also actively changing how we teach. It has great potential. And while a tech-enhanced educational future is exciting, we must approach it with care, curiosity, and a strong dedication to the true purpose of education.

7 Recommendation for Future Work

The literature review has shown that the use of generative AI brings great potentials, but also challenges, which in itself will lead to changes to the whole education system. Therefore, it is important to intensify research and also conduct practical experiments - of any kind - to further determine the possibilities and limitations. In particular, AI can be expected to go far beyond generative text creation, as we can already see today that AI-powered applications will play a major role in the creation of teaching and learning content, but also in providing individual support throughout the learning process (e.g. chatbots). We also recognize that teachers themselves will be able to generate metadata of courses and contents that can make matching or classification better. Last but not least, AI-supported tools will also change examination situations and here, too, educational institutions will have to adapt and rethink the current situation. In short, the use of AI will be indispensable tomorrow and there is a wide range of research needs to be addressed - moreless immediately.

Disclosure of Interests. The authors have no competing interests to declare that are relevant to the content of this article.

References

1. Ofosu-Ampong, K., Acheampong, B., Kevor, M.O.: Acceptance of artificial intelligence (ChatGPT) in education: trust, innovativeness and psychological need of students. Inf. Knowl. Manag. **13**, 37–47 (2023)
2. Rudolph, J., Tan, S., Tan, S.: War of the chatbots: bard, bing chat, ChatGPT, ernie and beyond: the new AI gold rush and its impact on higher education. J. Appl. Learn. Teach. **6**(1), 1–26 (2023)
3. Adams, C., Pente, P., Lemermeyer, G., Rockwell, G.: Ethical principles for artificial intelligence in k-12 education. Comput. Educ. Artif. Intell. **4**, 100131 (2023)
4. Akiba, D., Fraboni, M.C.: AI-supported academic advising: exploring ChatGPT's current state and future potential toward student empowerment. Educ. Sci. **13**(9), 885 (2023)
5. Aktay, S.: The usability of images generated by artificial intelligence (AI) in education. Int. Technol. Educ. J. **6**(2), 51–62 (2022)
6. Ashraf Alam. Possibilities and apprehensions in the landscape of artificial intelligence in education. In *2021 International Conference on Computational Intelligence and Computing Applications (ICCICA)*. IEEE, nov 2021
7. Ali, S.M., Hasan, Z.J., Hamdan, A., Al-Mekhlaf, M.: Artificial intelligence (AI) in the education of accounting and auditing profession. In: Alareeni, B., Hamdan, A., Khamis, R., Khoury, R.E. (eds.) ICBT 2022, vol. 621, pp. 656–664. Springer, Heidelberg (2023). https://doi.org/10.1007/978-3-031-26956-1_61
8. Alkhaqani, A.L.: ChatGPT: how can it impact nursing and health science education? Al-Rafidain J. Med. Sci. **5**, 112–113 (2023). (ISSN 2789-3219)
9. Aluga, M.: Application of CHATGPT in civil engineering. East Afr. J. Eng. **6**(1), 104–112 (2023)

10. Amri, M.M., Hisan, U.K.: Incorporating AI tools into medical education: harnessing the benefits of ChatGPT and dall-e. J. Novel Eng. Sci. Technol. **2**(02), 34–39 (2023)
11. Aristega, A.M.M., Aristega, J.E.M., Angulo, R.J.C., Rojas, M.T.C.: Artificial intelligence and its implications in basic education. Centro Sur. **7**(3), 24–43 (2023)
12. Athanassopoulos, S., Manoli, P., Gouvi, M., Lavidas, K., Komis, V.: The use of ChatGPT as a learning tool to improve foreign language writing in a multilingual and multicultural classroom. Adv. Mobile Learn. Educ. Res. **3**(2), 818–824 (2023)
13. Aydin, Ö.: Google bard generated literature review: metaverse. J. AI **7**(1), 1–14 (2023)
14. Bahroun, Z., Anane, C., Ahmed, V., Zacca, A.: Transforming education: a comprehensive review of generative artificial intelligence in educational settings through bibliometric and content analysis. Sustainability **15**(17), 12983 (2023)
15. Baker, B., Mills, K.A., McDonald, P., Wang, L.: AI, concepts of intelligence, and chatbots: the "figure of man," the rise of emotion, and future visions of education. Teach. Coll. Rec. Voice Scholarship Educ. **125**(6), 60–84 (2023)
16. Blythe, M.C.: An analysis of the suitability of philosophy as a core k-12 public school subject (2023)
17. Brusilovsky, P.: AI in education, learner control, and human-AI collaboration. Int. J. Artif. Intell. Educ. **34**, 122–135 (2023)
18. Tabrizi, T.B., Gocer, O., Sadrieh, A., Globa, A.: Leveraging AI to instruct architecture students on circular design techniques and life cycle assessment. In: 9th International Conference on Higher Education Advances (HEAd 2023). Universitat Politècnica de València (2023)
19. Bültemann, M., Rzepka, N., Junger, D., Simbeck, K., Müller, H.G.: Energy consumption of AI in education: a case study (2023)
20. Chan, C.K.Y., Hu, W.: Students' voices on generative AI: perceptions, benefits, and challenges in higher education. Int. J. Educ. Technol. High. Educ. **20**(1), 43 (2023)
21. Chen, L., Chen, P., Lin, Z.: Artificial intelligence in education: a review. IEEE Access **8**, 75264–75278 (2020)
22. Choudhary, N., Bharti, R., Sharma, R.: Role of artificial intelligence in chemistry. Mater. Today: Proc. **48**, 1527–1533 (2022)
23. Cooper, G.: Examining science education in ChatGPT: an exploratory study of generative artificial intelligence. J. Sci. Educ. Technol. **32**(3), 444–452 (2023)
24. Crompton, H., Burke, D.: Artificial intelligence in higher education: the state of the field. Int. J. Educ. Technol. High. Educ. **20**(1), 22 (2023)
25. Darvishinia, N.: Ai in education: cracking the code through challenges: a content analysis of one of the recent issues of educational technology and society (et&s) journal. Partners Univ. Int. Innov. J. **1**(4), 61–71 (2023)
26. Dehouche, N., Dehouche, K.: What's in a text-to-image prompt? the potential of stable diffusion in visual arts education. Heliyon **9**(6), e16757 (2023)
27. Dhanvijay, A.K.D., et al.: Performance of large language models (ChatGPT, bing search, and google bard) in solving case vignettes in physiology. Cureus (2023)
28. Dickey, E., Bejarano, A.: A model for integrating generative ai into course content development. arXiv preprint arXiv:2308.12276 (2023)
29. Dogan, M.E., Goru Dogan, T., Bozkurt, A.: The use of artificial intelligence (AI) in online learning and distance education processes: a systematic review of empirical studies. Appl. Sci. **13**(5), 3056 (2023)
30. dos Santos, R.P.: Enhancing physics learning with ChatGPT, bing chat, and bard as agents-to-think-with: a comparative case study. SSRN Electron. J. (2023)

31. Dydak, J.: Artificial intelligence and teaching of linear algebra (2023)
32. Eggmann, F., Weiger, R., Zitzmann, N.U., Blatz, M.B.: Implications of large language models such as scpChatGPT/scp for dental medicine. J. Esthetic Restorat. Dentistry (2023)
33. Flogie, A., Krabonja, M.V.: Artificial intelligence in education: developing competencies and supporting teachers in implementing AI in school learning environments. In: 2023 12th Mediterranean Conference on Embedded Computing (MECO). IEEE (2023)
34. Foltynek, T., et al.: ENAI recommendations on the ethical use of artificial intelligence in education. Int. J. Educ. Integrity 19(1), 1–4 (2023)
35. Freeman-Wong, J., Munguia, D., Mohr, J.J.: Building a strategy to harness chatgpt in education (2023)
36. Gao, R., Merzdorf, H.E., Anwar, S., Hipwell, M.C., Srinivasa, A.: Automatic assessment of text-based responses in post-secondary education: a systematic review. arXiv preprint arXiv:2308.16151 (2023)
37. Gartner, S., Krašna, M.: Artificial intelligence in education - ethical framework. In: 2023 12th Mediterranean Conference on Embedded Computing (MECO). IEEE (2023)
38. Gašević, D., Siemens, G., Sadiq, S.: Empowering learners for the age of artificial intelligence. Comput. Educ. Artif. Intell. 4, 100130 (2023)
39. Ghamrawi, N., Shal, T., Ghamrawi, N.A.R.: Exploring the impact of AI on teacher leadership: regressing or expanding? Educ. Inf. Technol. (2023)
40. Gupta, N., Gupta, P., Nadeem, D., Abuzar, A., Elahi, A.: Artificial intelligence in agriculture. SSRN Electron. J. (2023)
41. Hodges, C., Ocak, C.: Integrating generative AI into higher education: considerations (2023)
42. Holmes, W.: AIED—coming of age? Int. J. Artif. Intell. Educ. 34(1), 1–11 (2024)
43. Huallpa, J.J., et al.: Exploring the ethical considerations of using chat GPT in university education. Period. Eng. Nat. Sci. 11(4), 105–115 (2023)
44. Humphry, T., Fuller, A.L.: Potential ChatGPT use in undergraduate chemistry laboratories. J. Chem. Educ. 100(4), 1434–1436 (2023)
45. Hwang, G.-J., Xie, H., Wah, B.W., Gašević, D.: Vision, challenges, roles and research issues of artificial intelligence in education. Comput. Educ. Artif. Intell. 1, 100001 (2020)
46. Idroes, G.M., et al.: Student perspectives on the role of artificial intelligence in education: a survey-based analysis. J. Educ. Manag. Learn. 1(1), 8–15 (2023)
47. Inojosa, H., Gilbert, S., Kather, J.N., Proschmann, U., Akgün, K., Ziemssen, T.: Can ChatGPT explain it? use of artificial intelligence in multiple sclerosis communication. Neurol. Res. Pract. 5(1), 48 (2023)
48. Jahic, I., Ebner, M., Schön, S.: Harnessing the power of artificial intelligence and chatgpt in education-a first rapid literature review. Proc. EdMedia+ Innov. Learn. 1462–1470, 2023 (2023)
49. Johnson, W.L.: How to harness generative AI to accelerate human learning. Int. J. Artif. Intell. Educ. (2023)
50. Kaplan-Rakowski, R., Grotewold, K., Hartwick, P., Papin, K.: Generative AI and teachers' perspectives on its implementation in education. J. Interact. Learn. Res. 34(2), 313–338 (2023)
51. Kassymova, G.K., Malinichev, D.M., Lavrinenko, S.V., Panichkina, M.V., Koptyaeva, S.V., Arpentieva, M.R.: Ethical problems of digitalization and artificial intelligence in education: a global perspective. J. Pharmaceut. Negative Results 2150–2161 (2023)

52. Khurma, O.A., Ali, N., Hashem, R.: Critical reflections on ChatGPT in UAE education: navigating equity and governance for safe and effective use. Int. J. Emerg. Technol. Learn. (iJET) **18**(14), 188–199 (2023)
53. Kim, J.: Leading teachers' perspective on teacher-AI collaboration in education. Educ. Inf. Technol. (2023)
54. Kim, K., Kwon, K.: Exploring the AI competencies of elementary school teachers in South Korea. Comput. Educ. Artif. Intell. **4**, 100137 (2023)
55. Kortemeyer, G.: Could an artificial-intelligence agent pass an introductory physics course? Phys. Rev. Phys. Educ. Res. **19**(1), 010132 (2023)
56. Lai, T., et al.: The application of artificial intelligence technology in education influences Chinese adolescent's emotional perception. Curr. Psychol. **43**(6), 5309–5317 (2024)
57. Leung, C.H., Chan, W.T.Y., Xiao, J.J.: A study on perceived benefits and applications of generative artificial intelligence in education. Int. J. Educ. Sci. Res. **13**(1), 47–58 (2023)
58. Liang, Y.: Balancing: the effects of AI tools in educational context. Front. Humanities Soc. Sci. **3**(8), 7–10 (2023)
59. Lin, C.C., Huang, A.Y.Q., Lu, O.H.T.: Artificial intelligence in intelligent tutoring systems toward sustainable education: a systematic review. Smart Learn. Environ. **10**(1), 41 (2023)
60. Lin, S.M., Chung, H.H., Chung, F.L., Lan, Y.J.: Concerns about using ChatGPT in education. In: Huang, Y.M., Rocha, T. (eds.) ICITL 2023. LNCS, vol. 14099, pp. 37–49. Springer, Cham (2023). https://doi.org/10.1007/978-3-031-40113-8_4
61. Lin, Z.: Why and how to embrace AI such as ChatGPT in your academic life (2023)
62. Lou, Y.: Exploring the application of ChatGPT to English teaching in a Malaysia primary school. J. Adv. Res. Educ. **2**(4), 47–54 (2023)
63. Malinka, K., Peresíni, M., Firc, A., Hujnák, O., Janus, F.: On the educational impact of ChatGPT: is artificial intelligence ready to obtain a university degree? In: Proceedings of the 2023 Conference on Innovation and Technology in Computer Science Education, vol. 1. ACM (2023)
64. McGee, R.W.: What are the top 20 questions in sociology? a chatgpt reply. Technical report, Working Paper (2023). https://ssrn.com/abstract=4413441
65. Michel-Villarreal, R., Vilalta-Perdomo, E., Salinas-Navarro, D.E., Thierry-Aguilera, R., Gerardou, F.S.: Challenges and opportunities of generative AI for higher education as explained by ChatGPT. Educ. Sci. **13**(9), 856 (2023)
66. Molek, N.: AI and organizational transformation: anthropological insights into higher education. Chall. Future **8**, 148–177 (2023)
67. Nascimento, N., Alencar, P., Cowan, D.: Artificial intelligence versus software engineers: an evidence-based assessment focusing on non-functional requirements (2023)
68. Nazareth, J.L.: A shakespearean experiment with chatgpt (2023)
69. Nazir, T., Ahmad, U., Mal, M., Rehman, M.M.U., Saeed, R., Kalia, J.S.: Microsoft bing vs google bard in neurology: a comparative study of AI-generated patient education material (2023)
70. Nguyen, P., Truoing, H., Nguyen, P., Bruneau, P., Cao, L., Wang, J.: Evaluation of Google Bard on Vietnamese High School Biology Examination. Researchgate. Net (2023)
71. Nguyen, K.H., Nguyen, H.A., Cao, L., Hana, T.: Potential of ChatGPT in biology teaching and learning at the Vietnamese high school (2023)

72. Nguyen, P., Truong, H., Nguyen, P., Bruneau, P., Cao, L., Wang, J.: Google bard's performance on Vietnamese high school civic education examination (2023)
73. O'Leary, D.E.: An analysis of watson vs. BARD vs. ChatGPT: The jeopardy! challenge. AI Maga. (2023)
74. Oosterwyk, G., Tsibolane, P., Kautondokwa, P., Canani, A.: Beyond the hype: a cautionary tale of chatgpt in the programming classroom (2023)
75. Ouyang, F., Jiao, P.: Artificial intelligence in education: the three paradigms. Comput. Educ. Artif. Intell. **2**, 100020 (2021)
76. Page, M.J., et al.: The prisma 2020 statement: an updated guideline for reporting systematic reviews. Int. J. Surg. **88**, 105906 (2021)
77. Pavlik, J.V.: Collaborating with ChatGPT: considering the implications of generative artificial intelligence for journalism and media education. J. Mass Commun. Educ. **78**(1), 84–93 (2023)
78. Pizzolla, I., Aro, R., Duez, P., De Lièvre, B., Briganti, G.: Integrating artificial intelligence into medical education: lessons learned from a Belgian initiative. J. Interact. Learn. Res. **34**(2), 401–424 (2023)
79. Sudheesh, R., et al.: Analyzing sentiments regarding ChatGPT using novel BERT: a machine learning approach. Information **14**(9), 474 (2023)
80. Ratten, V., Jones, P.: Generative artificial intelligence (ChatGPT): implications for management educators. Int. J. Manag. Educ. **21**(3), 100857 (2023)
81. Rayhan, A., Rayhan, R., Rayhan, S.: Revolutionizing education: the power of artificial intelligence (AI). PhD thesis (2023)
82. Routray, B.B., Dash, J., Swain, T., Nanda, B.: Exploring the potential of generative AI (2023)
83. Schönberger, M.: ChatGPT in higher education: the good, the bad, and the university. In: 9th International Conference on Higher Education Advances (HEAd 2023). Universitat Politècnica de València (2023)
84. Scott-Branch, J., Laws, R., Terzi, P.: The intersection of AI, information and digital literacy: harnessing chatgpt and other generative tools to enhance teaching and learning (2023)
85. Smith, M.L.: Language models, plagiarism, and legal writing. Univ. New Hampshire Law Rev. **22** (2023)
86. Supriyadi, E., Kuncoro, K.S.: Exploring the future of mathematics teaching: insight with ChatGPT. Union: Jurnal Ilmiah Pendidikan Matematika **11**(2), 305–316 (2023)
87. Tartaro, A.: When things go wrong: the recall of AI systems as a last resort for ethical and lawful AI. AI Eth. (2023)
88. Thurzo, A., Strunga, M., Urban, R., Surovková, J., Afrashtehfar, K.I.: Impact of artificial intelligence on dental education: a review and guide for curriculum update. Educ. Sci. **13**(2), 150 (2023)
89. Toutain, O., Jabbouri, R.: Artificial intelligence and the transformation of management education. Manag. Int. **27**(2), 119–132 (2023)
90. Tupper, M., Hendy, I.W., Shipway, J.R.: Field courses for dummies: can ChatGPT design a higher education field course? (2023)
91. Tzirides, A.O., et al. Generative AI: implications and applications for education. Article In Review (2023)
92. Ugo, C.A.: An empirical investigation of the impact of artificial intelligence on accounting practice in Nigeria. Afr. J. Account. Finan. Res. **6**(3), 22–35 (2023)
93. Uzumcu, O., Acilmis, H.: Do innovative teachers use AI-powered tools more interactively? a study in the context of diffusion of innovation theory. Technol. Knowl. Learn. (2023)

94. Walczak, K., Cellary, W.: Challenges for higher education in the era of widespread access to generative AI. Econ. Bus. Rev. **9**(2), 71–100 (2023)
95. Wardat, Y., Tashtoush, M.A., AlAli, R., Jarrah, A.M.: ChatGPT: a revolutionary tool for teaching and learning mathematics. Eurasia J. Math. Sci. Technol. Educ. **19**(7), em2286 (2023)
96. Williamson, B.: The social life of AI in education. Int. J. Artif. Intell. Educ. (2023)
97. Dao, X.Q., Le, N.B.: Chatgpt is good but bing chat is better for vietnamese students (2023)
98. Xue, Y., Wang, Y.: Artificial intelligence for education and teaching. Wirel. Commun. Mob. Comput. **2022**, 1–10 (2022)
99. Zekaj, R.: AI language models as educational allies: enhancing instructional support in higher education. Int. J. Learn. Teach. Educ. Res. **22**(8), 120–134 (2023)
100. Zhang, B., Liu, T., Liang, P., Wang, C., Shahin, M., Yu, J.: Architecture decisions in AI-based systems development: an empirical study. In: 2023 IEEE International Conference on Software Analysis, Evolution and Reengineering (SANER). IEEE (2023)
101. Zhou, J., Zhang, J., Li, H.: Exploring the use of artificial intelligence in teaching management and evaluation based on citation space analysis. J. Educ. Edu. Res. **3**(2), 42–45 (2023)
102. Zhou, X.: Research on classroom teaching behavior analysis system based on artificial intelligence technology. In: Proceedings of the 2nd International Conference on New Media Development and Modernized Education. SCITEPRESS - Science and Technology Publications (2022)

Evolution of the Adoption of Generative AI Among Spanish Engineering Students

Faraón Llorens-Largo$^{(\boxtimes)}$ ⓘ, Rafael Molina-Carmona ⓘ, Alberto Real-Fernández ⓘ, and Sergio Arjona-Giner

Department of Computer Science and Artificial Intelligence, University of Alicante, 03080 Alicante, Spain

{faraon.llorens,rmolina,alberto.real}@ua.es, sag58@alu.ua.es

Abstract. The irruption of ChatGPT has led to a technological change that could affect all sectors, concretely education. University students are facing this change, and the adoption of generative AI will be key to both their learning and job performance. This paper aims to study the adoption and evolution of generative AI among engineering students by analysing two surveys conducted in 2022 and 2023. The results show that engineering students are mostly aware and they are using generative AI tools. On the other hand, it has been studied whether gender can influence their adoption, and the results do not indicate significant changes. Regarding the evolution of the adoption of generative AI, a great change is shown, since it is being more used in all fields, also in education. This change indicates the attitude of engineering students to explore and take advantage of innovative tools, which can have a current and future impact on their learning and development.

Keywords: Generative AI · Technology Adoption · ChatGPT

1 Introduction

The education sector is constantly evolving with the emergence of new technologies that have the potential to revolutionize the way we teach and learn [1]. One of the new disruptive technologies that have the transformative power is generative artificial intelligence (generative AI), which since the release of ChatGPT in November 2022 has triggered a boom in AI, causing a significant breakthrough in this branch of computer science. And while there have been many concerns about the use of generative AI in terms of loss of academic integrity, there is a growing understanding that this technology can improve student learning outcomes. It could also play an important role in the labour market, and universities have a responsibility to prepare students for this.

Generative AI can serve as an effective learning tool that reduces teachers' workloads and provides personalised learning experiences for students [2]. Moreover, its integration into education can not only make education more globally accessible, but also foster equal opportunities, improve communication between learners and facilitate the transition to a digital learning environment [3]. However, the integration of generative AI in education implies certain risks. Students may experience a decrease in personal interactions, which could hinder their socialisation. In addition, the use of such tools may lead to misinformation and loss of critical thinking due to possible biases, and there are also concerns about the violation of data privacy [4].

Nevertheless, in order to harness the full benefits and thus maximise student's learning, an adaptation process of the entire educational environment is necessary. It is essential that teachers acquire the necessary skills to use these tools efficiently in the classroom. Educational centres will need to adapt curricula and assessment mechanisms [5], and policies should be introduced to address issues such as data privacy and the ethical use of AI-based tools.

The purpose of this article is to analyse the adoption and its evolution of tools based on generative AI among engineering students in Spain. To this end, a comparison is made between two surveys conducted during the 2022–2023 and 2023–2024 academic years to engineering students at the University of Alicante.

To facilitate the understanding of the article, it has been structured as follows. Section 2 reviews Generative AI in the context of education and its adoption by students. Section 3 explains the research methodology for the paper and the design of the experiment. Section 4 shows the results in tables and graphs. Finally, Sect. 5 draws the main conclusions of the study.

2 Generative AI Overview: Education and Student Adoption

In this Review section, the comprehensive overview of generative AI is explored. From its conceptualisation, through its application in education, and finally, examining the acceptance of innovative technologies by students.

2.1 What is Generative AI?

Generative AI is a field of AI that focuses on generating original content from existing data. This technology uses advanced machine learning algorithms and deep neural networks to learn from text, images or sounds to generate new and unique content [6, 7]. Progress in generative AI has been impressive since the release of ChatGPT at the end of 2022 and is expected to continue to improve in the future. In fact, it is expected that 10% of all data generated in 2025 will come from generative AI tools [8].

ChatGPT, the best-known generative AI, is a chat system based on the Natural Language Processing (NLP) model GPT-3.5 (Generative Pre-training Transformer), developed by the company OpenAI. It is a model with more than 175 million parameters and trained with large amounts of text to perform language-related tasks, from translation to text generation. It is a chat to which you write through prompts and the chatbot generates a response as if it were a person. One of its most surprising features is that it is able to remember the context of the conversation through a neural network model called Attention [9].

Since its release ChatGPT has been improved. The GPT model has been updated to the GPT-4 version, making it more truthful and creative. In addition, the Vision feature has been added, allowing GPT to be able to analyse and interpret images in addition to text (multimodal). On the other hand, the versatility of ChatGPT has increased since the release of its API, being able to integrate it with any application via plugins. Additionally, since November 2023, OpenAI allows the community to create their own customised GPTs [10]. Also during 2024 ChatGPT will be able to both receive prompts and respond by voice [11].

It is important to note that although ChatGPT is the most renowned generative AI, there are currently many of alternative tools: Bing, Microsoft's chatbot; or Midjourney for creating images. Google has recently announced its new generative AI model, Gemini, which will be fully multimodal, being able to receive and respond with text, images, audio, video and programming languages [12], taking a step towards General AI.

The Gartner Hype Cycle [13, 14] is a graphical representation in the form of a curve that depicts the maturity and adoption of emerging technologies, so as to distinguish which technologies are hype from those that are viable. In this representation, generative AI in 2023 was currently in the Peak of Inflated Expectations phase [14]. However, it is expected to reach the productivity plateau within 2–5 years. Furthermore, Gartner considers it as one of the top 10 strategic technology trends for 2024.

2.2 Generative AI in Education

The high performance offered by generative AI models gives both hope and concern to the educational world. Table 1 shows a comparison table of Gemini and GPT-4 performance in several areas and the accuracy is very high in both models.

Table 1. Gemini and GPT-4 performance comparison

Capability	Benchmark	Description	Gemini	GPT-4
General	MMLU	Question in 57 subjects (STEM, humanities…)	90.0%	86.4%
Reasoning	Big-Bench Hard	Challenging tasks requiring multi-step reasoning	83.6%	83.1%
	DROP	Reading comprehension	82.4%	80.9%
	HellaSwag	Reasoning for everyday	87.8%	95.3%
Math	GSM8K	Arithmetic manipulations	94.4%	92.0%
	MATH	Challenging math problems	53.2%	52.9%
Code	HumanEval	Python code generation	74.4%	67.0%
	Natural2Code	Python code generation	74.9%	73.9%

Source: [12]

Generative AI in education has strategic value, bringing many advantages. It can serve as an effective learning tool that reduces teachers' workloads and provides personalised learning experiences for students [15]. Moreover, its integration into education cannot only make education more accessible globally, but also foster equal opportunities, improve communication between learners and facilitate the transition to a digital learning environment. Some of the concrete applications of generative AI in education include the creation of advanced curricula, personalised tutoring, more efficient assessments, adaptive learning, and the generation of student records and profiles to provide personalised education [3]. These applications not only make the learning process more effective, but also help to increase retention and comprehension of material, reduce the knowledge gap and improve overall academic performance. Some researchers wonder whether advances in AI will challenge teachers or even replace them. However, it is estimated that this will not happen, but that the role of the teacher will change from a transmitter of knowledge to a guide [16].

Despite the advantages discussed above, the integration of generative AI in education could carry certain risks. Firstly, there are concerns about breaches of data privacy, as AI systems require a large amount of information, including students' private data [17]. Furthermore, the risk of increased misinformation, technology dependency and loss of critical thinking because of incorporating AI in education has also been pointed out [3, 4, 18], as generative AI works with probabilistic models and can lead to misleading results that confuse the learner. Additionally, there is a risk that students will outsource AI tools to do work without learning, which could undermine their educational development and their ability to acquire critical skills.

2.3 Student's Acceptance to Innovative Technologies

Student acceptance is a key element in the development of technological innovations [19]. The Unified Theory of Acceptance of Technology Use (UTAUT) proposed by Venkatesh [20] seeks to explain user intentions to use technology (like generative AI) and subsequent usage behaviour. This theory derives four factors:

- Performance expectancy. Degree to which an individual believes that use of the system will be beneficial to him/her in work or professional performance.
- Effort expectancy. It refers to how easily a technology can be used.
- Social influence. It refers to the extent to which a person perceives the valuation of others with respect to the use of technology.
- Facilitating conditions. Degree to which an individual considers that the organisational and technical structure exists to support the adoption of the technology.

The variables of performance expectancy and effort expectancy have been studied in several research studies. Robey [21] focused on analysing the impact of performance expectation on the use of technology and concluded that if a technology does not help users develop in their work it will not be accepted despite efforts to implement it. Bandura [22] concluded that user acceptance behaviour will be predictable given expectations of effort and performance.

On the other hand, more specific current studies have been carried out on the acceptance of generative AI among students [19, 23, 24]. The results of the articles revealed a positive reception and use of generative AI technologies in terms of students' perception and use. Also in [23], it was found that students are committed to adopting generative AI, but concerned about preventing the development of skills such as teamwork, problem solving or critical thinking; and even developing dependency.

Finally, the paper by Huedo-Martínez et al. [25] concluded that engineering students were more likely to adopt a new innovative technology more quickly.

3   Experiment Design

The aim of this experiment is to observe the adoption by engineering students at the University of Alicante (Spain). To this end, two surveys on the knowledge and use of generative AI have been carried out in two consecutive years: 2022 and 2023.

Surveys are administered through the online platform LimeSurvey with encrypted communication over HTTPS strictly anonymised to ensure privacy and data security of the data collected and therefore, protect the identity of the participating students.

The questionnaires have been elaborated in collaboration with several Spanish universities in a joint project, although in this paper only the data obtained by the University of Alicante have been presented. Pooled data from all universities in the first survey have been published in [26], while data from the second survey are still awaiting publication.

3.1   Methodology

In order to produce the article in a coherent and high-quality manner, a three-phase methodology has been followed:

1. Conducting the surveys. In this first phase, the information necessary to carry out the study is collected from two surveys.
2. Analysis of results. At the end of the response period, the surveys will be closed, and the responses will be downloaded. This data will be subjected to a cleaning process, if necessary. Once the cleaning process is completed, several graphs will be generated to facilitate the drawing of conclusions for the study.
3. Conclusions. The graphs generated will provide a visual representation of the results obtained. From this visualisation, conclusions will be drawn that will address the research objectives and provide valuable insights into the topic at hand.

3.2   First Survey (S1)

The first survey (S1), conducted in 2022, includes both open-ended and closed-ended questions to gather information about the academic year and students' knowledge and current or future uses of ChatGPT. The survey consists of 7 questions (SQ) represented in Fig. 1. The full questionnaire is available in Appendix I.

3.3   Second Survey (S2)

The second survey (S2), conducted in 2023, asks questions about knowledge and use of generative AI and ChatGPT. It includes open-ended, closed-ended, multiple-choice and open-ended questions. A diagram of the survey is shown in Fig. 2. The full questionnaire is available in Appendix II.

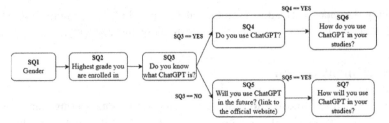

Fig. 1. Diagram of the questions in the first survey

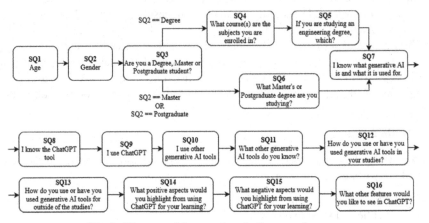

Fig. 2. Diagram of the questions in the second survey

4   Results and Discussion

This section presents the findings from the survey of engineering students. First, a contextual and demographic profile of the participants is presented. This is followed by an analysis of the evolution of knowledge and use of generative AI across the surveys. Subsequently, it explores whether gender has any association with ChatGPT knowledge and use in the first and second surveys. Finally, it explores the applications of ChatGPT in the context of engineering studies.

4.1   Demographic and Contextual Profile of Participants

This section shows the demographic data. Table 2 shows the distribution of participants in both surveys indicating the number of participants and their gender and average age distribution.

It is also interesting to know the course in which the students are enrolled. Figure 3 and Fig. 4 show the distribution of students in the courses based on the highest course enrolled.

Table 2. Distribution of participants, gender and average age

	First survey		Second Survey	
Gender	Participants	Average age	Participants	Average age
Female	22	-	26	18.92
Male	71	-	70	20.26
Non-binary	0	-	1	33
Not specified	1	-	3	22.33
Total	94	-	100	20.08

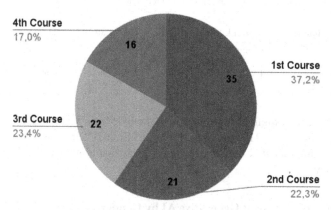

Fig. 3. Student distribution by course in S1

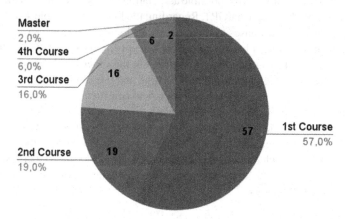

Fig. 4. Student distribution by course in S2

4.2   Evolution of Knowledge and Use of Generative AI

This section aims to analyse descriptively the evolution of the knowledge and use of ChatGPT. For this purpose, Table 3 shows a comparison of these two questions in both questionnaires. Since in the second questionnaire the question "I know the ChatGPT tool" is formulated on a Likert scale (SQ8) and in the first one as a nominal variable of Yes/No, to make a correct comparison, the Likert scale question has been transformed.

For this purpose, affirmative answers have been considered to be those that were answered as Strongly Agree or Agree, and negative answers have been considered to be Neutral, Disagree and Strongly Disagree.

Table 3. Comparison of knowledge and use of ChatGPT

	Know ChatGPT	Do not know ChatGPT	Use ChatGPT	Do not use ChatGPT
S1	88.30%	11.70%	48.19%	51.81%
S2	96%	4%	92%	8%

The results show a slight improvement in the knowledge of ChatGPT among students, increasing by almost 8%. However, student use of ChatGPT increased from 48.19% to 92%. This is a significant change and suggests a substantial increase in the adoption of this technology.

4.3   Knowledge and Use of Generative AI by Gender in S1

An interesting aspect to study is the possible association between gender and the adoption of Generative AI, in this case ChatGPT. Regarding the first survey, Table 4 shows a table with the frequencies of responses to these questions by gender. However, there are not many percentage differences between genders, except for "Not specified", although it should be noted that they are underrepresented. On the other hand, between men and women, men represent a slightly higher knowledge and use of ChatGPT.

Although there are some slight differences between men and women, we want to check whether these differences are statistically significant. To do so, a Chi-square test was performed (Table 5), in which the gender Not Specified was not considered because only one participant belongs to this gender and would bias the results. The values obtained for knowledge and use of ChatGPT are 0.617 and 0.935 respectively; both being greater than 0.05, so there is no significant change in the knowledge and use of ChatGPT between genders.

4.4   Knowledge and Use of Generative AI by Gender in S2

Before proceeding to the analysis of the data from the second survey, it is important to check whether the distribution of the results is normal due to the use of Likert scale questions. For this purpose, a Shapiro-Wilk normality test has been performed. The results from the Shapiro-Wilk normality test suggest that we can refute the assumption

Table 4. Knowledge and use of ChatGPT by gender in the S1

Question	Answer	Male	Female	Not Specified	Total
Do you know ChatGPT?	Yes	64	19	0	83
		90.1%	88.6%	0%	
	No	7	3	1	11
		9.9%	13.6%	100%	
Do you use ChatGPT?	Yes	31	9	0	40
		48.4%	47.4%	0%	
	No	33	10	0	43
		48.4%	47.4%	0%	

Table 5. Chi-square for use and knowledge of ChatGPT by gender in the S1

		Value	Deg. Freedom	Asymptotic significance (bilateral)
Pearson's Chi-square	Knowledge of ChatGPT	0.250	1	0.617
	Use of ChatGPT	0.007	1	0.935

of a normal distribution ($p < 0.05$). Nevertheless, the F-test has been shown to be robust against moderate departures from normality in cases where sample sizes are sufficiently large and comparable [25]. A sufficient sample size ($n = 100$) allows us to justify the use of these tests with sufficient confidence, despite not meeting the normality criterion.

Descriptive information on the knowledge and use of Generative AI is shown in Tables 6 and 7. In Table 6, the questions on the knowledge of Generative AI are shown. Since the questions are formulated on a Likert scale, in order to be able to perform the descriptive analysis, for each participant the answers have been coded as follows: Strongly disagree (1), Disagree (2), Neutral (3), Agree (4) and Strongly agree (5). As can be seen, the differences between genders are very subtle. However, the participants are clearer about what ChatGPT is than Generative AI except for the female gender. And regarding the question about the use of ChatGPT, now the female gender uses it more than the male gender.

Again, the corresponding statistical tests have been carried out to see if there are significant differences between genders and the knowledge and use of generative AI: ANOVA for Likert scale questions (Table 8 and Table 9) and Chi-Square for categorical questions (Table 10). In all tests the null hypothesis is accepted, so there are no significant differences between genders.

Table 6. Knowledge of Generative AI and ChatGPT by gender in the S2

Question	Measure	Male	Female	Non-binary	Not Specified
I know what generative AI is and what it is used for	Participants	70	26	1	3
	Mean	4	4.08	3	4
	Standard deviation	0.933	0.845	0	1
I know the ChatGPT tool	Participants	70	26	1	3
	Mean	4.74	4.65	5	5
	Standard deviation	0.846	0.846	0	0

Table 7. Use of ChatGPT by gender in the S2

Question	Answer	Male	Female	Non-binary	Not Specified	Total
I use ChatGPT	Yes	63	25	1	3	92
		90%	96.2%	100%	100%	
	No	7	1	0	0	8
		10%	3.8%	0%	0%	

Table 8. ANOVA knowledge of Generative AI

Variation source	Deg. Freedom	Sum squares	Squared mean	F-test	Sig. Level p
Inter-group	1,144	3	0,381	0,458	0,712
Intra-group	79,846	96	0,832		
Total	80,990	99			

Table 9. ANOVA knowledge of ChatGPT

Variation source	Deg. Freedom	Sum squares	Squared mean	F-test	Sig. Level p
Inter-group	0,454	3	0,151	0,216	0,885
Intra-group	67,256	96	0,701		
Total	67,710	99			

Table 10. Chi-square for use of ChatGPT by gender in the S2

	Value	Deg. Freedom	Asymptotic significance (bilateral)
Pearson's Chi-square	1.338	3	0.720

4.5 Applications of ChatGPT for Studies

Table 11 shows a comparison of the use of ChatGPT by students, indicating how many of them use ChatGPT in the study and outside the study, as well as their percentage of the total number of students using ChatGPT. Although there is a percentage improvement in the use of ChatGPT in the study, it is worth noting the adoption of the technology in other areas outside the study, which has increased from 12.5% to 68.48%.

Table 11. Comparison on the use of ChatGPT

	Use ChatGPT for the study		Use ChatGPT outside the study		Use ChatGPT
S1	37	92.5%	5	12.5%	40
S2	88	95.65%	63	68.48%	92

On the other hand, regarding the specific applications that students make of ChatGPT for study purposes, a comparative bar chart on specific applications of use can be seen in Fig. 5. In order to make a comparison, taking into account that the question on ChatGPT applications in S1 was open-ended and in S2 it was a multiple-choice question, the answers from S1 were analysed and included in the same categories of S2.

What can be seen from the graph is that students use ChatGPT much more in all its applications, especially in Self-Assessment and Suggestion of ideas. The most common uses include Resolution of doubts, Correction of code errors, use as a Source of information and Suggestion of ideas.

Finally, 47% of respondents in S2 use other generative AI tools, including Midjourney, Dall-E, Bard, Copilot and Bing. This information emphasizes the breadth of generative AI tool adoption among respondents in S2.

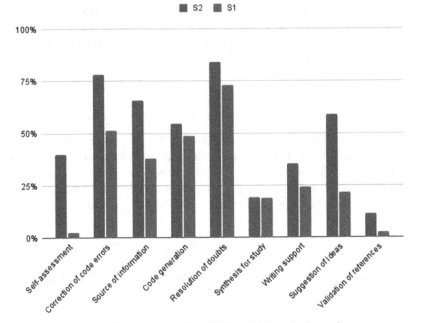

Fig. 5. Comparison of ChatGPT applications in the study

5 Conclusions

University students are facing a technological change that will affect all sectors, the boom of generative AI, and its acceptation will be key both in their learning and in their future career. This paper aimed to study the adoption of generative AI in engineering students, as well as its evolution in the period of one year, since the release of ChatGPT by analysing two surveys, in two consecutive years: 2022 and 2023.

The conclusions drawn after analysing the results are, firstly, that most respondents are aware of ChatGPT; with regard to its use, there has been a large increase in uptake from 48% of respondents in 2022 to 92% in 2023. Subsequently, an analysis has been made as to whether there is a difference in the knowledge and use of ChatGPT with respect to gender, reaching the conclusion that there are no statistically significant differences with respect to this factor. Also, we wanted to analyse the use that students make of ChatGPT regarding learning. Uses related to resolving doubts, correcting code or suggesting ideas stand out. On the other hand, there has been an enormous growth in terms of the applications of its use among the surveys. Finally, almost half of the respondents in 2023 use other generative AI tools.

These results suggest that the engineering student community is increasingly embracing generative AI technologies. The growing acceptance of generative AI in academic domain reflects an increased interest in its value. This shift indicates students' willingness to explore and leverage innovative tools, which could impact both education and future engineering and technology development. The successful integration of generative AI into academic curricula and research projects highlights the long-term relevance of these emerging technologies in the education of future engineers.

Acknowledgements. We would like to thank Daniel Amo-Filva (and *La Salle-URL* - https://www.salleurl.edu) for coordinating the data collection and leading the elaboration of the questionnaires common to all the universities participating in the project.

Appendix 1

First questionnaire (S1)
    1. Gender:
    ○ Male ○ Female ○ Not specified.
    2. Highest grade you are enrolled in:
    ○ 1 ○ 2 ○ 3 ○ 4.
    3. Do you know what ChatGPT is?
    ○ Yes ○ No.
    4. Do you use ChatGPT?
    ○ Yes ○ No.
    5. Will you use ChatGPT in the future (link to the website).
    ○ Yes ○ No.
    6. How do you use ChatGPT in your studies?
    _____ (free text).
    7. How will you use ChatGPT in your studies?
    _____ (free text).

Appendix 2

Second questionnaire (S2)
    1. Age: _____ (numeric field).
    2. Gender:
    ○ Male ○ Female ○ Non-binary ○ Not specified.
    3. Are you a Degree, Master or Postgraduate student?
    ○ Degree ○ Master ○ Postgraduate.
    4. What course(s) are the subjects you are enrolled in: (multiple choice).
    ○ 1 ○ 2 ○ 3 ○ 4 ○ 5.
    5. If you are studying an engineering degree, which?
    _____ (free text) ○ Other.
    6. What Master's or Postgraduate degree are you studying?
    _____ (free text).
    7. I know what generative AI is and what it is used for:
    Totally disagree ○ 1 ○ 2 ○ 3 ○ 4 ○ 5 Totally agree.
    8. I know the ChatGPT tool:
    Totally disagree ○ 1 ○ 2 ○ 3 ○ 4 ○ 5 Totally agree.

9. I use ChatGPT (multiple choice):

○ In my studies ○ In my personal life ○ In my working life ○ Other uses ○ No.

○ Other uses: _____ (free text).

10. I user other generative AI tools (multiple choice):

○ In my studies ○ In my personal life ○ In my working life ○ Other uses ○ No.

○ Other uses: _____ (free text).

11. What other generative AI tools do you know?

_____ (free text).

12. How do you use or have used ChatGPT or other generative AI tools in your studies?

○ Self-assessment ○ Correction of code errors ○ Source of information.

○ Code generation ○ Resolution of concrete doubts ○ Synthesis for study.

○ Writing support ○ Suggestion of ideas ○ Validation of references.

○ Personal use outside studies ○ Use required by the university.

○ Other uses: _____ (free text).

13. How do you use or have used ChatGPT or other generative AI tools outside of your studies?

_____ (free text).

14. What positive aspects would you highlight from using ChatGPT for your learning?

_____ (free text).

15. What negative aspects would you highlight from using ChatGPT for your learning?

_____ (free text).

16. What other features would you like to see in ChatGPT?

_____ (free text).

References

1. Haleem, A., Javaid, M., Qadri, M.A., Suman, R.: Understanding the role of digital technologies in education: a review. Sustain. Oper. Comput. **3**, 275–285 (2022). https://doi.org/10.1016/j.susoc.2022.05.004

2. García-Peñalvo, F.J., Llorens-Largo, F., Vidal, J.: The new reality of education in the face of advances in generative artificial intelligence. RIED-Revista Iberoamericana De Educación a Distancia. **27** (2023). https://doi.org/10.5944/ried.27.1.37716

3. Arjona-Giner, S., Molina-Carmona, R., Llorens-Largo, F.: Exploring the possibilities of ChatGPT in students' assignments: some simple experiences. In: Lecture Notes in Educational Technology. Springer, Portugal (2023)

4. Qadir, J.: Engineering education in the era of ChatGPT: promise and pitfalls of generative AI for education. In: 2023 IEEE Global Engineering Education Conference (EDUCON), pp. 1–9. IEEE, Kuwait, Kuwait (2023). https://doi.org/10.1109/EDUCON54358.2023.10125121

5. UNESCO-IESALC: ChatGPT, inteligencia artificial y educación superior. https://www.youtube.com/watch?v=Ij6o6DQg_ps/. Accessed 16 Apr 2023

6. Lim, W.M., Gunasekara, A., Pallant, J.L., Pallant, J.I., Pechenkina, E.: Generative AI and the future of education: ragnarök or reformation? A paradoxical perspective from management educators. Int. J. Manage. Educ. **21** (2023)

7. García-Peñalvo, F., Vázquez-Ingelmo, A.: What do we mean by GenAI? A Systematic mapping of the evolution, trends, and techniques involved in generative AI. IJIMAI **8**, 7 (2023). https://doi.org/10.9781/ijimai.2023.07.006

8. Gartner: Gartner Identifies the Top Strategic Technology Trends for 2022. https://www.gartner.com/en/newsroom/press-releases/2021-10-18-gartner-identifies-the-top-strategic-technology-trends-for-2022 (2021)

9. Vaswani, A., et al.: Attention is all you need. In: Advances in Neural Information Processing Systems. Curran Associates, Inc. (2017)

10. OpenAI: Introducing GPTs. https://openai.com/index/introducing-gpts/. Accessed 27 Nov 2023

11. OpenAI: ChatGPT can now see, hear, and speak. https://openai.com/index/chatgpt-can-now-see-hear-and-speak/. Accessed 04 Jan 2024

12. Google: Welcome to the Gemini era, https://deepmind.google/technologies/gemini/#capabilities. Accessed 05 Jan 2024

13. Dedehayir, O., Steinert, M.: The hype cycle model: a review and future directions. Technol. Forecast. Soc. Chang. **108**, 28–41 (2016). https://doi.org/10.1016/j.techfore.2016.04.005

14. Gartner: What's New in the 2023 Gartner Hype Cycle for Emerging Technologies, https://www.gartner.com/en/articles/what-s-new-in-the-2023-gartner-hype-cycle-for-emerging-technologies. Accessed 06 Jan 2024

15. Arjona-Giner, S., Llorens-Largo, F.: Explorando ChatGPT para la educación: su potencial en la redacción. In: Innovación educativa en los tiempos de la inteligencia artificial. Actas del VII Congreso Internacional sobre Aprendizaje, Innovación y Cooperación. CINAIC 2023, pp. 124–127. University of Zaragoza (2023)

16. Llorens-Largo, F.: Cavilaciones invernales sobre la escritura de trabajos académicos usando inteligencia artificial, https://www.universidadsi.es/cavilaciones-invernales/. Accessed 22 Jan 2023

17. Chen, X., Chen, P., Lin, Z.: Application and theory gaps during the rise of artificial intelligence in education. Comput. Educ. Artif. Intell. **1** (2020). https://doi.org/10.1016/j.caeai.2020.100002

18. Flores-Vivar, J.-M., García-Peñalvo, F.-J.: Reflections on the ethics, potential, and challenges of artificial intelligence in the framework of quality education (SDG4). Comunicar: Revista Científica de Comunicación y Educación. **31**, 37–47 (2023). https://doi.org/10.3916/C74-2023-03

19. Chan, C.K.Y., Hu, W.: Students' voices on generative AI: perceptions, benefits, and challenges in higher education. Int. J. Educ. Technol. High. Educ. **20**, 43 (2023). https://doi.org/10.1186/s41239-023-00411-8

20. Venkatesh, M.: Davis, davis: user acceptance of information technology: toward a unified view. MIS Q. **27**, 425 (2003). https://doi.org/10.2307/30036540

21. Robey, D.: User attitudes and management information system use. Acad. Manag. J. **22**, 527–538 (1979). https://doi.org/10.2307/255742

22. Bandura, A.: Self-efficacy mechanism in human agency. Am. Psychol. **37**, 122–147 (1982). https://doi.org/10.1037/0003-066X.37.2.122

23. Nacua Obenza, B., Salvahan, A., Nicole Rios, A., Solo, A., Ashlee Alburo, R., Gabila, R.J.: University students' perception and use of ChatGPT generative artificial intelligence (AI) in higher education (2023). https://doi.org/10.5281/ZENODO.10360697

24. Bonsu, E.M., Baffour-Koduah, D.: From the consumers' side: determining students' perception and intention to use ChatGPT in ghanaian higher education. Review **6**, 102 (2023). https://doi.org/10.21203/rs.3.rs-2686760/v1

25. Huedo-Martínez, S., Molina-Carmona, R., Llorens-Largo, F.: Study on the attitude of young people towards technology. In: Zaphiris, P., Ioannou, A. (eds.) Learning and Collaboration Technologies Learning and Teaching, LCT 2018. Lecture Notes in Computer Science, vol. 10925, pp. 26–43. Springer, Cham (2018). https://doi.org/10.1007/978-3-319-91152-6_3

26. Amo-Filva, D., et al.: Usos y desusos del modelo GPT-3 entre estudiantes de grados de ingeniería. In: Actas de las XXIX Jornadas sobre Enseñanza Universitaria de la Informática, pp. 415–418 (2023)

Anticipating Tutoring Demands Based on Students' Difficulties in Online Learning

Aluisio José Pereira[1] (iD), Alex Sandro Gomes[1] (iD), Tiago Thompsen Primo[2] (iD), Leandro Marques Queiros[1] (iD), and Fernando Moreira[3,4](✉) (iD)

[1] Informatics Center, Federal University of Pernambuco, Recife 50740-600, Brazil
{ajp3,asg,lmq}@cin.ufpe.br
[2] Technological Development Center, Federal University of Pelotas, Pelotas 83321-270, Brazil
tiago.primo@inf.ufpel.edu.br
[3] REMIT, IJP, Universidade Portucalense, Universidade de Aveiro, Porto, Portugal
fmoreira@upt.pt
[4] IEETA, Aveiro, Portugal

Abstract. Anticipating the tutoring needs in online learning is essential to provide adequate support to students. Feedback and even silence are valuable clues to reveal the level of engagement. Approaches based on Artificial Intelligence (AI) can process this information and alleviate the workload of human tutors. In this study, Natural Language Processing (NLP) techniques were used to assess the performance of classifying students' difficulties in an Educational Social Network. Difficulties were classified into categories such as "personal", "technical", and "others". The model's performance allows you to anticipate and direct tutoring.

Keywords: Human Tutors · Students · Natural Language Processing (NLP) · Interactions · E-Learning

1 Introduction

Student engagement in online learning can be affected by various difficulties [1, 2], highlighting the importance of identifying these challenges early to better direct tutoring activities. In this context, one of the responsibilities of human tutors is to establish contact to gather information that helps understand the difficulties students face [3]. By analyzing responses, it's possible to find reasons behind student disengagement in the teaching-learning process. However, it's challenging for human tutors to scale their tutoring efforts, especially in educational contexts with many students. The absence of an instructor and the feeling of being alone can create difficulties for students in online learning [4].

To efficiently and broadly handle student demands, it's necessary to adopt approaches that allow for individualized attention. A promising approach is the application of Natural Language Processing (NLP) techniques in the field of Artificial Intelligence in Education (AIEd) [5, 6]. In this study, these techniques can be used to classify different types

P. Zaphiris and A. Ioannou (Eds.): HCII 2024, LNCS 14724, pp. 321–332, 2024.
https://doi.org/10.1007/978-3-031-61691-4_21

of difficulties reported by students in virtual learning environments mediated by Educational Social Networks (ESN). Additionally, incorporating Intelligent Tutoring Systems (ITS) features can assist human tutors in handling a large volume of information about student engagement. Therefore, this article emerges in response to these challenges, motivated by the need to cooperate with tutors to promote more effective tutoring, and is guided by the following question: 'How can the difficulties faced by students in online learning, with interactions mediated in an Educational Social Network environment, be supervised and classified?

In the context of this article, a Natural Language Processing (NLP) component was developed to supervise and classify the difficulties faced by students in online learning, with interactions in a virtual Educational Social Network (ESN) environment. Through data analysis, a model was trained to identify patterns in student responses regarding difficulties, mainly in "personal", "technical", and "others" situations. Proper identification and classification of student difficulties is a crucial step in providing personalized and relevant tutoring, assisting in the learning process, and individual student monitoring.

The article is structured into four additional sections: Sect. 2 discusses related works, Sect. 3 describes the methodology used, including techniques and procedures, Sect. 4 presents the results, and Sect. 5 concludes with final considerations.

2 Related Works

Natural Language Processing (NLP) approaches are being used to create content and personalize instructional materials [7]. In Intelligent Tutoring Systems (ITS), they are applied in conversational dialogues [8] to understand student needs. In the context of online learning (e-learning), NLP allows for conversation analysis, identifying patterns in various situations. By analyzing phonology, grammar, semantics, and context, dialogue formation models can generate content, personalize instructional materials [7], identify sentiments in social network contexts [9], and classify comments, responses, and discussions to monitor student engagement. Liu et al. [10] explore student engagement through discussions on how they learn and understand content, as well as self-regulation strategies and perseverance in learning. The authors used mapping of student interest in subjects, satisfaction, and seriousness in following didactic activities. Although NLP is promising for deciphering collected textual information and highlighting the subjectivity of student difficulties, approaches that contribute to human tutoring are necessary, as learning difficulties may present in a social dimension where only interaction and the desire to communicate can reveal them.

3 Method

To identify and classify the difficulties that discourage students in online learning, monitoring was conducted during periods of school activities mediated by virtual environments. Understanding how human tutors identify student difficulties was key to proposing strategies using NLP techniques intertwined with the interdependent network of interactions between tutors and students in the virtual environment. It was investigated whether human tutors used specific approaches to understand student difficulties, and whether these approaches left recurrent clues in interactions that could be used for classification. This classification was crucial to identify factors that demotivate students in virtual environment interactions. Initially, understanding the instructional design of human tutors' interactions with students was necessary.

3.1 Study Context

The role of tutors in the design of online instructional content can create an interaction framework that directly impacts the identification of student difficulties. The interaction between human tutors and students can offer insights and patterns that assist in classifying these difficulties. This study focused on online learning for micro and small businesses, particularly in the metropolitan area of Recife, Pernambuco, Brazil, covering various thematic courses: The course "*Trilha: Como posso inovar?*" had 588 students, 3 tutors, and 1 teacher, focusing on how current innovation strategies can benefit businesses. "*Canvas You: Meu Modelo de Negócio Pessoal*" with 69 students, 2 tutors, and 1 teacher, outlined ways to reinvent careers, overcome obstacles, find new opportunities, and deliver value to clients. "*Como a Disrupção Pode Afetar o seu Negócio - Minicurso Online*" (132 students, 2 tutors, 1 teacher) explored strategies for dealing with technological innovations, consumer trends, and breaking market conventions and paradigms. "*Novos Comportamentos de Consumo - Minicurso Online*" (702 students, 3 tutors, 1 teacher) focused on understanding current consumption patterns, connecting with consumers, and ensuring the survival of micro or small businesses. "*Strategic Planning for Entrepreneurs*" (1105 students, 6 tutors, 2 teachers) focused on developing business strategies, vision, mission, objectives, and competitor analysis. "Digital Marketing for the Entrepreneur" (1340 students, 5 tutors, 2 teachers) aimed at reaching new customers in increasingly digital consumer markets. "*How to Develop High-Performance Teams*" (257 students, 2 tutors, 1 teacher) emphasized individual skills and innovative approaches to employee performance. "*Financial Strategy for Growth*" (897 students, 3 tutors, 1 teacher) concentrated on building a future vision for micro-businesses.

3.2 Data Collection and Analysis

The courses encompassed a diverse audience, but primarily women entrepreneurs with elementary and high school education levels. They helped build skills in leadership, communication, entrepreneurship, understanding consumer behavior, business models, customer understanding, finance, digital positioning and presence, business purpose, marketing, product validation, networking, digital-era finance, and advertising on Facebook and Instagram, among others. In this context, human tutors, among other activities, analyzed student completion percentages and collected responses to standardized messages in "*Active Search*" efforts by students, recording them in a spreadsheet (Fig. 1, screenshot of the tutor's spreadsheet template), during the monitoring period from December 2022 to May 2023, to understand the difficulties that were disengaging the students.

On a monthly basis, verification and qualification of reasons were conducted. The collection of module completion percentages allowed for weekly interactions every Monday, sending targeted messages to students whose module completion performance was below 75%. In addition to this message collection phase, steps were also taken to

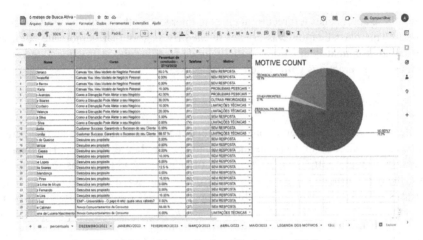

Fig. 1. Spreadsheet - Student "Active Search" Cycle.

analyze and define the NLP model (Fig. 2). The message collections corresponded to the responses of students to the messages sent by human tutors, which served as a data source for the analyses. Each message was labeled based on the joint perceptions of the human tutors and served as a source for the systematic analysis approach using NLP techniques. Section 4 presents the classification resulting from this stage of the study.

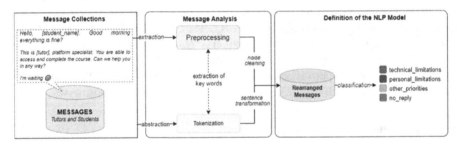

Fig. 2. Flowchart of data collection, analysis, and model definition for the analysis of tutoring messages and classification based on different types of difficulties.

The message analysis flow (Fig. 3), with the application of NLP techniques, involved text preprocessing through fundamental steps to prepare the data for analysis. These steps included removing unwanted information such as special characters, emoticons, excessive punctuation, and stop-words. After preprocessing, the text was tokenized using the Tokenizer library[1]. This step involved transforming sentences into sequences of tokens, which could be words or parts of words, limited by a vocabulary defined by the parameter num_words = 500. To feed the data into a Neural Network model, it was necessary to ensure that all token sequences had the same length. To achieve this, the

---

[1] https://www.tensorflow.org/api_docs/python/tf/keras/preprocessing/text/tokenizer

pad_sequences function was used, which adjusted the length of sequences by filling them with zeros when necessary.

3.3 Definition of the NLP Model

The model choice took into consideration current approaches used in Natural Language Processing (NLP). Some of these approaches include: Convolutional Neural Network (CNN), used for the discovery and recognition of patterns in textual elements [11]; Recurrent Neural Network (RNN), with feedback mechanisms that enable the retention of previous information when processing subsequent inputs; and Feedforward Multi-Layer Perceptron (MLP), with the capability to work with multiple layers for classification problems, considering the Long Short-Term Memory (LSTM) technique, which allows for the processing of input sequences and the recall of relevant information at different time steps [12].

In an experimental approach, a classification model based on word sequences (Keras Sequential) was used, with parameter variations, to find the best configuration for classifying students' difficulties based on the messages received from human tutors. Parameter variations involved tests on: Three different sizes (embedding_size = [64, 128, 256]) for the word representation vector (embedding). Three different quantities (lstm_units = [64, 128, 256]) of LSTM units, to capture context information in word sequences. Three dropout rates (dropouts = [0.2, 0.3, 0.4]) for regularization to help prevent overfitting by randomly deactivating a fraction of units during training. Three different optimizers (optimizers = ['adam', 'rmsprop', 'sgd']) to define how the model's weights would be updated during training in the quest to minimize the loss function.

Ultimately, the Dense layer had 3 neurons with sigmoid activation, indicating classification into three classes (representative of the types of difficulties: technical, personal, and others). During the execution of parameter variations, the model was built, trained, and evaluated using training data (80%) and test data (20%) with the Scikit-learn train_test_split function. The resulting accuracy in each iteration was compared to the best accuracy obtained previously, and if it was higher, the current parameters were updated as the new best-identified configuration. In the end, the best parameter configuration found was adopted for the subsequent analyses in this study, serving as the combination that maximizes the NLP model's performance in classifying students' difficulties. Section 4 presents the results of the analyses.

4   Results

In this section, the main results are presented regarding how human tutors actively sought interactions with students, mapped and classified the types of difficulties, providing information about the strategies and the overall performance of the NLP model.

4.1 "Active Search" by Students

The "active search" involved direct contact between tutors and students, allowing for individualized tutoring. Over a six-month observation period, tutors contacted 206 students from different courses. Among these, 101 students did not respond to the contact and were classified as "unresponsive" while a total of 105 students responded to the tutors' outreach. The difficulties faced by students who responded to the tutors' contact were classified into categories: "technical", "personal", and "others". The quantities and trends of these difficulties occurred as follows (Fig. 3).

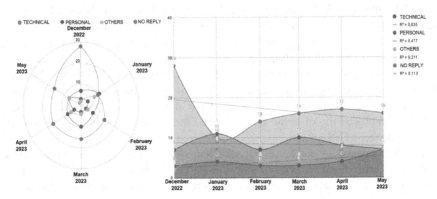

Fig. 3. Frequencies by types of difficulties classified over the course of the six-month monitoring period of human tutor activities.

When extracting messages from the students, there were responses that allowed human tutors to make inductive classifications of "technical", "personal" and "others" difficulties. Table 1 presents a selection of messages (verbatim as received), highlighting words or phrases used to classify students' difficulties.

Explored visually, word frequencies were obtained for each type of difficulty (Fig. 4). This allowed for the identification of specific words in the textual content of messages classified as "technical" difficulties which included words related to the platform, challenges in accessing it, availability of resources, and the level of familiarity with technologies, as well as perceptions regarding platform usage. In messages classified as "personal" difficulties, the presence of words related to the course itself and the use of personal pronouns was observed, which is essential for understanding the subjective dimension of students' engagement regularly and without the need for assistance. On the other hand, in messages classified as "others" difficulties, there was a frequency of words related to what students would like, including elements related to other interests, courses, and individual priorities.

In this sense, conceptually (Fig. 5), it is understood that technical difficulties may be related to digital literacy, with issues related to the use of tools and technological resources in the learning environment. Personal difficulties are related to autonomy and well-being, involving emotional aspects, motivation, organization, and autonomy. Difficulties classified as "other" refer to prioritization, encompassing difficulties that do not fit into the previous categories, such as prioritizing other activities, courses, and individual preferences. In cases of "no response", it is not possible to explicitly identify the difficulties.

Fig. 4. Most frequent words in each type of difficulty.

Table 1. Selection of messages returned by the students.

#	Mensagens dos estudantes	Classe
1	*Estou sem computador. No celular tá bem ruim de navegar. Poderias me auxiliar com passo a passo?*	technical
2	*Oi, [tutora]. Estou fazendo alguns seminários do [ambiente] já, por isso não acessei, mas vou.*	other
3	*Boa tarde! Tudo bem! Consegui sim, como ele é bem detalhado fiquei sem tempo de assistir com calma sabe. Mas pretendo concluir*	personal
4	*Sim. Só não tive tempo para concluir o curso*	other
5	*Sim consegui acessar normalmente. Porém, sem tempo.*	other
6	*Oi [tutora]. Sim, consegui acessar! Por enquanto, tudo certo. Mas estou tendo other demandas* 🙀	other
7	*Eu me inscrevi em 4 cursos. Consegui realizar só 2.*	other
8	*Ainda não. Me passa o link para entrar. E o passo a passo*	technical
9	*Oia boa tarde. Qual será o horário da aula por que estou na emergênciafea*	personal
10	*Olá! Consegui visualizar sim.*	other
11	*Consegui ainda não. Mas quero conseguir. Não sou familiarizada com tecnologia*	technical
12	*Não consegui acessar*	technical
13	*Eu não consigo acessar a página do [ambiente] Pois a confirmação do e-mail Pra trocar a senha não chega*	technical
14	*Bom dia!* 🙀 *Querida como faço?*	technical

(continued)

Table 1. (*continued*)

15	*Bom dia [tutora], quando eu tiver eu com **tempo livre eu acesso** sim ,obg*	other
16	*Bom dia! **Estou começando hoje o curso**. Com fé em Deus*	other
17	*Oi [tutora]! Vou bem e você? Bom [tutora] estava resolvendo algumas **pendências personal** antes de começar, acredito que ainda hoje eu entre.*	personal
18	*Boa tarde, eu **não consegui acessar a plataforma** Não sei como entra.*	technical
19	*Oi Foi sim, **não lembrava mais** Como faço?*	other
20	*Ola boa tarde Eu **não consigo fazer o acesso***	technical
21	*Sim realizei. Nenhum impedimento além do **tempo mesmo pra poder acessar**.*	other
22	*Não consegui acessar nao. **Nao entendo como mexe** Bom dia*	technical
23	*Bom dia! Ainda não realizei o acesso na plataforma, pois **fiquei doente** Como realizo*	personal
24	*Tem uma plataforma específica do [ambiente]? **Como entra?***	technical
25	*Bom dia E porque o **imel** que cadastrei **perdi e não conseguir recupera** lo*	technical
26	*Bom dia. **Não consegui acessar**. Pode sim me **ajudar** 🎧*	technical
27	*Fiz para me inscrever em uma palestra, ja vi ela. Mas **não tive mais interesse**.*	other
28	*Olá [tutora], boa tarde! Tudo bem, obrigada por perguntar. Eu fiz a inscrição e na verdade não soube bem o que era. Permine não entrando mas. Eu tenho uma página no Instagram que vendo bolsas e sapatos, **pensei** que fosse alguma coisa ligada a vendas. Deixei de lado estou se **concentrado no meu trabalho**.*	personal
29	*Olá [tutora], estou tendo **dificuldades para acessar a plataforma**. Parece que minha senha não está funcionando. Você poderia me ajudar a redefinir?*	technical
30	***Não consigo acessar** a plataforma desde que mudei meu endereço de e-mail. Pode atualizar meus detalhes?*	technical
31	*Eu tentei **baixar** o **aplicativo** no meu tablet, mas não consegui. Existe uma versão para tablet?*	technical
32	*[tutora], eu comecei um **novo trabalho** recentemente e estou um pouco **sobrecarregado**. Mas quero muito voltar em breve, posso?*	other

(*continued*)

Table 1. *(continued)*

33	*Olá, [tutora]. A **conexão** com a **internet** no meu local é muito fraca, e isso torna difícil acessar a plataforma. Tem app?*	technical
34	*Tive uma **emergência familiar** e não pude acessar a plataforma, **minha mãe ficou internada** esse tempo todo e tive que ficar com ela.*	personal
35	*Na verdade, eu comecei a acessar o curso, mas o conteúdo **não era o que eu esperava**. Você tem other opções que possam me interessar?*	personal
36	***Não** to **conseguindo acessar** com minha **senha** do **email**, oq faço?*	technical
37	*Estou focada em **outros** estudos no **momento**, mas pretendo acessar a plataforma assim que possível.*	other
...	...	...

Note: # - message enumeration; class - type of difficulty assigned by human tutors; ... - continuation; bold - main words or phrases observed by human tutors in the classification.

Fig. 5. Conceptualization of the types of student difficulties identified from interactions with human tutors in online learning.

The messages returned by the students and the categorization of types of difficulties carried out by human tutors allowed for the adoption of supervised NLP learning approaches. The following section presents the results of the application of the NLP model, where students' responses are input elements and types of difficulties are classes (Sect. 4.2).

4.2 Classification of Difficulties

The subsequent analyses were conducted based on the best parameter configuration for the NLP model (Fig. 6). A sequential approach was adopted, wherein the parameters of the best-tested configuration were assigned as follows: an embedding layer with 5000 units, a vector of size 256, and an input length equal to the number of columns in X; an LSTM layer with 256 units, a dropout rate, and recurrent dropout of 0.3; a dense layer

```
# Algorithm for message analysis
# Defining the model - Sequential
# Assignment of the best identified parameter configurations:
model = Sequential()
embedding_size=256
lstm_units=256
dropout= 0.3
optimizer='adam'

# EEmbedding with 5000 units, vector size of 256, and input equal to
the number of columns of X:
model.add(Embedding(5000, embedding_size, input_length=X.shape[1]))

# LSTM with 256 units, dropout rate, and recurrent dropout of 0.3:
model.add(LSTM(lstm_unit, dropout=dropout, recurrent_dropout=drop-
out))

# CDense layer with 3 units and sigmoid activation:
model.add(Dense(3, activation='sigmoid'))

# Compile the model with binary_crossentropy loss function, Adam
optimizer, and accuracy metrics:
model.compile(loss='binary_crossentropy', optimizer='adam', met-
rics=['accuracy'])

# Splitting into training and testing data:
Y = pd.get_dummies(df['classe']).values
X_train, X_test, Y_train, Y_test = train_test_split(X, Y,
test_size=0.2, random_state=80)

# Training the model:
model.fit(X_train, Y_train, epochs=10, batch_size=80)

# Evaluating the model - accuracy:
print('Model Accuracy - for tutoring style:')
print(model.evaluate(X_test, Y_test)[1])
```

Nota: X - representa o vetor do conjunto de mensagens retornadas pelos estudantes; Y - representa o vetor do conjunto de tipos de dificuldades classificadas pelos tutores humanos.

Fig. 6. Resulting Best Parameter Configuration for the Model.

with 3 units and 'sigmoid' activation; compiling the model with binary_crossentropy loss function, 'adam' optimizer, and accuracy metrics; converting the class variable into one-hot encoding format and assigning it to Y; splitting X and Y into training and testing sets using the train_test_split function with a 20% test size and an 80 random state; and training the model with training data X_train and Y_train, using 10 epochs and a batch size of 80.

From the model evaluation, it can be highlighted that it performs well, with a steady decline throughout the training and validation phases (Fig. 7).

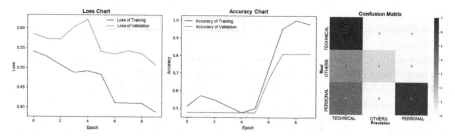

Fig. 7. Loss, accuracy, and confusion matrix of the model.

The model achieves accuracy levels (Acc) in the testing phase of approximately Acc ≈ 0.97 and in the validation phase of approximately Acc ≈ 0.81. However, it is still insufficiently capable of learning in a way that resembles the classifications made by human tutors. This becomes evident when analyzing the confusion matrix (Fig. 7), which shows the overall performance of the model in classifying students' difficulties. The approach was able to correctly classify in the validation phase (in the 20% data set, 21 messages): 7 instances as "technical", 6 instances as "personal" and 1 instance as "other". However, it made mistakes by classifying 3 instances of "other" difficulties as "technical" and 4 instances of "personal" difficulties as "technical" (Fig. 7). Therefore, it requires abstractions beyond the understanding of human tutors for accurate classification of difficulties.

5   Final Considerations

In this study, interactions between human tutors and students in the context of online learning mediated by a Learning Management System (LMS) were analyzed. The data collected through "active searching" allowed tutors to classify difficulties and served as input for the Natural Language Processing (NLP) approach analysis. The highlighted difficulties align with "technical", "personal", and "other" limitations, which suggest opportunities to enhance digital literacy, student satisfaction, and engagement with learning. Despite the overall performance of the model, it was found that the NLP approach can collaborate with the work of human tutors, enabling identification and classification of student difficulties based on messages requesting help, comments, and discussions in virtual environments. It is believed that identifying and classifying types of difficulties can help appropriately direct students to specialized tutors, recommend specific materials, or suggest peers for collaboration. However, considering that the classifications made by tutors are specific to a particular tutoring context, it is important to expand the dataset available for training and testing the classification model using data from various other online learning contexts in future work.

Acknowledgements. This work was supported by the FCT – Fundação para a Ciência e a Tecnologia, I.P. [Project UIDB/05105/2020].

References

1. Muilenburg, L.Y., Berge, Z.L.: Student barriers to online learning: a factor analytic study. Distance Educ. **26**(1), 29–48 (2005). https://doi.org/10.1080/01587910500081269
2. Panackal, N., Rautela, S., Sharma, A.: Modeling the enablers and barriers to effective E-learning: a TISM approach. Int. J. Interact. Mob. Technol. (iJIM) **16**(3), 138–164 (2022). https://doi.org/10.3991/ijim.v16i08.29455
3. Veloso, B., Daniel, M.I.L.L.: Tutoria no sistema Universidade Aberta do Brasil (UAB): uma análise dos tutores presenciais e virtuais. Revista de Educação Pública **29**, 1–17 (2020). https://doi.org/10.1111/bjet.12016
4. Pereira, A.J., Gomes, A.S., Primo, T.T., Rodrigues, R.L., Júnior, R.P.M., Moreira, F.: Learning mediated by social network for education in K-12: levels of interaction, strategies, and difficulties. Educ. Sci. **13**(2), 100 (2023). https://doi.org/10.3390/educsci13020100
5. Chen, X., Xie, H., Hwang, G.J.: A multi-perspective study on artificial intelligence in education: grants, conferences, journals, software tools, institutions, and researchers. Comput. Educ. Artif. Intell. **1**, 100005 (2020). https://doi.org/10.1016/j.caeai.2020.100005
6. Chiu, T.K., Xia, Q., Zhou, X., Chai, C.S., Cheng, M.: Systematic literature review on opportunities, challenges, and future research recommendations of artificial intelligence in education. Comput. Educ. Artif. Intell. **4**, 100118 (2023). https://doi.org/10.1016/j.caeai.2022.100118
7. Litman, D.: Natural language processing for enhancing teaching and learning. In: Proceedings of the AAAI Conference on Artificial Intelligence, vol. 30, no. 1 (2016). https://doi.org/10.1609/aaai.v30i1.9879
8. Wang, Y., Sun, Y., Chen, Y.: Design and research of intelligent tutor system based on natural language processing. In: 2019 IEEE International Conference on Computer Science and Educational Informatization (CSEI), pp. 33–36. IEEE. (2019). https://doi.org/10.1109/CSEI47661.2019.8939031
9. Ortigosa, A., Martín, J.M., Carro, R.M.: Sentiment analysis in Facebook and its application to e-learning. Comput. Hum. Behav. **31**, 527–541 (2014). https://doi.org/10.1016/j.chb.2013.05.024
10. Liu, Z., et al.: Dual-feature-embeddings-based semi-supervised learning for cognitive engagement classification in online course discussions. Knowl.-Based Syst. **259**, 110053 (2023). https://doi.org/10.1016/j.knosys.2022.110053
11. Alrajhi, L., Alharbi, K., Cristea, A.I.: A multidimensional deep learner model of urgent instructor intervention need in MOOC forum posts. In: Kumar, V., Troussas, C. (eds.) Intelligent Tutoring Systems. ITS 2020. Lecture Notes in Computer Science, vol. 12149, pp. 226–236. Springer, Cham (2020). https://doi.org/10.1007/978-3-030-49663-0_27
12. Hochreiter, S., Schmidhuber, J.: Long short-term memory. Neural Comput. **9**(8), 1735–1780 (1997)

Towards an Architecture for Educational Chatbots

José Fidel Urquiza-Yllescas[1], Sonia Mendoza[1]([✉])(iD),
Luis Martín Sánchez-Adame[2](iD), José Rodríguez[1], and Dominique Decouchant[3]

[1] Computer Science Department, CINVESTAV-IPN, Av. Instituto Politécnico Nacional 2508, San Pedro Zacatenco, Gustavo A. Madero, 07360 Mexico City, Mexico
{jose.urquiza,sonia.mendoza,jose.rodriguezgarcia}@cinvestav.mx
[2] Design and Building Division, FES-Acatlán, UNAM, Av. Jardines de San Mateo s/n, Sta. Cruz Acatlán, 53150 Naucalpan de Juárez, Mexico, Mexico
lmsanchez@sigchi.org
[3] Department of Information Technologies, UAM-Cuajimalpa, Av. Vasco de Quiroga 4871, Santa Fe, Cuajimalpa, 05300 Mexico City, Mexico
decouchant@cua.uam.mx

Abstract. Chatbots are gaining significant relevance due to their enormous potential in various sectors, particularly education. The COVID-19 pandemic led to suspending in-person classes for students and teachers, creating an opportunity for research in developing educational chatbots. However, the proposal of a widely accepted structure for chatbots poses a challenge due to the constant evolution of technologies and tools employed in their implementation and deployment. Moreover, generic chatbot architectures present limitations when instantiated in specific contexts. For instance, in the case of educational chatbots, it is necessary to have an architecture specifically tailored to the functionalities required in the academic domain. This article follows a formal approach to designing and implementing a software architecture for educational chatbots. We rely on an iterative method called ADD 3.0 to achieve this objective. Our proposal consists of a three-tier architecture to define the component distribution of chatbots and a six-layer architecture to specify their structure.

Keywords: Software Architecture · Method ADD 3.0 · Educational Chatbots · Layers · Distribution Structure

1 Introduction

Nowadays, the mention of chatbots has become increasingly common. Essentially, a chatbot refers to a program developed to engage in conversations with humans [8], whether in an open domain or a closed domain. In an open domain, the chatbot can converse on any topic the user desires. For instance, ChatGPT [20] is a prominent example that has garnered significant controversy. Conversely, in a closed domain, the chatbot is designed to address a particular topic

P. Zaphiris and A. Ioannou (Eds.): HCII 2024, LNCS 14724, pp. 333–351, 2024.
https://doi.org/10.1007/978-3-031-61691-4_22

specifically. Consequently, any queries outside the chatbot's scope would not receive an appropriate response. An example of this is a frequently asked questions (FAQ) chatbot that provides admission information for a university [23]. It is undeniable that chatbots are experiencing a surge in popularity, indicating they are here to stay for some time [28].

The education sector is particularly well-suited for using chatbots [18]. Students derive a significant portion of their academic training from online resources, including class topics, assignments, practice materials, quizzes, and essays. Consequently, chatbots have the potential to provide valuable assistance throughout the educational stage. On the one hand, chatbots can serve many students simultaneously by addressing their questions and providing answers. On the other hand, chatbots might help alleviate the shortage of teachers and course offerings in schools and universities worldwide [24]. As such, they represent a powerful tool. Although the use of chatbots is still relatively limited [30], teachers highly value their potential to enhance outcomes in the teaching and learning process [5]. Thus, the development of chatbots has become of great interest to universities [1, 16].

The emergence of the COVID-19 pandemic has compelled governments to implement mechanisms that enable students to continue their courses. Despite the closure of schools, education has persevered by adopting online classes. This sudden shift has directly impacted traditional educational models, which predominantly revolve around face-to-face instruction [26].

The construction of an educational chatbot necessitates the establishment of a robust software architecture. Every software system possesses an architecture, so chatbots are no exception. A software architecture comprises a collection of structures that facilitate reasoning about the system, including its software components, the relationships between these components, and their properties [4]. Consequently, a software architecture is a fundamental guide for system development, ensuring its coherence and effectiveness [4].

The proposal of a widely accepted general architecture for chatbots poses a challenge due to the constant evolution of technologies and tools employed in their implementation. In educational chatbots, the absence of a standardized architecture makes reuse difficult, as many existing solutions tend to be *ad hoc* and specific to particular cases, making them less functional in different contexts. This lack of standardization hampers accessibility and the transferability of solutions to diverse circumstances. For example, educational chatbots provide the community with commonly sought-after information. In contrast, others prioritize offering more sophisticated functionalities to enhance the teaching and learning process for students. In order to fortify education-focused chatbots, it is crucial to establish a structured reference model that facilitates the study of the chatbot itself and enables potential developments within the academic domain.

In this paper, we describe a comprehensive architectural proposal for educational chatbots. By analyzing the system requirements and thoroughly examining related works, we design a software architecture that addresses academic institutions' general needs and aims to enhance teachers' and students' experiences in the teaching and learning process. To achieve this proposal, we employ the ADD 3.0 method [6], which allows us to capture the system's structure, behavior, and interactions from multiple perspectives. This article is organized as follows. Section 2 presents an overview of the related work. Sections 3 and 4 elaborate on the design methodology employed and our approach to an educational chatbot architecture. Finally, Sect. 5 provides the conclusions and outlines future work.

2   Related Work

Inokuchi et al. [11] propose a chatbot architecture consisting of two main elements: chat services and a bot. According to this architecture, the user sends a command as a message through the chat service, which is then received by the bot. The bot performs the operations specified in the message and returns the result to the user. However, this proposal needs more rigor and comprehensive details to enhance its potential extensibility. Additionally, it does not address integrating natural language processing (NLP) into the chatbot, nor does it specifically mention utilizing resources such as databases or knowledge bases, which are needed to provide the chatbot with intelligent capabilities.

Veglis and Maniou [29] adopt a client-server architecture for chatbot development. The client can be a web page or a mobile application. On the server side, the architecture comprises the following components: 1) *Logic and Rules Analyzer*, responsible for recognizing the input text and generating a response based on predefined rules; 2) *Knowledge Base*, which provides intelligence to the chatbot; and 3) *Natural Language Processing*, which validates the input text by conducting sentiment analysis and instructs the Knowledge Base to respond accordingly. However, scalability and security should be thoroughly addressed in this proposal, as the focus primarily lies on Artificial Intelligence.

Matthies et al. [17] build upon the proposal by Inokuchi et al. [11] by introducing an additional element that involves obtaining additional information from third-party resources, such as a knowledge base or Internet resources. However, this proposal still needs to improve regarding extensibility and the integration of NLP from the previous work.

Khan [12] discusses emerging technologies and services for chatbot development and presents an architecture for implementing chatbot solutions in a general context. The author proposes a six-layer architecture: 1) *Presentation Layer*, which encompasses components responsible for implementing and displaying the user interface and managing user interaction; 2) *Business Layer*, consisting of components that process, format, and manage data; 3) *Service Layer*, providing components that facilitate access to internal and external data, business functionality, and connectivity for information exchange between applications and other services; 4) *Data Layer*, responsible for efficient and secure data access; 5) *Utility Layer*, which handles various system parameters such as security and configuration; and 6) *External Services Layer*, utilizing different external services depending on the type of chatbot solution. However, additional layers containing the necessary components and modules must be introduced for chatbots with more specific purposes to address the required functionality within a broader context.

Srivastava and Prabhakar [27] propose a reference architecture for chatbots, comprising five components: 1) *Voice Utilities*, responsible for converting the user's voice message to its text representation and vice versa, facilitating message delivery; 2) *Inputs*, which represent different kinds of expected user inputs, with parameters serving as attributes or details of a query, parsed from the inputs to generate a response or perform an action; 3) *Response Generator*, tasked with generating appropriate responses to the user after each input; 4) *Flow Manager*, responsible for tracking the current state of the conversation and determining the next step; and finally, 5) *Actions and Fulfilments*, bridging the core functionalities of the application with the chatbot components. Despite these components, common aspects such as security, data access, and component communication must be adequately addressed.

From this selection of works, it becomes evident that the study of educational chatbots encompasses various topics. However, in all these works, applying software engineering principles is crucial. These principles are necessary for the proposals to serve as immediate solutions but need more scalability, exhibit deficiencies in different areas, and become costly to maintain. Therefore, these studies highlight the gap that our work aims to address.

3   Preliminaries

Numerous methodologies for designing software architectures have emerged, predominantly from the industrial sector. These include the Attribute-Driven Design (ADD) [3], Siemens 4 Views [10], Rational Unified Process (RUP) 4+1 Views [13,14], Business Architecture Process and Organization (BAPO) [2,19], Architectural Separation of Concerns (ASC) [22], The Process of Software Architecting [7], Microsoft® Application Architecture Guide [21], and Viewpoints and Perspectives [25]. Conversely, a few methodologies have been proposed within the academic sector, such as the Architecture-Centric Design Method (ACDM) [15] and ADD 3.0 [6]. Upon an exhaustive analysis of the merits and limitations of these methods, our choice for designing the software architecture of educational chatbots is the ADD 3.0 method. Several considerations underpin this decision.

Primarily, ADD 3.0 offers an explicitly tailored, comprehensive framework for software architecture design, ensuring meticulous attention to detail throughout the design process, a facet occasionally neglected in alternative approaches. Moreover, ADD 3.0 is compatible with other design methodologies, enhancing overall architectural design. It presents a lightweight yet effective alternative to more cumbersome processes or frameworks. Significantly, ADD 3.0 advocates for the reuse of reference architectures and is bolstered by an exhaustive catalog of design concepts, including a diverse array of tactics, patterns, frameworks, reference architectures, and technologies. It is crucial to note that while company-provided guidelines can be biased towards their technologies, ADD 3.0 enables the adoption of a more generic, technology-agnostic architecture, mitigating the risk of such bias in the architectural design process.

3.1   ADD 3.0 Method

Before starting to apply the ADD 3.0 method to build our architectural proposal, it is necessary to define some important concepts [6]:

- *Design purpose:* Refers to what is intended to be achieved concerning the design of architecture, following one of these three approaches: 1) greenfield systems for a mature domain, where the architecture is built from scratch, but the domain, infrastructure, tools, technologies and knowledge base are known elements; 2) greenfield systems for a new domain, which are challenging and complicated, since architectural references might be few or non-existent, so the domain has a less established infrastructure and little knowledge base; or 3) existing or brownfield systems, which already have an architecture, so the intention is to maintain them and make changes to them.
- *Quality attributes:* Defined as measurable or verifiable properties of a software system, which indicate how well the system satisfies the needs of interested parties.
- *Architectural interests:* Cover additional aspects that must be considered as part of the architectural design but are not expressed as traditional requirements.
- *Constraints:* The software architect has little or no control over these decisions.
- *Reference architectures:* Plans that provide a general logical structure for specific types of applications.
- *Architectural design patterns:* Conceptual solutions to recurring design problems that exist in a defined context.
- *Deployment Patterns:* Provide models for physically structuring the system to deploy it.

ADD 3.0 consists of seven steps:

1. *Check the entries.* It is necessary to have a series of guidelines that serve as input, such as the design purpose, primary functional requirements derived from use cases, quality attribute scenarios, constraints, and architectural interests.
2. *Set the iteration goal.* Before starting a particular design iteration, the goal must be formalized by selecting guidelines.
3. *Select elements to refine.* This involves choosing one or more system elements that are instrumental in adhering to the specified guidelines.
4. *Choose design concepts to satisfy guidelines.* This requires the identification of potential design concept alternatives that can aid in achieving the iteration goal. Subsequently, a choice is made from these alternatives to meet the chosen guidelines.
5. *Create instances of architectural elements, assign responsibilities, and define interfaces.* This step involves instantiating necessary elements and ensuring their interconnectivity for collaboration. Responsibilities for each element are designated, and the interfaces for information exchange are defined.

6. *Record views and design decisions.* This entails the preliminary documentation of sketched views and the recording of significant design decisions made during the iteration, aiding in subsequent analysis and comprehension.
7. *Analyze the design and review the iteration goal and the design purpose achievement.* The architecture's state is reviewed following the design analysis to assess its alignment with the initial design purpose and iteration goal.

ADD 3.0 is an iterative method; therefore, once step 7 is completed, the designer must iterate, if necessary, repeating steps 2 through 7 for each guideline considered part of the entry. It is worth mentioning that, according to Cervantes and Kazman [6], there may be occasions when the order of steps 2 and 3 must be reversed, forcing the designer to start with step 3 first and then continue with step 2. This may occur because there are cases when designing a greenfield system for a new domain or when developing reference architectures, at least in the early stages of design, the designer will first begin the iteration by selecting a particular system element. Then, the designer will consider the drivers to be addressed.

The following subsections are the results we obtained after establishing and documenting the inputs required to launch the ADD 3.0 method.

3.2   Check the Entries

The purpose of this design in this first step is to create a type of greenfield system for a new domain. The goal is to produce a simple, essential design that contains general specifications about the necessary components for an educational chatbot to serve as a guide for building a prototype.

Use Cases: Are helpful to describe the interactions between the educational chatbot and users. To develop use cases, we have considered our proposal of educational chatbot classification [28] that distinguishes between school service-oriented and student/teacher-oriented.

The *school service-oriented* class groups chatbots that provide information about *calendar & schedule* (academic events, staff and facilities work schedules, vacation periods, and evaluation dates), *information* (fees, educational offerings, directory and study plans), *FAQs* (Frequently Asked Questions), and *procedures* (how to enroll in a class or requirements to obtain a certificate).

The *student/teacher-oriented* class groups chatbots that not only interact with students, but also with teachers, providing support for *evaluation* (assessment tools for students, e.g., exams, homework, quizzes, practices, and essays), *subjects* (interacting with the student about the classes they have registered), *Q&A* (concrete questions and answers to the student about a specific subject of a class), *feedback* (students receive feedback according to their progress in class), *health wellness* (channeling students to care for physical and mental health problems as a consequence of confinement, distance education due to COVID-19 or school bullying), *support* (providing students with some kind of technical assistance, e.g., how to connect an electronic device to the laboratory network), *reports* (details provided to the teacher about the progress of their students), and *tutorships* (offering students some form of educational or personal orientation).

The following use cases are fundamental functionalities integral to the architecture - based developments for our educational chatbots. These are bifurcated into the two classes explained above, each serving specific aspects of the educational ecosystem. The first one, *school service-oriented* class, encompasses the initial five use cases (0–4). These are designed to facilitate administrative and logistical aspects of the educational institution. Subsequently, the remaining use cases fall under the *student/teacher-oriented* class (5–12). This one focuses on more personalized interactions with students and teachers. All use cases represent tasks that have the purpose of improving the teaching and learning process (Table 1):

Quality Attributes: Once the use cases are identified, discussing the significant quality characteristics that should be prioritized in all systems developed using our architecture becomes essential. Furthermore, it is crucial to establish clear boundaries for the functionalities of our solution, ensuring focused development and avoiding unnecessary complexities.

Quality attributes are fundamental elements in architectural design since they are measurable properties of a software system, which indicate how well the system meets the needs of interested parties. Furthermore, it is relevant to highlight the existence of quality attribute scenarios, which are brief descriptions of how the system must respond to specific stimuli [6]. There are various lists of quality attributes since their relevance depends on the application domain and specific business objectives. However, those widely used are [4]: availability, portability, modifiability, performance, security, testability, usability, variability, portability, scalability, and maintainability.

Verifying that there is no potential conflict between quality attributes is crucial, as this can impact the architectural design. Therefore, for this first design stage, it is most convenient to prioritize the quality attributes [9]. On the other hand, an essential aspect in creating the quality attribute scenarios is the participation of stakeholders, who can be any person, e.g., individuals, groups, organizations, or entities interested in a project's success or failure. However, in our case, during this early design stage, access to stakeholders was not feasible. In such circumstances, deciding how to address and prioritize the system's numerous challenges becomes imperative. Following the recommendations of Cervantes and Kazman [6], creating a utility tree is a helpful technique in these situations.

We have proposed 17 quality attribute scenarios, from which seven were selected, as shown in Table 2, focusing on those scenarios that can help generate a structure with the essential components for an educational chatbot. The *ID* column corresponds to the quality attribute identifier, *Quality Attribute* presents the chosen attribute, *Scenario* describes the system's response to a stimulus, *Associated Use Case* indicates which use case the quality attribute reaches, and *Priority* categorizes each quality attribute in two dimensions: busi-

Table 1. Use Cases for an educational chatbot.

ID	Use Case
UC0	*Login:* Both student and teacher users access the chatbot using a username and password
UC1	*Schedule Inquiry:* Both student and teacher users can inquire about the available schedules for the current academic term, academic events, examination periods, or vacations
UC2	*Obtaining General Information:* Both student and teacher users can acquire comprehensive information regarding the institution's history, educational offerings, directory, and curriculum plans
UC3	*Responding to FAQs:* Both student and teacher users can pose inquiries and receive answers. The type of questions and answers involved in this use case are commonly referred to as FAQs, such as laboratory schedules, library information, and medical services
UC4	*Displaying General Procedures:* A student or teacher user requires a comprehensive guide containing specific information to carry out procedures, such as enrolling in an academic term, selecting a group or class, language options, or extracurricular activities. Additionally, it encompasses procedures for obtaining a student ID card, requesting book loans or educational materials, and obtaining a school certificate
UC5	*Conducting Assessments:* A student user can undertake examinations or submit assignments, tasks, quizzes, and essays
UC6	*Displaying Course Information:* A student user can access information regarding the subjects they must take during the semester
UC7	*Posing Inquiries and Obtaining Responses:* A student user can pose a specific question and receive a precise response
UC8	*Receiving Feedback:* A student user can receive feedback based on their progress
UC9	*Providing Support for Physical and Mental Health Issues:* A student user can request a referral to a psychologist for assistance with any issues they may be facing
UC10	*Providing Technical Support:* A student user can receive assistance, such as guidance on connecting a device to the laboratory's wireless network
UC11	*Displaying Student Progress:* A teacher user can request information regarding a student's academic progress
UC12	*Providing Support and Guidance through Tutoring:* A student user can receive educational or personal guidance and assistance through tutoring services, ensuring continuous monitoring and support

ness importance and technical risk. Each dimension is assigned a value of 'High' (H), 'Medium' (M), or 'Low' (L), resulting in paired classifications (e.g., (H, H)) to indicate the priority level in both contexts.

As can be seen in Table 2, for this first stage, we select four quality attributes as a basis: availability, portability, security, and usability, and the scenarios that were chosen are those whose priority is a combination of (H, H), (H, M) and (M, H): QA3, QA4, QA7, QA12, QA13, QA16 and QA17. *Availability* denotes the software system's readiness and capacity to execute its functions at a moment's notice. *Portability* is the extent to which multiple systems can efficiently exchange and use information through interfaces in a specified context. *Security* measures the system's effectiveness in safeguarding data and information from unauthorized access, encompassing protection of user information and access to authorized systems. *Usability* pertains to the degree of ease and intuitiveness with which users can navigate and operate within the system.

Constraints: Represent factors over which architects have minimal influence. Recognizing and cataloging these constraints is critical to the architectural design process. They can take various forms, such as mandatory technologies, interoperability requirements with existing systems, adherence to legal standards and regulations, and availability of human resources. For our project, specific constraints have been identified to ensure that the resulting architecture aligns seamlessly with the educational context. Table 3 enumerates these constraints, which are crucial for adherence during the implementation of the ADD 3.0 methodology:

- CT1 is derived from the nature of chatbots, as they are usually available online and accessible through web browsers on various operating systems.
- CT2 is rooted in the benefits of cloud-based natural language processing services tailored for chatbot development. These services, such as Dialogflow or Watson, often entail costs, with limitations on functionality or access in their free versions.
- CT3 arises as an extension of the CT2 constraint since the possibility of more fluid integration with storage and database services opens up when using cloud services.
- CT4 is immediate because of the CT2 and CT3 constraints.
- CT5 is proposed as a user control measure.
- CT6 is intended to be used in the first tests.
- CT7 is derived first to prevent inappropriate use of language and, therefore, to avoid more significant problems in the future.
- CT8 is a significant constraint to consider since, in an educational context, the ideal is to focus on some educational model, but that requires the participation of experts in the area, which would further increase complexity. However, it is more than enough as it has coherently aligned essential educational elements.
- CT9 is an essential constraint for the design and must be complied with.

Table 2. Quality attribute scenarios for an educational chatbot.

ID	Quality Attribute	Scenario	Associated Use Case	Priority
QA3	Availability	Students studying outside the educational facilities depend on the educational chatbot for help with their schoolwork. The chatbot must be available 24/7 to provide ongoing assistance and support education	All	(H, H)
QA4	Availability	Students use the educational chatbot to study for their exams. The chatbot must remain operational, allowing students to learn and practice whenever convenient	7 & 8	(H, M)
QA7	Portability	Students can access the chatbot from various devices, such as desktop computers, tablets, and smartphones. The chatbot must be interoperable on different platforms and devices, guaranteeing a uniform experience no matter how students access it	All	(H, H)
QA12	Security	Students provide personal information to the educational chatbot. The chatbot must guarantee the security of this data and protect the information from students against unauthorized access	5, 8, 9 & 10	(H, H)
QA13	Security	An unknown user without registration attempts to enter the login screen in a normal operating environment. The system must prevent access and display a message only registered students and teachers can enter	0	(H, M)
QA16	Security	A student turns to the chatbot to request educational, personal, or sensitive guidance. The chatbot must provide an accurate referral to ensure the student receives appropriate care	12	(H, M)
QA17	Usability	A student uses the chatbot to reinforce their learning on educational or informational topics. The chatbot should offer intuitive navigation and allow the student to find the answers to their questions easily	8	(H, H)

Table 3. Constraints for an educational chatbot.

ID	Constraint
CT1	Accessibility through a web browser on various operating systems
CT2	Utilization of cloud services for natural language processing in chatbot development
CT3	Employment of cloud-based storage and non-relational database services
CT4	Basic knowledge of cloud services is required for chatbot developers
CT5	User account registration for authentication in the educational chatbot
CT6	Support for a minimum of 15 simultaneous users
CT7	Implementation of language analysis to point out violent, hateful, or harassing content
CT8	Incorporation of pedagogical elements to enhance the teaching and learning process, e.g., stimulus-response model or reinforcement theory
CT9	Adherence to our concept of educational chatbot "An educational chatbot is a closed domain software that interacts in real-time with students and teachers using natural language in order to support the teaching and learning process and assist the school community in various topics of common interest"

Architectural Concerns: are those factors to be considered in the design since they act as guides. There are several concerns: general, specific, and internal, among others. We focus on an architectural interest of the general type, whose primary purpose is to establish the structure of an educational chatbot (Table 4).

Table 4. Architectural concerns for an educational chatbot.

ID	Architectural Concern
AC1	Establish an initial high-level general structure for an educational chatbot

4   Proposed Architecture for Chatbots

This section presents the design process to develop a generic architecture for educational chatbots. Previously, the inputs required to launch ADD 3.0 were established and documented. From this point, we develop steps 2 to 7, which mark the beginning of the first iteration of the design process.

4.1   Set the Iteration Goal

This is the first iteration in designing a greenfield system for a new domain, so the goal focuses on establishing an initial general structure of the chatbot. A first iteration will be sufficient to define this initial general structure and will be governed by the guidelines established in the first step (see Sect. 3.2).

4.2   Select Elements to Refine

As this is the first iteration and a greenfield development, the element to refine is the complete system.

4.3   Choose Design Concepts to Satisfy Guidelines

Since the goal is to create the general structure of an educational chatbot, a design concept that satisfies the guidelines must be chosen. This step is crucial because it is the starting point of the general design that will be established in the architecture. In this case, it is convenient to present the available options to analyze and briefly explain why they could be used or not. Cervantes and Kazman [6] provide a list of reference architectures to analyze and choose the most appropriate one. From this list, we can mention *Rich Client Applications, Rich Internet Applications, Mobile Applications, Service Applications*, and *Web Applications*.

According to the use cases analyzed for the system, it requires access through a web browser (cf. constraint CT1). Therefore, the best option is to use the *Web Applications* reference architecture, an application accessed through a web browser that communicates with a server using the HTTP protocol-no installation is required on the client side. The application resides in the server and typically employs a layered architecture. This reference architecture is the one that comes closest to what is established in our requirements.

On the other hand, deployment patterns describe the physical structure: *Non-Distributed* and *Distributed*. In the Non-Distributed pattern, all components in the different layers reside on a single server, except the functionality of the data storage. However, the application components reside on separate physical levels for the Distributed pattern. In our case, the three-tier distributed deployment pattern is used. This pattern defines a pre-established software architecture for web applications in three logical levels: *Client or presentation level, Application level* where data is processed, and *Data level* where the data associated with the application is stored and managed.

In this way, the constraints that the chatbot can be accessed from a web browser (CT1) and can use cloud services for both natural language processing (CT2) and database management (CT3) are being respected.

4.4 Create Instances of Architectural Elements, Assign Responsibilities, and Define Interfaces

In this step, the design decisions considered are established:

- Create the component for the login procedure in the presentation layer (UC0),
- Create the component for role-based user access in the business layer (QA12, QA13, CT5),
- Configure user access through *Auth* services (UC0) so that the corresponding student information is linked solely to their account (QA12). Thus, if a student wants to know about other students, the chatbot should not allow it.
- Create the components for the functionality of the student and teacher users in the orientation layer (UC5 - UC12).
- Create the component to manage the chatbot services in the services layer (CT2).
- Create the components for data access and knowledge base access in the data layer (CT3).

For this iteration, we are not required to define interfaces because we are focused on establishing the general structure of the system.

4.5 Record Views and Design Decisions

Figure 1 illustrates an educational chatbot's physical structure and distribution. The interaction flow begins with a user who sends a text or voice message through a Web browser or client-side application. The chatbot receives this message, hosted on an application server, which executes the necessary operations to generate a response. These operations may involve parsing the message or utilizing a cloud-based chatbot service to match the message expression with the most appropriate *intent* of the *agent* or *assistant*. From there, requests are made to extract relevant information from cloud services and the database or knowledge base. Finally, the chatbot formulates a response and delivers it back to the user.

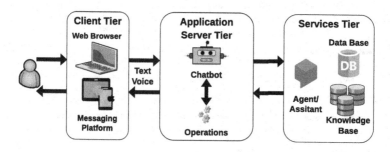

Fig. 1. Three-tier distribution architecture for educational chatbots.

Figure 2 shows a sketch view of the proposed layered architecture, according to the design decisions, taking the chosen reference and deployment architectures as a starting point. This architecture resides on the server side and is composed of the following elements and responsibilities:

1. **Presentation Layer:** This layer encompasses the components responsible for implementing and displaying the user interface. It consists of the following:
   - *Web:* This component facilitates the display of the chatbot through a web browser.
   - *Messaging platforms:* This component enables the presentation of the chatbot through various messaging applications such as Telegram, WhatsApp, or Facebook Messenger.
   - *User interface:* It implements mechanisms to enhance user interaction with the chatbot, regardless of whether it is accessed through a web browser or a messaging platform.
2. **Business Layer:** This layer incorporates the components responsible for handling user requests. It includes the following:
   - *User access:* This component manages user access based on their roles, distinguishing between students and teachers.
   - *Student:* It provides functionality specific to students.
   - *Teacher:* This component implements functionality tailored for teachers.
   - *Message Processing and Formatting:* It analyzes user messages to detect and prevent using offensive, hateful, or harassing language.
3. **Orientation Layer:** This layer comprises two primary components that define the educational chatbot's functionality:
   - *School Services:* This component is responsible for providing information to the school community and external users regarding:

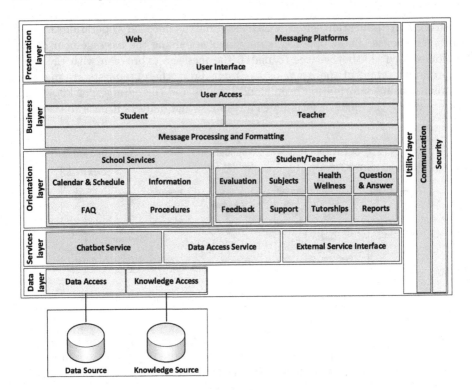

Fig. 2. Layered software architecture for educational chatbots.

- *Calendar & Schedule:* It displays activity-specific information, such as academic events, staff and facility work schedules, vacation periods, and exam dates.
- *Information:* This component presents information about the educational offerings, directory, and curricula.
- *FAQ:* It collects frequently asked questions and corresponding answers.
- *Procedures:* This component offers functionality to guide students through specific procedures, such as enrollment, certificate issuance, student card processing, and health insurance application.
- *Student/Teacher:* This component caters to students and teachers, providing functionality related to:
  - *Evaluation:* It facilitates the evaluation of students through exams, assignments, quizzes, practices, and essays.
  - *Subjects:* This component enables interactions with students regarding their enrolled classes.
  - *Question & Answer:* It handles specific questions from students and provides concrete answers on particular topics.

- *Health Wellness:* This component directs students to seek attention for physical and mental health issues resulting from confinement, distance education due to COVID-19, or even instances of bullying.
- *Feedback:* It allows teachers to provide feedback to students based on their progress in the class.
- *Support:* This component offers technical support to students, assisting them with tasks such as sharing videos over the network.
- *Reports:* It provides teachers with student progress information.
- *Tutorships:* This component offers students educational or personal guidance.

4. **Service Layer:** This layer comprises components that grant access to internal and external data, business functionality, and other services. It includes the following:
   - *Chatbot service:* This component manages the chatbot services in the cloud.
   - *Data access service:* It provides functionality for transforming messages into a format that other components can understand. As the chatbot is integrated with a cloud service, an adapter may be required to convert data from the services into a compatible format.
   - *External service interface:* This component is designed to supplement the chatbot's functionality, allowing the integration of additional services beyond those originally intended. It is important to note that technology advances rapidly, and access to services may change accordingly.
5. **Data Layer:** This layer encapsulates the functionality required for communication with the component responsible for storing and managing data and knowledge, enabling access to relevant information.
6. **Utility Layer:** This transversal layer incorporates components that handle communication and security between the various layers.

4.6 Analyze the Design and Review the Iteration Goal and the Design Purpose Achievement

In the description of ADD 3.0, it is recommended to use a Kanban board to resume the status of the architectural guidelines and the decisions made during the iteration. Table 5 contains columns showing whether the guidelines have been partially, completely, or not addressed in the iteration. Our goal for this first iteration is to establish an initial general structure of an educational chatbot, identifying its essential components without delving into implementation details. Therefore, a second iteration is unnecessary, and we conclude the design process.

Table 5. Kanban board for the first iteration.

Partially Addressed	Completely Addressed	Design decisions made during the iteration
QA3, QA4	CT1	The *Web Applications* reference architecture was selected, and the *Web* component was defined at the presentation layer
QA7		Thanks to the *Web* component, the chatbot can operate independently of the hardware platform. Also, the *Messaging Platforms* component was added to the presentation layer so that the chatbot can be used through Telegram, WhatsApp, or Facebook Messenger
QA17		The *User Interface* component was added to the presentation layer
	UC0	The *User Access* component was defined in the business layer, using *Auth* services
QA3, QA4, QA12, QA13, QA16, CT5		The *User Access*, *Student*, and *Teacher* components were defined in the business layer, as well as the *Tutorships* component in the orientation layer for the channeling of students. Also, the *Security* component was added to the utility layer
CT7		The *Message Processing and Formatting* component was added to the business layer
UC1 - UC4		The *School Services* component and the preliminary modules *Calendar & Schedule*, *Information*, *FAQ*, and *Procedures* were defined in the orientation layer
UC5 - UC12		The *Student/Teacher* component and the preliminary modules *Evaluation*, *Subjects*, *Health Wellness*, *Question & Answer*, *Feedback*, *Support*, *Tutorships*, and *Reports* were added to the orientation layer
CT2		The *Chatbot Service* and *External Service Interface* components were defined in the services layer
	CT6	Structuring the chatbot in a three-tier architecture allows multiple clients to connect to the application server
CT3		The physical structure of the chatbot was selected using the distributed deployment pattern, and the data layer was defined
	AC1	The *Web applications* reference architecture, the *Three-tier Distributed deployment* pattern and the *Layered Architecture* were selected
	CT8	The *Student/Teacher* component and the preliminary modules *Evaluation*, *Questions & Answers*, *Feedback* and *Tutorships* allow managing the stimulus-response approach
	CT9	The orientation, services, and data layers, together with the *Student* and *Teacher* components, are sufficient to cover the definition of an educational chatbot

5   Conclusion and Future Work

In this paper, we have presented a comprehensive architectural proposal for educational chatbots. Analyzing the system requirements and thoroughly examining related work, we have designed an architecture that addresses academic institutions' general needs involving academic services and activities concerning the teaching and learning process.

We began by discussing the importance of chatbot technology in the educational domain and its potential to provide personalized support, facilitate information retrieval, and improve administrative tasks. Subsequently, we identified and analyzed the critical use cases that our architecture should encompass, ranging from schedule inquiries and obtaining general information to conducting assessments and providing support for physical and mental health issues.

We employed the ADD 3.0 method to design our six-layer architecture, which allowed us to capture the system's structure, behavior, and interactions from multiple perspectives. We also proposed a three-tier distribution architecture consisting of a client, an application server, and a set of cloud services, each with well-defined responsibilities and components.

Our proposed architecture provides a solid foundation for developing an educational chatbot system that effectively meets the requirements of academic institutions. By leveraging chatbot technology, we could improve student involvement, simplify administrative tasks, and offer tailored help and guidance. Our modular and scalable architecture ensures flexibility, maintainability, and future extensibility.

In terms of future work, implementing a prototype of our architecture is the priority. Developing a series of tests, first in a controlled environment and then in an actual educational institution, will allow us to obtain technical and stakeholder feedback to refine our proposal.

References

1. Admithub: Harvard innovation lab, admithub (2018). https://www.admithub.com. Accessed 15 Mar 2019
2. America, P., Rommes, E., Obbink, H.: Multi-view variation modeling for scenario analysis. In: van der Linden, F.J. (ed.) PFE 2003. LNCS, vol. 3014, pp. 44–65. Springer, Heidelberg (2004). https://doi.org/10.1007/978-3-540-24667-1_5
3. Bass, L., Clements, P., Kazman, R.: Software Architecture in Practice. Second Edition, Addison-Wesley Professional (2003)
4. Bass, L., Clements, P., Kazman, R.: Software Architecture in Practice, 3rd edn. Addison-Wesley Professional (2012)
5. Bii, P., Too, J., Mukwa, C.: Teacher attitude towards use of chatbots in routine teaching. Universal J. Educ. Res. **6**(7), 1586–1597 (2018)
6. Cervantes, H., Kazman, R.: Designing Software Architectures: A Practical Approach. Addison-Wesley Professional (2016)
7. Eeles, P., Cripps, P.: The Process of Software Architecting. Addison-Wesley Professional (2010)

8. Fryer, L.K., Nakao, K., Thompson, A.: Chatbot learning partners: connecting learning experiences, interest and competence. Comput. Hum. Behav. **93**, 279–289 (2019). https://doi.org/10.1016/j.chb.2018.12.023

9. Henningsson, K., Wohlin, C.: Understanding the relations between software quality attributes-a survey approach. In: Proceedings 12th International Conference for Software Quality (2002)

10. Hofmeister, C., Nord, R., Soni, D.: Applied Software Architecture. Addison-Wesley Longman Publishing Co. Inc., USA (1999)

11. Inokuchi, A., Tamada, H., Hata, H., Tsunoda, M.: Toward obliging bots for supporting next actions. In: 2016 4th Intl Conf on Applied Computing and Information Technology/3rd Intl Conf on Computational Science/Intelligence and Applied Informatics/1st Intl Conf on Big Data, Cloud Computing, Data Science Engineering (ACIT-CSII-BCD), pp. 183–188 (2016)

12. Khan, R.: Standardized architecture for conversational agents aka chatbots. Int. J. Comput. Trends Technol. **50**(2), 114–121 (2017)

13. Kruchten, P.: The 4+1 view model of architecture. IEEE Softw. **12**(6), 42–50 (1995). https://doi.org/10.1109/52.469759

14. Kruchten, P.: The Rational Unified Process: An Introduction. Addison-Wesley Professional (2004)

15. Lattanze, A.J.: The Architecture Centric Development Method. Carnegie Mellon University, School of Computer Science (2005)

16. Maderer, J.: Jill Watson, round three, Georgia tech (2017). https://www.news.gatech.edu/2017/01/09/jill-watson-round-three. Accessed 15 Mar 2019

17. Matthies, C., Dobrigkeit, F., Hesse, G.: An additional set of (automated) eyes: chatbots for agile retrospectives. In: Proceedings of the 1st International Workshop on Bots in Software Engineering, BotSE 2019, pp. 34–37. IEEE Press (2019). https://doi.org/10.1109/BotSE.2019.00017

18. Molnar, G., Szuts, Z.: The role of chatbots in formal education. In: 2018 IEEE 16th International Symposium on Intelligent Systems and Informatics (SISY), pp. 197–202. IEEE, Subotica, Serbia, September 2018. https://doi.org/10.1109/SISY.2018.8524609

19. Obbink, H.T., Muller, J., America, P., Copa, R.V.O.: A component-oriented platform architecting method for families of software-intensive electronic products (2000)

20. OpenAI: Chatgpt: Language model for conversational ai (2021). https://openai.com/blog/chatgpt/. Accessed 13 June 2023

21. Patterns, M., Team, P.: Microsoft® Application Architecture Guide. Microsoft Press (2009)

22. Ran, A.: ARES conceptual framework for software architecture In: Azayeri, M., Ran, A., Van Der Linden, F., Van Der Linden, P. (eds.) Software Architecture for Product Families: Principles and Practice. Addison-Wesley Reading (2000)

23. Ranoliya, B.R., Raghuwanshi, N., Singh, S.: Chatbot for university related faqs. In: 2017 International Conference on Advances in Computing, Communications and Informatics (ICACCI), pp. 1525–1530. Udupi, India, September 2017. https://doi.org/10.1109/ICACCI.2017.8126057

24. Reyes, R., Garza, D., Garrido, L., De la Cueva, V., Ramirez, J.: Methodology for the implementation of virtual assistants for education using google dialogflow. In: Martínez-Villaseñor, L., Batyrshin, I., Marín-Hernández, A. (eds.) Advances in Soft Computing, pp. 440–451. Springer International Publishing, Cham (2019)

25. Rozanski, N., Woods, E.: Software systems architecture: working with stakeholders using viewpoints and perspectives. Addison-Wesley (2012)

26. Silva de Souza, G.H., Bento Marques, Y., Siqueira Jardim, W., Cesar Lima, N., Lopes Junior, G., Silveira Ramos, R.: Brazilian students' expectations regarding distance learning and remote classes during the covid-19 pandemic. Educ. Sci. Theory Practice **20**(4), 66–80 (2020)
27. Srivastava, S., Prabhakar, T.: A reference architecture for applications with conversational components. In: 2019 IEEE 10th International Conference on Software Engineering and Service Science (ICSESS), pp. 1–5 (2019). https://doi.org/10.1109/ICSESS47205.2019.9040822
28. Urquiza-Yllescas, J.F., Mendoza, S., Rodríguez, J., Sánchez-Adame, L.M.: An approach to the classification of educational chatbots. J. Intell. Fuzzy Syst. **43**(4), 5095–5107 (2022). https://doi.org/10.3233/JIFS-213275
29. Veglis, A., Maniou, T.A.: Embedding a chatbot in a news article: design and implementation. In: Proceedings of the 23rd Pan-Hellenic Conference on Informatics, PCI 2019, pp. 169–172. Association for Computing Machinery, New York (2019). https://doi.org/10.1145/3368640.3368664
30. Yang, S., Evans, C.: Opportunities and challenges in using ai chatbots in higher education. In: Proceedings of the 2019 3rd International Conference on Education and E-Learning, ICEEL 2019, pp. 79–83. Association for Computing Machinery, New York (2019). https://doi.org/10.1145/3371647.3371659

Author Index

P. Zaphiris and A. Ioannou (Eds.): HCII 2024, LNCS 14724, pp. 353–355, 2024.
https://doi.org/10.1007/978-3-031-61691-4

Printed in the United States
by Baker & Taylor Publisher Services